# Pharmaceutical Engineering

# Pharmaceutical Engineering

**D. K. Tripathi** M.Pharm, PhD.
Director, Pharmacy
Santosh Rungta Group of Institutions
Bhilai, CG

**Nirmalya Tripathi**
Assistant Professor
Amity University
Kolkata

**PharmaMed Press**
*An imprint of Pharma Book Syndicate*
**A unit of BSP Books Pvt. Ltd.**
4-4-309/316, Giriraj Lane,
Sultan Bazar, Hyderabad - 500 095.

**Pharmaceutical Engineering**

***by* D. K. Tripathi and Nirmalya Tripathi**



***Published by***

**PharmaMed Press**

*An imprint of Pharma Book Syndicate*

**A unit of BSP Books Pvt. Ltd.**

4-4-309/316, Giriraj Lane, Sultan Bazar, Hyderabad - 500 095.
Phone: 040-23445600, 23445688; Fax: 91+40-23445611
E-mail: info@pharmamedpress.com
www.pharmamedpress.com/pharmamedpress.net

**ISBN : 978-93-91910-66-2**

# Preface

The content of the book has been prepared as per the syllabus of Pharmaceutical Engineering, prepared by the Pharmacy Council of India for $4^{th}$ semester of Bachelor in Pharmacy course. Each and every topic of the syllabus has been covered and discussed adequately. In pharmaceutical science, there is requirement of basic knowledge of engineering; for example, the student should know what is crystallization and precipitation. There are fourteen chapters. Each of the chapter covers the entire syllabus for the subject. At the end of each chapter a set of questions including multiple choice questions (MCQs) have been provided for practice and to build up the confidence. Sufficient care has been taken during preparation of the content in terms of language, so that the students can easily understand.

However, the authors would be thankful for any kind of suggestion given for further development of the book as well as for the benefit of the students.

***Authors***

# Contents

## CHAPTER 3: SIZE SEPARATION



## CHAPTER 4: MIXING

# Introduction

Pharmaceutical engineering involves the study of industrial processes usually carried out in pharmaceutical and allied industries. In pharmaceutical formulation industries the raw materials are converted into dosage forms. In bulk manufacturing industries pharmaceutically important materials such as drugs and excipients are prepared. Whether it is formulation manufacturing or bulk drug/excipient manufacturing, various processes are performed using various equipments and machineries. For example, mixing tank or crystallizer, filtration machine, or tablet press, ointment mill, etc. are used. These are manufactured by engineering companies. As a user, if the industrial pharmacist does not know fundamentals of engineering processes and of the relevant equipments, it would be difficult to operate these machines and understand their operations.

Usually, each process or activity involves a number of steps and each step is carried out separately. Thus, the activities can be divided into two categories

- Unit process, and
- Unit operation

## Unit Process

Unit process can be defined as an activity in which various steps or unit operations take place in sequences. Unit process may be physical or chemical. The unit operations in combination make the process success.

## Physical Process

The processes which take place without chemical reaction, are called physical process. For example, recrystallization of salt. The operations sequentially performed are:

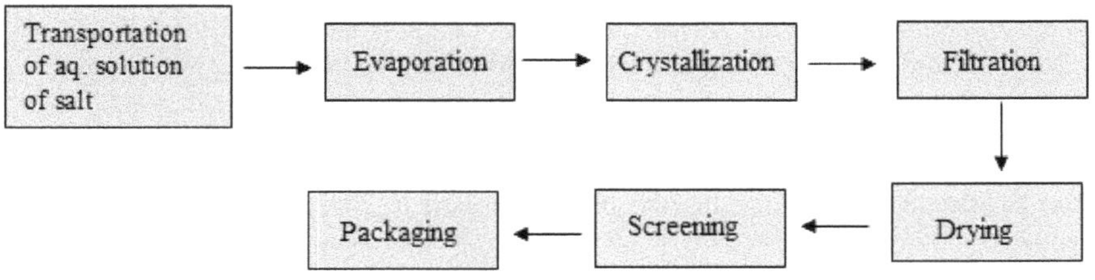

## Chemical Process

The processes which take place through chemical reactions are called chemical process. For example, manufacture of paracetamol.

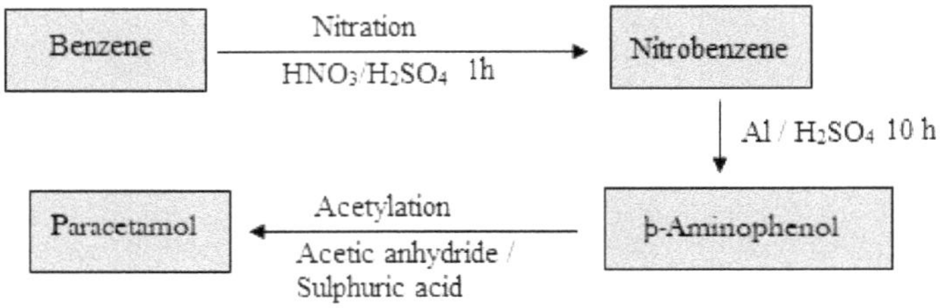


## Unit Operations

A unit operation is a basic step in a process. Unit operations involve a physical change or chemical transformation such as crystallization, evaporation, filtration, polymerization, isomerization, and other reactions in a process of separation. For example, in milk processing, homogenization, pasteurization, and packaging are each unit operations which are connected to the overall process. A process may require many unit operations to obtain the desired product from the starting materials, or feedstocks.

Thus, unit operation refers to individual step of a chemical process. For example, making tablets by granulation is a process in which sieving of powders, mixing of powders, preparation of wet granules, drying of wet granules, size reduction, blending of dried granules, compression of granules in form of tablets are various *unit operations* (steps) are involved.

In a unit process a number of unit operations may take place simultaneously or in a sequential manner, mechanism of these operations is based on some fundamental laws. In pharmaceutical manufacturing industries following activities are the unit operation:

*Size reduction:* This operation is done to reduce the particle size of drug or processes drug to achieve appropriate size range suitable for particular dosage form. For example, to prepare emulsion or ointment, the drug should be finely powdered. For oral suspension, the size of drug should be of coarse powder. It is a physical process. The drug may be synthetic or extracted from plant or animal source.

*Drying:* Drug or excipient used to prepare dosage form should have limited moisture content. Similarly, while preparing bulk drug or excipients, the product is dried at suitable temperature, so that the product (drug or excipient) contain limited moisture content. For this purpose, drying operation is very much important in pharmaceutical manufacturing unit. To manufacture tablet by wet granulation method, the wet granules are dried to remove unwanted amount of moisture. The moisture or solvent is evaporated out from the solid surface on heating.

*Evaporation:* This operation is usually carried out to remove the solvent at a temperature below the boiling point of the solvent to be removed. It is a surface phenomenon. Hence, rate of evaporation is proportional to the surface area exposed to air. The extract prepared from plant is evaporated to make it concentrated.

*Distillation:* It is a unit operation carried out mainly for preparation of distilled water or for removal of the solvent other than water from the extract prepared from plant. The extract is distilled to concentrate the extract and to recover the solvent. This operation is commonly done to obtain essential oil from plant parts.

These operations are very much common in nature and extensively used in pharmaceutical, food, and chemical industries.

## Basic Laws

Generally, the law of conservation of mass and the law of conservation of energy are applicable to every process. These laws are used in engineering in following ways:

1. Material balance (as per law of conservation of mass), and
2. Energy balance (as per law of conservation of energy).

## Material Balance

This is governed by the law of conservation of mass which is stated as *the material can neither be created, nor be destroyed, only it can be changed from one form to another.* In other words, the total quantity of materials used as input in a particular process shall be equal to the total quantity of output material, provided there is no loss of material during processing.

### Illustration:

Say, 5.0 kg of Material A,

0.75kg of Material B and

1.5 kg of Material C is being mixed in a mixer;

then, after mixing, the total mass of mixed materials would be = (5.0 + 0.75 + 1.5) kg = 7.25 kg, assuming that there is no loss of material during mixing or handling.

Now, if the total amount of mixture is found to be 7.23 kg, then 7.25 – 7.23 = 0.02 kg would be considered as handling loss. Theoretical output (yield) would be 7.25 kg and practical output (yield) is 7.23 kg.

**Note:**

1. The practical yield may be equal to the theoretical yield,
2. The yield may be less than the theoretical yield, indicating that there is loss of material during processing.
3. In case of radioactive process, the concept of material balance does not stand true.

## Mole

In a chemical reaction, concentration of reactant(s) and product(s) are expressed in molecular units; that is, in gram terms of molarity, molality or mole fraction.

In material balance calculations moles is used to express the amount of reactant or product in a chemical reaction.

Mole of an individual component is the number of gram molecular weight present in a particular amount (g) of the substance. Thus, 2g of oxygen means $\frac{2}{32}$ = 0.0625 mole of oxygen (molecular weight of oxygen is 32) and 5 g of carbon means $\frac{5}{12}$ = 0.417 moles of carbon (molecular weight of carbon is 12).

$$\text{Therefore, gram-moles of a substance} = \frac{\text{Mass in grams}}{\text{Molecular weight of the substance}}$$

If in a reaction there are multiple reactants, gram-moles or moles of each reactant should be calculated, to be added to find out the total moles of reactant(s).

## Molarity

Molarity of a particular solute of a solution is *defined as the number of moles of solute present per kg of solvent*. Thus, molality, $m = \frac{\text{Number of moles of the solute}}{\text{Number of kg of medium (solvent)}}$

## Mole Fraction

The concentration of one of solute(s) in a solution (mixture) can be expressed as

$$\text{The mole fraction of A, } X_A \text{ in a mixture of A and B} = \frac{\text{Number of moles of A}}{\text{Total number of moles of A+B}}$$

### Illustration

Say, 5.3 g of sodium chloride and 2.5 g of potassium chloride are present a mixture.

Number of moles of sodium chloride in the mixture = $\frac{5.3}{58.5}$ = 0.90 [Molecular weight of NaCl is 58.5]

Number of moles of potassium chloride in the mixture = $\frac{2.5}{74.55}$ = 0.03 [Molecular weight of KCl is 74.55]

$$\text{Mole fraction of sodium chloride in the mixture} = \frac{0.90}{(0.90+0.03)} = \frac{0.9}{0.93} = 0.97$$

$$\text{Mole fraction of potassium chloride in the mixture} = \frac{0.03}{(0.90+0.13)} = \frac{0.03}{0.93} = 0.032$$

Say, these materials are present in 500 g of water.

Mole of water present in a mixture $= \frac{500}{18} = 27.78$ [Molecular weight of water is 18]

Mole fraction of water present in a mixture $= \frac{27.78}{(0.90 + 0.03 + 27.78)} = \frac{27.78}{28.71} = 0.967$

Sum of the mole fractions of all the components must be equal to 1 (unity).

In this case, total mole fractions of all the components (sodium chloride, potassium chloride and water)

$= 0.031 + 0.001 + 0.967 = 0.999$ (approximately 1.0)

## Energy Balance

Energy *is the capacity to exercise a force through a distance and demonstrates itself in various forms*. The unit of energy in SI system is J (Joules). Thus, the energy per unit mass is known as *specific energy*. The unit of specific energy is J/kg. Characteristics of energy are:

- Energy cannot be destroyed, it has different forms such as mechanical, chemical, thermal, electrical, radiation.
- Energy can be converted from one form to another,
- Energy can be transferred or conveyed from one place to another,
- Energy can be stored in various forms utilizing a working substance.

The first law of thermodynamics is the law of conservation of energy. It also states that energy can be transformed into work.

Thus, when one kind of energy is destroyed or consumed, an equal amount of another kind must be formed.

## Some Basic Concept

### Rate of a Process or Reaction

The rate of a chemical reaction can be realized and expressed by understanding the change of concentration of the reacting species with time. Thus, the rate of a reaction can be expressed mathematically as:

$$\text{Rate of a reaction} = \frac{dC}{dt}$$

Where C is the concentration and dC is very small change in concentration at a time, dt. This concept of rate can be expressed in

$$\text{Rate of a process} = \frac{dF}{R} = \frac{\text{Driving force}}{\text{Resistance}}$$

That is, any action to happen there must be a sufficient reason (according to the Newton's law of motion), behind the progress, the reason works as the driving force. For example, the flow of water or flow-current in a river depends on 1. the quantity-difference of water and 2. height-difference between two locations of the river. If there is sufficient difference in height, water from higher site will flow to the lower site and if there is no continuous supply of water after certain, upper sites of the river will dry up. Similarly, if a metallic-spoon is left as such within a hot liquid, the end of the inside the air, become hot due to flow of heat from one end to the other end of the spoon. This happen because the material of construction of spoon is a good conductor of electricity and the temperature difference between two points at two ends of the spoon.

### Steady State

Whether it is heat or water, it moves from its higher state (level) to lower state. The movement continues till both the states become same or until an equilibrium is reached. That is, heat will go on moving till the temperatures at two points of two ends remains different, with passage of time this difference of temperature will reduce and ultimately will become equal. Thus, the quantity of heat flowing (net flow of heat) from hot region to cold region will gradually reduce and finally become zero. This final state is called steady-state. If the movement of energy or material is considered two-way action, it is expressed by two arrows at opposite direction shown in figure below.

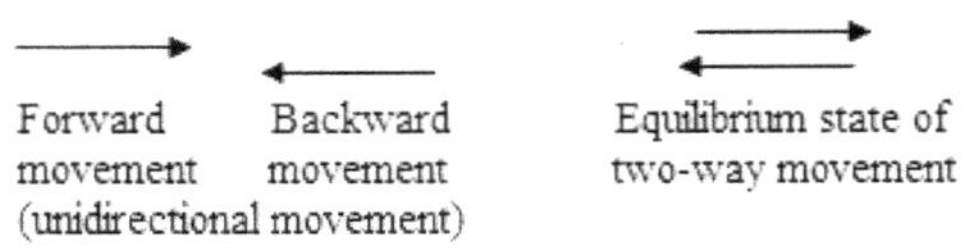


Direction of movement.

When the equilibrium is reached; that is, the rate of forward reaction becomes equal to that of backward reaction, it is considered to attain *steady state*. In other words, steady state of a reaction is a condition when the concentration of the reactants or products does not change with time. On the other hand, if the operating condition vary with time, in a system, the system is considered as *unsteady state* or *state*. For example, water is boiling in a container. Before boiling, heat was transferred from source to water in the container and the temperature of water is gradually being increased. At this condition the system (water being heated) is under unsteady condition. Once the temperature of water is raised to the boiling point of water, water starts boiling. At this condition, no virtual movement of heat will take place from source to water, a dynamic equilibrium is attained. This condition is said to be *steady state*. Provided that the pressure above the water remains same.

## Units, System and Conversion

Physical quantity measured must have a particular unit. The units may be length, mass, temperature, time or any other. For example, acceleration is the rate of change of velocity $\left(\frac{v-u}{t}\right)$ ft/sec$^2$ or cm/sec$^2$or momentum is the product of velocity, v and mass, m (mv) gm.cm/sec or lb. ft/sec. In engineering, different units are used even when only one system, either the metric or the British system, is commonly used. Thus, conversion of one simple unit, say 1 cm to another unit, say inch is required either by dividing or multiplying by a conversion factor.

Dimension requires measurement; measurement requires expression of the measured quantity using relevant unit; unit refers to the system; for better understanding conversion of the measured quantity should be converted to required system.

There are three systems used to measure a quantity.

1. CGS (Centimeter-Gram-Second) system, also known as metric system
2. FPS (Foot-Pound-Second) system, also known as British system
3. MKS or SI (Meter- Kilogram-Second) system, also known as Modern system.

Fundamental quantities measured are length, mass and time. In different systems, their values are different. The units used to express in a particular system may be divided into two categories:

1. **Primary units:** The units mentioned in any system to express the physical quantities such as length, mass and time are called *fundamental or primary units*. For example, cm-g- sec. or m-kg-sec.
2. **Derived units:** Certain physical quantities are expressed in terms of derived from fundamental units; for example, area and volume are derived from length unit, momentum from mass, length and time; density from mass and volume, etc. These units are called *derived units or secondary units*.

Physical quantities have two parts –

- Number such as one, two, three, four, etc.
- Unit indicating the system used to measure the quantity such cm/m/ft etc.

Combination of both indicates the actual value.

## Illustration

Say mass of a liquid is 25g, it occupies a space measuring 2cm × 2cm × 5cm. That is, the volume of 25g of the liquid is 20cubic.cm or 20ml.

Then, the density of the liquid would be $= \frac{\text{Mass}}{\text{Volume}} = \frac{25\text{g}}{20\text{ml}} = 1.25\text{g/ml}$ (derived unit)

Basic units in different systems are shown below in tabular form.

| Quantity/Measurement | CGS System | MKS / SI System | FPS System |
|---|---|---|---|
| Length (L) | Centimeter (cm) | Metre (m) | Foot (ft) |
| Mass (m) | Gram (g) | Kilogram (kg) | Pound (lb) |
| Time (t) | Second (S or Sec) | Second (S or Sec) | Second (S or Sec) |
| Temperature | Centigrade (°C) | Kelvin (K) | Fahrenheit (°F) |
| Luminous intensity | | Candela (cd) | |
| Electric current | | Ampere (A) | |
| Molar mass | | Mole (mol) | |

It is necessary to know the different units in different system and use a particular system for units. Some of the most commonly useful derived units in SI system are shown below

| Measurement / Quantity | Unit | Symbol |
|---|---|---|
| Electrical charge | Coulomb | |
| Electrical potential | | |
| Electrical resistence | | |

## Conversion of Units

Conversion of units from CGS system to British system and vice versa

| | | | | |
|---|---|---|---|---|
| Length | | | | |
| | 1 millimeter (mm) | 0.0394 inch (in) | | |
| | 1 centimeter (cm) | 0.3937 in | | |
| | 1 meter (m) | 1.0936 yards (yds) | 3.281 ft | 39.369 in |
| | 1 kilometer (km) | 0.62137 mile | 1760 yds | 5280 ft |
| | 1 in | 2.54 cm | | |
| | 1 foot (ft) | 30.48 cm | | |
| | 1 yd | 91.44 cm | 3 ft | 36 in |
| | 1 mile | 1760 yds | 5280 ft | 1.609 km |
| Mass | | | | |
| | 1 ounce | 28.349 grams (g) | | |
| | 1 pound (lb) | 0.4536 kg | 453.6 g | |
| | 1 cwt | 50.80 kg | | |
| | 1 ton | 1. 016 metric tonnes | | |
| | 1 g | 0.03527 ounce | | |
| | 1 kg | 2.205 lbs | 0.01968 cwt | |
| | 1 metric tonne | 0.9842 ton | | |
| Time | | | | |
| | 1 minute (min) | 60 seconds (s or sec) | | |
| | 1 hour | 60 min | 3600 sec | |
| | 1 day | 24 hours (hr) | 1440 min | 86 400 sec |
| Temperature | | | | |
| | 1°C | 33.8 °F | | |
| Area | | | | |
| | 1 sq in | 6.4516 sq cm | | |
| | 1 sq ft | 929.0304 sq cm | | |
| | 1 sq yd | 0.8361 sq m | 8361 sq cm | |
| | 1 sq mile | 2.589 sq km | 30 97 600 sq yds | 2 78 78 400 sq ft |

*Contd...*

| | | | | |
|---|---|---|---|---|
| | 1 hectare (ha) | 2.4711 acres | 1 07 645.831 sq ft | 10 000 sq.m |
| | 1 acre | 4840.212 sq yds | 43 561.908 sq ft | 4047 sq m |
| | 1 sq cm | 0.155 sq in | 100 sq mm | |
| | 1 sq.m | 1.1960 sq. yds | 10.764 sq ft | 10 000 sq.cm |
| | 1 sq km | 0.386 sq mile | 1 07 61 062.4 sq ft | |
| Volume | | | | |
| | 1 cubic inch | 16.387 cubic cm | | |
| | 1cubic ft (c ft) | 28.316 cubic decimeter(cdm) | | |
| | 1 pint | 0.568 liter | 568 ml | |
| | 1 imperial gallon | 4.546 lt | 4546 ml | |
| | 1 cubic cm (cc) | 0.0610 cubic inch | | |
| | 1 cdm | 0.035 c ft | | |
| | 1 lt | 1.76pint | | |
| | 1 lt | 0.220 imp gallon | | |

## Gas Laws

Usually ideal gas law is expressed as: PV = nRT; where P is pressure, V is the volume, T is absolute temperature ($^oK = ^oC + 273.1$ or $^oRankine = ^oF + 459.6$), R is the universal gas constant, n is the number of moles of gas.

Although this gas law (ideal gas law) does not apply everywhere (particularly, to any real gas); in general, the law is most commonly used for engineering calculation and the law gives sufficiently correct answers in most of the cases. The law tells that

1. The volume of a gas is directly proportional to the number of moles of the gas present,
2. The volume is directly proportional to the absolute temperature,
3. The volume is inversely proportional to the pressure.

To calculate the volume of a gas at different temperature and pressure, the statement 2 and 3 become very necessary. The above gas equation can be written as;

$$\frac{P_1V_1}{T_1} = \frac{P_2V_2}{T_2}$$

Where $V_1$is the volume of a gas at temperature $T_1$ and pressure $P_1$; the volume changes to $V_2$ when the temperature changes to $T_2$ under the pressure $P_2$. Thus, if the value of the temperatures are known and any of the pressures and corresponding volume of the gas is known, then other volume can be easily calculated.

### Illustration

Say, the volume of a gas changes from 250 cc to 325 cc, the temperature changes from 25°C to 35°C, if the initial pressure is 1 atm, find out the final pressure.

Thus, $P_1$ = 1 atm = 76 cm of Hg

$T_1 = 25 + 273 = 298^{\circ}K$

$T_2 = 35 + 273 = 308^{\circ}K$

$V_1 = 250$ cc,

$V_2 = 325$ cc

$P_2 = ?$

We know that,

$$\frac{P_1V_1}{T_1} = \frac{P_2V_2}{T_2}$$

Or,

$$= \frac{76 \times 250}{298} = \frac{P_2 \times 325}{308}$$

So,

$$P_2 = \frac{250 \times 76 \times 308}{325 \times 298}$$

$$= 60.42 \text{ cm of Hg}$$

## Mole Volume

According to the ideal gas equation, PV = nRT, one mole of a gas under particular temperature and pressure always occupies a definite volume irrespective of the nature of the gas. This volume is called the mole volume.

1-gram mole of an ideal gas occupies 22.41 lt at 0°C and 1 atm (76 cm of Hg) pressure.

1 lb mole of an ideal gas occupies 359 c ft at 32°F and 76 cm of Hg pressure.

### Dalton's Law of Partial Pressure

According to Dalton's law, the total pressure exerted by a mixture of ideal gases shall be equal to the sum of the pressures that would be exerted by each of the gases if it alone were present and occupied the total volume. Amagat's law of partial volume is similar to Dalton's law. Amagat's law states that in a mixture of ideal gases, each gas can be considered to occupy a fraction of the total volume equal to its own mole fraction and to be at the total pressure of the mixture. Thus, in a mixture of ideal gases each one of the mixtures occupies the entire volume at its own partial pressure, or a combination of partial volumes of the individual gases. Each partial volume is taken at the total pressure. As in the case of a pure gas, one lb mole is that weight of a gas mixture that will occupy 359 cft under one atmospheric pressure at 32°F. This may be called average molecular weight of the gas. From this statement of relationship, it can be stated that in a mixture of ideal gases

Volume % = Pressure % = Mole %

For example, air contains 79% of nitrogen and 21% of oxygen by volume. That is, under a pressure P atm, one cu. ft of air may be considered to be a mixture of 0.21 cu. ft of $O_2$ at P atm and 0.79 cu. ft of $N_2$ at P atm. It can also be considered as a mixture of 1 cu. ftof $O_2$ at 0.21 P atm and 1 cu. ft of$N_2$ at 0.79 P atm;% of total pressure is due to $N_2$.

Thus, 1 mole of air contains 0.21 mole of $O_2$ and 0.79 mole of $N_2$ at all temperatures and pressures.

## Exothermic and Endothermic Reactions

In chemical reactions or processes, heat may be evolved or absorbed. The reactions which generate heat, are called *exothermic reactions*; while the reactions absorb heat are called *endothermic reactions*. For example, sodium hydroxide when dissolved in water, heat is produced. While ammonium chloride is dissolved in water, it absorbed heat. The $\Delta H$ becomes positive in case of exothermic reactions and negative in case of endothermic reactions. In the reaction of one mole of solid carbon (in form of graphite) reacting with one mole of oxygen (gas), one mole of carbon dioxide (gas) is formed ($C + O_2 = CO_2$) and the standard heat of this reaction, $\Delta H$ is – 94.052 kcal at 25°C. The negative sign indicates that the heat is evolved in the reaction (exothermic reaction). This means that the reactants, carbon and oxygen, contain 94.052 kcal in addition to the product, one mole of carbon dioxide. This heat is evolved during the reaction. If this reaction is reversed, that is, one mole of carbon dioxide (gas) is converted into one mole of carbon (solid) and one mole of oxygen (gas), the reaction will absorb the same amount of heat 94.052 kcal. Thus, the reaction would be endothermic one and $\Delta H$ would be positive.

## Hess's Law of Heat Summation

Hess demonstrated that since $\Delta H$ depends only on the initial and final states of a system, thermodynamic chemical equations for several steps in a reaction can be added or subtracted to obtain the overall heat of reaction. This principle is called *Hess's law of heat summation*. This principle is used to obtain the heat of reactions that cannot be easily measured directly. If a reaction cannot be performed in a calorimeter, the $\Delta H_{25^\circ C}$ for the reaction can be obtained as indicated below:

$$\text{C (solid)} + O_2\text{(gas)} = CO_2 \text{ (gas)} \quad \Delta H_{25}{}^\circ C = -94.052 \text{ kcal} \qquad .....(1)$$

$$\text{CO (gas)} + \frac{1}{2}O_2 \text{ (gas)} = CO_2 \text{ (gas)} \quad \Delta H_{25}{}^\circ C = -67.636 \text{ kcal} \qquad .....(2)$$

If the eqn.2 and its heat of combustion are subtracted from the eqn.1and its heat of combustion, we get

$$\text{C (solid)} + \frac{1}{2} O_2 \text{ (gas)} = \text{CO (gas)} \quad \Delta H_{25}{}^\circ C = -26.416 \text{ kcal}$$

**Hess's law of heat summation may also be defined as:** If a chemical change take place in two or more different ways, then in the total change, the amount of heat absorbed or evolved may be same; it does not depend on the method by which the change has been carried out. Thus, thermochemical reactions may be added or subtracted.

## Dimensional Analysis

There are some problems which cannot be solved completely either by theoretical or mathematical methods, these require empirical experimentation. For example, the pressure of a liquid is reduced due to friction during the flow of a liquid through a long, straight, round, smooth pipe due to the following factors:

- Length and diameter of the pipe,
- Density of the liquid flowing,
- Viscosity of the liquid flowing,
- Rate at which the liquid flows,

If any one of these factors varies, the pressure drop will also change. The empirical method to get an equation that can correlate the pressure drop with the effects of all these factors, is that the effect of each factor on the pressure drop is to be determined separately. The effect one factor is to be determined by keeping other factors constant. This process is very laborious and it is very difficult to obtain a useful relationship by correlating all the results obtained.

Thus, intermediate between complete mathematical development and total empirical studies, there is a method called dimensional analysis. It is based on the fact that, if a theoretical equation exists among the variables that affect a physical process, that equation must be dimensionally homogeneous. As such it is possible to group the factors affecting the process into smaller number of dimensionless groups and these groups enter the final equation, not the factors separately. The benefit of this method is to reduce drastically the number of independent variables that effect the problem. However, dimensional analysis does not bring about a numerical equation and experiment is necessary to complete the solution to the problem.

Dimensional analysis shows that the variables must enter the final equation. In the above example, the variables shown are diameter of the pipe (D), velocity of the liquid (v), density (ρ) and viscosity of the liquid (η) must appear as a dimensionless group $\frac{D\,V\,\rho}{\eta}$.

A dimensional analysis cannot be made unless the physics of the process is known sufficiently to decide which factor would be important in the problem and what physical laws would be involved in a mathematical solution if one were possible. The method used to construct a dimensionless equation is important in research and development activities.

## Dimensionless Groups

By use of dimensional analysis and other means, various important dimensionless groups have been developed. For example, Reynolds number $\frac{D\,V\,\rho}{\eta}$,

Fanning friction factor $\frac{\Delta P_f g_C D}{2V^2 L\rho}$,

Grashof number $\frac{L^3\rho^2 g\beta\Delta t}{\eta^2}$

Nusselt number $\frac{hD}{k}$,

Prandtl number $\frac{C\mu}{k}$,

Power number $\frac{P_{g_C}}{\rho N^3 D^5}$,

Schmidt number $\frac{\mu}{\rho DL}$, etc.

For a particular case, the numerical value of a dimensionless group does not depend on the unit of primary quantities present in the group, provided that consistent units are used within that group. However, the units used in one group may not be same and consistent with those used in other groups. For example, meters are used in one group while feet can be used in another group.

## Use of Mathematical Methods

In the treatment of unit operations following mathematical methods are used:

1. Graphic method of integration (Graphical integration)
2. Graphical treatment of exponential functions.

1. **Graphic method of integration (Graphical integration):** In this method, integral calculus used shows that the value of a definite integral $\int_{x_2}^{x_1} f(x)dx$ represents the area bounded by the curve of f(x) vs x, the ordinates $x = x_1$and the $x= x_2$ and the x axis. Any definite integral can therefore be calculated numerically by plotting f(x) vs x, drawing two vertical lines corresponding to the limits, and the area is determined between the curve, the limits and the x axis, as shown below in the figure, without using the table. Thus, in the figure, if the curve MNOPQR expresses the plot of f(x) against x. If the lines MT and RS represent the values of $x_1$ and $x_2$ respectively, the complete area MNOPQRST becomes integrated value.

   The area may be determined by splitting it into a series of rectangles such as the one shown cross-hatched in the figure.

   The height of this rectangle is such that the area of the small triangle omitted between the rectangle and the curve is almost equal to the area of the small cross-hatched triangle within the rectangle above the curve. This can be observed by the naked eye. The area desired is thus, the sum of all such rectangles as the one shown in below.

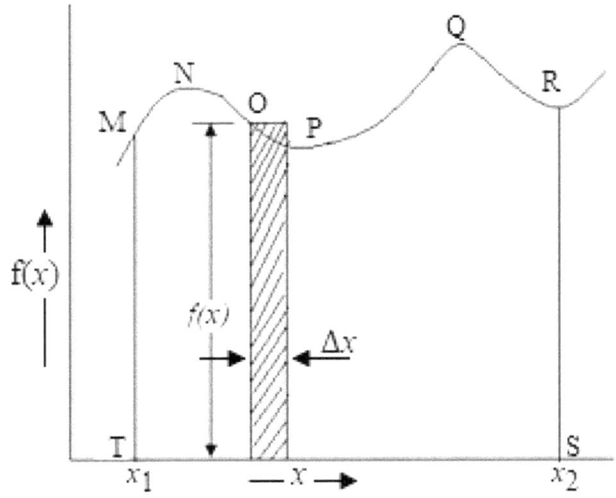


Concept of graphical Integration

***Mean values***: It becomes necessary to use the average values in many engineering calculations. In fact, averaging of values of some variables such as density, viscosity, velocities, etc. are required to obtain a reliable result. In some cases, averaging cannot be done easily; particularly, where the changes of the variable are represented by;

$$y = f(x) \qquad \text{.....(1)}$$

In such cases, the average value of $y$ is calculated when $x$ changes from $x_1$ to $x_2$ as follows

$$y_{av} = \frac{\int_{x_2}^{x_1} f(x)dx}{x_2 - x_1} \qquad \text{.....(2)}$$

The equation 2 can be used when $f(x)$ can be expressed by a mathematical function. In such case, formal integration should be used. If the relationship is known only as a curve and equation of the curve (the form of $f(x)$) is unknown, then the methods of graphic integration, must be used.

**2. Exponential Equations and log-log plots**

In many cases, experimental data including the variables $x$ and $y$ fit an equation of the form

$$y = a.x^n \qquad \text{.....(3)}$$

where a and n are constants. It is possible to duplicate many curves by an equation of the type:

$$y = a + bx + cx^2 + dx^3 + \ldots\ldots \qquad \text{.....(4)}$$

In many cases, the eqn. 4 can fit more accurately than the eqn. 3. Yet, the following eqn.3 can fit many experimental data closely enough to permit its use; this can be explained below. The constants of eqn.3 can be determined quickly. On the other hand, fitting the eqn.4 to experimental data is a tedious process and often requires the use of a large number of terms.

The eqn.3 may be rewritten as:

$$\log y = \log a + n \log x \qquad .....(5)$$

If log x is plotted against log y, the eqn.5 is the equation of a straight line with a slope of n and log a is the intercept, when x = 1. It is possible to plot log y against log x. However, for this purpose log-log paper can be used. The disadvantage of the logarithmic plot is that the scales normally used cannot be read too closely. In most cases, the points can be plotted with an accuracy comparable to the accuracy of normal engineering data. Advantage of log-log plots is that deviations from a curve of a given distance represent deviations of a constant per cent of the total value of the variable at that point, irrespective of the part of the plot in which they may lie.

# CHAPTER 1

# Flow of Fluid

Types of Manometers, Reynolds Number and its Significance, Bernoulli's Theorem and its Applications, Energy Losses, Orifice Meter, Venturi Meter, Pitot Tube and Rotameter.

## Types of Manometers

Manometer is one of the earliest devices used for measuring fluid pressure difference consisting of a hollow U-tube having one or more fluid (may be liquid or gas) of different specific gravities. It can provide a very accurate result. A U-tube manometer is recognized by NIST as a primary standard due to its inherent accuracy and simple operation. The manometer has no movable parts that can subject to wear. Manometers works on the *Hydrostatic Balance Principle: a liquid column of known height will exert a known hydrostatic pressure when the weight per unit volume of the fluid is known.* The fundamental relationship for pressure expressed by a fluid column is:

$$p = P_1 - P_2 = \rho \times h \times g$$

Where

p is the differential pressure,
$P_1$ is the pressure at the low-pressure connection
$P_2$ is the pressure at the high-pressure connection
$\rho$ is the density of the liquid
g is acceleration due to gravity, and
h is the height of the liquid column

All forms of manometers such as Piezometer, U-tube manometers, differential manometer, well-type, and inclined, etc. contain two liquid surfaces. Pressure determinations are made by how the fluid moves when pressures are applied to each surface. For gauge pressure, $P_2$ is equal to zero (atmospheric reference), simplifying the above equation to

$$p = \rho hg$$

In manometer, a known pressure (which is generally atmospheric pressure) is applied to one end of the manometer tube and the unknown pressure (to be determined) is applied to the other end.

The manometers measure the differential pressure; that is, only the difference between the two pressures. There are primarily four types of manometers:

1. Simple u-tube manometer – Piezometer
2. Differential U-tube manometers
3. U-tube with one leg enlarged (Well type manometer), and
4. Inclined U-tube manometer

The U-tube manometer may be of three types:

(a) Two fluid U-tube manometer,

(b) Four-fluid U-tube manometer, and

(c) Differential U-tube manometer

**1. Simple u-tube manometer – Piezometer:** It is used to measure the pressure in a static fluid by using the height of a column of a liquid as shown in Figure 1.1.

Pressure at A = Pressure at B

$= \rho.g.h$

Where, $\rho$ is the density of the liquid

g is acceleration due to gravity

h is the height of the liquid column

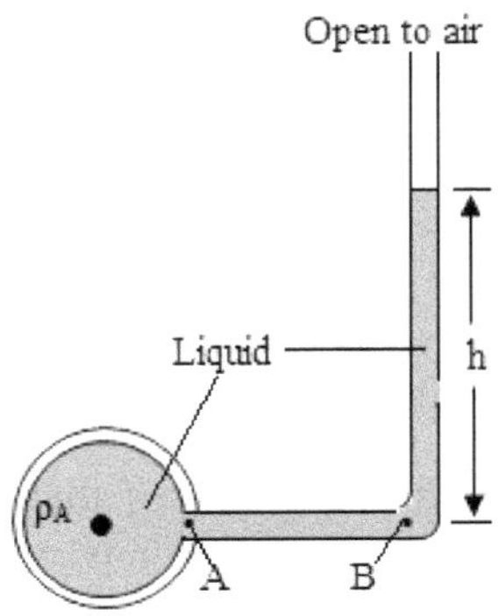


**Fig. 1.1** Piezometer

**2. Differential U-tube manometers:** The principles of manometry can be easily established in the U tube manometer shown in Figure 1.2. It is simply a glass-tube bent to form the letter U and partially filled with a liquid. If both the legs of the manometer are kept open to atmosphere or exposed to the same pressure, the levels of the liquid remain exactly on the same line or with a zero difference. As illustrated in Figure 1.3, if the pressure is more to the left side of the apparatus, the fluid level comes down to a lower level in the left leg and raises in the right leg. The fluid moves until the weight of the fluid as indicated in figure exactly balance the pressure. This is known as hydrostatic balance. The height of fluid from one side to the other is the actual height of fluid opposing the pressure. The pressure is always indicated by the height of fluid regardless of the shape or size of the tubes, as illustrated in Figure 1.3. Manometers in Figure 1.3 are open to atmosphere on both legs indicating the fluid level in both legs. Because of the variations in the volume of the manometer legs, the distances moved by the fluid columns are different. However, the total distance between the fluid levels, H, remains identical in all the manometers.

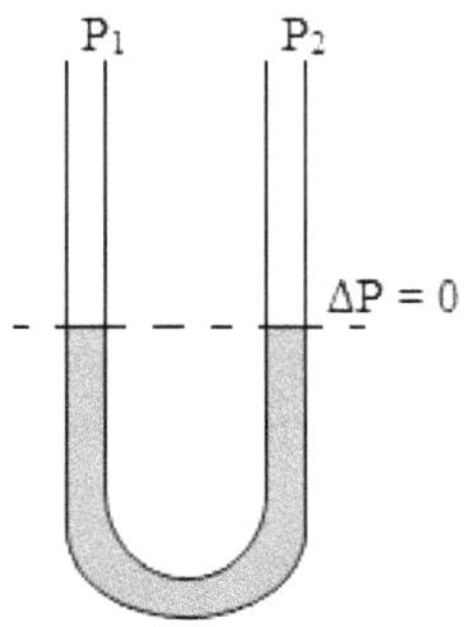


**Fig. 1.2** U-tube manometer

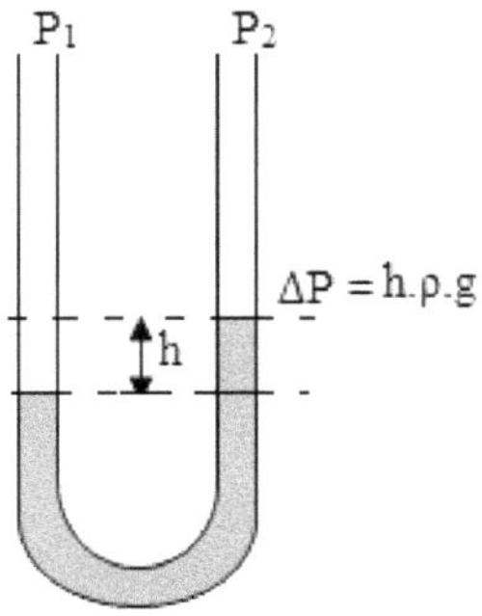


**Fig. 1.3** U-tube manometer

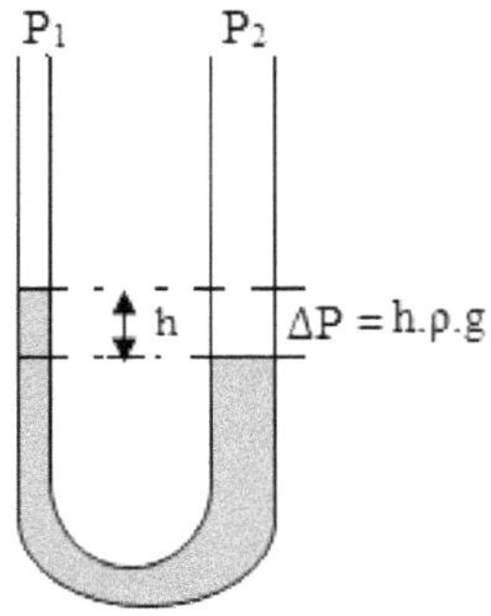


**Fig. 1.4** U-tube manometer

3. **U-tube with one leg enlarged (Well type manometer):** To provide convenience and to meet other requirements this type of manometer has been used. The well-type manometer is one of the various types of manometers. The schematic diagram of this type of manometer has been shown in Figure 1.5. The cross-sectional area of one leg of the manometer is many times larger than that of the other leg. The leg with a larger area is called the well. As pressure is applied to the larger leg, the fluid moves down compared to the increase in height of the smaller leg.

   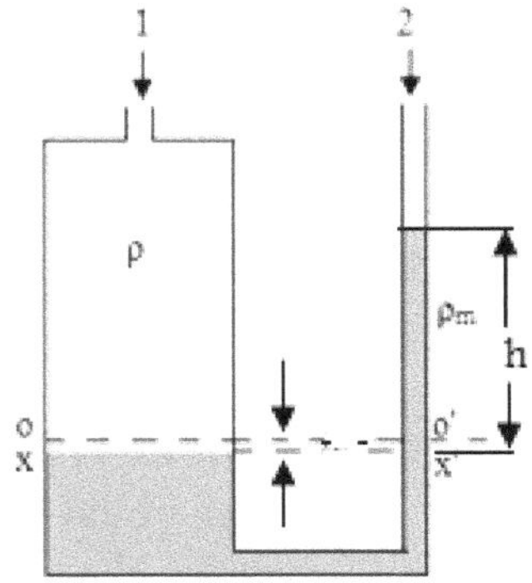
   
   **Fig. 1.5** Well type manometer

   The true pressure reading follows the principles, previously described and is measured by the difference between the fluid surfaces h. As the pressure is applied at 1 there must be some drop in the well level from O to X. This is readily compensated for by spacing the scale graduations in the exact amount required to correct for this well drop. To ensure the accuracy of this correction, the well area and internal diameter of the indicating tube must be carefully controlled.

   Thus, the well type manometer offers itself to be used with direct reading scales graduated in units for the process or test variable involved. It does require certain operational restrictions not found on the U-tube. A pressure higher than atmospheric pressure is always connected to the well; a pressure lower than atmospheric is always connected to the top of the tube. For a differential pressure, the higher pressure is connected at the well. A raised well manometer, however, allows both gauge and vacuum measurements off of the well port.

4. **Inclined U-tube manometer:** In many cases, accurate measurement of low pressure such as drafts and very low differentials are required. To handle these applications better the manometer is arranged with the indicating tube inclined, as shown in Figure 1.6. It provides better resolution. This arrangement can allow 12" of scale length to represent 1" of vertical liquid height. With subdivisions of scale, even up to a pressure of 0.00036 psi (one-hundredth of an inch of water) can be read.

   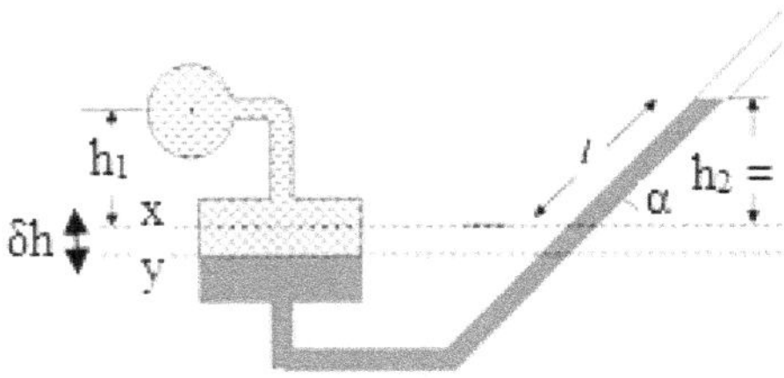
   
   **Fig. 1.6** Inclined U-type manometer

## Absolute Manometer

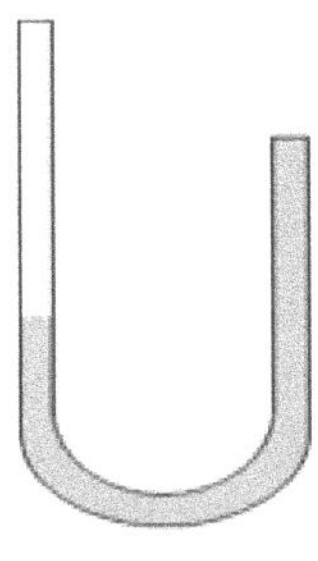
**Fig. 1.7** Absolute manometer

Absolute zero pressure refers to the pressure at a perfect vacuum. In an absolute pressure manometer, the pressure being measured is compared to absolute zero pressure in a sealed leg above a mercury column, as shown in Figure 1.7. The term absolute zero pressure is derived from the definition, that is, a perfect vacuum is the complete absence of any gas. The most common form of sealed tube manometer is the conventional mercury barometer used to measure atmospheric pressure. Mercury is the only fluid used in this application. In this type of manometer, there is only one connection from which both pressures above atmospheric pressure and pressure below atmospheric can be measured. Absolute manometers are available in well type or U tube configurations.

## Indicating Fluid

The sensitivity, range, and accuracy of the manometer can be improved by selecting an appropriate indicating fluid. Indicating fluids are available with densities varying from 0.827 $g/cm^3$ (Red Oil) to 13.54 $g/cm^3$ (Mercury). The pressure range would become three times greater and the resolution would be one third as great if an indicating fluid is three times heavier than water. If the density of an indicating fluid is less than water, the pressure range will decrease and the resolution (sensitivity) will increase. Thus, for a given size of the instrument, the pressure range can be increased by using a fluid with higher density and reduced by using a fluid with lower density.

## Correction of the Manometer

Manometry measurements depend on both density and acceleration due to gravity. The values of the density and acceleration due to gravity are not always constant. Density is a function of temperature, and acceleration due to gravity is a function of latitude and elevation. Due to this relationship, specific ambient conditions must be selected as standard, so that a fixed pressure can be maintained.

Standard conditions for mercury: Density of mercury at 0°C is 13.5951 $g/cm^3$;

Acceleration due to gravity at sea level and at 45.544° latitude is 980.665 $cm/sec^2$

Standard conditions for water:

Density of water at 4°C is 1.000 $g/cm^3$;

Acceleration due to gravity at sea level and at 45.544° latitude is 980.665 $cm/sec^2$

Generally, the manometers may be read outside standard temperature and acceleration due to gravity and corrections should be made to improve the accuracy of a manometer reading at any given condition.

## Correction of Fluid Density

Manometers indicate the correct pressure at only one temperature. This is because the indicating fluid density changes with temperature. If water is the indicating fluid, an inch scale indicates one inch of water at 4°C only. On the same scale, mercury indicates one inch of mercury at 0°C only. A reading using water or mercury taken at 20°C (68° F) is not an accurate reading. The error introduced is about 0.4% of reading for mercury and about 0.2% of reading for water. Since manometers are used at temperatures above and below the standard temperature, corrections are needed. A simple way of correcting for density changes is to ratio the densities. At a particular place where the value of g is constant,

$$\text{(Standard) } \rho_c g h_c = \text{(Ambient) } \rho g h$$

$$h_c = \frac{\rho}{\rho_c} \times h$$

Where,

$\rho_c$ = Density of indicating fluid at standard temperature,

$h_c$ = Corrected height of the indicating fluid at standard temperature,

h = Height of the indicating fluid at experimental temperature, and

$\rho$ = Density of indicating fluid at the experimental temperature

This method is very accurate when density-temperature relations are known. Data is readily available for water and mercury.

The density (g/cm$^3$) of mercury can be corrected as a function of temperature ($0^\circ$C) as

$$13.556786\ [1 - 0.0001818(T - 15.5556)]$$

Density (g/cm$^3$) of water can be corrected as a function of temperature ($0^\circ$C) as 0.9998395639 + 6.798299989 × 10$^{-5}$ (T)

$$- 9.10602556 \times 10^{-6}(T^2) + 1.005272999 \times 10^{-7}(T^3) - 1.126713526 \times 10^{-9}(T^4) + 6.591795606 \times 10^{-12}(T^5)$$

## Reynolds Number

The Reynolds number is defined as *the ratio of inertial forces to viscous forces and consequently quantifies the relative importance of these two types of forces for given flow conditions.*

When liquids flow through a pipe or tube or channel, the character of the flow varies depending on certain conditions. This was first demonstrated by Osborne Reynolds in the year 1883. He carried out the experiment using a long glass tube. The tube was connected to water reservoir to maintain a constant supply pressure. A jet was inserted into the inlet of the tube as shown in figure 8. The position of the jet was so adjusted that it can inject the dye solution at the center of the tube. The outlet of the tube was attached to a valve to control the flow of water. Thus, two liquids (water and dye solution) were flowing through the tube. Reynolds observed how the flow property of the dye solution varied with flow property (velocity) of water.

When the velocity of water was less, the dye solution flew steadily, having a thread-like appearance and remained undisturbed in the center of the water stream. This can be imagined as if water has been flowing in a series of concentric layers, like the draw-tube of a telescope. This type of flow is called *streamline, laminar*, or *viscous flow*.

When the velocity of water was increased moderately, a point was reached at which the thread started to become a wave-like appearance without mixing with water. The velocity of water at this point was called *critical velocity* and the phase of the flow was called as *transitional flow*.

When the velocity of water was further increased to a high degree, eddies (vortices) began to start in the flow and the dye solution started mixing with water just after leaving the orifice of the jet. This was the state of complete turbulence and flow is called *turbulent flow*.

Figure 1.8 shows the schematic diagram of Reynolds apparatus. Based on the observations made in his experiment, Reynolds concluded that the flow of liquid could be affected by the following four factors;

Diameter of the pipe,

Velocity of the fluid,

Density of the fluid, and

Viscosity of the fluid.

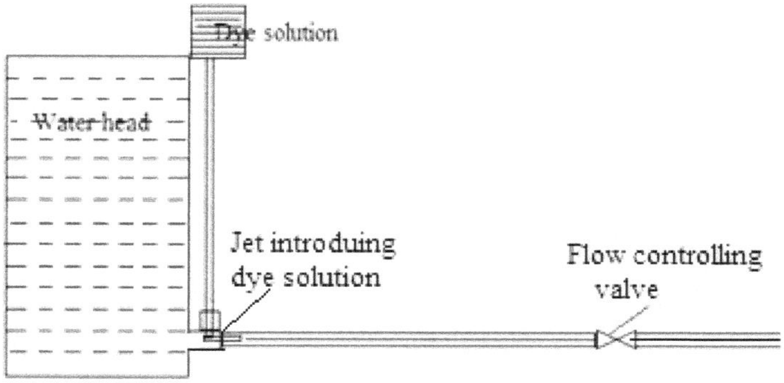


**Fig. 1.8** Reynolds apparatus

Reynolds connected all these factors, grouped together and expressed in the form of the following equation:

$$Re = \frac{\rho u d}{\mu}$$

Where Re is the Reynolds Number,

$\rho$ is the density of the fluid, kg/m$^3$

u is the velocity of the fluid, m/s

d is the diameter of the pipe, m and

$\mu$ is the viscosity of the fluid, kg/m.s.

Hence, the unit of Reynolds Number would be $\frac{kg}{m^3} \times \frac{m}{s} \times m \times \frac{m.s}{kg}$. Thus, Reynolds Number has no unit; that is, dimensionless.

## Significance of Reynolds Number

It is very important to know whether the flow is streamlined or turbulent and the significance of Reynolds Number is that it can be used to predict the character of flow in a particular set of conditions. Generally, the significances of the Reynolds Number are that:

If the Reynolds Number is less than 2000, the flow will be streamlined or laminar.

If the Reynolds Number is more than 4000, the flow will be turbulent.

If the Reynolds Number is more than 2000 but less than 4000, the type of flow will depend on the form of the flow channel.

If there is no disturbance of any kind the flow pattern may be streamlined even at Reynolds Number is more than 2000.

If the internal surface of the pipe is rough, the flow may be turbulent.

If there are bends in the pipe, the flow may be turbulent.

If there are other pipe fittings attached to the pipe, the flow may be turbulent even the Reynolds Number is less than 2000.

The major difference between the streamline and turbulent flow is that in streamline flow there is no velocity component at right angles to the direction of flow. Hence, in case of streamline flow, there will no movement of fluid between the walls and center of the pipe or tube, and the dye solution will appear like a thread at the center of the tube in the Reynolds experiment. While in case of turbulent flow there will be greater movement of fluid across the direction of flow, eddies would be set up, and there will be a mixing of two liquids.

## Bernoulli's Theorem

According to Bernoulli's theorem, if there is an increase in the speed of the liquid, there would be a simultaneous decrease in the potential energy of the fluid or there is a decrease in the pressure of the fluid. Basically, it is the principle of conservation of energy in the case of ideal fluids. If the fluid flows horizontally such that there is no change in the gravitational potential energy of the fluid then increase in velocity of the fluid results in a decrease in pressure of the fluid and vice versa. In the year 1726 Daniel Bernoulli postulated three basic equations of hydrodynamics (properties of moving fluids – liquids and gases).Bernoulli's principle is applied to various types of fluid flow and there are different forms of Bernoulli's equation for different types of flow. In fact, Bernoulli's equation can be derived from the principle of conservation of energy. It states that, *in a steady flow, the sum of all forms of energy in a fluid along a streamline is the same at all points on that streamline*. That is, the sum of kinetic energy, potential energy, and internal energy would remain constant.

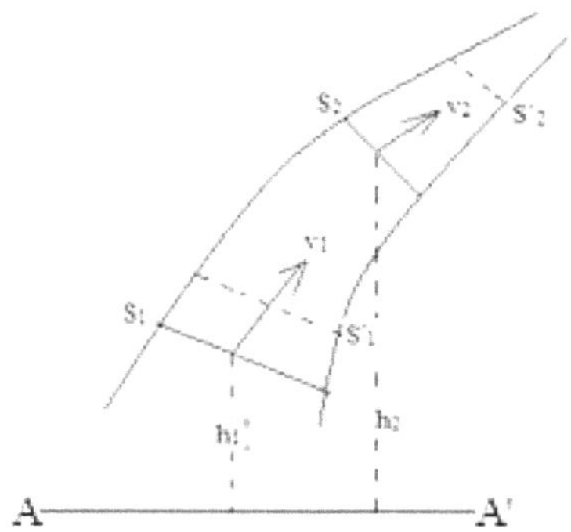


**Fig. 1.9** Schematic diagram of Bernoulli's equation

### Derivation of Bernoulli's Equation

Let us assume that a fluid is flowing through a pipe; at a point X the velocity, pressure, and area of the fluid column are $v_1$, $p_1$, and $A_1$ respectively. Similarly, let us assume that at another point Y the velocity, pressure, and area of the fluid column are $v_2$, $p_2$, and $A_2$ respectively.

Let the volume of the fluid is bounded by XY and it is moving towards MN, and there the fluid is bounded by MN.

Let us further assume that $XM = L_1$ and $YN = L_2$.

Now, if we can compress the fluid; then,

$$A_1 \times L_1 = A_2 \times L_2$$

We know that the work done by the pressure difference per volume of the unit is equal to the sum of the gain in kinetic energy and gain in potential energy per volume of the unit.

This indicates that

$$\text{Work done} = \text{force} \times \text{distance}$$

Or, $$\text{Work done} = p \times \text{volume}$$

Therefore, network done per volume = $p_1 - p_2$

The kinetic energy per unit volume = $\frac{1}{2}\ m\ v^2$

Therefore, we have,

The kinetic energy gained per unit volume = $\frac{1}{2}\ \rho\ [(v_2)^2 - (v_1)^2]$

And potential energy gained per unit volume = $pg\ (h_2 - h_1)$

where $h_1$ and $h_2$ are heights of X and Y above the reference level taken in common.

Finally, we have

$$p_1 - p_2 = \frac{1}{2}\ \rho\ [(v_2)^2 - (v_1)^2] + pg\ (h_2 - h_1)$$

$$\text{or, } p_1 + \frac{1}{2}\ \rho\ (v_1)^2 + \rho\ g\ h_1 = p_2 + \frac{1}{2}\ \rho\ (v_2)^2 + \rho\ g\ h_2$$

$$\text{or, } p + \frac{1}{2}\ \rho\ v^2 + \rho\ g\ h \text{ is a constant}$$

When $h_1 = h_2$

Then, we have, $p + \frac{1}{2}\ \rho\ v^2$ is constant.

*This proves the Bernoulli's Theorem*

Therefore, the Bernoulli's equation is,

$$p_1 + \frac{1}{2}\rho v_1^2 + \rho g h_1 = p_2 + \frac{1}{2}\rho v_2^2 + \rho g h_2$$

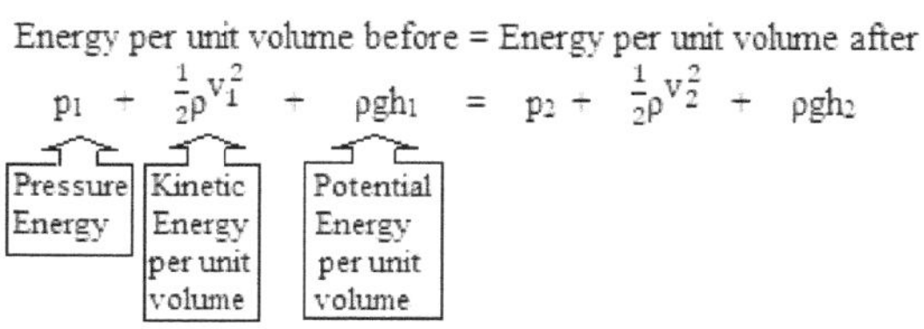

The Bernoulli's equation no 7 is applicable in the following situations:

The velocity of fluid flow is high and the pressure is low

Flow rate is small but the pressure is high

The fluid is automatically flowing from high pressure to low pressure.

An ideal fluid flows as a stationary if the level of fluid flow or the influence of the height difference is not significant (such as gas flow).

*Bernoulli's Theorem basically relates the pressure, velocity, and elevation in a moving fluid (liquid or gas), the compressibility and viscosity (internal friction) of which are negligible and the flow becomes steady, or laminar.*

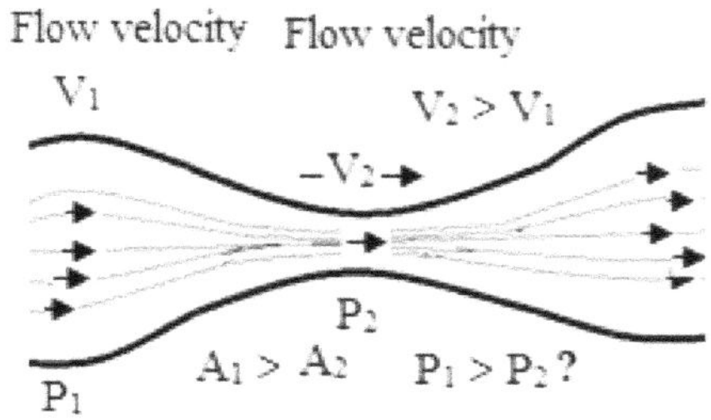


**Fig. 1.10** Increased fluid velocity, decreased internal pressure

## Applications of Bernoulli's Theorem

It can be used to calculate the pressure or velocity of the fluid:

**Air flight:** When an aircraft flies, the air flight can be explained by Bernoulli's principle with the architecture of the wings of the plane. The top of the wing is somewhat curved, while the bottom of the wing is completely flat. In the sky, air moves across both the top and the bottom simultaneously. Different design of both the top part and the bottom part of the plane allows the air to move on the bottom at a relatively slower rate, which creates more pressure on the bottom, and allows the air on the top to move faster, which creates less pressure. This ultimately creates lift, which allows the planes to fly. An airplane is also acted upon by a pull of gravity in which opposes the lift, drag, and thrust. Thrust is the force that enables the airplane to move forward while drag is air resistance that opposes the thrust force.

**Baseball:** Baseball is another example of an application of Bernoulli's principle which is very visible in everyday life. In the case of baseball, the curveball plays the role. Since the stitches of the ball actually form a curve, it helps the pitcher to grip the seams of the baseball. By gripping the baseball, the pitcher can make the ball to spin. This allows the friction to cause a thin layer of air to engulf the misunderstanding of the baseball as it is spinning; since the ball is spinning in a certain manner, this allows for more air pressure on the top of the ball and less air pressure on the bottom of the ball. Therefore, according to Bernoulli's principle, there should be less speed on the top of the ball than on the bottom of the ball. What emerges out of this is that the bottom part of the ball accelerates downwards faster than the top part, and this phenomenon allows for the ball to curve downward, causing the batsman to miscalculate the ball's position.

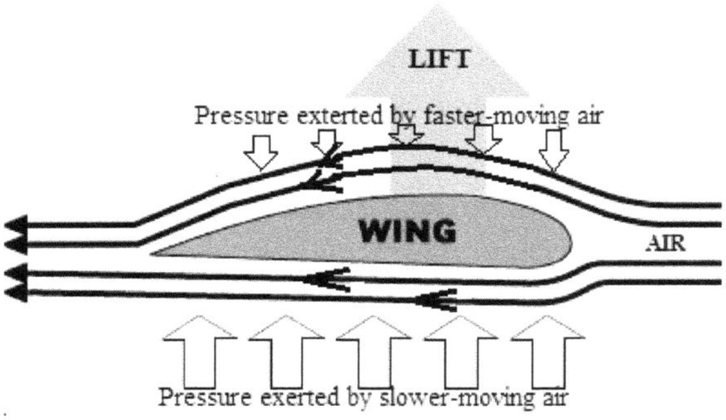


Fig. 1.11 Application of Bernoulli's theorem (Air fight)

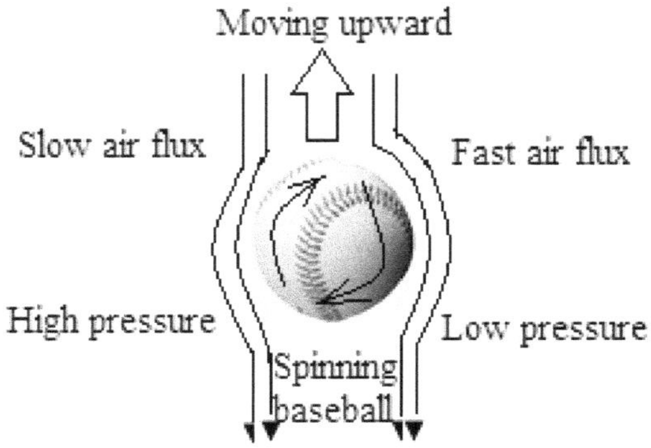


Fig. 1.12 Application of Bernoulli's theorem.

**Draft:** Another example of Bernoulli's principle in our everyday lives is in the case of someone feeling a draft. We all at least one time or another, have experienced the feeling of a draft, and it is because of Bernoulli's principle. Let's say that a room is really hot, but it is nice and cool both outside of the window and outside the door. If the window is opened up and fresh air is allowed to enter into the room. Then, there would not be much change in temperature, unless the door of the room is opened up to let the hot air out of the room. The reason why it works in this way is that if the front door is closed, the room will become an area of high pressure built up from the hot air, and outside the door, there is little pressure, which means that the rate at which the air enters with high speed. When the door is opened up, the inside pressure is reduced and the hot air exits quickly. When the hot air exits the pressure of air in the room becomes more because within a while the cool air come in. Once the hot air flows out, the cool air comes in at a faster rate. Thus, a draft result.

**Engines:** In many reciprocating engines the carburetor used contains a venturi that creates a region of low pressure to draw fuel into the carburetor and mix it thoroughly with the incoming air. The low pressure in the throat of a venturi can be explained by Bernoulli's principle; in the narrow throat, the air is moving at its fastest speed and therefore it is at its lowest pressure.

**Venturi meter:** The flow speed of a fluid can be measured using a device called venturi meter. It works on Bernoulli's principle.

## Energy Losses

When a fluid flows through a pipe, some of the energy of the fluid is lost due to resistance to the flow. Two types of energy-losses are there – major and minor. The major energy loss takes place due to friction. While minor energy losses take place due to sudden expansion, sudden contraction, bent in the pipe, pipe fittings, and obstruction in flow in the pipe.

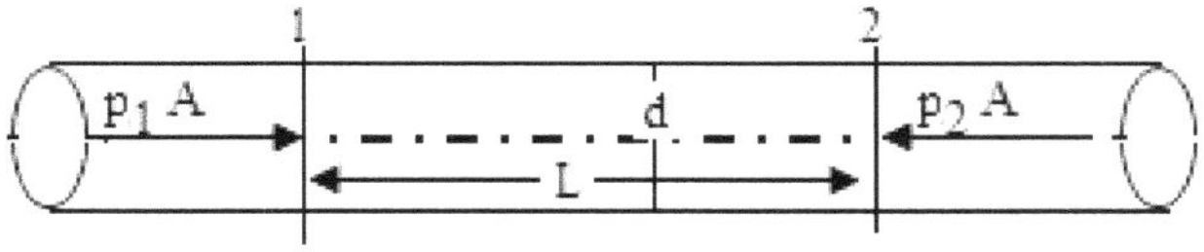


Horizontal pipe in which the fluid is in steady flow

## Major Energy Loss

Loss in energy due to friction in the flow through pipe is caused due to the viscosity. Viscosity causes frictional loss. The frictional loss can be expressed using Bernoulli's equation for real fluid at points 1 and 2 (as shown in the figure) as:

$$\frac{p_1}{\rho_g} + \frac{v_1^2}{2g} + z_1 = \frac{p_2}{\rho_g} + \frac{v_2^2}{2g} + z_2 + h_f$$

where, L = length of the pipe between section 1 and 2

d = diameter of the pipe

f = friction factor

$h_f$ = loss of head due to friction

$p_1$ = pressure at section 1

$v_1$ = velocity at section 1

$p_2$ = pressure at section 2, and

$v_2$ = velocity at section 2.

But, $z_1 = z_2$ and $v_1 = v_2$, since the pipe is horizontal and at both the sections the diameter is same, the above equation is reduced to

$$h_f = \frac{p_1}{\rho_g} - \frac{p_2}{\rho_g}$$

According to Darcy-Weishbach, head loss due to friction can be expressed as:

$$h_f = f\frac{LV^2}{d_2 g} = 4C_f\frac{LV^2}{d_2 g}$$

Where,

L = length of the pipe,

V = mean velocity of the flow,

d = diameter of the pipe, and

$C_f$ = the skin friction coefficient

For fully developed laminar flow when f is the friction factor:

$$F = \frac{64}{Re} \text{ (for Re < 2000 and Re} = \frac{\rho u_{avg} d}{\mu}\text{)}$$

Minor energy loss due to sudden expansion

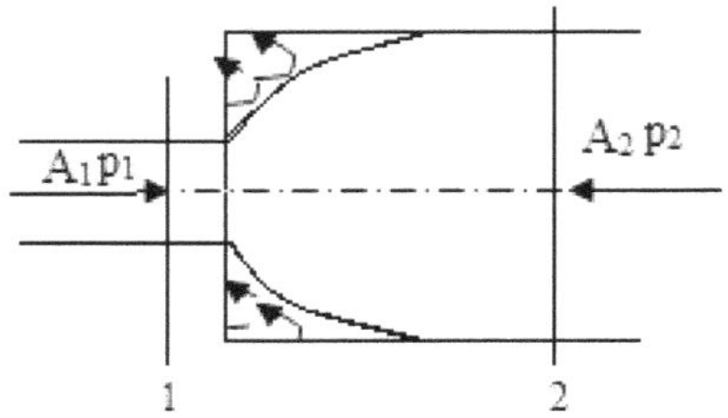


Let $A_1$ = Area at section 1,

$p_1$ = pressure at section 1,

$v_1$ = velocity at section 1,

$A_2$ = Area at section 2,

$p_2$ = pressure at section 2, and

$v_2$ = velocity at section 2.

Applying Bernoulli's equations for real fluid at section 1 and 2, we get

$$\frac{p_1}{\rho_g}+\frac{v_1^2}{2g}+z_1=\frac{p_2}{\rho_g}+\frac{v_2^2}{2g}+z_2+h_e$$

or,

$$h_e=\frac{p_1-p_2}{\rho_g}+\frac{v_1^2-v_2^2}{2g}$$

Minor energy loss due to sudden contraction

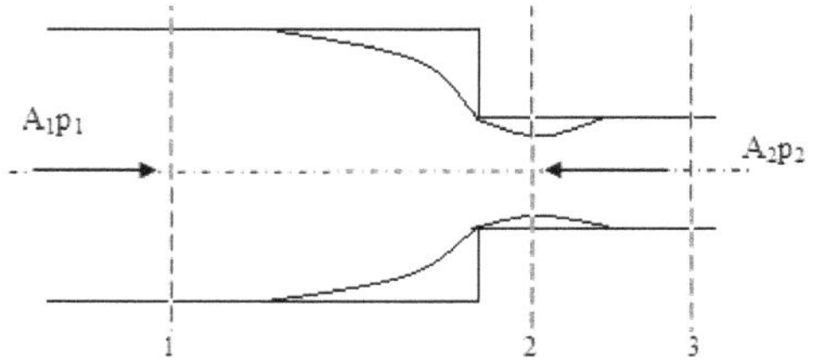

Horizontal pipe with a sudden contraction

Let, $A_1$ is the area at section 1, $p_1$is pressure at section 1, $v_1$ is the velocity of fluid at section 1, $A_2$is the area at section 2,$p_2$ is the pressure at section 2, $v_2$is the velocity of fluid at section 2, and $A_3$, $p_3$, $v_3$are the corresponding values at section 3.

Now, $A_2v_2 = A_3v_3$

Or,

$$\frac{v_2}{v_3}=\frac{A_2}{A_3}=\frac{1}{C_a}$$

Hence, the head loss due to expansion from section 2 to 3 can be expressed as:

$$h_3=\frac{(v_2-v_3)^2}{2g}=\frac{v_2^2}{2g}\left(\frac{v_3}{v_2}-1\right)^2=\frac{v_2^2}{2g}\left(\frac{1}{C_2}-1\right)^2=k\frac{v_2^2}{2g}$$

Where, $k=\left(\frac{1}{C_2}-1\right)^2$ ; the value of k varies from 0.5 to 0.7.

Head loss at the entrance of the pipe

$$h_i=0.5\frac{v^2}{2g}$$

Where, v is the velocity of the fluid in the pipe

Head loss at the exit of the pipe

$$h_\rho=\frac{v^2}{2g}$$

Head loss due to bend in the pipe

$$h_b = \frac{kv^2}{2g}$$

Where $v$ is the velocity of the flow, k is the coefficient of the bend which depends on the angle of the bend, radius of curvature of the bend and diameter of pipe.

Head loss due to pipe fittings

$$h_f = \frac{kv^2}{2g}$$

Where $v$ is the velocity of the flow, k is the coefficient of pipe fitting.

## Orifice Meter

An *orifice meter* consists of a flat plate that has a sharp-edged hole accurately machined in it. It is placed concentrically in a pipe as shown in Figure 13. As the liquid flows through the pipe, the flow suddenly contracts as it approaches the orifice and then suddenly expands after the orifice back to the full pipe diameter. This forms a *vena contracta* or a throat immediately past the orifice. This reduction in flow pattern at the vena contracta causes increased velocity and hence lower pressure at the throat, similar to the venturi meter.

The pressure difference between section 1, with the full flow and section 2 at the throat, can then be used to measure the liquid flow rate, using equations developed for the venturi meter and the flow nozzle. Because of the sudden contraction at the orifice and the subsequent sudden expansion after the orifice, the coefficient of discharge for the orifice meter is much lower. Moreover, depending on the pressure tap locations, section 1 and section 2, the value of coefficient of discharge becomes different for orifices. The diameter of orifice is generally 0.5 times the diameter of the pipe (D), although it may vary from 0.4 to 0.8 times the pipe diameter.

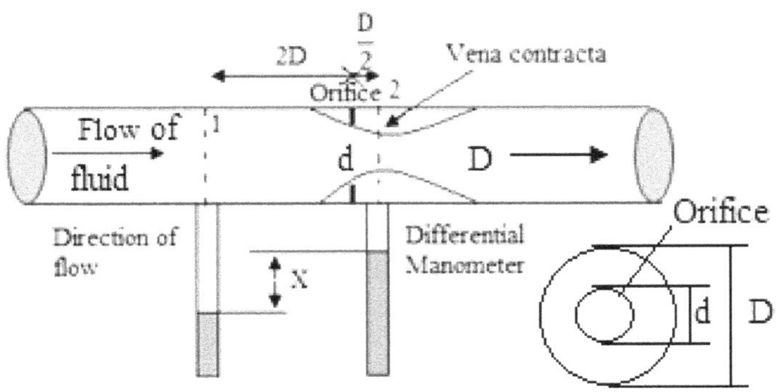


**Fig. 1.13** Schematic diagram of Irifice meter

## Advantages of the Orifice Meter

Well documented in standards;

It has wide acceptance; people working in the industry should have the knowledge about use and maintenance;

Relatively low cost,

Easy to install;

No moving parts in the flow stream; and

When built to standards' requirements, does not require calibration beyond confirming mechanical tolerances.

## Disadvantages of the Orifice Meter

Low rangeability with a single device;

Relatively high-pressure loss for a given flow rate, particularly at lower beta ratios;

More sensitive to flow disturbances at higher beta ratios than some meters; and

Flow pattern in the meter does not make meter self-cleaning.

## Calculation

Let us assume that, $d_1$ and $d_2$ = Diameter at section1 and section2 respectively,

$p_1$ and $p_2$ = Pressure at section1and section2 respectively,

$v_1$ and $v_2$ = Velocity of fluid at section1 and section2 respectively,

$A_1$ and$A_2$ = Area at section1 and section2 respectively,

On application of the Bernoulli's equation at section1 and section2,

$$\frac{p_1}{\rho_g}+\frac{v_1^2}{2g}+z_1=\frac{p_2}{\rho_g}+\frac{v_2^2}{2g}+z_2$$

Or,
$$\left(\frac{p_1}{\rho_g}+z_1\right)-\left(\frac{p_2}{\rho_g}+z_2\right)=\frac{v_2^2-v_1^2}{2g}$$

Or, The differential head, $h=\frac{v_2^2-v_1^2}{2g}$

and
$$v_2=\sqrt{2gh+v_1^2}$$

Say, $A_o$ is the area of the orifice; then Coefficient of contraction, $C_c=\frac{A_2}{A_0}$

Now,
$$A_1v_1=A_2v_2$$

$$v_1=\frac{A_oC_C}{A_1}V_2$$

Hence, $$V_2 = \sqrt{2gh + \frac{A_o^2 C_C^2 V_2^2}{A_1^2}} = \frac{\sqrt{2gh}}{\sqrt{1 - \frac{A_o^2 C_C^2}{A_1^2}}}$$

If Q is the discharge, then $Q = A_2 v_2 = v_2 A_o C_c$

$$= \frac{A_o^2 C_C^2 \sqrt{2gh}}{\sqrt{1 - C_C^2 \frac{A_o^2}{A_1^2}}}$$

If $C_d$ is the coefficient of discharge for orifice meter, then

$$C_d = C_C = \frac{\sqrt{1 - \frac{A_o^2}{A_1^2}}}{\sqrt{1 - C_2^2 \frac{A_o^2}{A_1^2}}} \quad \text{or,} \quad C_c = C_d = \frac{\sqrt{1 - C_2^2 \frac{A_o^2}{A_1^2}}}{\sqrt{1 - \frac{A_o^2}{A_1^2}}}$$

Therefore, $$C_d = \frac{A_o A_1 \sqrt{2gh}}{\sqrt{A_1^2 - A_0^2}}$$

The coefficient of discharge of orifice meter is much smaller than that of a Venturimeter.

## Venturi Meter

Venturi meter and orifice meter are commonly used to measure the flow of liquid or to measure the flow rate of the fluid flowing. These flow meters are also known as *variable head meters*.

The venturi meter has a converging conical inlet, a cylindrical throat and a diverging recovery cone. It has no projections into the fluid, no sharp corners and no sudden changes in contour. The figure 1.14 shows the venturi meter with uniform cylindrical section before converging entrance, a throat and divergent outlet.

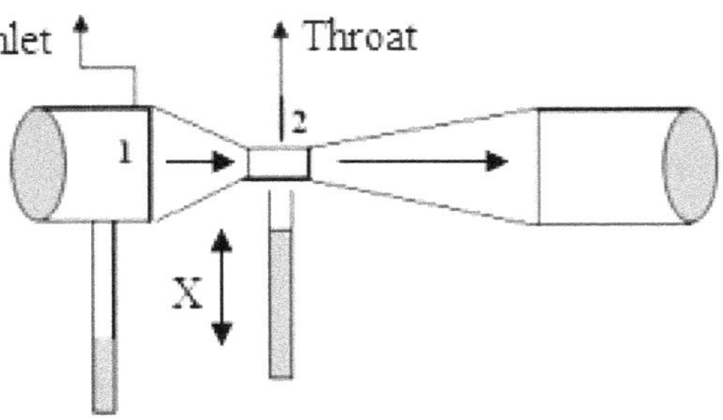


**Fig. 1.14** Schematic diagram of Venturimeter

The converging inlet section decreases the area of the fluid stream, resulting the increase of velocity and decrease in the pressure. The low pressure is measured at the center of the cylindrical throat where the pressure is the lowest. Neither the pressure nor the velocity would change. As the fluid enters the diverging section the pressure increases with lowering the velocity of the fluid. The Venturi effect is the reduction in fluid pressure that occurs when a fluid flows through a constricted section of pipe. The velocity of fluid increases through the constriction to satisfy the equation of continuity; while its pressure must decrease due to conservation of energy: the gain in kinetic energy is balanced by a drop-in pressure or a pressure gradient force. An equation for the drop-in pressure due to Venturi effect may be derived from a combination of Bernoulli's principle and the equation of continuity. The equation for venturi meter is obtained by applying Bernoulli equation and equation of continuity assuming an incompressible flow of fluids through manometer tubes. If $V_1$ and $V_2$ are the average upstream and downstream velocities and $\rho$ is the density of the fluid, then using Bernoulli's equation we get,

$$\alpha_2 V_2^2 - \alpha_1 V_1^2 = \frac{2g(p_a - p_b)}{\rho} \qquad \text{.....(1.2)}$$

Where $\alpha_1$ and $\alpha_2$ are kinetic energy correction factors at two pressure tap positions. Assuming density of fluid to be constant, the above equation can be written as;

$$V_1 = \left(\frac{D_2}{D_1}\right)^2 V_2 \qquad \text{.....(1.3)}$$

Where $D_1$ and $D_2$ are the diameter of pipe and throat in meters respectively. Eliminating $V_1$ from equation 1.2 and 1.3, we get

$$V_2 = \frac{1}{\sqrt{\alpha_2 - \alpha_1\beta^4}} \sqrt{\frac{2(p_1 - p_2)}{\rho}} \qquad \text{.....(1.4)}$$

Where $\beta$ is the ratio of the diameter of throat to that of diameter of the pipe.

If we assume small friction lose between two pressure taps, the above equation 4 can be corrected by introducing imperial factor $C_v$ and written as;

$$V_2 = \frac{C_v}{\sqrt{1 - \beta^4}} \sqrt{\frac{2(p_1 - p_2)}{\rho}} \qquad \text{.....(1.5)}$$

The small effect of the kinetic energy factors $\alpha_1$ and $\alpha_2$ are also taken into account in the definition of $C_v$. The volumetric flow rate $Q_a$ can be calculated as:

$$Q_a = V_2 S_2 = \frac{C_v S_2}{\sqrt{1 - \beta^4}} \sqrt{2g\Delta H} \qquad \text{.....(1.6)}$$

Where $\Delta H$, the manometric height difference = specific gravity of manometric fluid – specific gravity of manometric fluid of water.

## Pitot Tube

Pitot tube is composed of two tubes inserted into a pipe carrying a liquid as shown in Fig 1.15. Tubes inserted at right angle to the direction of flow can measure the pressure head inside the pipe. The tube pointing up stream shall measure the pressure head and velocity head. The reading h of the manometer will therefore indicate the velocity head, and $\Delta H_P$ measures the pressure head. $\Delta H_P$ corresponding to h can be calculated as;

$$\Delta H_p = \frac{u^2}{2g_c} \qquad .....(1.7)$$

The orifice meter and venturi meter measure the average velocity of the whole stream of fluid, whereas pitot tube measures the velocity at single point only. The velocity of the fluid depends on the cross section of the pipe. Hence, the true average velocity of the fluid flowing in the pipe can be measured by one of the two methods:

The pitot tube should be inserted at the centre of the pipe and the average velocity is to be calculated from the semi-logarithmic graph indicating the relation between u/u' and Reynolds number. When this method is followed, the pitot tube must be inserted carefully so that the velocity of the fluid is not disturbed in any way. There should be normal velocity distribution in the pipe.

The pitot tube should be adjustable and readings should be taken at different points in the cross section of the pipe. The mean velocity is to be calculated by graphic integration. This method is commonly used when gases flow in large ducts at low pressure.

In fact, the pitot tube as shown in Fig 1.15 is not practically suitable. The pitot tube itself causes too much of disturbance in the movement of fluid; and hence in the measurement. For measuring the flow of low-pressure gases, the apparatus commonly used is shown in Fig 1.16. The diameter of the static holes should not be more than 0.02 in. The leading edge of the pitot tube may be sharp or hemispherical.

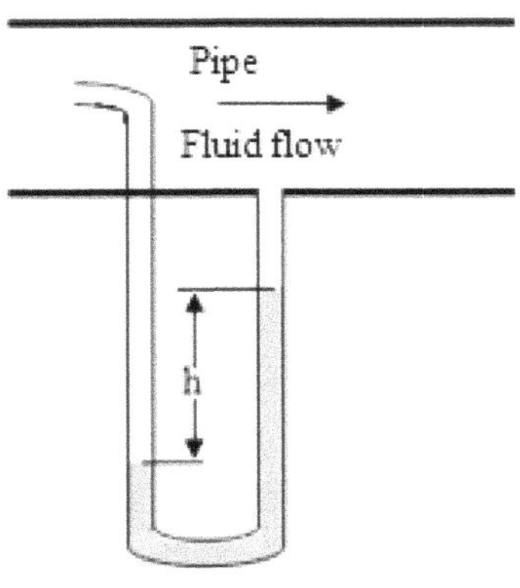


**Fig. 1.15** Schematic diagram of Pitot tube

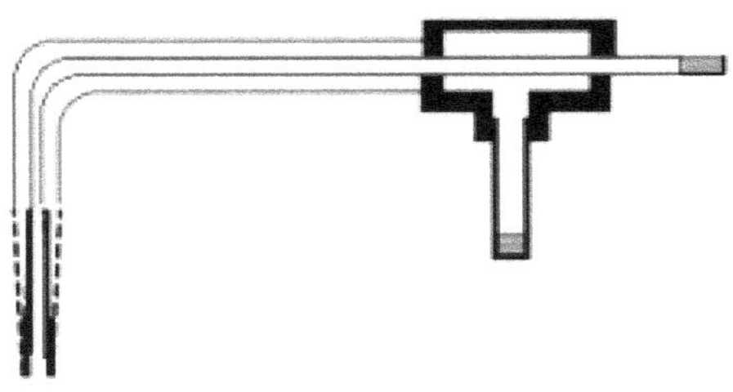

**Fig. 1.16** Pitot tube

A perfect pitot tube should obey exactly the eqn.7, but all the practical instruments should be calibrated and the corrections should be made.

### Advantages

Pitot tube is most convenient to use,

If the pressure of a liquid or gas is high, pitot tube can be suitable for measurement,

### Disadvantages

It fails to provide the average velocity directly,

In case of low-pressure gases, its readings are small.

For measurement of low pressure, either differential or inclined manometer should be used.

## Rotameter

The measurement of a variable pressure difference by orifice meter and venturi meter depends on the fixed constriction placed in the flow in a pipe. These are frequently called "variable-head meters"; because the velocity of the fluid varies with pressure-difference. In case of rotameter, the area of flow of fluid is varied to produce constant pressure difference; for which rotameters are alternatively called "variable-area meters".

It can only be used in a vertical pipeline. Its accuracy is also 98% of other types of flow meters. As shown in Fig 1.17, a rotameter primarily consists of the following measurement components – Float 1. meter tube 2. flowrate scale 3. fittings 5. flanged or threaded, for mounting in the pipeline and O-Rings 7. to provide the seals. The movement of float is restricted by the float stops 4. and a protective housing 6. surrounds the meter tube.

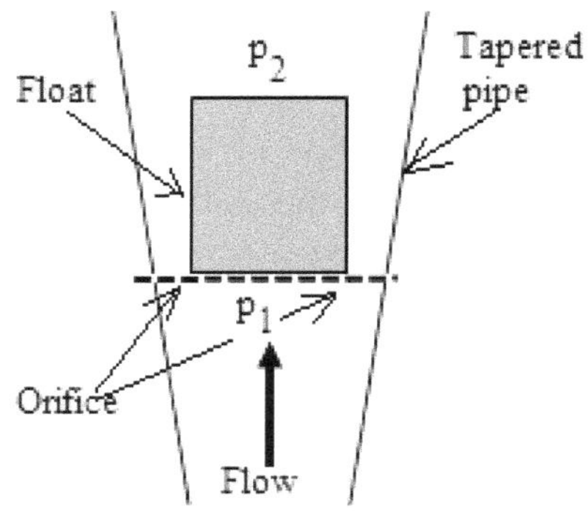

**Fig. 1.17** Schematic diagram of a rotameter

The flowrate scale for flowmeters with glass meter tubes is preferably applied directly on the meter tube.

When the fluid flows upward through the gap between the tube and the float, the float moves up or down depending on the rate and results a change in the gap; as a result, the area of the orifice changes. In fact, the float settles down at a position, where the pressure drop across the orifice creates an upward thrust and that will balance the downward force due to the gravity. The position of the float is calibrated with the flow rate.

The float position, which is a measure of the instantaneous flow-rate, is indicated external to the metal meter tube by a transmission system.

The tapered tube's gradually increasing diameter provides a related increase in the annular area around the float, and is designed in accordance with the basic equation for volumetric flow rate:

$$Q = kA\sqrt{gh}$$

Where,

Q is the volumetric flow rate,

k is a constant,

A is the annular area between float and the tube wall,

g is the gravitational force, and

h is the pressure drop across the float.

The performance of a rotameter depends greatly on the two basic components that are the *tapered metering tube* and the *float.* Tube sizes vary from $^1/_{16}$ to 4 in., most commonly $^1/_8$ to 2 in. Of course, each model has limitations as to capacity, temperature, pressure, and, in the case of liquids, viscosity. In general, a float should be designed in such a way that: it must be held vertical, it should create uniform turbulence so as to make it insensitive to viscosity, it should make the rotameter least sensitive to the variation of the fluid density.

As regards tapered tubes, there are different types of tapered tubes made of different materials for different purposes.

Glass tube rotameters are commonly used for simple but reliable indication of flow rate with a high level of repeatability. Alarm contacts can be easily added to provide high-, and/or low-flow signals, in which the contact is activated as the flow rate either drops below or rises above the set point.

Plastic tube rotameters can be an entirely suitable, very cost-effective alternative to glass or metal meters for a wide variety of fluid measurements. One popular model is made of a single piece of clear acrylic that is practically unbreakable in most industrial process applications. Frequently used as a purgemeter, this type is a low-cost and reliable.

Metal Tube Rotameters, also known as *armored* meters, are designed for applications where the temperature or pressure exceeds the limits of glass tubes. Flow rate is indicated by a pointer on an indicating scale by means of a magnet inside the float, magnetically linked to the pointer. Designed for indication only, metal tube meters require no external source of electric power. They may also be specified in applications requiring remote transmission of the measured flow rate, a feature not generally available with glass tube meters.

## Advantages

It is simple in construction, ready to install and the flow rate can be directly seen on a calibrated scale, without the help of any other device, e.g. differential pressure sensor etc.

It is useful for a wide range of variation of flow rates (10:1).

### Disadvanges

Accuracy of rotameter is about 98% of that of other instruments used to measure the flow of fluid.

## Short Questions

1. 'The manometers measure the differential pressure.' Explain the statement.
2. What are different types of manometers? Mention their applications.
3. How does a suspended particle flow with a flowing liquid?
4. What is Reynold's Number? Name the factors on which flow of fluid depends.
5. What are the significances of Reynold's Number?
6. Define Bernoulli's theorem. Under which situations Bernoulli's theorem is applicable?
7. What is meant by the term 'energy loss'?
8. What is 'vena contracta or throat'? Write down the functions of the apparatus to which the terms 'vena contracta or throat' are related.
9. What for a Venturimeter is used? Write down the advantages and limitations of a venturi meter.
10. What are the advantages and disadvantages of a metal tube rotator?

## Long Questions

1. Is Bernoulli's theorem is applicable in all cases? Explain briefly the applications of Bernoulli's theorem.
2. Explain the terms, major energy loss and minor energy loss under different situations.
3. Draw a schematic diagram of a venturi meter and explain how does it work.
4. With the help a diagram, write down how does an orifice meter work. What are its advantages and disadvantages?
5. For what a pitot tube is used? How is it used? What are its merits and demerits?
6. Why is a rotameter used? With the help of a diagram explain how does it work.
7. What is armored meter? What are its advantages and limitations?
8. What are different types of manometer? Draw the diagram of a well type manometer and describe how does it work.
9. What is an 'indicating fluid'? How can a manometer be corrected?
10. With the help of a diagram explain the Reynold's Number.

# CHAPTER 2

# Size Reduction

Objectives, Mechanisms & Laws Governing Size Reduction, Factors Affecting Size Reduction, Principles, Construction, Working, Uses, Merits and Demerits of Hammer Mill, Ball Mill, Fluid Energy Mill, Edge Runner Mill & End Runner Mill.

## Objectives

Size reduction, alternatively called *comminution* of materials means a reduction of larger particles to appropriate or required size range; that is, reduction to coarse particles, or to powders. The role of particle size in the pharmaceutical formulation is enormous. For example, for the manufacture of tablet we require larger to coarse particles; for preparing oral suspension fine particles; while for making emulsions and parenteral suspensions very fine powders are required. Therefore, size reduction is an important operation in pharmacy. The properties of powders depend directly on the size of the particles or, indirectly on the surface area which is again dependent on the particle size.

The objectives of particle size reduction can be summarized as follows:

- Size reduction increases the surface area of drugs which helps rapid solubilization of the drug.
- The extraction from animal glands such as liver and pancreas, and from crude vegetable drugs can be increased by increasing the surface area because the solvent can easily penetrate into the tissues.
- The therapeutic effectiveness of certain drugs can be increased by reducing the particle size, for example, the dose of griseofulvin can be reduced by reducing its particle size.
- Mixing of several solid ingredients becomes easier to make the more uniform mixture by reducing the particle of all the ingredients to the same size. For example, in the case of powdered pharmaceutical dosage forms, the crystalline drugs are powdered before mixing them with other drugs to prepare a uniform mixture of all the drugs.
- Relatively few drugs can be compressed directly to manufacture tablets. Drugs are mixed with the excipients and converted to granules of suitable size range which are subsequently compressed.
- The stability of emulsions can be enhanced by reducing the particle/globule size of the dispersed phase.
- In the case of suspensions, if the particles are fine, they may form a deflocculated suspension.

- The physical appearance of ointments, pastes, and creams can be improved by reducing the particle size of the dispersed phase.
- All the ophthalmic preparations and preparations meant for external application to the skin must be finely powdered.
- The rate of absorption of a drug depends on the particle size. The smaller the particle, quicker and greater will be the rate of absorption.

### Advantages of Size Reduction

- Uniformity of content
- Uniformity of flow property
- Effective extraction of drug
- Effective drying
- Improvement of physical stability
- Decreases the rate of sedimentation
- Increases the rate of dissolution
- Increases the rate of absorption (smaller the particle size, greater is the absorption)
- Increases the surface area and viscosity of the material
- Improves bioavailability

### Disadvantages

- Rate of degradation of drug increases
- Causes poor mixing
- Chance of contamination increases

## Mechanisms of Size Reduction

In general, to perform size reduction four different processes are there and thus, four mechanisms are involved:

1. **Cutting:** As the name speaks, in this method the material is cut into pieces with the help of sharp blade or blades. Fig 2.1 demonstrates the mechanism of cutting process of size reduction.

**Fig. 2.1** Mechanism of cutting

2. **Compression:** This process is involved in crushing the feed material with the application of pressure. The Fig 2.2 demonstrates the mechanism of the compression process of size reduction.

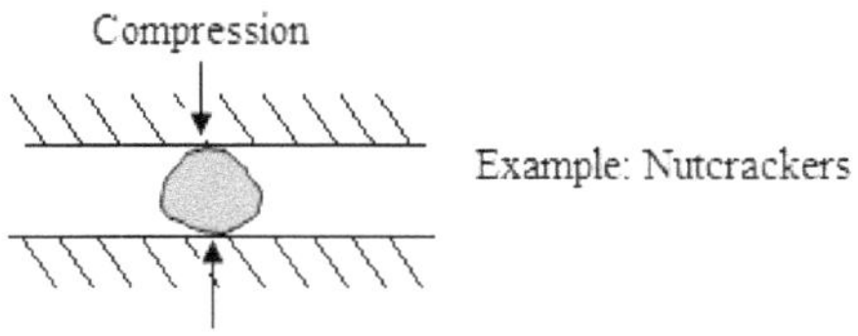


**Fig. 2.2** Mechanism of compression

3. **Impact:** When the feed material is more or less remains stationary and it is hit by a hammer moving at a high speed or the feed material is moving and hits a stationary surface, an impact occurs. In both the cases, the feed material is crushed into small pieces; because the material is hit by the hammer and the particles formed are then thrown into the casing of the machine.

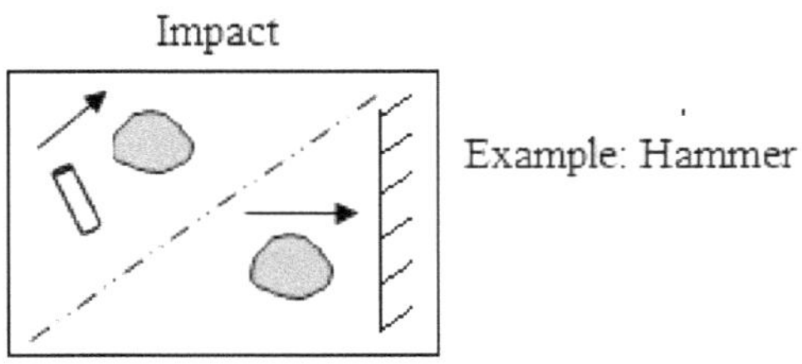


**Fig. 2.3** Mechanism of impact

4. **Attrition:** In this method, the particles are broken with the help of the sheer force. The material is exposed to pressure, as in case of compression, and surfaces are made to move relative to each other. This results in the development of shear force. These four mechanisms are explained diagrammatically with the help of Fig 2.1 to 2.4. The fineness of the product increases as indicated below:

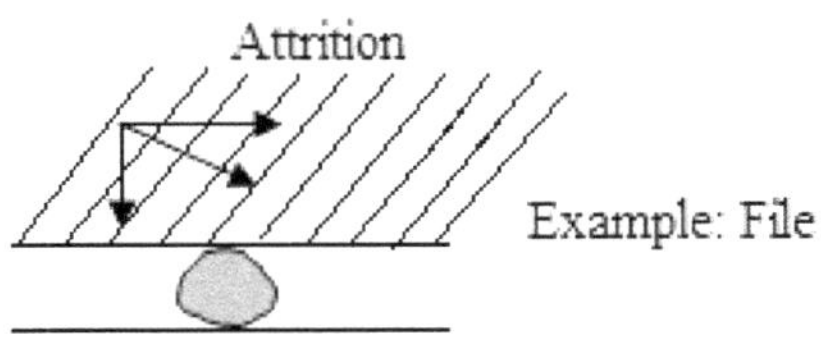


**Fig. 2.4** Mechanism of attrition process

Cutting ⟶ Compression ⟶ Impact ⟶ Attrition

1. **Cutting:** On a small scale, for size reduction, the cutting process can be done by a knife or a root cutter which is a simple form of the guillotine. *Cutter mill* can be used on a large-scale operation. As shown in Fig 2.5, there are two types of knives attached to the rotor, one set works as stationary and other as rotating. Stationary knives are mounted in the casing of the machine. Rotating knives are attached to a horizontal rotor which rotates at high speed. The upper part has a hopper to feed the material and at the bottom, there is a detachable screen which allows the passage of product of appropriate size.

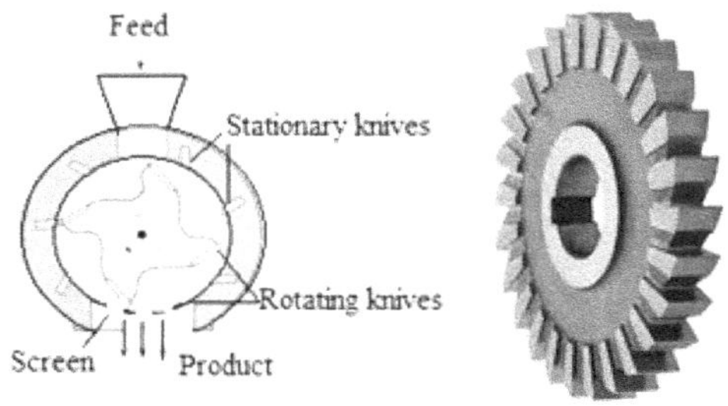


**Fig. 2.5** Schematic diagram of cutter mill

Materials of oversize are retained over the screen until these are cut to the required size. This method or mill is used to cut the feed material to produce coarse or relatively larger particles. Usually, plant material such as bark, root or stem of plants is used as feed material. The product thus obtained become suitable for extraction.

2. **Compression:** Size reduction by compression method in the laboratory is done by using mortar and pestle. In the pharmaceutical industry, this method is done by using a roller mill.

   Roller mill consists of two cylindrical rolls made of stone or metal. The rolls are mounted horizontally. The rolls rotate on their longitudinal axes. Usually, one roll is driven directly and the one rotates freely. As a result, when the feed material is placed above the rolls, the material is drag inside through the nip of the first roll and then the second roll starts rotating by friction. The diameter of the rolls may vary from few centimeters to a meter or more. The gap between the rolls can be adjusted as per the required size range of the particles of the product. The roller mill is generally used for crushing the material such as seeds for extraction of oil, sugar cane to extract its juice.

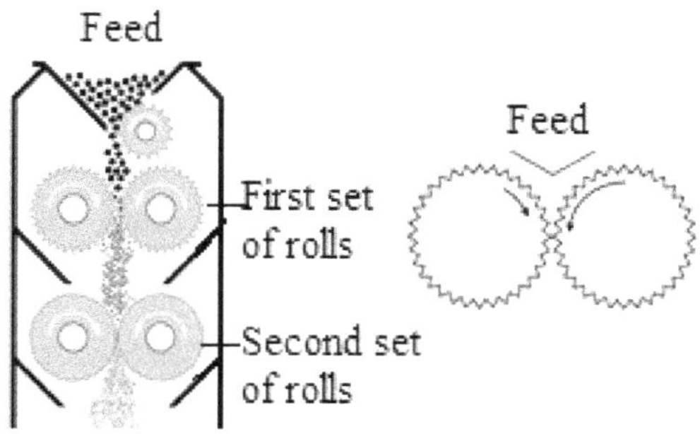


**Fig. 2.6** Roller mill

   However, this type of mill is not used for milling the ointments. For milling the ointment in a roller mill, both the rolls of the mill are driven, but at different speeds, so that size reduction takes place by attrition.

3. **Impact:** The shattering of brittle substances is done by using a hammer or pestle and mortar. Otherwise, there is no equipment or apparatus that can be used by hand. The industrially used machines such as hammer mill with low capacity are used in the laboratory.

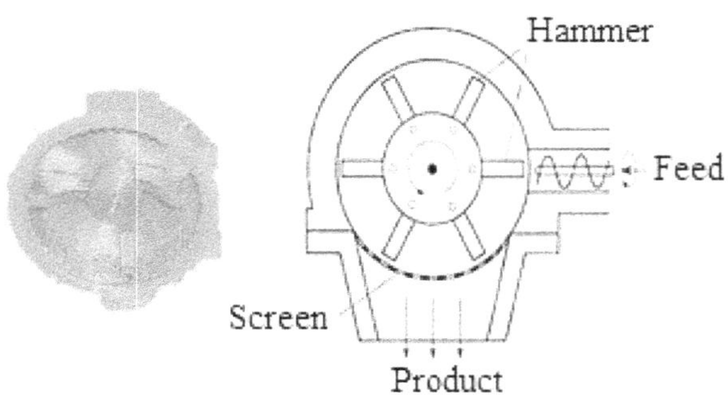


**Fig. 2.7** Schematic diagram of hammer mill

The **hammer mill** consists of a stout metal casing which encloses a central shaft. Four to six hammers are attached to the central shaft. The hammers are mounted with swivel joints, so that the hammers can swing out to a radial position when the shaft is rotated. There is a screen at the lower part of the casing. Through this screen, the product can be collected. The screen can be changed as per the required size range of the particles of the product.

According to the requirement, the hammers may be square-faced, tapered to a cutting edge, or may have a stepped form. An alternative form with rigid beaters is known as a *disintegrator*; but this type of machine may be damaged by any hard material, if present, in the feed.

The interior of the casing may be circular in shape with slightly rough surface. It ensures repeated impacts as the particle is thrown repeatedly between the hammers and the casting, with this the efficiency may be increased.

The rotor moves at relatively high frequency, usually about 80 per second. However, the actual speed of the rotor depends on the diameter of the rotor.

4. **Attrition:** Effective size reduction can be done by hand, if mortar-pestle is used. For a small-scale method, the roller mill can be used.

   **Roller mill** utilizes the principle of attrition for size reduction of solids in suspensions, pastes or ointments. Two or threerolls, usually made of metal or porcelain, are mounted horizontally with a very small, but the adjustable gap between the rolls. The rolls rotate at different speeds so that the material is sheared as it passes through the gap. During the movement, the material is transferred from the slow-moving roll to fast-moving roll, from where the material is removed with the help of a scraper. This method is very effective for reducing the size and dispersing solids in the semi-solid media.

## Types of Crushers and Grinders

Particle size can be reduced by the operation known as *crushing and grinding* using different types of devices mentioned below.

1. Coarse crusher
   - Jaw crusher
     (i) Blake
     (ii) Dodge

2. Intermediates
   - Rolls
   - Disc crushers
   - Edge runner
   - Disintegrators (cage)
   - Hammer mills
3. Fine grinders
   - Centrifugal
     (i) Raymond
   - Buhrstones
   - Roller mills
   - Ball mills and Tube Mills
   - Ultrafine grinders

## Laws Governing Size Reduction

There are two most popular laws of comminution; first is proposed by Kick, and second is by Rittinger. There is another law proposed by Bond, so we are having three laws of comminution and we call it Kick's law, Rittinger's law, and Bond's law.

1. **Rittinger's law:** According to this law, *the work required for size reduction is directly proportional to the new surface created.* The Rittingers law is more accurate as far as size reduction or comminution is concerned. Although the crushing and grinding of materials have been done widely in various industries well as at homes since long, the development of a suitable formula took place quite later.

   Mainly there are two theories, Rittinger's law and Kick's law. Even then, none of these laws can exactly express the performance of any grinding machine.

   Rittinger proposed the law on the basis of an assumption that the energy required for crushing a material is proportional to the surface sheared. As per Fig 2.8, let us assume that a cube of X inches (each side) is crushed into four smaller cubes. Each of the smaller cubes has a dimension of $x$ inch. Thus, X: $x$ = 4:1. Let the ratio X:$x$ is represented by n. The Fig 2.8 shows that there are (n – 1) planes of fracture in each of the three directions. This can be alternatively said that to crush this larger cube into smaller cubes, the surface of the cube needs to be sheared with a force amounting $3(n-1)X^2$ square units must be applied.

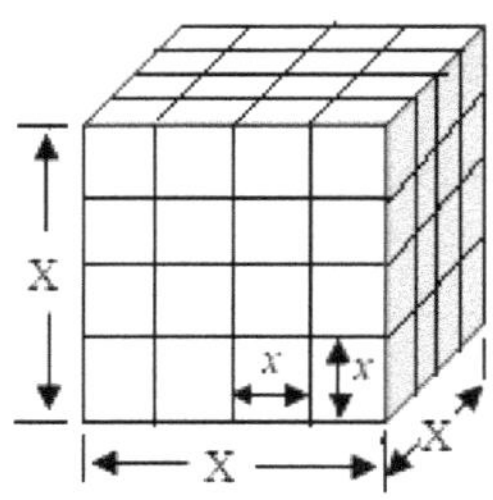


**Fig. 2.8** Cube undergoing crushing and grinding.

Let us also assume that for this crushing B ft-lb work is done to produce 1 sq. inch new surface. Thus, the work required to crush a cube of X inches (dimension) would be $3BX^2$ (n – 1).

So, Work done = $3BX^2(n-1)$ .....(2.1)

If 1 cu. inch of material is crushed, there would be $\frac{1}{x^3}$ of the larger units. This may also be assumed that if the units are not perfectly cubes, the ratio of the area of the actual unit to the area of a cube of the same major dimension would be same for all the sizes. This ratio is represented by K and $n = \frac{1}{x}$. Thus, by taking all these into consideration, the equation 1 can be written as;

$$\text{Work done/ cu. in} = \frac{1}{x^3}(3BX^2K)(n-1)$$

$$= 3BK\left(\frac{1}{x} - \frac{1}{X}\right) \quad .....(2.2)$$

This is Rittinger's law.

A factor, C related to specific gravity can be used to convert the equation 2 to express in form of horsepower per ton from work per cubic inch as;

$$\text{hp/ton} = C\left(\frac{1}{x} - \frac{1}{X}\right) \quad .....(2.3)$$

A test is conducted on a particular ore using a particular crushing machine and the equation 3 is used to calculate the change in power by adjusting the mill to the product size. If more amounts of fine particles are finer than $x$, that is, the total surface is in the fraction is finer than $x$, the results could never comply with the Rittinger's law. Hence, the validity of the law remains questionable. With the decrease in particle size, the ratio X: $x$ decreases. A constant ratio equal to K for all size ranges should not be used; it is better to use an appropriate value of K for each size range. Of course, the value of this ratio is a function of size.

2. **Limitation of Rittinger's law:** Mechanical losses due to friction and inertia in the grinding equipment are not considered in the Rittinger's law. These mechanical losses of the crusher can be predicted by running the crusher without any charge (empty). Thus,

$$\text{Overall energy efficiency} = \frac{\text{Energy required to create a new surface}}{\text{Total energy supplied}} \text{ and}$$

$$\text{Theoretical effectiveness} = \frac{\text{The energy required to create a new surface}}{\text{Total energy supplied} - \text{Energy required for running the empty mill}}$$

Rittinger's law is applicable mainly to the process, where the new surface is being created and is the most suitable for fine grinding, that is, the increase in surface per unit mass of material is predominant. Thus, it gives better results for fine grinding where there is a much greater change in surface area. This law is the most suitable for the feed size of less than 0.05mm.

3. **Kicks law:** The law can be applied to crushing. It says that *the work required for crushing a given quantity of material is constant for given reduction ratio irrespective of the original size.*

That is, whatever energy is required, whatever work is required for reducing the size of a material depends on the size of the feed as well as the size of the product. The law is based on the assumption that the energy necessary for crushing a material is proportional to the logarithm of the ratio between initial and final diameters of the particles. Thus, the same amount of energy would be required to reduce a particle weight of $1-\frac{1}{2}$ inch cubes to $\frac{1}{2}-\frac{1}{4}$ inch cubes, or of $\frac{1}{4}-\frac{1}{8}$ inch cubes, and so on.

According to Kick's law, the energy required for producing a three-fold reduction should be half of that required for reduction of particles to nine-fold. The Kick's law can be expressed as:

$$\text{hp} = \text{K} \log \frac{\text{X}}{x} \qquad \text{.....(2.4)}$$

Where, K is a constant, X is the initial dimension of the particles and $x$ is the final dimension of the product.

The surface of final particles after crushing of quartz has been measured by the method of solubilization in hydrofluoric acid. This method was used to find out the validity of Rittinger's law. The new surface produced was plotted against net energy input. The plots obtained were not completely linear when extended to a large range of energy input, this indicates that the Rittinger's law is not completely valid. The ratio of the size of feed to product can be defined as the reduction ratio. Therefore, the work required is proportional to the reduction ratio, it does not vary with the original size of the feed. The Kicks law can be defined mathematically as follows:

$$\frac{E}{M} = K_k \ln \frac{D_F}{D_p} \qquad \text{.....(2.5)}$$

Where,

E is the energy required for crushing M kg of material,

$K_k$ is the Kick's constant, and

$\frac{D_F}{D_p}$ is the reduction ratio, R

Thus, the above equation can be written as $\frac{E}{M} = K_k \ln R$ .....(2.6)

In other words, the energy consumption is proportional to the reduction ratio, and here the proportionality is equated with the constant that is the Kick's constant. Therefore, comminution energy depends only on the reduction ratio and is independent of the original size of the feed.

When the particle size is smaller and is converted to a further smaller size, it requires more collision for reduction purpose. That is, the reduction ratio is same to crush 200 mm particle to 50 mm will require less energy in comparison to the reduction of 2 mm particle to 0.5 mm product. Although the reduction ratio is the same, obviously energy consumption will significantly be high. Because in case of the smaller particle, the more collisions are required and many of these collisions will be wasted also and they do not participate in size reduction.

In fact, a higher amount of energy is required for reducing fine particles to finer sizes than for breaking down large pieces of rock. So, Kick's law can be applied to coarse crushing where the reduction ratio is small.

4. **Bond's law:** An intermediate and more realistic method of predicting power consumption for crushing and grinding was proposed by Bonds in the year 1952. It states that *the work required to form a particle of size from a very large particle size is proportional to the square root of the surface to volume ratio of the product.*

   According to Bond's law, the work required to form particles of size, $d_P$ from very large particle is proportional to the square root of the surface to volume ratio of the product, $S_P/V_P$. So,the surface, as well as volume ratio and work required for crushing the feed of large size to the product of size $d_P$, will be proportional to the square root of surface to volume ratio $\sqrt{S_p / V_p}$ , of the product. The law can be expressed mathematically as:

$$\frac{S_P}{V_P} = \frac{6}{d_P}$$

$$\frac{E}{M} = K\left(\sqrt{\frac{S_P}{V_P}}\right)_P = K\sqrt{\frac{6}{d_P}}$$

## Factors Affecting Size Reduction

In many industries other than pharmaceutical industries the size reduction operation is well standardized, for example, in flour, cement, and coal industries. In pharmaceutical industries, various types of materials are in use; for example, chemical substances, plant drugs, animal tissues, etc. The plant drugs or crude drugs may be seeds, barks, peels, etc. Out of these seeds are hard, barks are fibrous; while peels are of spongy type. Thus, the method used for size reduction would differ depending on the type of material to be crushed.

The factors that can influence the size reduction operation can be categorized broadly into three types:

- Physiochemical properties of the material,
- Physiological effect, and
- Ratio of feed size to product size
- **Physiochemical properties of material**
  - ➢ ***Bulk density:*** Usually, the lot size of solid materials is expressed in terms of weight but the capacity of a grinding mill depends on the volume of the material to be ground. Therefore, even all the factors remain favorable and constant, the output of the grinding mill will depend on the bulk density of the material to be ground.
  - ➢ ***Hardness:*** Hardness is a surface property of the material. Sometimes, it is confused with the property of the material responsible for its strength. If a hard material is found to be brittle, no special arrangement would be required for its size reduction, or its size reduction would cause no problem.

    An arbitrary scale of hardness known as *Moh's Scale* has been devised for size reduction.

According to this scale, mineral substances are assigned hardness number between 1 to 10. The material may vary from graphite to diamond.

- The material having hardness number from 1 – 3are called *soft* and can be marked with a finger nail.
- Materials with hardness number from 3 to 7 are *intermediate.*
- The materials with hardness number more than 7 are called *hard*. The hard materials cannot be marked even with a knife blade. It is difficult to reduce the size of the hard materials.

➢ **Toughness:** Toughness is more important than hardness. Thus, if the material is soft but tough, it is difficult to reduce its size. If the material is hard but brittle, it is easy to crush. For example, it is easy to crush the black-board chalks but not the rubber.

Many pharmaceutical substances are found to have toughness. For example, fibrous crude drugs; their toughness depends on their moisture content. For example, the toughness of a green twig may become brittle on drying.

In some cases, the tough materials can be reduced after treating the material with liquified gas such as liquid nitrogen. This indicates that on cooling at a temperature between –100°C to –150°C, the substances can be made brittle. With this method, the rubber becomes brittle like glass. This method has also the following advantages:

1. Decomposition of thermolabile materials can be reduced to a great extent.
2. The loss of the volatile component of the material can be arrested.
3. Oxidative decomposition of the constituent of the material can be reduced.
4. The risk of explosion is negligible.
5. Due to cost and engineering problem, the method is rarely used in practice.

➢ ***Abrasiveness:*** Usually, abrasiveness is a property of hard materials, particularly if it is obtained from mineral. Type of machinery to be used depends on the type of material. Generally, metal powders is found in the final product obtained after grinding, because the metal is worn from the grinding mill and this contamination with metal may increase up to 0.1% if, very abrasive materials are ground in a grinding mill.

➢ ***Stickiness:*** The term ‘stickiness’ is not scientific, yet its meaning can be understood by the term. During size reduction(grinding), this property can causea substantial problem. For example, the material can adhere to the grinding surfaces, can deposit on the apertures of the screen resulting in choking of the aperture, etc. Generally, resinous or gummy substances possess this property and cause a problem during grinding, particularly if heat is generated during size reduction. To reduce such a problem either the material should be completely dried or inert substances can be added during grinding. Sometimes, the addition of inert substance can reduce the problem considerably. For example, the addition of kaolin in grinding of sulfur or DDT has been found to be more beneficial.

➢ ***Slipperiness:*** This is a property just opposite to stickiness. The material having adequate slipperiness, show problem during grinding; because such material acts as a lubricant and can reduce the efficiency of the grinding surfaces.

➢ ***Softening temperature:*** In many cases, during size reduction processes the heat is generated. As a result, some substances become soft at a higher temperature. The temperature at which the substance softens is important. Thus, the size reduction process may be affected. For example, a waxy substance such as stearic acid, or crude drugs containing fats or oils becomes soft at a higher temperature during grinding. In such cases, the mill should be kept cool during size reduction either by circulating cold water through a water jacket or by circulating air or liquid nitrogen through the jacket.

- ***Moisture content:*** The moisture content of the substance can greatly influence certain properties of the substance that can ultimately affect its size reduction process. The properties such as hardness, toughness, stickiness, etc. depend on the moisture content of the material. There may be dry grinding or wet grinding. In case of dry grinding the moisture content of the materials should ordinarily be not more than 5%; while for wet grinding the moisture content may be more than 50%.
- ***Structure of the material:*** The characters of some substances are homogeneous. Most of the substances have a special structure. For example, mineral substances may have lines of weakness along which the materials split to form flake-like particles; while vegetable drugs possess a cellular structure which frequently produces long fibrous particles.
- ***Purity of the material:*** The grinding surfaces of some grinding machines may wear during grinding. Such machines should not be used to grind the material, if a high degree of purity of the material is required to be maintained. Similarly, there are some grinding machines which cannot be properly cleaned after grinding of material and before grinding of another. These machines should not be used when a high degree of purity of the material is necessary to be maintained even after grinding.
- ***Flammability:*** Under certain conditions, fine particles become a potentially explosive mixture. For example, dextrin, starch, sulfur, etc. All electrical switches should be explosion proof and mill should be well grounded.

- **Physiological effect**

  There are certain very potent drug substances such as podophyllum resin, hormones, etc. A small amount of such drug in the form of dust can exert an effect on the operators. In such cases, to avoid dust an enclosed mill should be used or special air extraction system should be provided. However, wet grinding of such potent drug or its formulation can be used to avoid the problem completely.

- **Ratio of feed size to product size**

  Usually, a size reduction machine, used for producing a fine product, cannot work with large size of feed material. Hence, it works satisfactorily when feed size is reasonably less. As a result, more than one machines are to be used for a particular lot. One is used for crushing the feed to produce coarse material, the second one makes the coarse particles to fines and lastly the third one is used to produce very fine particles of the desired size range.

## Ball Mill

### Principles

The effect of impact and attrition are combined in a ball mill. The particles receive the impacts of the balls and thereafter, these particles are subjected to attrition when the balls slide over each other in a ball mill.

## Construction

The ball mill consists of a horizontal cylinder with its diameter almost equal to its length. It is mounted in such a way that it can rotate on its horizontal axis, as shown in Fig 2.1. The cylinder is lined with a heavy liner plate. Some models are very large, with cylinders 3 m in diameter, but about 1 m is more common in pharmaceutical industries. There is a feed end at the right side as shown in the figure. The feed end is connected to a helical feed scoop which introduces the feed through the spiral feed liner. The cylinder contains balls that occupy 30 to 50% of the mill volume. The load of the balls, their size, the speed of revolution of the cylinder, and the rate at which feeding to be done, are adjustable factors. These factors are controlled as per the size and rate of producing the product. At the discharge end, a screen of larger mesh (less than the size of the balls) is attached to prevent the ball from coming out with the product. The screen is placed above the discharge funnel. Usually, the balls of approximately 75mm in size are provided to a mill 1 m in diameter, for larger cylinders the larger balls of 150mm diameter are also used. The balls would be of different size ranges. Since the balls are regularly worn away due to attrition, these should also be replaced as and when required, so that a range of sizes exists from about 20 mm upwards.

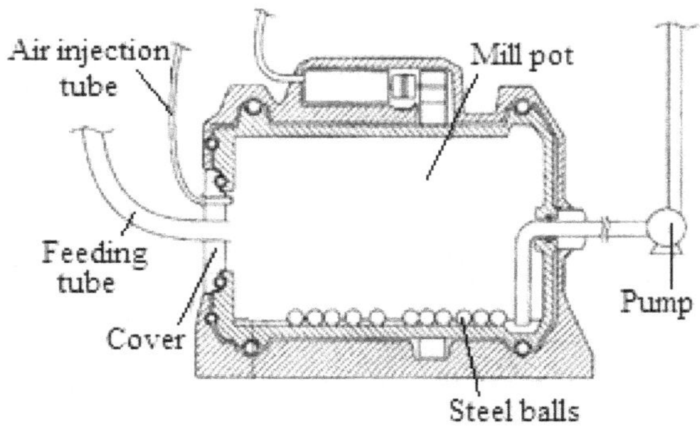


**Fig. 2.9** Schematic diagram of Ball Mill

This gives a better product. Since the larger balls crush the feed and the smaller ones form the fine product. There is a gear that rotates the mill. The cylinder may be made of metal, porcelain or of rubber, to reduce abrasion. Similarly, the balls may be of metal, porcelain or, sometimes pebbles. When the mill contains pebbles, it may be called as a pebble mill. The amount of the material in the mill is of considerable importance, too much of a cushioning effect and too little lead to loss efficiency and to abrasion.

## Working

The mill and the balls to be used for grinding the material should be cleaned thoroughly and dried before introducing the feed material. The amount of feed depends on its density. There should be sufficient space for movement of the balls. The mill should be run at the desired speed depending on the required size of the powder. For the production of fine powders, the mill is run at higher speed and for a longer time.

### Uses

The ball mill is used for grinding the materials such as coal, pigments, drugs, and drug products. Grinding can be carried out either wet or dry condition, but the former is performed at low speed. For systems with multiple components, ball milling has been shown to be effective in increasing solid-state chemical reactivity. Additionally, ball milling has been shown effective for the production of amorphous materials.

### Merits of Ball Mill

- Useful for grinding of a wide range of materials with different degree of hardness and related characteristics.
- Being a closed system of grinding may be suitable for grinding toxic substances,
- Can produce fine powders,
- Can be used for continuous operation,
- The classifier can be attached to the mill to separate the undersize particles from oversize ones and to feed the mill with oversize particles for further grinding,
- Equally useful for both wet and dry grinding.

### Demerits of Ball Mill

- Contamination of product may occur as a result of wear and tear of the balls which occurs principally and partially from the casing.
- High level of machine noise occurs, if the hollow cylinder is made of metal; but much less, if the rubber is used.
- Not suitable for soft and sticky materials; because such material either adheres to the sides of the mill or stick to balls and creates problem in milling.
- It requires a relatively long time of milling.
- It is difficult to clean the machine after use

## Hammermill

### Principles

The basic principle of hammer mills is very straightforward. This includes a wide variety of crushing and shredding equipment. These work by the impact. The hammer mill can be used as a primary, secondary, or tertiary crusher.

Depending on the design, the hammer mill will move into the crushing chamber either by gravity or controlled/metered process. The ganged hammers or chopping knives hit the material separately. Theses knives or hammers rotate at a high-speed reducing material to the desired size. Only the particles having diameter same as to that of the screen size will pass through. Otherwise, the hammer will continue to hit these materials until they are reduced to the required size. Basically, within this chamber, the material is hit by a repeated combination of knives/hammer impact and collision with the wall of the milling chamber.

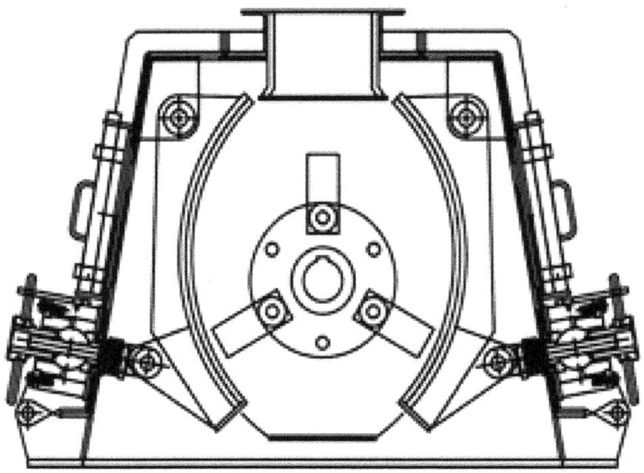

**Fig. 2.10** Schematic diagram of Hammer Mill

Inter-particulate collisions play an important role in the size reduction process. This is a mechanical process where the particles are hit with high-speed knives. Depending on the size and design of the metal screen, it allows the required size of particles to pass through while retaining course material.

The crushing chamber should not be opened when the machine is in operation; because the flying particles will hit the crushing hammers/knives at very high speed. The output of the milling chamber is attached to a perforated metal screen. They are also referred to as the bar gates. The Fig 2.2 shows the diagram of a typical hammer mill.

The material that passes through is basically the finished product. It can either be packed using capsule filling machines or processed further depending on the specific requirements.

## Construction

A number of discs are attached to a central shaft. Between these discs, the hammers are hinged. The hammers are in the form of plain rectangular steel bars. The thickness of the bars varies from 1/8 to 1/2 inch. The breaker plates made of white cast iron or manganese steel are on one side of the casing. Around the bottom, there is a cage that contains hard screen bars. The shaft rotates at a high speed, and the centrifugal force causes the hammers to swing out radially. The construction of the mill should be such that the hammers can be easily replaced when they have worn. In some mills, the part of the screen cage is hinged in such a way that it can be lowered so that from the mill any hard material can be removed that cannot be pulverized.

For crushing and grinding of the brittle material like limestone, the cross section of the screen bars is commonly rectangular; while for shredding fibrous materials, the screen bars may have a cutting edge. However, the mills may be of different types with respect to the construction and shape of the hammer bars; but the function of the mills remain the same.

## Working

A hammer millis essentially a steel drum containing a vertical or horizontal rotating shaft or drum on which hammers are mounted. The hammers are free to swing on the ends of the cross, or fixed to the central rotor. The rotor is spun at a high speed inside the drum, while the material is fed through the feed hopper. The material is impacted by the hammer bars, shredded and expelled through screen of selected size attached to the drum.

Brittle and friable material like coal, limestone, or similar substances is crushed inside the mill by impact against the breaker plates or against the screen bars. The crushing is continued until whole of the material passes through the screen. By using hammers of appropriate weights and screen bars of different cross-sections, the machine can be used to crush the material ranging from brittle such as coal to fibrous such as ginger.

## Uses

- It is used to produce the intermediate grades of powders of various substances such as plant bark, leaves, roots, crystals, etc. except the sticky substances which can choke the screen.
- Grinding of legumes and other dry products.
- The hammer mill can be used satisfactorily for granulation with the help of cutting edges of the hammers. The damp masses are cut to granules by the hammers and uniform granules are obtained. This method has been found to be better than sieve granulation.

## Merits of Hammer Mill

- The process is rapid and can be used to grind many different types of materials.
- The equipment or machinery for crushing and grinding can be easily installed and operated. The operation can be made continuous.
- There is a negligible chance of contamination of the product with metal abraded from the mill, if the mill is thoroughly checked to ensure that there is no worn in metal part that can contaminate.
- The particle size of the material being reduced can be controlled easily by using appropriate hammer, and type, shape, and size of the screen, and running the mill at a suitable speed of the rotor.

## Demerits of Hammer Mill

- The mills being run at high speed can generate heat that may affect the stability of thermolabile materials or drugs containing gum, fat or resin. The mill may be cooled with water or air to reduce this heat damage.
- The rate of feed must be controlled carefully, since this may result in choking of the mill, and thus, decreased efficiency or even damage may be resulted.
- The hammer mill is susceptible to damage by foreign objects such as stones or metal in the feed if it is run at high speed.

## Fluid Energy Mill

### Principles

Fluid energy mill is also known as micronizer or jet mill. It utilizes the combined effect of impact and attrition. Solid is pulverized in jets of high pressure superheated steam or compressed air, supplied up to 35 bars. The pulverization takes place in a shallow cylindrical chamber with a number of jets arranged tangentially at an equal interval around the circumference. The solid is thrown to outside the walls of the chamber. Thus, fine particles are formed by the shearing action resulting from the differential velocities within the fluid stream.

The particles are driven to the peripheral wall forming a circulating particle layer. The particles located near the grinding air nozzles are accelerated to higher velocities by two grinding air streams compared to other particles and those high-speed particles are more expected to hit the wall or collide with others, due to the velocity difference. The distribution of the particle velocities becomes broader with the increase of the operating pressures, leading to a higher probability of the establishment of the relative velocities and higher relative velocities to some extent. Both the particle-particle collisions and the particle-wall collisions play important role in the particle size reduction. Commonly particle-particle collisions can be considered to be *side swipe collision*, and mainly lead to particulate abrasion, instead of cleavage or fracture. The feed air stream is not as efficient and effective as the grinding by the air stream takes place in terms of facilitating particle breakage.

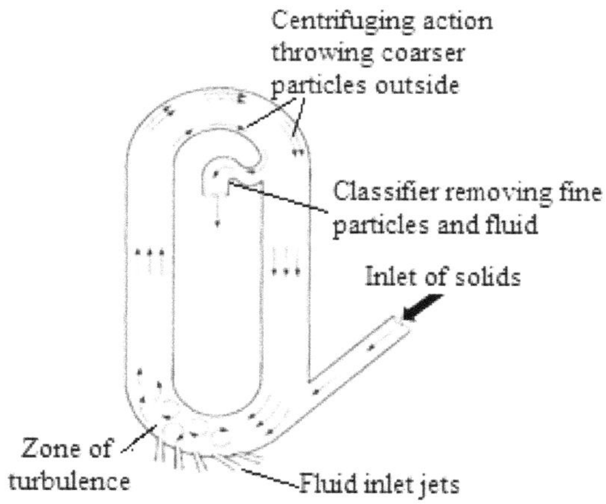


**Fig. 2.11** Schematic diagram of Fluid Energy Mill

### Construction

It consists of a loop of a pipe. Its diameter ranges from 20 to 200 mm, depending on the overall height of the loop. It may be up to about 2 meters. A fluid, usually air is injected at high pressure through nozzles at the bottom of the loop, giving rise to a high-velocity-circulation in a very turbulent way, as shown in Figure 2.11. Solids are introduced into the stream. Due to the higher degree of turbulence, the impact and attritional forces occur between the particles. A classifier is attached to the system so that the particles of the larger size range are retained until become sufficiently fine.

The feed to the mill needs to be pre-treated to reduce the particles size to the order of 100 mesh. This allows the process to produce a product as small as 5 micrometers or less. In spite of this, the mills are available which are capable of producing fine particles up to 4 mg per hour.

### Working

Fluidized energy mill consists of a hollow toroid which has a diameter of 20 – 200mmdepending on the height of the loop which can be up to 2m. It operates by particles impaction and attrition. A fluid or milling gas, usually air or inert gas is injected at a high-pressure jet through nozzles at the bottom of the loop. The powder particles in the mill are accelerated to high velocity. The kinetic energy of the air plus the turbulence created inside the mill causes inter particle (particle-particle collision) and particle-wall collisions that reduces the size of the particles up to between 2 and 10 micrometers. The fluidized effect transports the particles to a classification zone where the size classifier retains the particles until they are made sufficiently fine to be removed. The particle size and size distribution are controlled by;

- The speed of air/inert gas
- Feed rate and size
- The configuration of the mill
- Design of the classifier
- The position of the nozzle
- The impact between the feed and air

### Uses

- ➢ Fluidized energy is used for milling thermolabile materials.
- ➢ It is chosen when a higher degree of drug purity is required
- ➢ Fluidized energy mill is used for the fine grinding of frits, kaolin, zircon, titanium and calcium, alumina.

### Merits of Fluid Energy Mill

- ➢ The particle size of the product can be made smaller than that produced by any other method of size reduction.
- ➢ Expansion of gases at the nozzles can cause cooling; hence, the heat is not generated usually generated due to friction.
- ➢ The size reduction takes place through a process of inter-particulate attrition. There is little possibility of abrasion of the mill and so, practically there is no chance of contamination of the product.
- ➢ In case of very oxygen-sensitive materials, inert gases can be used to maintain stability.
- ➢ A classifier is an integral part of the system, this permits close control of particle size and particle size distribution.

➢ The method is suitable where fine powders of pharmaceutical substances such as antibiotics, sulphonamides, and vitamins, are required.

### Demerits of Fluid Energy Mill

➢ There is a tendency of forming aggregates or agglomerates after milling.
➢ Generates amorphous content due to high energy impact.
➢ Forms ultra-fine particles

## Edge Runner Mill

### Principles

A number of mills and mixing machines belong to this class. *Arastra* is the oldest and basic type. It consists of two circular, heavy, flat, slabs made of stone. At the center of the slab, a vertical post is there. Horizontal arms are extended from this post. A mule or an ox hitched to a long sweep causes the central post and its arms to rotate and drag the stones over the material lying on the floor. Such a primitive machine has been used to extract oil from the seeds.

This machine was modified later on primarily in two aspects –

1. The central post was driven by power instead of animals.
2. The slabs made of stone were replaced by heavy wheels. This type of modified mill was called a *Chilean mill* and has been used extensively for crushing the hard-rock. The putty chaser is the real representative which has been used for a long time. It is more mixer than a grinder.

The dry pan may be of two types

1. The entire bottom of the pan may be solid and the apparatus or machine works in batches. When one batch is completed it is scooped out by hand.
2. The space between the wearing ring and the outside of the pan be covered with perforated plates. Any material that becomes fine enough to pass through these perforations is removed. Only the material that is not yet been ground fine enough remains to be scraped back under the mullers. Thus, the pan works continuously work both in dry or wet condition.

### Construction

The putty chaser consists of a stationary pan that can hold much of material which is technically called as*charge*. A vertical shaft attached centrally to the pan can be rotated with the help of a bevel gear and pinion. A short horizontal shaft is attached to the vertical shaft. A heavy steel or granite wheel is carried on the horizontal shaft. This wheel rotates freely about its own axis as well as about the vertical axis. Usually, a type of blade or plow is attached towards the vertical axis of the wheel. The blade scrapes the material from the outer edge of the pan back into the path of the wheel. The wheel exerts a rubbing action along with crushing action. Thus, this mill or machine can be used as a mixer for stiff materials. In this type of crusher, the pan rotates and the horizontal axis of the grinding wheels remains stationary. In clay industries, such a machine is widely used and called as *dry pan* or *wet pan* depending on whether water is used or not during crushing.

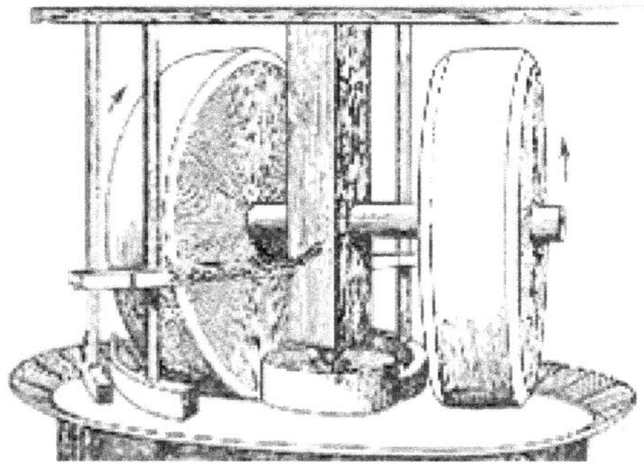

**Fig. 2.12** Schematic diagram of Edge Runner Mill

### Working

A dry pan consists of two heavy frames connected at the top by a yoke. The yoke carries a bearing for the central vertical shaft. The bearing is for the horizontal jack shaft that carries the pully and drives-pinion of the bevel gear. The central shaft stands in a step bearing at the bottom and carries the pan. The pan may be of 4 – 12 ft diameter and from 6 – 12 inch deep. There is a wearing ring near the center of the pan made of steel or white cast-iron plate on which the heavy cast-iron wheels or mullers run. These mullers are attached (mounted) to the short shafts that rest in the bearing boxes at either end. The bearing boxes are not fixed. These are free to move up and down in vertical slots to adjust the mullers to the load in the pan. A scraper is there to work the material in front of the mullers continuously when the pan rotates.

### Uses

- Useful for very tough and fibrous barks, roots, and fibrous roots.
- Can be used both for wet and dry grinding.
- Useful for grinding paints, clays and sticky materials.

### Merits of Edge Runner Mill

- Can produce very fine powder
- Grinding requires less number of operations
- Easy to clean and operate
- Low maintenance
- Does not show any problem of chocking

### Demerits of Edge Runner Mill

- Consumes more energy
- Wet material is necessary for grinding.
- Due to shear, heat is generated,
- Not suitable for thermolabile materials.

## End Runner Mill

### Principles

End-runner mill (also known as Roller stone mill) is the mechanized forms of mortar and pestle, and it works on the principle of compression comminution. This milling equipment consists of two heavy wheels made of either stone or metal, connected by a shaft. The wheels rotate at its axis in a shallow circular pan. The material to be milled is fed into the center of the pan and is thrown outwards by the action of the wheels. Scrapers are used for scraping the material continuously from the bottom of the wheel and vessel after which it is fed into the vessel where it gets crushed to powders.

The principles of size reduction applied by these mills is the result ofthe heavy weight of the stones or metal and shearing force (due to the movement of these stones or metal). In the End-runner mill, a weighted pestle is turned by the friction of material passing beneath it, and the mortar rotates the powder within it.

### Construction

This milling equipment consists of two heavy wheels made of either stone or metal, connected by a shaft. The wheels rotate at its axis in a shallow circular pan. The material to be milled is fed into the center of the pan and comes outwards by the action of the wheels. Scrapers are used for scraping the material constantly from the bottom of the wheel after which it is feed to the vessel where it is crushed and made powders.

The principles of size reduction applied by these mills crush due to the heavy weight of the stones or metal and shearing force which is as a result of the movement of these stones or metal. In the End-runner mill, a weighted pestle is turned by the friction of material passing beneath it as the mortar rotates under the powder. The Edge-runner mill has the paste equivalent mounted horizontally and rotating against a bed of powders.

### Working

Mortar revolves at high speed and revolving mortar causes the pestle to revolve.

### Uses

It is used in the size reduction of non-sticky materials.

### Merits of End Runner Mill

- ➢ It produces fine particles
- ➢ Requires less attention during the milling operation

### Demerits of End Runner Mill

- ➢ It is not suitable for milling sticky materials
- ➢ Machine noise leading to noise pollution

## Short Questions

1. Why comminution is done?
2. Briefly explain with suitable milling machine that works through compression mechanism.
3. What are different types of crushers and grinders.
4. Explain the limitation of Rittinger's law.
5. Explain the Bond's law governing size reduction of particles.
6. What are the effects of physiological effect and ratio of feed size to product size.
7. Write down the advantages and disadvantages of ball mill.
8. Write down the advantages, disadvantages and uses of fluid energy mill.
9. Write down the construction and uses of edge runner mill.
10. What is the role of impact in size reduction? Name a machine that works on impact.

## Long Questions

1. Explain the mechanisms of size reduction with the help of diagram.
2. Write down the objectives of comminution.
3. Explain Rittinger's law that governs the size reduction.
4. Explain Bond's law and Kick's law that govern the size reduction.
5. Explain the physicochemical properties of material that influence size reduction process.
6. Write down the construction, working, and uses of ball mill.
7. Write down the construction, working, and uses of hammer mill.
8. Write down the principle, construction, and working of fluid energy mill.
9. Explain the principle and construction of edge runner mill.
10. Explain the principle, construction of end runner mill.

# CHAPTER 3

# Size Separation

Objectives, Applications and Mechanism of Size Separation, Official Standards of Powders, Sieves, Size Separation Principles, Construction, Working, Uses, Merits and Demerits of Sieve Shaker, Cyclone Separator, Air Separator, Bag Filter and Elutriation Tank.

## Objectives

There are various methods used to separate the solids on the basis of their sizes. If the solids are insoluble in water, their dispersions are kept undisturbed for some time. The particles according to their size range would settle under the force of gravity, and the samples drawn from respective layers will indicate their presence quantitatively. Another method for this purpose is the use of screens of appropriate size. Screens are usually used for separation of dry powders. Hence, the screens must be a standard one and their aperture size must be known.

For a particular purpose, the fine powders or coarse powders are used in pharmaceutical industries. For example, tablets are manufactured by compressing the granules. Granules are prepared either by compaction of solid powders mixed with an appropriate solid binder or the powders are mixed and granulated by mixing with a paste of an appropriate binder. The size range of these granules has a relation with the average weight of the tablet. While for preparing a semisolid preparation, emulsion, ointments, etc. fine or ultrafine powders are required. Simple household's preparation such as the body talcum powder requires ultrafine powders of talcum. Therefore, size separation is an important activity in pharmaceutical industries and various machines are used for these purposes and their basic principles should be known.

### Particle Size Analysis

There are a large number of methods by which the particle size of powders can be analyzed but sieving method is commonly used in industries; while sieving and sedimentation method is used in the laboratories.

### Sieving

Sieving is the most widely used method for particle size analysis in a powder sample because the method is cheap, simple and rapid. The variation between the operators is also slight. Sieving or sifting is a process by which different grades of powders are separated from each other. In the laboratory different grades of sieves are used for sifting the powders and for preparing the granules of required particles size. After comminuting any material, it is passed through a specific sieve to get the particles (granules)of required size. The bigger particles, retained over the sieve are returned to the machine for regrinding. After final grinding and sieving, the particles which do not pass through the sieve is known as *tailing* which should never be rejected because they may contain the therapeutically active constituents. The tailing may be added to the next batch of the drug for grinding. Most of the sieves used are of the wire mesh type, the number of the sieve indicates the number of meshes (apertures) present in a length of 2.54 cm (1 inch) in each direction parallel to the wires. It refers to the number of apertures that is specified and not the number of wires. Thus, a No. 10 sieve has 10apertures per inch in each direction.

## Applications of Size Separation

Various dosage forms are designed and prepared in pharmaceutical industries. Pharmaceutical ingredients including drug and excipients are mostly available in solid state. For processing, each type of dosage form, powders of the definite particle size range are required. The applications of size separation process are mentioned below:

- For determination of particle size and size distribution for the production of tablets and capsules.
- For analysis of raw material, it is used as a quality control tool.
- To avoid or reduce powder segregation.

## Mechanism of Size Separation

Solid particles can be commonly separated as per their size by sieving method, if the meshes of a screen are not damaged. However, the particles should not be forced through a sieve. Small particles can easily pass through a sieve, if the sieve is shaken, tapped, or brushed.
Mechanical sieving is done by agitation, brushing, or by centrifugation.

**Agitation method:** The sieves of different mesh nos. are arranged in a descending way, that is, the sieve of highest mesh no is kept at the top, while the sieve of lowest mesh no is kept at the bottom. A receiver tray is attached to the bottom most sieve and a lid to top most sieve. The powder material to be sieved is taken in the sieve kept at the top. The entire set is agitated in a number of ways, such as

- ***Oscillation:*** In a frame, the set of sieves is mounted and is oscillated mildly back and forth. The method is simple, the particles roll on the surface of the sieve, the fibrous material particularly takes a ball-shape. If the shape of the particles is spherical and smaller in size, it can pass through the aperture of the sieve.
- ***Vibration:*** In this method, the mesh is vibrated at high speed with the help of electrical means. The rapid vibration is conveyed to the particles on the sieve and the particles are less likely to block the mesh.
- ***Gyration:*** In the gyratory method, the sieve mounted with rubber is connected to an eccentric flywheel. Thus, the sieve becomes under a rotary motion of small amplitude, but of considerable intensity. This gives a spinning motion to the particles. This motion increases the

chance of the orientation of a particle to pass through the mesh. Thus, the output is usually greater than that obtained with oscillatory or vibratory sieves. If the sieve is inclined, agitation methods may be made continuous and provide separate outlets for undersize and oversize particles. This happens irrespective of the method of agitation.

**Brushing method:** When a brush is used to move the particles over the surface of the sieve, it makes the apertures of the screens open. To make effective brushing, across the diameter of an ordinary circular sieve, a single brush is rotated about the mid-point. But in case of large-scale production, a horizontal cylindrical sieve is to be used with a spiral brush that rotates on the longitudinal axis of the sieve.

### Centrifugal Method

In this method, the apparatus uses the centrifugal force for the separation of liquid from solid, powders of different size range. Primarily this is a development of a gravity filter.By utilizing centrifugal force, the force acting on the materials can be increased enormously and the materials which may be even a mixture of two immiscible liquids can be separated. This type of mechanical sieves commonly consists of a vertical cylindrical sieve having a high-speed rotor inside the cylinder. The centrifugal force throws the particles outwards. This movement creates the current of air,helps sieving also. Thus, it is useful for separation of very fine powders. The force developed by centrifugal action can be expressed as:

$$F_c = \frac{Wu^2}{g_c r}$$

Where Fc is the force developed, lb

W is the weight of the rotating assembly plus load, lb mass

u is the peripheral velocity of the basket, ft

r is the radius of the basket, ft

gc is the dimensional constant, 32.2 (lb mass) (ft)/ (lb force)($sec^2$)

If N is the speed (rpm), then $u = 2\pi rN/60$. Now substituting this for u and 32.2 for gc in the above equation, we get

$$Fc = 0.000341WrN2$$

## Official Standards of Powders

For official purposes, the standards for powders are laid down in different Pharmacopoeias. The degree of fineness or coarseness of a powder can be differentiated and expressed in terms of size of the mesh of the sieve through which the powder can pass.

| Grades of powder | Sieve through all the particles must pass (Mesh number) |
|---|---|
| Coarse | 10 |
| Moderately coarse | 22 |
| Moderately fine | 44 |
| Fine | 85 |
| Very fine | 120 |

According to the Indian Pharmacopoeia, there are five grades of powder as per their ability to pass through a mesh of particular aperture.

It would not be wrong to think that this type of definition is not adequate to define powder. Because powder that passes through mesh number 85 is called fine; but the same powder can also pass through mesh number 22; whether the powder should be called moderately coarse or fine? Although a definite size is being assigned to the powder, it is practically a mixture of powders of different sizes. Hence, there should be a clear definition of the size of powder and a limit should be fixed. For this reason, the Pharmacopoeias specify two consecutive sieves; all the particles of the powders must pass through a sieve, but at least 60% must be retained over the sieve of the immediate smaller mesh size. For example, the powder that completely passes through a sieve of mesh 10 and if not more than 40% of the particles do not pass through a sieve of mesh no.44, it is considered to be coarse powder. This definition fixes a limit of under sider size particles. Accordingly, the powders may be classified as mentioned below:

| Grades of powder | Sieve through all the particles must pass (Mesh number) | Sieve through which not more than 40% of particles can pass (Mesh number) |
|---|---|---|
| Coarse | 10 | 44 |
| Moderately coarse | 22 | 60 |
| Moderately fine | 44 | 85 |
| Fine | 85 | Not specified |
| Very Fine | 120 | Not specified |

## Sieves

The most common method used in industries and laboratories for size separation of powder or standardization of powders is sieve analysis. Hence, specifications of sieves have been stated by different Pharmacopoeias. Most of the sieves used are made of mesh wire and the number is assigned on the basis of a number of meshes made per 2.54 $cm^2$ (square inch). That is, the mesh number indicates the number of holes of the same size present per sq. inch. The sieve no. 10 contains 10 meshes (holes) per sq. inch. Sieves may be perforated plate or woven. The wires used to prepare sieve must be of uniform and specified diameter.

Now, stating the number of mesh per unit length to indicate the sieve number is not enough. Although the passage of the particles through a particular sieve depends on various factors, the diameter of the wire used to make the sieve is most important. Because of this, the Pharmacopoeias has mentioned the specifications for the wires to be used to prepare the sieve. As shown in figure1, the sieves can be prepared in ways:

1. Woven with wire, and
2. Perforated plate

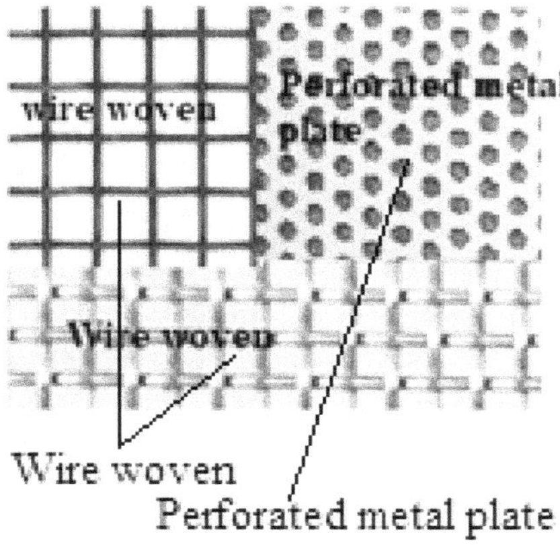


Fig. 3.1 Two types of sieves

### Standards for Sieve

It is necessary that the cross-section of the wire used to prepare the wire-mesh sieves must be uniform and perfectly circular. Irrespective of number, each sieve must follow the following standards:

- **Number of Sieves:** This states the number of meshes (holes) in each length of 25.4 mm (1 inch), in each direction parallel to each wire.
- **Nominal Aperture size:** This indicates the distance between the two wires. It states the length of the side of the square aperture. The size of the aperture says how large a sphere can pass through it. Of course, this is related to the dimension of the particles; because plate-like, needle-like, fibrous particles can pass through a mesh if they are suitably oriented. For example, a plate-like particle can pass through diagonally, a needle-like particle can pass through length-wise.
- **Nominal Diameter of the wire:** The basic standards of a sieve depend on the dimension and number of meshes. The diameter of the wire is to be so selected that the required number of apertures with defined size would be produced after waving the sieve. At the same time, the strength of the wire should be such that it is not distorted after or during use for a prolonged period of time. Such wire bears a Standard Wire Gauge number representing a particular number related to the diameter of the wire.
- **Approximate Screening Area:** This is another standard which expresses the area of the meshes in terms of percentage of the total area of the sieve. It depends on the size of the wire used for a particular sieve number and it remains within 35 to 40%. This provides sufficient strength to the sieve leaving the adequate area of meshes as well as the area of the sieve.
- **Average Aperture Tolerance:** In fact, despite taking all sorts of precautions some variation in the aperture size cannot be avoided. Such variation is expressed as a percentage and is known as the aperture tolerance average. The term tolerance is mostly used in engineering activities to indicate the limits within which a particular attribute or dimension is allowed to vary and yet become acceptable for the purpose it is used. The degree of tolerance is more in case of fine wires. The variation increases with a decrease in the diameter of wires. Hence, fine meshes

cannot be woven with the same accuracy as a coarse one. Therefore, average aperture tolerance is smaller for sieves of 5 or 10 mesh than for sieves of 200 mesh.

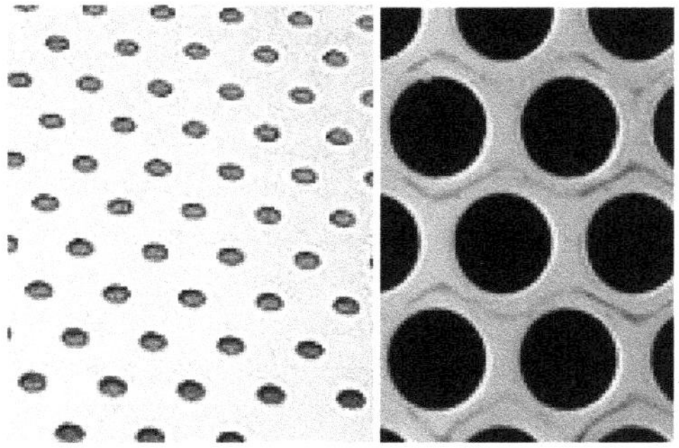

**Fig. 3.2** Perforated plate sieve

## Perforated Plate Sieves

This type of sieves is prepared by drilling holes in a metal plate. This type of sieve provides a perfectly *circular* aperture as against *square* apertures of the woven sieve. Generally, this type of sieves is used for larger sizes and made with greater accuracy than wire-mesh sieves. Another advantage of this type of sieves is that these sieves rarely distort or deform during long use and is able to withstand more friction. For this reason, these are generally used as screen in impact mills in pharmaceutical industries. If these sieves are viewed from the top, the holes are found to form the centers of apices of equilateral triangles; as shown in Fig 3.2, the holes are equidistantly placed. Further, the standards for plate thickness and a nominal width of the bridge as indicated in Fig. 3.3 can improve the strength of the sieve.

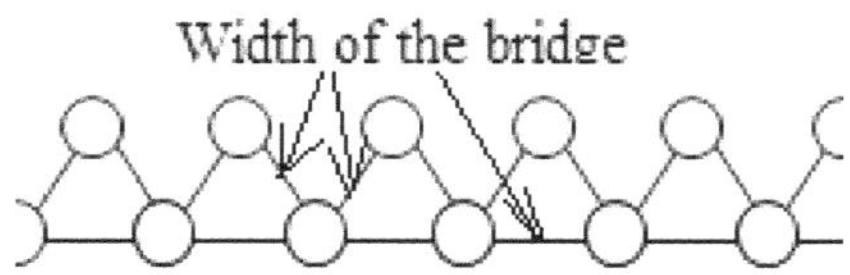


**Fig. 3.3** Width of the bridge

## Material used for Sieves

For making wire-sieves both metals and non-metals may be used. As per the Pharmacopoeial standards, the materials used for making sieves should be strong enough and the diameter of the wire used should be uniform and of perfectly circular.

Metals such as iron, coated iron, copper, copper alloys, stainless steel are used make the sieves. Iron is cheap but very susceptible to rusting which is most undesirable. Rusting of iron can be avoided by coating. Coating of iron can be done by galvanizing or tinning. The major disadvantage of coating is variation in the thickness of the wire. Copper wire is readily available and not susceptible to rusting. The material is soft, the sieve obtained can be distorted easily. Alloys of copper such as bronze, brass are resistant to corrosion and have greater strength. Hence, these can be used to prepare sieves. The sieves prepared should not distort on long use. Stainless steel although usually expensive is most suitable for making sieves. It has all the required qualities also.

The non-metal materials used to make sieve include synthetic fibers such as nylon, terylene, etc. These materials have good strength and are resistant to corrosion. These materials can be extruded in different, uniform diameters and a wide variety of sieves can be prepared with such materials.

## Size Separation Principles

Various methods are used for size separation. Particles may remain in powder form or in form of a dispersion in liquid. Accordingly, the method of size separation varies. Most commonly the methods used for separation of particles are:

- Mechanical sieving methods (Dry sieving)
  - Oscillation
  - Vibration
  - Gyration
- Wet sieving
  - Sedimentation methods
  - Elutriation methods

### Dry Sieving

- **Mechanical sieving method:** This method utilizes the devices which separate the particles into different sizes. Agitation, brushing the sieve or using centrifugal force are the principles or mechanisms involved in size separation of particles.

  Agitation method includes oscillation, vibration, and gyration.
  - *Oscillation:* In a frame, the sieve is mounted, the frame oscillates back and forth. The method is simple. The material rolls over the surface of the sieve and fibrous materials, in particular, tend to 'ball'.
  - *Vibration:* By electrical means, the sieve is vibrated at high speed. The rapid vibration is conveyed to the particles on the sieve and the particles are less likely to block the mesh.
  - *Gyration:* In this method, the sieve is mounted with rubber and connected to an eccentric flywheel. The sieve is under a rotary movement of small amplitude, but of considerable intensity. This spin the particles. As a result, the particles orient and get a chance to pass through the mesh. The output of this method is much more than that of oscillatory or vibratory sieves.
  - By inclining the sieve, the agitation method can be made continuous and separate outlets can be provided for undersize and oversize particles.
- **Brushing method:** This method utilizes a brush to move the particles on the surface of the sieve and to keep the mesh clean. Across the diameter of the sieve, if a single brush rotates about the mid-point, an effective sieving action would be achieved. In industries a horizontal cylindrical sieve is used, with a spiral brush rotates on the longitudinal axis of the sieve.

- **Centrifugal method:** The sieves are vertical and cylindrical type and attached to a high-speed rotor which is centrally fixed inside the cylinder. When the sieves are rotated, the centrifugal force throws the particles outwards. The current of air developed by the movement of the sieve helps to sieve of the particles also. This method is practically suitable for separation of fine powders.

## Wet Sieving

Size separation in wet sieving method is relatively more efficient than of the powders in the dry state. Because there are some substances which create problem during size separation of their powders. Inter particle adhesion or adhesion of particles with mesh becomes a problem.

When the powders are dispersed in an insoluble liquid, particles in the micro range move differently in the liquid. The behavior of powders having a spherical shape in the liquid can be expressed by the Stoke's law. The law is applicable to a single spherical particle falling from a height in a liquid.

- **Sedimentation method:** This method can be used both in the laboratory as well as in industrial scale. In the laboratory, an Andreason pipe or pipette is used whereas in industrial scale a sedimentation tank is used. A dispersion or suspension of the powders in a liquid, most commonly water, is used. The dispersion is taken in a tank. The dispersion is not disturbed for sufficient time, so that the dispersed particles can settle. The upper and clear layer is removed, this provides a single separation. However, the dispersion/suspension may be sampled at different heights, if the tank has pump inlets at those points. The pump inlet remains just below the liquid surface so that the liquid can be removed without any movement or disturbance of the remaining liquid layer. The suspension at the lower level contains relatively coarser particles. The process is simple but fails to provide a clear separation of particles with respect to their size. If the layers at which particles of the required size range are likely to remain dispersed, is known, removal of the respective layer would be able to provide the particles of the required size range. The disadvantage of this method is that until one lot is completely washed away or freed from undesirable particle size, another lot cannot be processed. The process is repeated until particles of the required size range is remained in the dispersion. When only coarser particles are required, continuous sedimentation method can be used. Sedimentation tank is also known as *Gravitation Settling Chamber*. When the desired particle size is around 100μm, this method is found to be useful. Centrifugal devices available are suitable for separation of relatively smaller particles of about 5 – 10 μm. Sedimentation balances provide the means of directly weighing the particles at predetermined time intervals as they fall in a liquid medium. For continuous observations, automatic recording balances are available. An instrument, known as *Micromerograph*, is available in the market for measuring sedimentation of particles in the air stream. The sedimentation method is a rapid one and is used in commercial production. But the method has the following disadvantages:
  - If the powder contains a wide range of particles, sedimentation of the particles may deviate from Stoke's law.
  - There may be hindered settling.
  - Particles can show impaction against the inner walls of the setting tank.

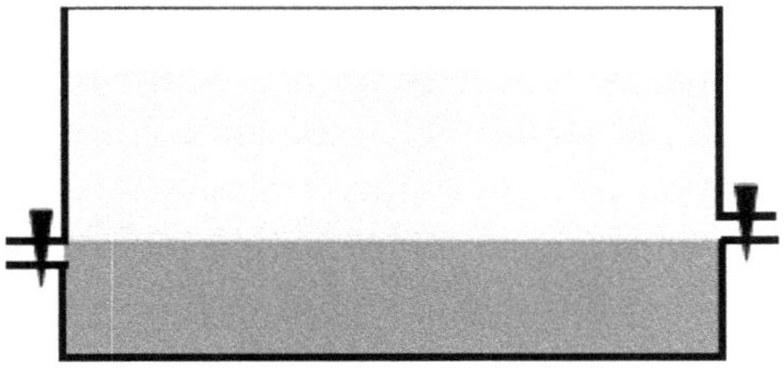

**Fig. 3.4** Schematic diagram of sedimentation tank

## Continuous Sedimentation Tank

The continuous sedimentation tank is shallow and is attached to inlet and outlet pipes as shown in figure 3.5. The liquid (water) remains flowing in the tank. Thus, the particles when enters into the tank, are exposed to two forces – horizontal force due to the flow of liquid and another one is vertical due to gravity. Depending on the size of the particle, it may either move with the flowing liquid or fall downwards, that is, settle down.

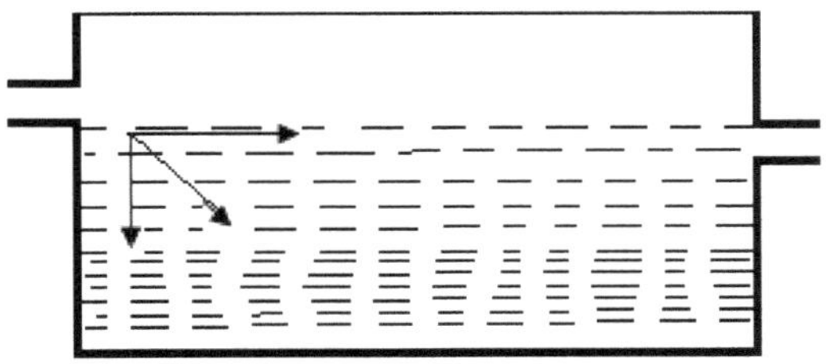

**Fig. 3.5** Schematic diagram of continuous sedimentation tank

Hence, the larger particle settles down at the bottom of the tank. The fall of the particle follows the Stoke's law. The fall of the particle will be proportional to the diameter of the particle. Thus, the smaller particles will be at the nearest to the outlet and the larger particles at the bottom of the tank.

The apparatus is very simple and inexpensive, and the method has the merit of being continuous is able to give a clear separation of particles into as many size fractions as may be required.

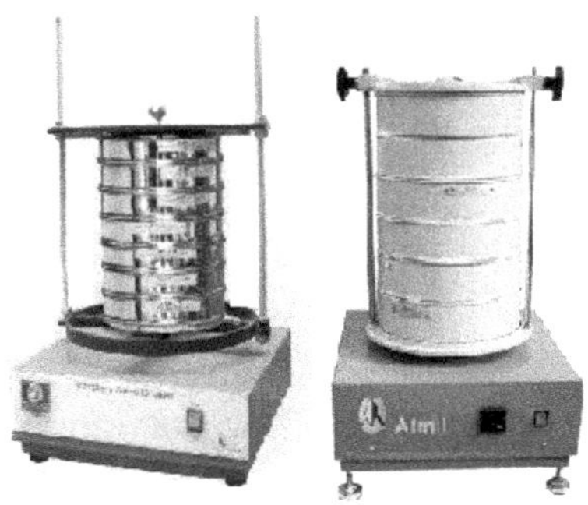

**Fig. 3.6** Schematic diagram of Sieve shaker

### Sieve Shaker

Screens are used when the size of the particles are within 1.27 cm and less. Sieving can be performed with the help of a flat or slightly inclined screens with a reciprocating motion. Screens may be of different types such as wire mesh, perforated plates, etc. But most of the screens are simple. Since the screens are subjected to reciprocating motion and the assembly is called *sieve shaker*.

Sieving is a simple 'go/no go'process. This divides the powder into two fractions above and below a specific sieve. It is necessary to carry out a series of screening to get a particle size distribution of a given a powder sample.

### Construction

Fig 3.6 shows the diagram of mechanical sieve shaker. Various screens of different mesh no are attached to a frame of iron channel and is suspended by hanger rods so that it can move freely. The sieves are shaken under a reciprocating motion for a predetermined period of time. As per mesh no. or sieve no., the particles are either retained or pass through the screens. Since a sieve shaker consists of a number of sieves, the particle of different size ranges can be obtained. The sieves may be made from wire, or other material such as nylon, or a plate perforated with holes.

### Working

The screens of different mesh numbers are assembled in such a way that the screen with the smallest aperture is placed at the top (highest mesh no) and the screen with the largest aperture is placed at the bottom (smallest mesh no). The screens are arranged in the descending order of mesh no. The assembly of screens is suspended by hanger rods so that it can move freely. According to the size distribution, the finest particles are collected at the top and the largest size particles are retained at the bottom screen. In any case, sieving for a prolonged time results in the formation of some fine particles due to attrition of the coarser particles among one another and against the sieves. The sample powder is weighed and then poured into the screen placed in the top, covered tightly. For a period of predetermined time, the sieves are shaken. The particles retained over each screen are weighed individually and the fines collected in the pan below the bottom-most screen are collected and weighed. Percentages of the fraction found oversize and undersize are plotted against particle size range.

### Uses

Mechanical sieve shaker is widely used in chemistry / plastics, construction materials, engineering / electronics, environment / recycling, geology / metallurgy, glass / ceramics.

- A typical sieve shaker separates particle by passing them through a series of screens with different mesh no and agitating the sample in order to achieve complete separation.
- Sieve shakers are used for separation and size determination of particles.
- Depending on the equipment, there are options for sieving both solid and liquid samples.
- Equipment can differ in the type of sieving, the maximum and minimum particle size that can be processed, and level of automation.
- Choice of equipment will depend on the type of laboratory and the samples being processed.

### Merits of Sieve Shaker

- Suitable for dry and wet sieving
- Software is also available
- Easy to sieve and easy to evaluate and record the results
- Maintenance-free
- Excellent separation efficiency even with short sieving times
- RETSCH's CET Technology is available for controlled amplitude even with high loads (up to 25 kg)
- Can separate up to 12 – 14fractions in one sieving operation
- Free digital adjustment of all process parameters (time, amplitude or sieve acceleration, interval)
- Digital sieve shaker has long memory for up to 9 SOPs
- Mobile operation panel for comfortable handling can also be provided.

### Demerits of Sieve Shaker

- Aggregation of the particles takes place due to electrostatic attraction.
- The aggregates formed do not pass through a particular mesh, through which individual particles pass through.
- Humidity may cause the formation of aggregates of the particles if, the material is hygroscopic in nature.
- For passing through a screen, the shape of the particle has an important role. Spherical particles can easily pass through a screen. Otherwise, orientation of particles is required.
- Particle size distribution affects the sieving process greatly. Particles well below the mesh size will pass through easily, while the particles that are greatly oversize will not block the meshes. But the particles that are 1.5 to 1.75 times the mesh opening can block the mesh.
- Similar to particle shape, the shape of the aperture can affect the rate of sieving. Usually, wire mesh sieves have the square aperture; while the perforated sieves have a circular opening. Square openings or in some cases herring-bone slots can be used.
- The process of sieving needs to be standardized with respect to the duration of shaking for achieving reliable results.

## Cyclone Separator

### Construction

Cyclone separator is composed of a cylindrical container whose base is of cone shape (conical). The schematic diagram of the cyclone separator is shown in Fig 3.7. The feed material is introduced tangentially with high speed and a rotary movement takes place within the container. The rotary or circular movement within the vessel separates the particles towards the walls and make the fluid out of the top through a central outlet. The solid particles thrown on the walls, fall down to the conical base and finally exit through the outlet at the bottom.

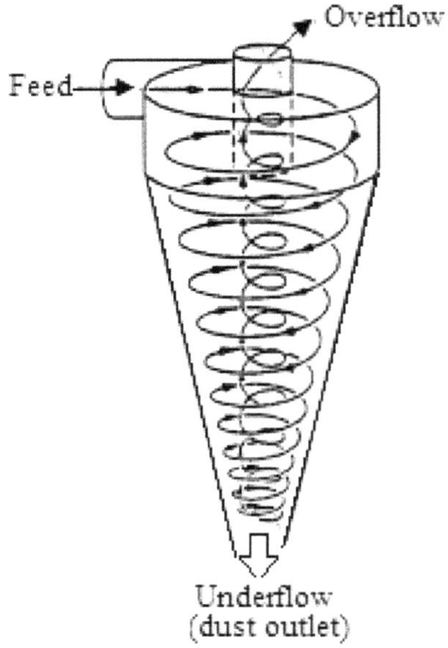


**Fig. 3.7** Schematic diagram of Cyclone separator

## Working

The suspension/dispersion is introduced tangentially at moderately high speed. As a result, a rotary movement occurs within the vessel. The fluid is removed from a central outlet at the top. The rotatory flow within the cyclone takes place. The particles move by centrifugal force, solids are thrown out to the walls and fall on to the conical base and come out to the solid discharge.

## Uses

Cyclone separators can be used for separation of solids from the medium of the suspension containing solids dispersed in a liquid. Most commonly solids are separated from a gas, commonly air. Cyclone separator causes the solids to form sediment with the help of centrifugal force. Although gravitational force exists, it does not have greater effect. Thus, this separator can almost completely separate all the solids depending on the consistency of the suspension or velocity of the fluid. With this process, the fine solids can be separated and removed from the top being carried with the fluid; while the coarser particles are removed from the bottom.

## Merits of Cyclone Shaker

- Able to arrest and remove very fine particles that are difficult to control using wet methods.
- The choice of reintroducing the material arrested back into the production process or dumping the material, is possible, so that it does not cause damage later to the process.
- Reliable performance in cold weather conditions because of not being greatly impacted by low temperatures, as well as wet conditions.
- For some operations whose product is hygroscopic or suffers serious consequences from even small percentages of moisture (e.g., clay or shale operations), it works.

### Demerits of Cyclone Shaker

- Have low collection efficiency for respirable particulates
- Suffer decreased efficiency if gas viscosity or gas density increases
- Are susceptible to erosion
- Have drastically reduced the efficiency due to reduction in airflow rate
- Cannot process sticky dust.

## Air Separator

Cyclone separator alone fails to separate the particles into various size ranges. A current of air with centrifugal force is used to separate the fine particles. The schematic diagram of an air separator is shown in Fig 3.8. As shown in the figure the material is fed through the feed hopper and falls on to the rotating plate. The same shaft drives a set of fan blades. The blades produce a current of air. The fine particles are picked up by the blades and carried into the space, marked as settling chambers. In this space, the velocity of air is sufficiently less. Thus, the material sent to this space, drops and then are removed at the outlet for fine product. Heavy particles picked up by the air stream, fall to the bottom and are removed through the outlet for coarse product.

### Construction

The size separation of fine particles cannot be done accurately by using cyclone separator alone. For this purpose, the air stream and centrifugal force should be combined. The combination of centrifugal force and the air stream is utilized in air separator. The schematic diagram of an air separator is shown in Fig 3.10.

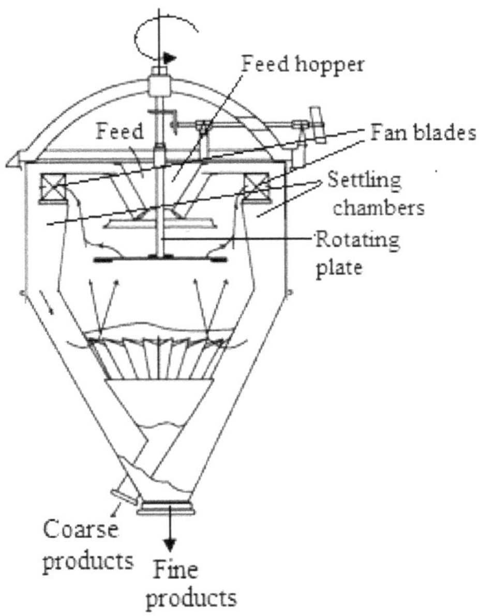


**Fig. 3.8** Schematic diagram of Air separator

### Working

The feed material is introduced through feed hopper and feed material falls on to a rotating plate. the same shaft drives a set of fan blades. This generates a current of air which is indicated by the arrows. Fine particles are picked up by the air and sent to space where settling of fine particles occur (settling chambers).Here the velocity of air is sufficiently less. Thus, the fine particles drop and removed through the outlet for fine product. the particles that are too heavy and cannot be picked up by the air stream directly fall on to the bottom and are removed through the outlet for coarse product. In modern machines the drive is more carefully designed so that the operation can be done more perfectly.

### Uses

Mostly used for separation of fine particles.

### Merits of Air Separator

- High collection efficiencies for coarse and fine particles, around 99.5%.
- Capable to handle large gas flow rates, about 1 – 1000 $m^3/s$
- Can be operated at high temperatures even up to $1000^0$ C and high pressure or under vacuum
- Low capital cost
- Low energy consumption
- Can work at low-pressure drop
- Capable of p roving constant flow rate
- Easy to maintain
- Dry and wet collection are possible
- Relatively small space is required
- Simple to operate
- Recovery of collected material for subsequent processing and disposal are convenient.

### Demerits of Air Separator

- Inability to handle sticky materials
- Wear problems in some place

## Bag Filter

Cyclone separator, air separator, and bag filters do not separate the particles into different and defined size ranges. All these can separate the particles from the medium where the particles are suspended. For example, cyclone separator can take out the coarse particles from which fines are separated and removed by the bag filter. If a bag filter is attached to an air separator and the air separator is designed in such a way that the very fine particles carried by the air stream can be discharged to a bag filter. In this case, the air separator can separate the suspended particles in two fractions, and it is attached to dust removal equipment which is the third component of the assembly. In such a system, air is filtered through a long, cylindrical bag made of cotton or wool.

The dust is removed from the air and stays inside the bag. At a regular interval of time, the bags are shaken and the dust adhered to the surface is removed through the discharge into a collecting outlet. Ordinary vacuum cleaner being used in homes, belongs to the category of simple bag filter.

## Construction

Fig 3.9 shows a design of a typical bag filter in which a number of cylindrical fabric bags A are there. The bags are suspended in a metal container B. Normally, the gas or air to be filtered is introduced through the hopper C, the air moves up inside the bags and accumulates at the top of the casing D to which suction fan is attached. The suction fan is so designed that the whole apparatus works under a pressure less than 1 atm.

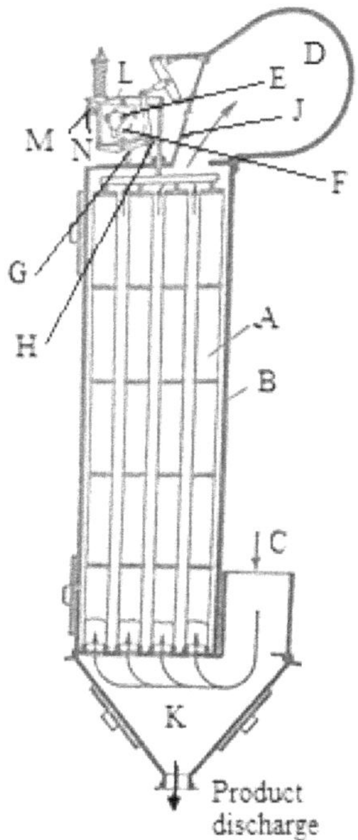


**Fig. 3.9** Bag filter, A: filter baga; B: Casing; C: Inlet connection; D: Manifold discharge; E: Slow-speed shaft; F: Cam; G: Bell-crank lever; H: Bell-crank lever pivot; J; Damper; K: Dust hopper; L: Shaking lever; M: Shaking cams; N: Cam shaft ; P: Product discharge

## Working

While working, the bags are suspended rigidly. The shaft E rotates slowly and at a regular interval (say, 3-4 min) the cam F presses against the bell-crank lever G which rotates around its fulcrum H so that the position of the damper J is changed as shown in the figure. This is called *shaking period*. Since the entire apparatus works under reduced pressure, air enters into the casing and passes into the bags, so that the dust accumulated in the bag-surface can be displaced or removed. The dust-loaded air passes into the hopper K and to the other units for filtration. At the same time, depression of horizontal arm of the bell-crank lever G brings the bar L against the cams M on the rapidly rotating shaft N. Thus, violent jerking of the bags occurs while the dusts are removed from the bag. Most of the dust fall into the hopper K, from where it is removed at definite intervals by a gate attached at P. The functioning of such machine may be completely automated and can be designed so as to afford very large filtering surfaces per unit floor space.

### Uses

- Bag filters are being used in many industries such as Pharmaceutical industries, Food industry, Woodworking, Sinter plants, Metal working, Foundries, Textile industries, Chemical industry, Coal-fired boilers, Asphalt batch plants, etc.
- It is used in settling chambers (it separates the dust particles using gravity),
- It is used as the precipitator (using the internal force),
- It is used as a cyclone dust collector (using centrifugal force),
- It is used as the foam separator (using spray washing with water to effect particles),
- It is used as the filter bags (using filtration of particles as per their sizes),
- It is used as an electrical precipitator (using electric field of particle separation).

### Merits of Bag Filter

- Have high collection efficiency for respirable dust
- Strong woven bags if used, it can withstand intensified cleaning cycle to reduce residual dust built up
- Simple to operate
- Have low pressure drop for equivalent collection efficiencies

### Demerits of Bag Filter

- Have low air-to-cloth ratio (1.5 to 2 ft/min)
- Cannot be used in high temperatures
- Require large areas of space
- Need large numbers of filter bags
- Consist of many moving parts
- Require frequent maintenance
- Personnel must enter bag house to replace bags, creating potential exposure to toxic dust
- Can reduce the cleaning efficiency even if a slightly positive pressure exists inside the bags

## Elutriation Tank

Elutriation is a process for separating particles on the basis of their size, shape, and density under the gravitational force. In this process, a stream of gas or liquid flowing in a direction, usually opposite to the direction of sedimentation, is used. A typical elutriation tank is shown in Fig 10. Thus, in this method, the particles are suspended in a liquid which is in motion. Elutriation may be of four types:

1. Vertical,

2. Horizontal,
3. Centrifugal, and
4. Felvation

1. In *vertical elutriation*, the particles of smaller size range move upwards with the fluid at a particular velocity; while larger particles settle down under the influence of gravity.

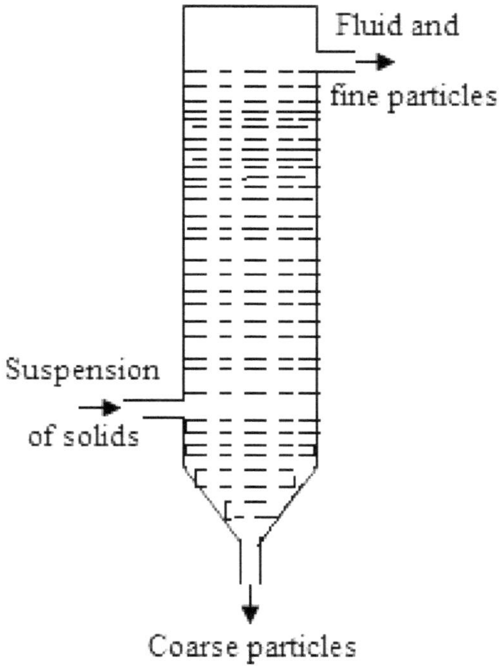


**Fig. 3.10** Schematic diagram of Elutriation

2. In *horizontal elutriation*, a stream of suspended particles is placed in a settling chamber or sedimentation tank. The larger particles leave the stream and settle down. These larger particles are collected at the bottom of the tank. Irrespective of the type of elutriation, both undersized and oversize particles are found in each fraction; thus, recycling becomes necessary for getting a clean cut.

   If the velocity of the fluid is changed gradually, the particles can be separated in fractions, their size range and the amount present in each fraction can be determined by Stoke's law and also by microscopy. Compared to liquid (water) elutriation method, air elutriation gives a sharper fractionation within a shorter time.

3. *Centrifugal elutriation* is primarily the same process; in this case, the fluid stream is made to spin so that comminution takes place at a high centrifugal force to separate the suspended particles. Too large particles separate out on the walls or bottom of the elutriator or cyclone. These particles are expected not to follow the direction of flow. The finer particles follow the stream and escape out. Certain centrifugal separators can separate the particles of about 0.5µm. The Dorr Clone is an example of the centrifugal classifier. Inertial elutriators use an abrupt

change in direction of the fluid to produce separation. Such elutriator is effective for the particles of about 74 μ(200mesh). Similar to other elutriators, a clean cut is not obtained without recycling.

4. *Felvation* is a unique process, it combines both elutriation and sieving along with a varying fluid flow rate. As a result, a turbulent fluidized bed is achieved and particles separate. Within felvation column the particles are fluidized. When the fluid flow rate is gradually increased, the very fine particles come closer and then set into the upper section of the column through the sieve surface. Subsequently, these fines are filtered out of the fluid stream. If the fluid flow rate is further increased, it causes larger particles to move through the sieve. At the final stage, the particles just larger than the sieve aperture are elutriated up to the sieve.

## Advantages

- The process can be made continuous
- As per the necessity, the number of stages can be increased.
- Compared to sedimentation, this method can separate the particles quickly.
- Apparatus is very simple and compact.

## Disadvantages

- The method requires diluted dispersion/suspension.
- Dilution of suspension may not be desirable in some cases.
- The method cannot be suitable for every case.

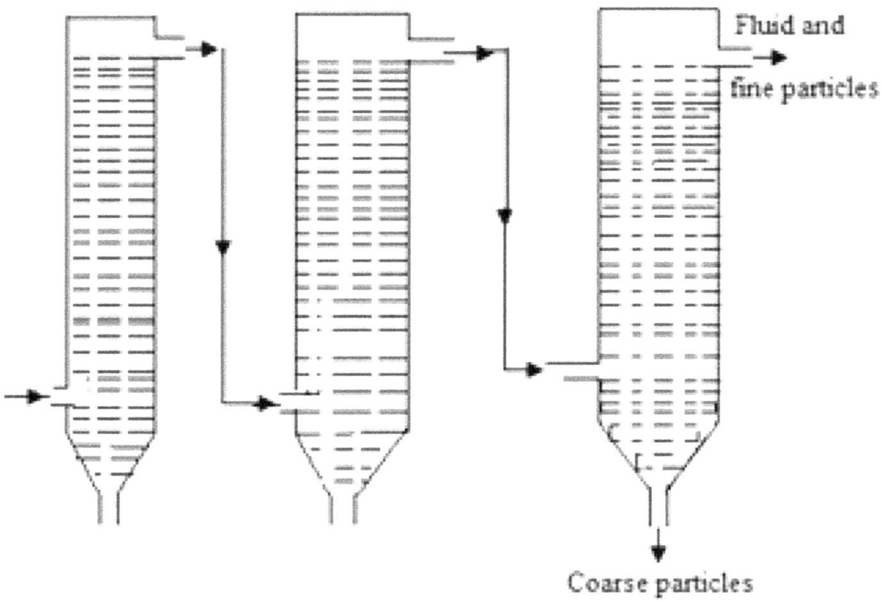


**Fig. 3.11** Multi-state Elutriator

### Application of Elutriation

This method is used for the separation of fine particles of oversize from a powder sample. These oversize particles are returned back for further grinding. For measurement of the particles size range by this method, insoluble solids are dispersed in a liquid (water). For example, kaolin is first subjected to wet grinding and then, dispersed in more of water for sedimentation or elutriation study.

The method is also used to determine the size range of particles present in a sample of air or gas. The particles should separate slowly in liquid. The particles should be fine. A cyclone or mechanical air separator can be used in combination to separate and then return back the particles of oversize.

It is mentioned above the elutriation takes place due to natural settling; that is, gravitational force acts as the driving force for settlingof the particles. The particles settle as per their sizes; the larger particles settle first and at a relatively faster rate and fine particles at a slower rate. Usually, two types of settling are observed in natural settling – (1) free settling, and (2) turbulent or hindered settling.

**Free settling:** Free settling means that the particles settle independently as per their sizes under the force of gravity from their dispersion. Other particles present in the dispersion do not interfere in the settling or sedimentation process. When a particle moves down, it replaces same volume of liquid which goes up. During the upward movement of liquid, if there is any particle, the liquid pushes it up. Thus, the settling of that particle is obstructed. This can be avoided, if the number of particles or quantity of particles in the dispersion is very less. In other words, the free settling requires lesser number of particles in the dispersion so that each particle can move freely. If the particles are of narrow size range, their concentration would be less, and Stoke's law can be used to determine the sedimentation velocity of the particles. The particles start settling in laminar flow and the velocity at which the particles settle is called *terminal settling velocity*. The Stoke's law is expressed as;

$$v = \frac{D^2(\rho_S - \rho_1)g}{18\eta}$$

Where,

$v$ = sedimentation velocity or terminal settling, $cm^2/sec$

D = diameter of settling particle, cm

$\rho_S$ = density of the solid particles, $gm/cm^3$

$\rho_1$ = density of the medium, $gm/cm^3$

g = acceleration due to gravity, $cm/sec^2$

$\eta$ = viscosity of the medium, Pa. sec

There are two types of flow regions – laminar flow region and turbulent flow region.

- Laminar flow region indicates the region where the velocity of the particles is equal to the square of the particle diameter.
- Turbulent flow region refers to the region where the velocity of the particles is almost equal to diameter of the particles.

Usually, the particles settle at slower velocity and the larger particles settle first; while at last the fine particles settle. It is very difficult to separate the particles according to their sizes. However, their velocity of settling can be determined by using Stoke's law with an assumption that the particles are of uniform size range and fine.

**Turbulent/Hindered settling:** When the quantity of solid particles is more in a dispersion, or in other words, when the concentration of solid particles is more, the settling of particles is affected by inter particle collisions and collisions with the walls of the container. Thus, the particles cannot settle freely. These collisions put hindrance to their free settling. When a particle moves down (settles) same volume of the liquid (medium) is pushed up and obstructs the movement of the particle settling later. For this reason, such settling is called hindered settling. As a result, Stoke's law cannot be used in this case. In case of hindered settling, the settling velocity can be calculated only when the particles are spherical in shape. But, if the shape of the particles is irregular, size distribution is wide or if the fine particles remain flocculated in the dispersion. It is very difficult to calculate the settling velocity. When the diameter of the particles is less than 5.0mμ, the Brownian movement will dominate over the gravitational settling. If fine particles form agglomerates, the agglomerates will fall rapidly than the individual particle. Hence, determination of particle size or their sedimentation rate under these conditions will be misleading.

## Short Questions

1. What is the purpose of size separation in pharmacy?
2. What do you understand by particle size analysis?
3. How can the particles be separated by agitation?
4. What are the methods used for separation of particles?
5. What is application of continuous sedimentation tank?
6. Write down the application, advantages and limitations of sieve shaker.
7. What are the advantages and limitations of an air separator?
8. What is a bag filter? What are its applications and advantages?
9. Why elutriation tank is used?
10. What are free settling and hindered settling?

## Long Questions

1. Explain briefly the methods used for separation of particles.
2. Explain the official standards of powders.
3. Discuss the various standards for sieve.
4. Discuss dry sieving and wet sieving methods used for separation of particle size.
5. Discuss the principle, construction and working of sieve shaker.
6. Discuss the principle, construction and working of cyclone separator with the help of a suitable diagram.
7. Why air separator is used? Write down the principle, construction and working of an air separator.
8. Explain various types of elutriation tank.
9. Describe the method, uses and advantages of bag filter.
10. Write down the short notes on sieve shaker and cyclone separator.

# CHAPTER 4

# Mixing

Objectives, Applications & Factors Affecting Mixing, Difference between Solid and Liquid Mixing, Mechanism of Solid Mixing, Liquids Mixing and Semisolids Mixing. Principles, Construction, Working, Uses, Merits and Demerits of Double Cone Blender, Twin Shell Blender, Ribbon Blender, Sigma Blade Mixer, Planetary Mixers, Propellers, Turbines, Paddles & Silverson Emulsifier.

## Objectives

In any manufacturing industry mixing is the most common and widely practiced activity. Hardly any product can be prepared without mixing at any stages of its preparation. Mixing may be defined as *an activity or operation in which two or more substances are intermingled together to form a uniform mixture*. That is, one particle of one substance is most closely associated with that of another substance at every portion of the mixture. The latter refers to the degree of mixing. How the particles of the components would be present in the mixture depend on the purpose or objective of mixing. The objective of mixing may be broadly classified into four categories:

1. To obtain a simple physical mixture,
2. To effect a physical change
3. To make a dispersion, and
4. To facilitate a reaction.

1. To prepare a simple physical mixture, two or more miscible liquids or two or more powders are taken and blended in such a way that a uniform mixture is obtained. In case of liquid mixtures, the components are mixed in a tank with the help of a stirrer; while in case of powder mixing, there are certain rules of mixing to be followed. For example, if their quantities are widely different, or if their sizes are widely different. Say, one gm of a substance is to be mixed with ten kgs of another. Usually, this type of mixing is done in the pharmaceutical industry just to ensure uniform distribution of the drug in the mixture of excipients to ensure the uniform dose size of a drug. In preparation of a tablet, various excipients along with the drug in different quantities are mixed; if the drug is not mixed with these excipients uniformly, the dose of the drug will not be uniform. Similarly, to effect uniform mixing of two powders having different particle size, the powders are screened through a particular screen of same mesh no before mixing.
2. To effect a distinct physical change, mixing is done. The classical example is a solution of solid in a liquid. Solids have some distinct physical properties which are not visible in their solutions. To make this type of mixture, mixing efficiency is not so important, because mixing can occur during a long period of time through the diffusion process. Agitation or stirring can

only reduce the mixing time. Of course, in some cases, agitation improves the mixing uniformity.

3. To make a dispersion of one substance into another, mixing is necessary. For example, to make a suspension formulation of a drug, the powders of the drug are mixed with the dispersion medium effectively, so that the drug remains suspended uniformly for a prolonged period of time, till it expires. Similarly, to produce an emulsion two phases are mixed intimately so that one phase remains dispersed in the form of globules into another phase and the mixture does not change its physical stability. Thus, in both the cases, an effective mixing is required to ensure the desired stability.
4. To promote the reaction between two reactants, mixing is required. In fact, mixing encourages the reactants to react to each other. Because, mixing breaks up the substance into small particles and increases the surface area of the reactants and hence, the rate of reaction increases. For example, a solution of sodium phosphate can be quickly prepared, if it is mixed with water with constant stirring. Formation of ferric chloride by the reaction between iron and hydrochloric acid can be easily completed, if the iron filings are stirred in dilute hydrochloric acid.

## Types of Mixtures

Different mixture behaves differently. On the basis of the behavior, the mixtures can be classified primarily into three types:

1. Positive mixture
2. Negative mixture, and
3. Neutral mixture

1. *Positive mixtures* are the product of positive mixing. This type of mixing takes place slowly and there is no work done, if it happens during a long period. For example, the mixing of gases or the mixing of gas and liquid through diffusion. Since in this type of mixing no work is done, the process does not cause any problem and is irreversible in nature. The mixture thus obtained, is found to be stable.
2. *Negative mixtures* are relatively more difficult to obtain. Sufficient work must be done to produce a negative mixture. Degree of uniformity of mixing depends on the efficiency of the method used. As a result, this type of mixtures is not thermodynamically stable. A suspension formulation is a very good example of the negative mixture. The solid particles are dispersed in a liquid (aqueous) medium. Both phases (dispersed phase and dispersion medium) are mixed thoroughly for a long period of time using an appropriate mixing machine.
3. *Neutral mixtures* are not dynamic in nature, they are static in their behavior. The components neither have a natural tendency to mix one another nor segregate after mixing. Due to the difference in the physical properties of the components of the mixture, many variations may take place among the mixtures of this type. Again, pharmaceutical suspensions belong to this group and is a very good example. The properties of the mixture that can vary are density, viscosity, particle size, etc. due to the difference in these properties of constituents of the preparation. For example, wetting abilities of all drugs are not the same, the densities of all the excipients and drug are not same, viscosities of the components present in the mixture and so on. Among all these properties or factors, some are dependent on circumstance. For example, density and viscosity depend on temperature, viscosity is further dependent on the rate of shear, etc.

## Applications

Generally, the mixing is done to prepare the following types of products:

1. Two or more than two miscible liquids are to be mixed together to produce a true solution.
2. Two immiscible liquids are to be mixed in the presence of an emulsifying agent to produce an emulsion.
3. A solid is dissolved in a solvent/vehicle to prepare a solution.
4. An insoluble solid is mixed with a vehicle to prepare a suspension/dispersion.
5. A solid or liquid is mixed with a semisolid base to prepare an ointment or a suppository.
6. Two or more solid substances are mixed together to produce a powder mix which when filled into a capsule shell is called capsules and when compressed under heavy pressure is called tablet.

### Liquid Mixing

In case of mixing of two or more liquids, no difficulty is observed; particularly if, they are mutually miscible or soluble. However, the mixture of solid and mobile liquid is rarely found to be permanent. There are two requirements for the mixing process to occur:

1. Localized mixing which requires the application of sufficient shear to the particles of the fluid.
2. General mixing requires movement of sufficient material into the bulk through the shearing zone, so that a uniform mixture is obtained.

On small scale preparation of emulsions, a pestle and mortar are suitable. The shear forces are produced between the head of the pestle and bottom of the mortar. A general movement is required by a continuous movement of the pestle along the sides of the mortar by which the material attached to the sides can be returned to the bottom of the mortar. Generally, the emulsions are prepared in two stages –

1. Primary emulsion,
2. Secondary emulsion.

In the primary stage, the two immiscible liquids are triturated with an emulsifying agent to produce a primary emulsion, which is subsequently diluted by adding more of the vehicle. After the preparation of an emulsion which is coarse in nature may be placed into a homogenizer to obtain a homogeneous emulsion of desired particle size.

In some cases, the only flow of a liquid may be sufficient to produce a mixture. Liquid mixing may be divided into following two subgroups:

### Mixing of Liquids and Liquids

(a) Mixing of two miscible liquids is easy. This may occur by diffusion. This type of mixture can be obtained without any problem. Simple shaking or stirring would be enough, but if the liquids are not readily miscible or if they have very different viscosities, an electric stirrer may be useful. In such mixing, turbulence may be created in the liquids being mixed. Turbulence is a function of velocity gradient between two adjacent layers of a liquid. Thus, if a rapidly moving stream of liquid is in contact with a nearly stationary liquid, there will be a high-velocity gradient at the boundary layer. This results in tearing off portions of the faster moving stream and then sending it off to the slower moving areas in form of vortexes or eddies. These eddies persist for some time and ultimately disperse with generation of heat. Formation of vortex or eddies may be due to the differences in static pressures created as in case of an ejector. Most of the mixing equipment is designed on the basis of ability to provide high local velocities and directing them in such a way that they can ultimately carry the turbulence or the eddies may be created during mass mixing.

(b) Mixing of two immiscible liquids may be done to produce an emulsion. When two immiscible liquids are mixed, it causes the transfer of a dissolved substance from one liquid to another. For example, during the extraction of the acid form of penicillin from aqueous solution into the organic solvent, amyl acetate promotes a chemical reaction after the transfer of a component, and heat is transferred from one liquid to another. Another example is the preparation of emulsion. When two immiscible liquids are mixed together in the presence of an emulsifying agent, an emulsion is produced. For the production of a stable emulsion, the efficient and continuous mixing is required, because the components tend to separate out.

## Mixing of Liquids and Solids

(a) Mixing of liquids and soluble solids
(b) Mixing of liquids and insoluble solids

(a) Mixing of liquids and soluble solids to make the homogeneous mixtures such as solutions. In this case, the soluble solids are dissolved in a suitable liquid with the help of stirring. A physical change occurs, a solid is converted to a solution.

(b) Mixing of liquids and insoluble solids produces heterogeneous mixtures such as suspensions. When insoluble solids are mixed with a liquid, a suspension is produced which is the thermodynamically unstable system. The ingredients of a suspension have a tendency to separate out, if it is allowed to stand for some time. Thus, the addition of a suitable suspending agent is required to produce a stable suspension. On a small scale, suspensions may be prepared using a pestle and mortar.

**Table 4.1** Shows the classification of mixing equipment.

| Type of mixing | Name of the mixer | Applications |
|---|---|---|
| Liquid-liquid mixing | • Shaker mixers<br>• Propeller mixers<br>• Paddle mixers<br>• Turbine mixers<br>• Sonic and ultrasonic devices such as Rapisonic homogenizer | Used in the preparation of emulsions, antacid suspensions, mixtures such as anti-diarrheal bismuth-kaolin mixtures, etc.<br>The rapisonic homogenizer is particularly used in the mixing of immiscible liquids i.e. preparation of emulsions. |
| Solid-solid mixing | • Agitator mixers<br>• Tumbling mixers<br>• Double-cone mixers<br>• V-blender | Used for the mixing of dry powders. |
| Semisolid-solid mixing | • Agitator mixers like sigma mixers and planetary mixers<br>• Shear mixers like colloidal mills and triple roller mills | These mixers are used for wet granulation process in the manufacture of tablets, in the production of ointments.<br>Sigma mixers can also be used for solid-solid mixing. |

There are three velocity components:

- Radial components, acting in a direction vertical to the impeller shaft.
- A longitudinal component, acting parallel to the impeller shaft.
- A tangential component, acting in a direction, tangential to the circle of rotation around the impeller shaft.

A satisfactory flow pattern depends on the balance of these components. The impeller shaft is vertical. If the solids are present, excessive radial movement will take the materials to the container wall and they will fall to the bottom. Entire mass may rotate below the impeller. If the tangential component is dominant, a vortex will form. The vortex may extend until it reaches the impeller when aeration occurs. If the longitudinal component is inadequate, liquids and solids may rotate in layers without mixing. This stratification may occur even when rotation is rapid. In the presence of vortexing, it would appear that mixing is vigorous and satisfactory. The flow pattern will be influenced by the factors such as the form of the impeller and its position. For example,

- High or low mixing in the vessel,
- Mounting of the impeller centrally or to one side,
- The shaft is positioned vertically or in inclined way.
- Container shape and
- The presence of baffles

The flow characteristics and mixing behavior of fluids are governed by three primary laws or principles:

- Conservation of mass,
- Conservation of energy, and
- The classic laws of motion

## Mixing of Powders

Mixing of the powders is different from that of the liquids. As such, powder mixture is a heterogeneous mixture. The powders are commonly mixed to prepare tablets, capsules, and granules or powder dosage forms. When the weight of the active ingredient is around 0.5% of the total weight of a formulation, the uniform mixing of solids becomes challenging and critical. Non-uniform solid mixture means somewhere the active ingredient is more and somewhere less. The portion of the mixture containing a high proportion of active ingredient becomes toxic, sometimes may be lethal and the portions where drug content is less becomes therapeutically ineffective. Thus, maintaining the uniformity of dose becomes difficult. In most powder mixtures, a common phenomenon called *particle segregation* is observed. This problem can be avoided by mixing the particles of different substances having similar particle size and density. Moreover, the duration of mixing is equally important.

When different substances are ground, mixing take place simultaneously. Two or more substances are fed to the mill one after another. To obtain a homogenous powder mix, the following factors and physical properties of drugs must be considered.

- Powders of different substances should be of similar weights; equal weights of two substances should be taken for mixing.
- Particles of two substances to be mixed should be of similar size,
- Substances to be mixed should have similar densities.
- The stickiness of the components to bemixed is also important.
- Prolonged mixing, in some cases, becomes necessary for effective distribution of materials like lubricants and wetting agents into tablet granules.

Blending or mixing of powders becomes very difficult due to wide differences among their properties. Significant factors that influence the homogeneity of mixing are

- Particle size distribution,
- Shape,
- Surface characteristics such as surface area and electrostatic charges, etc.
- Flow characteristics such as the angle of repose (ability to flow),
- The abrasiveness of one ingredient upon the other,
- State of agglomeration of the ingredients,
- Moisture content,
- Density,
- Surface tension and operating temperature of any liquid added, and
- Mixing equipment

Selection of mixing equipment and the properties of the blending ingredients play an important role in a mixing operation.

## Degree of Homogeneity

There are many proposals to express mathematically the degree of homogeneity of powders in a powder mix. The Standard Deviation can be considered as a representative index to express the degree of homogeneity. It is determined by using a set of 'n' samples. If the sample number 'i' shows the composition '*xi*', and all the samples are of uniform size, the standard deviation in the sample can be expressed as:

$$s = \sqrt{\sum_{i=1}^{n} (x_i - \bar{x})^2 (n-1)}$$

Where, $\bar{x}$ is the mean composition determined from the sample. It must be ensured that the sample drawn statistically represent the composition of the powder throughout the powder bed.
Danckwerts described two major concepts related to mixing uniformity –

(a) The scale of segregation, and (b) Intensity of segregation

If the zones show uniformity but different in composition, the scale of segregation becomes the function of the composition of the zones. On the other hand, the intensity of segregation becomes a function of the composition difference among the zones.

## Mixing of Semi-solids

Mixing of semi-solid materials depends on the property of the materials. The properties may vary considerably. Among these properties the rheological property of materials has a greater influence on the mixing of semisolids. The dilatant and Newtonian materials are difficult to mix uniformly. The thixotropy of the semi-solids can make the mixing process easier.
Some of the factors to be considered during selection of an appropriate equipment are:

- The amount of formulation to be prepared.
- The rheological characteristics of the final product.
- The need to incorporate ingredients such as powders.
- The operating temperature, and
- Whether the processing is batch-wise or continuous operation. It is easier to produce a fine semisolid by using homogenizer.

## Factors Affecting Mixing

According to the principle of mixing, equal numbers of say, grey and white particles should be mixed so that the best conditions for mixing can be achieved. If the places of two particles change, there would be a major reason to lose the homogeneity of the mixture. Actually, it becomes a major problem or issue when 1% or less of a substance has to be mixed with a diluent.

Usually, to prepare homogeneous mixture of multiple components of unequal quantities, the component of lesser amount is mixed with similar amount of other one, and then with similar amount of another component to obtain the homogeneity. In practice, good mixing can be achieved when the components are mixed at 1:1 ratio. Generally, there are four conditions which influence the homogeneity in mixing:

- **Nature of the product:** If the surface of one of the components is rough, it does not make proper mixing. The reason for this is that the active substance may enter into the pores of the other ingredient. A substance that can adsorb on to its surface, can decrease aggregation; for example, addition of colloidal silica to strongly aggregating zinc oxide can make it a fine dusting powder which can be easily mixed.
- **Particle size:** Variation in particle size leads to the separation of particles, since the small particles move downward through the spaces between the bigger particles. As the particle size increases, flow properties also increase due to the influence of gravitational force on the size. It is easier to mix two powders having approximately the same particle size.
- **Particle shape:** For uniform mixing, the particles should be spherical in shape. The irregular shapes can become interlocked and there are fewer chances of separation of particles once they are mixed together.
- **Particle charge:** Some particles exert attractive forces due to electrostatic charges on them. This results in separation or segregation of particles of different sizes.
- **The volume of mixer:** The volume of mixer used should be such that it can permit sufficient space for dilation of the bed. The efficiency and uniformity of mixing shall be reduced due to overfilling.

- **Type of mixer:** To ensure both local mixing and convective movement of the particles in the bulk, hence a suitable mixer should be used. Any mixer used, would apply shear forces to effect mixing, but each has its own mechanism. The physical characteristics of the powder should match with the mechanism of the mixer.
- **Duration of mixing:** This is another important parameter in industrial manufacturing. In industries, time management is very much important; that is, a step or operation should be completed within minimum possible time. In fact, unnecessary prolonged mixing has a negative impact on mixing and mixture. The heat generated during mixing can affect the stability of the product. For example, if dextrose is mixed with other components such as sodium chloride, potassium chloride, etc. for a prolonged period, heat generated can caramelize the dextrose and the product become brownish in color. Hence, to ensure uniform mixing the duration of mixing must be optimized.
- **Handling of powder mix:** After mixing, the powder mix is not always used immediately. It may be stored or transported in bulk. In such cases, segregation or demixing of powders may occur. Thus, to ensure the delivery of uniform powder mix to the customer, it is recommended to re-mix the bulk mixture.

## Difference between Solid and Liquid Mixing

| Mixing of solids | Mixing of liquids |
|---|---|
| • To some extent, mixing of solids looks like the mixing of low-viscosity liquids.<br>• Solids cannot be perfectly mixed like liquids, because there is no flow-current.<br>• There are three primary mechanisms of mixing of solids– convection, diffusion, and shear.<br>• To varying extents, these three mechanisms occur depending on the type of mixers or blenders used and the characteristics of the solids to be mixed. | • Liquids of low viscosity are mixed due to the creation of flow current that transports unmixed material to the mixing zone adjacent to the impeller.<br>• The liquid mixing technology has been improved to produce a well-mixed, homogeneous liquid mixer with uniform composition.<br>• Uniformity of liquid mixer depends on the consistency and solubility characteristics of the liquids. |

## Mechanism of Mixing of Solid In Liquid

When powders of different solids are agitated, a static bed of particles will undertake the closet form of packing under the effect of gravity. This is known as *rhombohedral packing*. The porosity of this type of packing is only about 25%. The further movement of the particles during mixing lead them to pack in the form of *cubical packing* with a porosity of about 50%. Therefore, the porosity of the bed dilates; that is, the volume of the powder bed increases.

Practically, the mixing of powders is done to achieve a similar result as is achieved in mixing of liquids. But for this, a localized shear force would be required. The localized shear can change the packing arrangement and movement of the particles. Through general movement, the particles accumulate in the intense mixing zone. By two ways the localized shear force can be developed:

1. **Diffusive mixing:** In diffusive mixing, the material is to be tilted beyond its angle of repose. Thus, the gravitational forces can cause the upper layers to slip over the lower layers. Then the particles in motion can mix each other. This results in small-scale movement and, due to this the molecules of liquid diffuse through the solid particles. This is similar to molecular diffusion of liquids and gases.
2. **Shear mixing:** The shear mixing can be achieved by using an agitator arm or a blast of air which can generate shear forces in the material being mixed.

   However, a general convective movement must occur in both cases.

## Mechanism of Powder Mixing

It has been generally accepted that in all the mixtures, solid mixing can be achieved by a combination of two or more of the following mechanisms:

- **Convective mixing:** In convective mixing, transfer of groups of particles takes place from one location to another by means of blades or paddles of the machine.
- **Shear mixing:** In shear mixing, slip planes are set up within the mass of material.
- **Diffusive mixing:** In this mechanism, mixing occurs by diffusion process by random movement of particles within a powder bed and cause them to change their relative positions.

Due to the influence of gravity, a static bed of particles will assume the form of packing, which is known as *rhombohedral packing* with a porosity of about 25%. Mixing causes the movement of particles, so that *cubical packing* results, where the porosity is about 50%. Hence, dilation of the bed occurs resulting to an increase in the total volume occupied by the powder.

The actual mixing will be similar to the mixing of liquids, because localized shear forces will be required to produce the change to open packing and movement of the particles relative to each other. During mixing a general agitation causes circulation of the material through the intense mixing zone. However, localized shear forces may result in two ways – shear mixing and diffusive mixing.

### Material Density

If the components are of different density, the denser material will descend through the lighter one depending on the relative positions of the materials in the mixer. If the denser particles are present in the lower layer in a mixer, at the beginning of mixing operation, the degree of mixing will increase gradually until an equilibrium is attained, but not necessarily the mixing process is completed. If the denser component is present at the top layer, the degree of mixing increases to a maximum, and then will drop to equilibrium as the denser component falls through the lighter one. This indicates that segregation has started. This factor is of practical significance in charging and operating a mixer in commercial manufacturing.

### Particle Size

Segregation of particles may also take place due to the difference in particle size. The smaller particles can fall through the voids between the larger particles. Depending on the packing, there will be an optimum particle size that does not pass through the voids. If a bed of particles is agitated or disturbed, dilation takes place and the open packing creates greater porosity. Through this greater porosity, even larger particles can move down and segregation can occur.

### Particle Shape

Ideally, the particle should be spherical in shape. But in practice, this rarely happens and the irregular shape of the particles offers greater difficulty in mixing. However, such irregularity in shape causes interlocking of the particles and does not allow particle segregation after completion of mixing.

### Particle Attraction

Due to adsorbed liquid film or electrostatic charges some particles can exert attractive forces. As a result, the particles possess a tendency to attract and form aggregates. This is being a surface property, the effect of attraction increases with decrease in particle size.

## Mechanism of Liquids Mixing

Turbulence is a function of velocity gradient between two adjacent layers of a liquid and the method of mixing depends on the degree of turbulence created. When a rapidly moving stream of liquid comes in contact with a liquid which is almost stationary, at the boundary there will be a high-velocity gradient. As a result, two types of observations would be there –

1. The attractive force will break down some of the portions of the fast-moving stream and send it to slower-moving areas in form of vortexes or eddies. The eddies formed will persist for a considerable period and then, dissipate when all the energy is converted into heat.
2. According to Bernoulli's theorem, the high-velocity liquid will ultimately carry their own turbulence or possess a lower static pressure than the surrounding liquid moving at a lower velocity. Subsequently, the stagnant liquid possesses a higher static pressure than the high-velocity liquid. As a result, the slow-moving liquid will be drawn into the high-velocity jet.

For this reason, most mixing equipment is designed on the basis of producing high local velocities, but they will ultimately carry their own turbulence, or the turbulence of the eddies they create, throughout the mass to be mixed.

### Mechanism of Semisolids Mixing

The mixing of semisolids depends on the properties of the materials being mixed. The property varies considerably. Very little difference between the liquids of high viscosity and semisolids with respect to their flow ability is present. When powder and a liquid are mixed, initially it seems that powders are being mixed.

The rheological properties of non-Newtonian materials may have an important effect on the mixing process. Thus, plastics or dilatant materials are usually much more difficult to mix than Newtonian liquids; but thixotropy may make the mixing process easier.

In mixing of insoluble powders with a liquid, different stages can be observed with an increase in the content of the liquid.

**Pellet and powder state**

When a small amount of liquid is added to the bulk of dry powders, the solids ball up and form small pellets. The pellets are embedded in a matrix of dry powders. This shows a cushioning effect and makes the pellets difficult to break up. The solid remains free-flowing and the rate of homogenization becomes low.

**Pellet size**

On further addition of liquid, more amount of dry powders is converted into a pellet and finally, all the material transforms into a pellet. The mass acquires a coarse granular appearance. The pellets do not cohere and further agitation breaks down the aggregates into granules.

**Plastic state**

With the increase in liquid content, the property of the mixture changes markedly. Aggregates start adhering, the granular appearance is lost gradually, and the mixture becomes homogeneous. A clay-like consistency appears. Thus, plastic properties are observed. The mixture becomes difficult to shear, flow at low stresses; but break under high stresses. Homogenization of the mixture can be obtained more rapidly than in earlier stated cases. For example, this type of state is obtained when a pill-mass is made.

**Sticky state**

Continuous addition of liquid makes the mixture to achieve a sticky state. A paste-like appearance with the shiny surface is obtained. The mass can flow easily even under low stresses, but homogeneity is reached at a relatively slow rate.

**Liquid state**

Continuous addition of liquid dilutes the consistency of the mixture and finally, a fluid state is obtained. In this state, the mixture flows under its own weight and can drain off vertically. Rate of homogenization is faster. The mechanisms of mixing of liquids with powders sometimes can bring about a potentially dangerous situation which must be controlled carefully.

Say, a potent soluble drug is being granulated by wet granulation method. If an insoluble diluent such as starch is present, the process will start by mixing the soluble and insoluble powders first until a homogeneous mixture is obtained. Now, if small amounts of liquid is mixed, it results in the formation of pellets and powders.

In continuous mixing, the pellets start collecting soluble material on their surface, which will subsequently dissolve since pellets contain a higher proportion of water (moisture). As a result, a greater concentration of soluble material in the pellets will be found as compared with the powder matrix. There will be a decrease in the degree of mixing. Homogeneity would be found when water content will increase. But, in case of granulation for tablets, mixing should be continued till pellets are formed. Therefore, mixing needs to be controlled carefully to achieve a good degree of mixing.

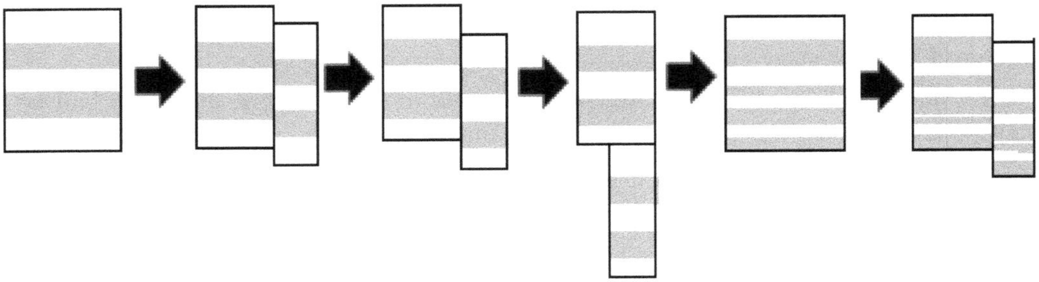

Fig. 4.1 Mixing of plastic solids

### Mixing in the Plastic State

Mixing of plastic materials can be explained better with the help of a diagram shown in Fig 4.1. Let us assume that the number of materials is represented by two white and two grey color blocks. When a shear force (agitation) is applied, the blocks will move as mentioned below:

1. A part of the material-block will start moving.
2. This part will be displaced by shearing action.
3. The material will be circulated due to continuous shearing (stirring).
4. Distortion of the mass takes place.
5. Further movement occurs due to continuous shearing.

The process continues until complete and uniform mixing is achieved.

## Twin Shell Blender

It belongs to tumble blenders. It is also called a twin-shell V-blender(because the vessel has twin-legs and V-shaped).This batch-blender rotates and tumble the ingredients to mix them. The baffles may be attached to the blender. The baffles are breaker bars. However, other components may be attached to break up agglomerates and facilitate mixing. It is generally used for blending dry ingredients but may also be fitted with liquid-addition equipment. There are three popular shapes of tumble blenders:

1. The V-Blender,
2. The double cone, and
3. The slant cones

The V-blender is an efficient and versatile blending machine for homogeneous mixing and lubrication process of dry powders. Approximately two-thirds of the volume of the blender is filled with powders to ensure proper mixing. The V-blender gives the best result for powders due to suitable medium speed and V shape of the container. Tumble blenders depend upon the gravity to cause the powder to cascade within a rotating vessel.

**Fig. 4.2** Twin-shell V-blender

## Principles

Primarily the blending in a V-blender takes place through diffusion process. Diffusion blending is considered by small scale random motion of solid particles. The movements of the blender increase the movement of the individual particles and thus, promote diffusive blending. Diffusive blending happens where the particles are distributed over a freshly developed interface. In the absence of segregation effects, the diffusive blending will result in high degree of homogeneity.

V-blenders are therefore chosen when the precise blending of the formulations is required. These are also suitable for applications where some ingredients may be as low as five percent of the total blend size. Normal blending time typically vary from 5 to 15 minutes depending on the properties of the material to be blended. The schematic diagram of a twin- shell V-blender is shown in Fig 4.2.Inter-shell flow is the slowest step in a V-blender, because it is dispersive in nature, while intra-shell flow is convective. Both processes can be described mathematically as:

$$\sigma^2 = Ae^{-kN}\sigma$$

Where

σ is mixture variance,

N is the number of revolutions,

A is an unspecified constant, and

k is the rate constant.

The orders of magnitude of the rate constants for convective mixing are greater than that for dispersive mixing. Thus, due to unequal loading across, the symmetry plane highlights the dispersive mixing and is comparatively slow as compared to top-to-bottom loading, which favors convective mixing.

## Construction

Double cone blender is an effective and commonly used machine for homogeneous mixing of the dry powder and granules. All the contact parts of these blenders are made of stainless steel of the highest grade such as SS-316 and internally polished to a 240-grit sanitary finish. The exterior is polished to an easily cleaned 150-grit finish. The intensifier bars do not allow agglomeration of the powders as required. These blenders are immensely used in food, pharmaceutical, cosmetic and chemical industries. The V-blender is made of two hollow cylindrical shells joined at an angle of 75° to 90°. The blender container is mounted on trunnions to allow it to tumble. As the V-blender tumbles, the material continuously separates and recombines. As a result, mixing occurs as the material free-falls randomly inside the vessel. The repetitive converging and diverging motion of the material combined with increased frictional contact between the material and the vessel's long, homogenous blending occurs as shown in Fig 4.3. All units are provided with appropriate safety railings and suitable safety interlocks. Stop-Start and E-Stop pushbuttons are included in all blenders.

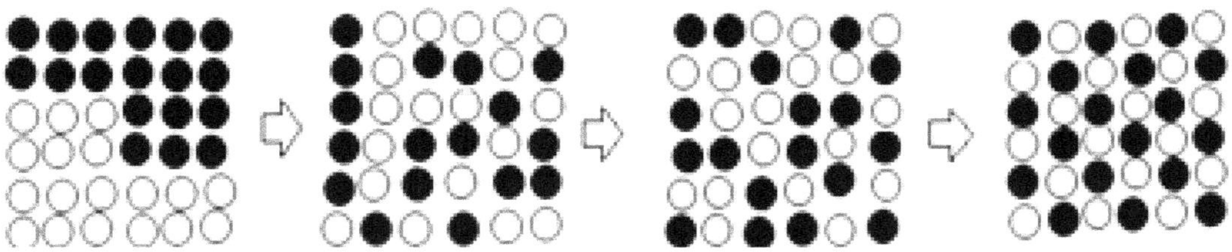

**Fig. 4.3** Different stages of powders mixing

## Working

The 2/3rd of the volume of V-blender is filled to ensure appropriate mixing. The solid (powders) being blended with other materials. Normal cycle-time is typically in the range of 15 min; however, the mixing time can be less depending on the property of the materials. V-blenders can have 5, 10, and 15 cu.ft. capacity. Discharge is accomplished through a manually operated butterfly valve. The valve is generally positioned at 2 ft from the floor in the bottom position. Powder cohesion properties also can affect the velocity gradient, where inter-particulate forces dilate the powder bed density. This may have further implications on downstream processing. Optimization of the blending process requires the understanding of blending mechanisms and critical variables.

## Uses

- Dry powders are mixed for making tablets and capsules formulations.
- Dry granules sub-lots mixing can be done to increase the batch size at bulk lubrication stage of tablet granules.
- Dry powder to wet mixing. The designs of V-blenders are most often used for the dry blending of free-flowing solids.
- This blender is often used for pharmaceuticals, but the mixing can slightly limit the use of V-blender for some very soft powders or granules.
- V-Blenders are generally used for the materials such as milk powder, coffee, dry flavors, ceramics, powders, pigments, pesticides and herbicides, plastic powders, animal feed, spice blends, fertilizers, baby foods, cosmetics, polyethylene, etc.

### Merits of Double Cone Blender

- Particle size reduction and attrition are minimized due to the absence of any moving blades.
- It can be used for fragile materials.
- Charging and discharging of material is easy.
- The V-blender is good for blending dry powders and granulated products
- The shape of the body of blender results in a near complete discharge of product material.
- The absence of shaft projection eliminates product contamination.
- V-blenders are easy to clean.
- Internal attachments like lump breakers and liquid dispensers widen the applications of this blender.

### Demerits of Double Cone Blender

- They require high head-room for installation and operation.
- They are not suitable for blending particles of different sizes and densities which may segregate at the time of discharge.

## Ribbon Blender

Similar to V-blender, the Ribbon blender is used for effective and versatile blending or mixing of dry granules and powder homogeneously. Approximately, two-thirds of the volume of the ribbon blender container is filled to ensure proper mixing. The ribbon blender provides the best result for mixing of dry powder and granules due to the design and shape of the blender and product container. It can be used for pharmaceutical, food, chemical, and cosmetic products, etc.

Available in two shapes - U and W. The U-shaped blender is used mainly for low to medium volume capacity (single shaft); while the W-shaped blender may be large to mega volume capacity (double shaft). Batch size is based on 65% of blender's volume. All contact parts are of stainless steel 316. Bearing is mounted on lanterns out of mixing zone to avoid cross-contamination. For feeding, a charging port is mounted on top of the blender. Monoblock design avoids cross-contamination and meets all cGMP standards. Air purge on the side entry seals the blender and provides better control of cross-contamination. Continuous ribbon design is made for complete discharge of the finished product. Variable frequency drive can be provided for fine-tuning of the shear energy at different stages of blending.

### Principles

The classical ribbon blender has multi-purpose uses in the manufacture of food, beverage, pharmaceutical, cosmetic, chemical, plastic, agricultural and other products. Due to the usefulness and economy, the ribbon blender is of the choice for most straight forward blending processes. In a well-made ribbon blender, properly designed and fabricated with close-tolerance, ribbons turn within a horizontal trough to produce a balanced lateral and radial movement of the batch materials. Blending cycles are relatively fast and the quality of the mix is not difficult to replicate from batch to batch. In fact, it requires very little maintenance even when with frequent product changeovers.

Scaling up operation from a pilot ribbon blender, the large commercial production becomes simple. Despite these established advantages, the process equipment, optimal mixing performance in the ribbon blender still requires proper sizing, specification, and customization. Ribbon blenders consist of a U-shaped horizontal trough and an agitator made up of inner and outer helical ribbons. They are inclined to move the material axially, in opposing directions, and also radially. This combination promotes fast and thorough blending. Typically, the size of the blender ranges up to 300 feet/min. Mechanism followed by this type of blender is shear-mixing. The shear is transferred by moving blades. High shear rates are effective in breaking the lumps. However, convective mixing occurs as the powder bed is lifted and allowed to force to the bottom of the vessel.

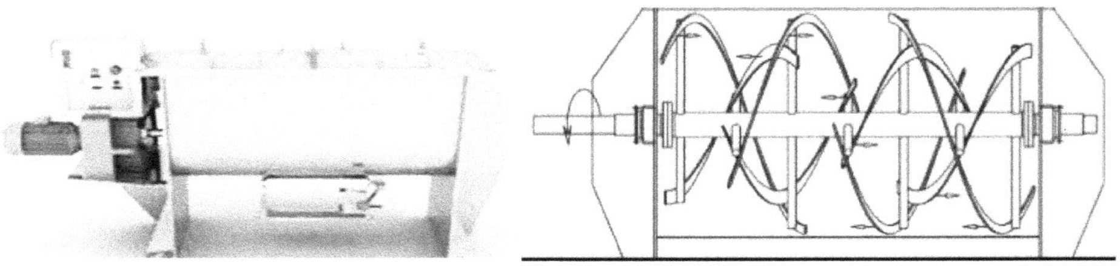

**Fig. 4.4** Schematic diagram of ribbon blender and blades

## Construction

The unit consists of one electrical motor, one reduction gear, belt-drive between motor and gear, couple-drive between gear and (ribbon) mixing stirrer. A container having four legs with a discharge valve and top cover. Both ends of mixing shaft are sealed with bush and PTFE. The gland housing and safety guards are provided on all moving parts.

It consists of horizontal cylindrical trough usually open at the top. It is fitted with two helical blades; the blades are mounted on the same shaft through the long axis of the trough. The blades have both right- and left-hand twists. The blades are connected to a fixed speed drive. It can be loaded by top loading and emptying is done through the bottom port.

## Working

Perhaps the most common operation done on the ribbon blender is mixing of the dry ingredients; for examples, baking mixes, tablet formulations, powdered flavors, protein supplements, chemical additives, etc. A typical mixing-cycle usually takes 15 minutes and, with the ribbon agitator continuously running, the operation may also be completed quickly. It is a simple process and a ribbon blender can easily work with required satisfaction provided the bulk density and particle size of the ingredients are within the range. However, depending on the characteristics of the powders, some discretionary features should be considered, these are:

- To reduce the dusting, option for a dust-tight discharge valve and clamps to secure the gasket cover.

- Lantern rings are installed on the packing gland when handling fine or abrasive powders.
- A slight positive pressure of air maintained during blending which will prevent particles from penetrating the stuffing box and protect the shaft from wear.

The material should be charged from the top, the port/ports are provided on the top cover to charge the material as well as for air outlet. One discharge valve is provided at the center of the bottom-side in centre of the container. As per requirement, the discharge height should be adjusted. The material is discharged in the container directly so that material handling time for discharge is reduced considerably and the operation becomes dust free. In ribbon blender the powder moves from center to the end of the container and again from the end to the center of the container. Hence, the total mixing time is very less and the RPM required is also very low. The dry material moves continuously due to the shape and movement of the ribbon and shape of the container. This provides good quality of blending.

The method of loading the materials into the blender vessel-top to bottom or left to right is a parameter that can affect the mixing performance of tumbling blenders. In the top-to-bottom configuration, one powder is initially loaded into the vessel. Above this powder bed, another powder is added. In the left to right configuration, a separator is initially inserted into the vessel where one side of the mixer is loaded with one powder and into the other side with another. The top-to-bottom loading provides significantly faster mixing rates than left-to-right loading.

## Uses

- Ribbon Blender can be used to coat solid particles with a minor component which can be another solid which is significantly smaller in size. For example, coating of polyethylene beads with a fine powder lubricant or a liquid ingredient such as spraying the flavoring oil into roasted coffee beans. In these kinds of processes, the presence of a minor or trace ingredient necessitates more accurate mixing.
- Lubrication of dry granules in large quantity
- Mixing of solids of different shapes and sizes
- For the preparation of a suspension of solid in liquid, equipped with a liquid-tight flush valve, Ribbon Blenders built for this type of application can include jacketing around the trough to control product temperature. For examples ready-to-eat soups, pasta sauces, pet food, etc. can be mixed.
- Mixing of slurries and pastes such as food recipes like cake butter, egg salad, etc. in industrial formulations such as carbon black dispersions, specialty adhesives, and plaster slurries.
- Dry mixing of free-flowing powders using low shearing force.
- The dry blending of capsule formulation, that is, powder blending.
- Mixing of cosmetic powders
- The vacuum drying process can be done using horizontal blenders equipped with a ribbon agitator, paddle blades or a combination of both.
- It is an efficient method for removing volatile components from pharmaceutical granulations, chemicals, plastics, ceramics, metals, and other materials. The combination of reduced pressure and constant agitation accelerates drying even at low temperatures.

### Merits of Ribbon Blender

- High shear can be applied by using perforated baffles. These baffles can rub and breakdown the large aggregates.
- This type of blender requires less space.
- It protects the motor and ribbon blender from overload. When the load is too large to block and rotate, the working liquid is ejected from the fusible plug to separate the working machine and the load, so that the motor and equipment will not be damaged when starting and overloading. In this operation, the speed difference caused by the impact will be alleviated by coupling.
- Stable start loads equipment, in the equipment startup and operation process, effective isolation of the impact and torsional vibration of the equipment.
- When overloaded, the working liquid does not spatter.
- A hydraulic lift is stable, flexible, easy to operate and maintain, guide safe and reliable.
- Small vibration mixing system, low noise.

### Demerits of Ribbon Blender

- It is a poor mixer.
- Shearing action is less than that in a planetary mixer.
- Dead spots are found in this mixer, but these are less.
- It has a fixed speed drive.
- The hydraulic coupler is not loaded with the inverter in general, and cannot adjust the rotating speed of the ribbon blender effectively.
- As the loading of hydraulic couplings is easy to form multiple transfer kinetic energy, resulting in power consumption, so it cannot improve the start-up performance of the ribbon blender.
- Unable to click the ribbon blender during use.

## Sigma Blade Mixer

Sigma mixers are also known as Universal mixers, because they have practically unlimited applications. They are equipped to process the materials of wide viscosity range in batches. The universal mixer and kneading machine consist basically of a rectangular trough curved at the bottom to form two half-cylinders. It is fitted with two blades horizontally placed and driven by suitable gear. The gear may be attached either on one or both ends of the trough. On every revolution, the blades sweep the entire area of the half-cylinder, revolving toward each other at unequal speed and conveying both with transverse and lateral motion. Clearance between blades and trough is veryless, so that no particle of the materials can escape the mixing action of the blades. When the blades move, every particle is inconstant motion. An intensive kneading action is carried out at the same time. In this mixing, the material is pulled and pushed (squeezed) against the blades, saddle, and sidewalls. Sigma mixer can efficiently handle and mixes the materials of different range in consistency, starting from dry powders to very stiff plastic masses. In many industries, vacuum mixers serve a very definite purpose of mixing operations. Sometimes, it is advantageous, and in many times the mixing is essential to be carried out under vacuum conditions. A material should be economically dried under vacuum to remove solvents or moisture before mixing with other material. Oxidation-sensitive materials can be prevented from oxidation by vacuum mixing; occluded gasses can also be efficiently removed and the air cannot interact with the material during mixing.

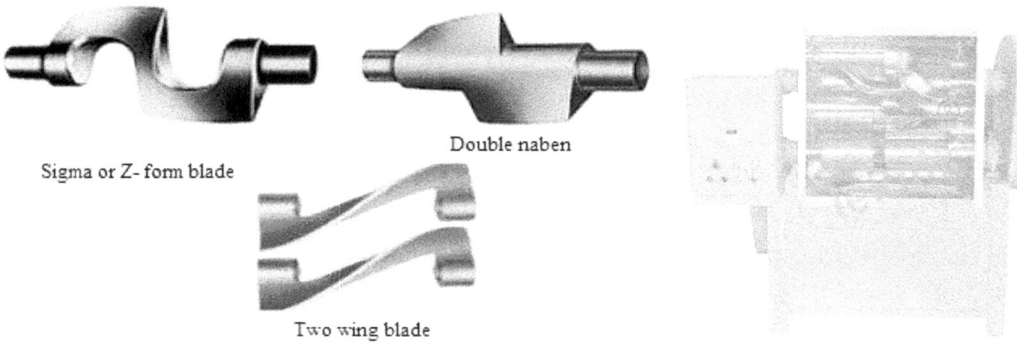


**Fig. 4.5** Type of sigma or kneading blades and sigma blade mixer

## Principles

This type of mixers can handle and mix very viscous materials. Mixing in a sigma blade mixer promotes both lateral and transverse motion of the material. The design and profile of the sigma blade are made in such a way that the viscous material is pulled, sheared, compressed, kneaded, and folded by the action of the blades against the walls of the mixer trough. The functions of a sigma blade mixer depend on:

1. The action of the blades – tangential or overlapping, and
2. The ratio of the speed of rotation to the blades.

The helix angle of the blade can be modified depending on the required shearing.

## Construction

Working capacity of this type of mixer can vary up to 1,000 gallons. However, customized models are also available. Choice of stationary or tilting units for loading and unloading are also available to suit the needs during production. The unit has a valve at the bottom for discharge. Mono-screw extruder models are available. Jacketed trough for heating or cooling, vacuum or pressure designs are also available. The models with independent blade arm drive with differential rotating speeds and the adjustable ratio are available. Two sigma shaped blades are fitted horizontally in each trough of the bowl. The complete mixer is mounted on steel fabricated stand of suitable strength to withstand the vibration and to give noise free performance.

## Working

For operation, the material is loaded through the top of the container up to 40 to 65 percent of the mixer's total volume. The blades rotate through heavy-duty drive systems. Typically, such a mixer consists of a motor, gearbox, couplings, and gears. The maximum speed of the sigma mixer is generally limited to 60 meters per minute. Mixing may be carried out at ambient temperature or under controlled temperature. In such cases, the mixer troughs with jackets for circulation of hot or cold media to maintain the required temperature conditions within the mixer can be used. The discharge of the material from the mixer container is made either by tilting of the mixer container, bottom discharge valve, or through an extruder/screw located in the lower portion between the two trough compartments. The mixer may be equipped with any one of these discharge arrangements. The tilting discharge arrangement is most common. The tilting arrangement of the container may be designed for manual operation or may be mechanized using motorized or hydraulic arrangement.

### Uses

- The sigma mixer is most suitable for mixing the materials like pasty, sticky, and gritty slurries with high viscosities such as adhesives, biscuit dough, butyl rubber, carbon pastes, ceramics, chemicals, chewing gum, crayon and pencil lead, explosives, fiberglass resin doughs, food and confectionery products, gaskets and gland packings, grinding wheel preparations, hot-melts, inks and pigment products, marzipan, mastics, metal powders, molding preparations, pencil erasers, pharmaceuticals, plastics, putties, refractories, sealing compounds, silicone rubber, soaps and detergents, solid propellants, sugar pastes, viscous rubber solutions, etc.
- The sigma mixer is used in wet granulation process for the manufacture of tablets, pill masses, and ointments.
- It is used primarily for liquid-solid mixing,
- It can be used for solid-solid mixing.

### Merits of Sigma Blade Mixer

- It creates a minimum dead space during mixing.
- It has close tolerance between the blades and side wall along with the bottom of the mixer shell.

### Demerits of Sigma Blade Mixer

- It works at a fixed speed.

## Planetary Mixers

Planetary mixer is ideal for mixing of wet/dry materials. It exerts a homogeneous mixing action. The planetary motion of the beater enables faster and better mixing of material in a considerably less time. Slow speed is used for dry mixing where less dust is generated. Higher speed causes kneading during wet granulation. Portable mixing bowl with top mounted agitator has a dual advantage of material transfer and there is no risk of gland packing contamination.

Planetary mixers are very widely used in many chemical industries where a very intimate physical mixing of various ingredients is essential. The stirrer has two blades – One blade moves around the circumference of the vessel in which the material is placed. Another one moves around its own axis (body) too. The motion is like, the earth revolving around the Sun. While doing so, the earth moves around its own axis. For this reason, this equipment has been name das *planetary*(like planet).The quality of the composition after mixing with this mixer would be more uniform and very effective mixing will take place. The mixing of various ingredients in which more amount of the solid is to be mixed with a lesser amount of the liquid and effective mixing is desired. There are many other industrial applications of this type of mixer where the quality of mixing is very important.

## Principles

All contact parts of the bowl and attachments are made of SS 316. Scrapping blades can also be provided. Mixing bowl can be jacketed for electric/steam heating or for circulation of cold water. Manual lifting arrangement for agitators up to 50 Lt, and hydraulic motorized lifting arrangements for capacities of 100 Lt and above are also available. Charging port on top of the mixing bowl with a stainless-steel lid is provided. The mixing bowl is provided with castor wheels and a locking arrangement for easy handling. Totally enclosed drive frame that eliminates the chances of cross-contamination. Effective design of the mixer can speed up the process of mixing.

The surface finish of 0.3 Ra having the discharge of the binder paste makes it easy. Flush bottom ball valve with a clear 4 ″ openings make the flow ability easy. Complete steam trap arrangement is supplied along with the system.

**Fig. 4.6** (a) Planetary mixer (Before operation) (b) Planetary Mixer (in operation)

## Construction

Planetary mixer primarily consists of a bowl of varying capacity and an agitator. The bowl remains static, while the agitator moves rapidly within the bowl to mix the materials present inside the bowl. The body of the mixer is constructed with a non-corrosive material. This is supported with robust construction with mechanically welded strong metal frame. The motor is having high start-up torque with the speeds from 20 to 180 rpm (planetary movement), to be set according to the need and the mixture hardness. It may be made water protected. Planetary movement is provided by self-lubricating gears, eliminating any risk of leaks. Overload is protected by the planetary system and motor. Adjustable feet are provided to make it perfectly stable. There may be single or double planetary blades, floating scraper blade which adjust itself to bowl curve. Since it is provided with a single base structure, manually and hydraulically operated lift using air or oil electric pump, durable special steel planetary gears with long life are also heat treated and hardened, multiple blade options like stirrup, vertical, or a combination, it gives high mixing efficiency. Moreover, the speed of the blades can be controlled, a control panel to limit the motion, it is very easy to handle, clean and maintain, it ensures uniform consistency and a homogeneous mixing. Planetary movement is provided by self-lubricating gears, eliminating any risk of leak. Overload is protected by the planetary system and motor.

## Working

A vertical designed mixer has no shaft seals, bearings, packing glands or stuffing boxes submerged in the product zone. In addition, the agitators are raised and lowered in/out of the mixing vessel by a hydraulic lift, that enables easy access for cleaning between batches. Vessels are interchangeable and can be dedicated to a particular formulation, so batch-to-batch cross-contamination risks are reduced. The blades move horizontally in circulatory motion; since the blades are attached to the shaft at an inclined direction, the components are mixed both horizontally and vertically. The planetary mixer can be operated at a variable speed. At slower speed it is used to mix the powders, and at higher speeds it is used for the kneading action required during the wet granulation process. One of the advantages of the planetary mixers is that the mixing bowl has no dead spaces. How the blade of the mixer moves with the movement of the gear is shown in Fig 4.7.

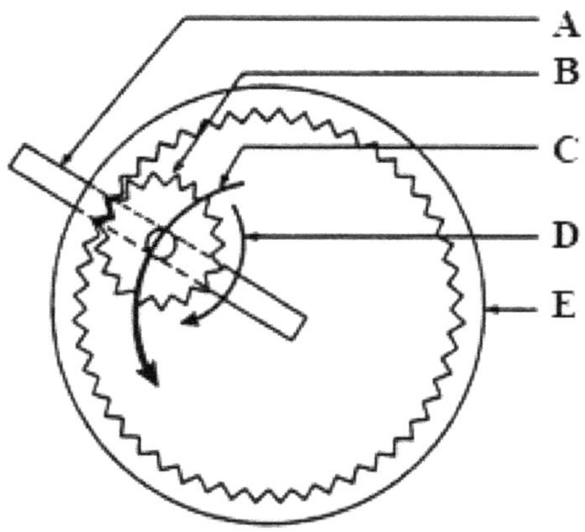


**Fig. 4.7** Planetary motion (Mechanism of movement of blades) A: Mixer blade, B: Planetary gear, C: Direction of drive, D: Direction of rotation of planetary gear, E: Stationary ring gear

In the bowl the ingredients are placed. A mixing element such as hook, flat beater, etc. is attached. One motor is attached to enable the whisks moments. One operator box is also provided to control mixing process, timing, speed, etc. Moreover, there are also several accessories such as a dough hook which is handy to knead bread dough, cakes, pizza, cookies, etc. A mixing paddle helps the mixing of cream, etc. The whisk accessory allows to beat egg white portion, also mayonnaise (a thick, white cream made from oil, vinegar, and the yellow part of eggs, usually cold) and soft cream, etc.

## Uses

Planetary mixers are more useful than other common spiral mixers, because they are able to mix a wide variety of ingredients. Planetary mixers can be used to whip and blend, whereas spiral mixers fail to do so. Type of blades for a mixer is also variable. It can also be of different shape and size and is mounted on a unique axis or shaft. This has many applications such as in a bakery due to few interchangeable utensils and the several accessories that are easily available. The mixer can be used for mixing in following industries/products:

- Pharmaceuticals, Cosmetics products, creams, lotion etc.,
- General Chemical Industries
- Biotech industries, Emulsions, Explosives.
- Adhesive and Sealant
- Caulking and Wax Compound
- Dental Fillers, Powder Coating, Blending powders
- Battery Pastes, Gel Products
- Food products, Bakeries
- Agricultural pesticide products
- High-Viscosity product
- Colors, Resins.

## Merits of Planetary Mixers

- Easily cleanable.
- The footprint of the double planetary mixer is considerably less than that of a sigma blade mixer.
- It saves energy. Since the double planetary mixer uses less motor horsepower to operate, everyday energy costs will be less and these savings can become significant over time.
- With the use of extra mix vessels, the double planetary mixer can produce material in a semi-continuous basis: one vessel may be charged with raw materials while other vessels in the loop are under the mixer. It can be at the discharge station or being cleaned for the next cycle.
- Depending on the specifications, a double planetary is generally one half to one-third the cost of a comparably sized sigma blade kneader.

## Demerits of Planetary Mixers

- Limited batch size that can be prepared at one time.
- Several sublots are prepared using this equipment, and then the final blend of the sublots is done in a large tumbling mixer.

## Fluid Mixing Equipments

Fluids can be mixed by use of impeller-based mixer. The equipments/apparatuses used for mixing of liquids consists of 2 components – 1. one vessel or container, 2. mixing device or impeller. On the basis of shape and pitch, the impellers are classified into three types:

- Propeller mixer,
- Turbine mixer, and
- Paddle mixer

**Propeller mixer** consists of number of blades, usually 3 blades. Such design is most commonly used for liquids. Depending upon the slant of their blades, may be right or left-handed. Two bladed propellers are used when the depth of the mixing tank is large. Size of propeller may be small from few centimeters to as large as 0.5metresdepending upon the size of thetank. Small size propellers can rotate up to 8000rpm and produce longitudinal movement. Propeller mixer is useful when high mixing capacity is required. It is effective for liquids which have maximum viscosity of about 2.0 pascal.sec or slurry up to 10% solids of fine mesh size. At laboratory scale dispersion of gas in liquid can be made successfully by using this mixer. Limitation of this mixer is observed when liquids having high viscosity of about 5.0pascal.sec such as glycerin, castor oil, etc. are to be mixed.

Depending on the type of impeller the type of flow varies.

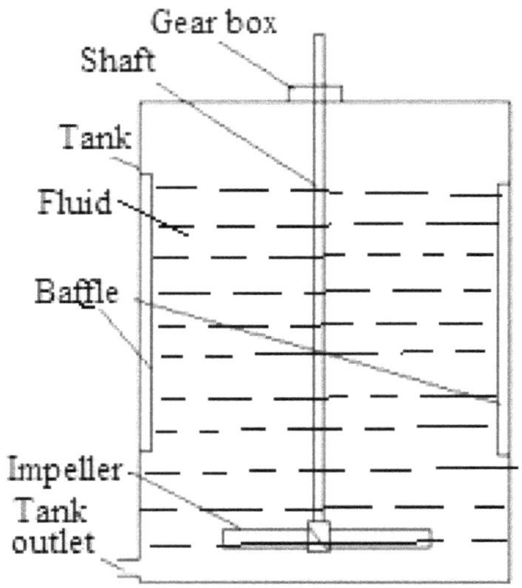


**Fig. 4.8** Schematic diagram of impeller mixer

## Turbines

A turbine is composed of a circular disc to which a number of short blades are attached. Blades may be straight or curved. The diameter of the turbine can range from 30 – 50%of the diameter of the vessel. Turbines rotates at a lower speed than the propellers (50 – 200rpm). Flat blade turbines produce radial and tangential flow. As the speed increases radial flow predominates. Pitched blade turbine produces axial flow. Near the impeller zone of rapid currents, high turbulence and intense shear is produced. Shear produced by turbines can be enhanced further by using a diffuser ring (stationary perforated ring which surrounds the turbine).

| Type of impeller | Glow Pattern |
|---|---|
| Propellers | Axial |
| Turbines | Axial or tangential or both |
| Paddles | Radial and tangential |
| Paddles with picth | Radial, tangential and axial |

## Principles

The turbine mixer contains a circular disc impeller, to this impeller a number of short, vertical blades, which may be straight or curved are attached. The turbine impeller is usually rotated at a somewhat lower speed than the propeller type. The ratio of the impeller to the diameter of the container is usually less. The blades may have a pitch to give some axial flow. But most of the turbine impellers have flat blades. In these cases, a very little axial or tangential flow would take place. The liquid moves very rapidly in a radial direction. Turbine-type impellers produce a shear force greater than the propellers and these forces can also be increased further by attaching a *diffuser ring.*

**Fig. 4.9** Turbine type impeller (a) Ruston impeller (b) High-shear impeller blades

Turbine mixers are useful for mobile and viscous liquids. For example, liquid glucose has viscosity of about 100 Ns/m$^2$ can be satisfactorily mixed by using turbine mixer; while propeller mixer cannot be used.

## Construction

Motion is produced as a result of rotary action of the impeller. Turbines have different physical dimensions such as diameter, number of blades, blade angle, blade shape, open or closed core, etc. The primary dimension of the turbines can be understood by seeing the Fig 4.9 and the flow pattern in the turbine mixer can be understood by seeing the Fig 4.10. Flow pattern developed under gassed conditions is a function of geometry, stirrer speed, gas flow rate, and gas bubble size. Turbine (Rushton turbine) with 90 degree angled flat blades can generate a strong radial flow pattern only and have limited mixing performance. The 100% radial flow pattern turbine design are based on a flat disk with 6 flat blades vertically mounted symmetrically on the disc. A cost-effective design with normal performance is generally limited by pockets or cavities, which adhere to the back of the blade at high gas flow rates and/or RPM. When gas flow gets too high, the pockets can bridge between blades, resulting in flooding and severe mechanical instability. Symmetric angled flat blade turbine (Jacob's) combines the radial flow with axial flow by selective angling of the blades. This is an open design that improves the aeration performance. Gas injected under the turbine are sucked into the fully open core volume of the turbine and distributed through the entire turbine exhaust.

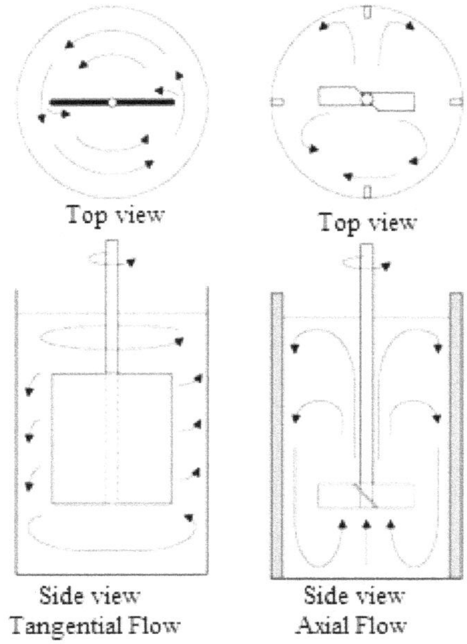


**Fig. 4.10** Flow pattern in turbine mixer (a) Tangential around the circumference of the vessel (b) Axial in the direction of the impeller shaft

## Working

The liquids to be mixed or the ingredients are transferred into the vessel or container. The mixer is allowed to run at a predetermined speed and time. Care should be taken that no vortex is formed; if formed it should be within limit. Both time and power (energy/time) are important parameters in mixing with turbine mixer. In case of improved turbine mixer with curved agitating blades, power is transferred from impeller to fluid. Depending on the type of product or constituents, these parameters are validated. A supporting ring concentric with the pivot is attached below and at the radial extremities of the agitating blades. These shearing blades are provided on the ring intermediate the peripheral extremities of the agitating blades. Each of the shearing blades is mounted on the ring in an angularly disposed position generally to extend in the direction of the adjacent rearward agitating blade. The shearing blades have sharply formed leading and trailing edges which shear lumps or agglomerates dispersed in the liquid. In addition to over-all re-enforcement for the agitating blades and a mounting for the shear blades, the ring provides substantial axial clearance between the blades, their pivot and the ring itself, allowing the axial as well as radial motion for the mixing medium.

### Uses

- Turbine mixers are used in liquid mixing, blending and related operations. Turbine having an improved arrangement of agitating and shearing blades promote a high degree of shearing action on lumps or agglomerates in liquids. This increases the liquid mixing efficiency and speed.
- The materials to be mixed if contain a relatively high percentage of lumps or agglomerates, the agitation of the mechanical devices alone usually is not sufficient to provide the degree of mixing required for many types of materials. The improved turbine mixer induces a high order of shearing action of the agglomerates or lumps through direct impact and shearing action of the blades that results in more efficient and better mixing.
- The improved turbine mixer comprises a number of curved agitating blades attached centrally to the shaft. These curved blades impart a high degree of centrifugal action in various liquids undergoing mixing. The agitating blades have a substantial curved slope with respect to radii extending from their pivot, presenting a convex forward face.

### Merits of Turbines

- Turbine mixers produces greater shearing forces than propeller mixers through the less pumping rate. Therefore, suitable for emulsification.
- Turbines are effective for high viscous solutions with a wide range of viscosities up to 7.0 pascal. second.
- During mixing of low viscous materials of large volumes, the turbine produces a strong current which spread throughout the tank destroying stagnant pockets.
- The turbine can handle slurries with 60% solids.
- Turbines are suitable for liquids of large volume and high viscosity, if the tank is baffled.

### Demerits of Turbines

- Turbine mixers are not commonly suitable for suspending heavy solids.
- It produces vortex.

## Paddles

A paddle consists of a central pivot with long flat blades attached to it vertically. Two blades or four blades are common. sometimes the blades are pitched and may be dished or hemispherical in shape and have a large surface area in relation to the tank in which they are used. Paddles rotates at a low speed of 100rpm. They push the liquid radially and tangentially with almost no axial action unless blades are pitched.

In deep tanks several paddles are attached one above the other on the same shaft. At very low speeds it gives mild agitation in unbaffled tank but as for high speeds baffles are necessary.

## Principles

Commonly a rotational mixer is used for mixing of liquids. This mixer provides the necessary shear forces. The mixer should be of suitable shape, able to act as an impeller to produce an appropriate pattern of mixing. At any point, the movement of the liquid in the vessel will have three velocity components and the complete flow pattern depends on these three components in different parts of the vessel. These three velocity components are;

**Radial components:** This acts in the direction vertical to the impeller shaft. Excessive radial flow takes the material to the container wall then material falls to the bottom and continues to rotate as the mass beneath the impeller.

**A tangential component:** This acts in the direction tangent to the circle of rotation around the impeller shaft. If shaft is placed centrally and vertically, the tangential flow will occur following a circular path around the shaft and a vortex in the liquid will be created.

**Axial component or longitudinal or vertical:** This acts in the direction parallel to the impeller shaft. Inadequate longitudinal component causes the liquid and solid to rotate in layers without mixing. Adequate longitudinal pattern is appropriate to generate strong vertical currents particularly when suspending solids are present in a liquid .Different types of flow patterns observed in paddle mixer are shown in Fig 4.11.

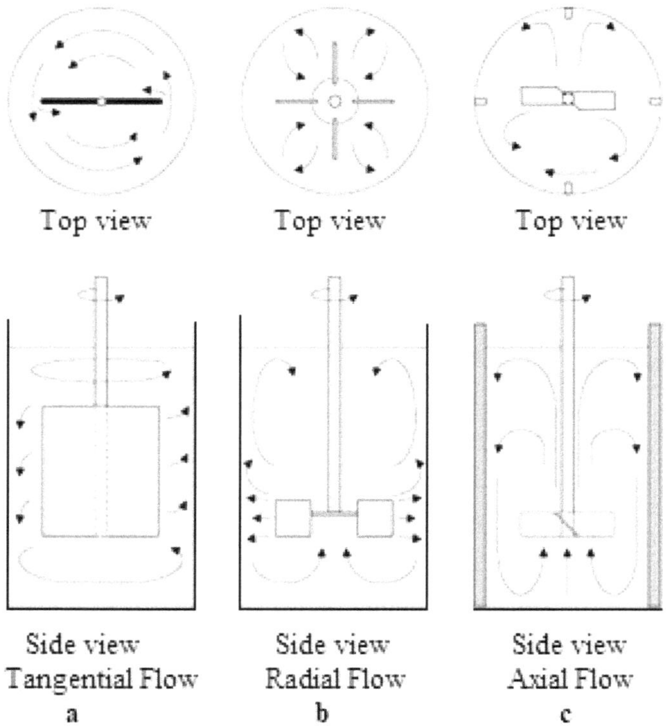


**Fig. 4.11** Flow pattern in paddle mixer (a) Tangential around the circumference of the vessel (b) Radial centrifugal off the peripheral tips of the blade, (c) Axial in the direction of the impeller shaft

### Construction

Usually paddle mixer consists of flat blades attached to a vertical shaft. The shaft with blades rotates at a relatively lower speed such as 100rpm. It works as an agitator. Simple flat blades are used for liquids of low viscosity. However, the importance has been given to produce radial and tangential movement with very little longitudinal effect. Such movement can be increased by using paddles with a slight pitch. For more viscous liquids, the paddles having different shape of blades can be used. The shape of the blades may be such that it can fit closely to the internal surface of the container so that no *dead-spot* or deposited solid can be found in the container during mixing. When the liquid is rotated at lower speed, the baffles are normally not required. When higher speed is required, baffles are attached, because the presence of baffles can avoid or reduce swirling and vortexing.

For more viscous liquids, an alternative mixer called *planetary motion mixer* can be used. This planetary motion mixer consists of a small paddle that rotates on its own axis like a planet moving round the sun, but travels in a circular path within the mixing vessel. Since it rotates like a planet, it is called planetary. The agitator is shaped to the side of the container so that the *dead-spots* can be avoided. The width of the agitator ranges from half to two-thirds of the internal diameter of the container. By reducing the size of the paddle, the mixing efficiency of the agitator can be improved, the overall power consumption can also be reduced. Different agitator-shapes are available as per the type and viscosity of the product.

### Working

The liquids along with necessary soluble solids (for making solution) are placed in the mixer of adequate capacity. The volume of the ingredients should such that they can occupy about 80% of the volume of the mixing tank. The mixer is allowed to run till a uniform solution is obtained. The speed of the blades is adjusted according to the requirement. As mentioned above the time and speed of mixing vary on the basis of viscosity of the product, type of product, etc. However, care should be taken to avoid vortex and entrapment of air. Because, mixing at very high-speed results air entrapment and it becomes a problem to remove the entrapped air later on, particularly if the viscosity of the product is high.

### Uses

Paddles are used in the manufacture of antacid suspensions, purgatives containing agarand pectin, antidiarrheal mixtures containing bismuth-kaolin, etc.

### Merits of Paddles

- Vortex formation does not occur with paddle impellers, because of low speed mixing.
- Provides better mixing efficiency,
- Dead spots and solid-deposits are rare.

### Demerits of Paddles

- Mixing of the suspension is poor; therefore, baffled tanks are required.

## Silvers on Emulsifier

Practically all emulsions are prepared by mixing with equipments which can be classified into four categories:

1. Pin mills, Silverson emulsifier, etc. are used as disintegrator;
2. Homogenizers are used for passing the fluid through fine orifices under pressure;
3. Colloid mills which by centrifugal force forces the mixture to flow between a stator and a fast-rotating rotor put close together;
4. Sonic and ultrasonic devices disintegrate the particles into fines.

### Principles

Silvers on mixer cum homogenizer belongs to the first category of the equipments used for preparing the emulsions. It can produce high shearing force and turbulence by its high-speed rotor. Within the mixing work-head the high-speed rotation of the rotor blades creates a powerful suction; as a result, the solid and liquid materials move upwards from the bottom of the vessel into the centre of the work-head. Then, the centrifugal force drives the material towards the periphery of the work-head where the materials are milled as per the clearance provided between the ends of the rotor blades and inner walls of the stator. The material is then forced out through the perforations in the stator and circulated into the main body of the mixture. This is done by the intense hydraulic shear. The materials expelled from the head are projected radially at high speed towards the side of mixing tank. To maintain the continuous mixing cycle, fresh material can be fed to the work-head. The effect of horizontal (radial) expulsion and suction into the head is to set up a circulatory pattern of mixing below the surface. For this reason, no unnecessary turbulence occurs at the surface.

If the machine is correctly selected on the basis of size and power, the entire contents of the tank will pass hundreds of times through the work-head during the mixing operation to give uniform progressive processing and homogenization. There is another benefit is that aeration can be reduced by using controlled mixing.

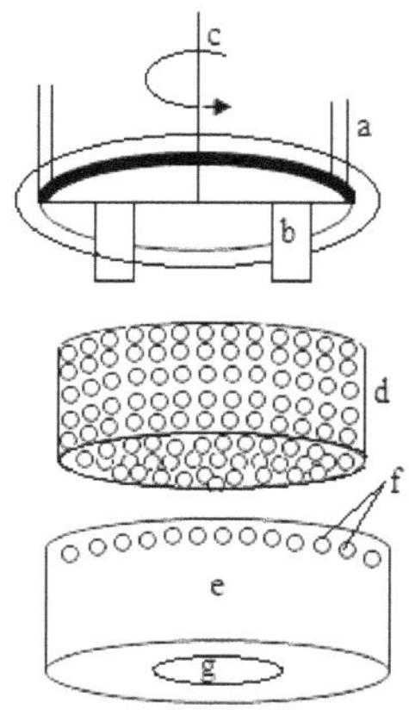


**Fig. 4.12** Schematic diagram of expanded head of Silverson emulsifier (a) Supporting column, (b) Turbine blades, (c) Turbine shaft, (d) Mesh (e) Cover (f) Outlet opening, (g) Inlet

## Construction

A comprehensive range of work-heads and screens is available for all Silverson rotor/stator mixers. The Fig. 4.12 shows the schematic diagram of the detonated head of Silverson emulsifier. These can be easily interchanged and the work-head scan be created as per the requirement. Thus, wide range of mixing operations including emulsifying, homogenizing, disintegrating, dissolving, dispersing, blending, particle size reduction and de-agglomerating can be performed. General purposed is integrating head is the most versatile of all the heads. It gives an exceptionally vigorous mixing action. In fact, it is ideal for general mixing applications.

For the disintegration of fibrous materials, such as animal and vegetable tissue, as well as the disintegration and solubilization of elastic materials such as rubbers and polymers, slotted disintegrating head would be more suitable. Square hole high shear screen provides exceptionally high shear rates which is necessary for the rapid size reduction of soluble and insoluble granular solids. It is also suitable for the preparation of emulsions and fine colloidal suspensions.

Standard Silverson mixer consists of column 'a' which supports the head. Inside the head 'a' the turbine blades 'b' is driven using a motor placed above the supporting column. The column drives the turbine shaft 'c'. The contents are expelled by the centrifugal force through the mesh 'd' and on to the cover 'e'. Large shearing and impaction forces produce a fine emulsion which emerges from the opening 'f'. circulation of the material through the head is maintained by the suction produced in the inlet 'g' at the bottom of the head.

This may have a capacity from few ml up to10 liters/min and with the ability to mixin-line with flow rates up to 20liters/minute. They provide excellent reproducibility when scaling up activity during formulation development and provide an accurate and easy means of forecasting the performance of larger Silverson machines under full-scale working conditions.

## Working

The speed of the regulator should be turned to zero, and the machine off, when not in use. The machine should be switched off when adding or removing attachments. Never touch any moving parts. Always operate the mixer with mixing head assembly, completely submerged in liquid, to prevent overheating and seizure of the mixing assembly. Before operation, ensure shaft coupling sleeve is secure and covers the coupling pin. It is to be made sure that no obstructions are there at the zone just below the mixing head; particularly when lowering the mixer body. Ensure that the liquid to be mixed is in a large enough container. The mixer is not explosion or flame proof. Hence, the work should always be done in a well-ventilated area if flammable solvents are present. Users should be aware that extended high speed mixing could cause significant heating of mixtures. Mixing of volatile solvents or toxic ingredients should be done in a fume cupboard. Dusting of powders can occur significantly. Always start mixer at lowest speed, and then gradually increase speed until desired setting, to prevent splashing. Clean mixing head and assembly as soon as possible after use, to prevent corrosion. The mixer is splash proof, but not waterproof. Never immerse unit in water or spray with hose. Take care when changing mixing heads, as the rotor blades may be sharp.

### Uses

It is especially useful for all emulsions.

- Silverson mixer is suitable for preparing emulsions of low viscosity. The Silverson High Speed Mixer is used for mixing liquid/liquid or liquid/solid mixtures at speeds of up to 8000 rpm.
- For blending liquids of similar or widely varying viscosities can be mixed rapidly to produce homogeneous product.
- The emulsions of particle/globule size range within 2.0 and 1.5 μ can be prepared successfully by the high speed Silverson mixer.
- The Silverson mixer can be used for disintegration of solids and the preparation of gels and thickeners, suspensions, solutions and slurries.

### Merits of Silverson Emulsifier

➢ The Silverson mixer can be used for disintegration of solids and the preparation of gels and thickeners, suspensions, solutions and slurries.

### Demerits of Silverson Emulsifier

➢ Sometimes there is a chance of clogging of pores of the mesh.

## Short Questions

1. What are the applications of mixing in pharmaceutical industries?
2. Write down the different types of mixtures used in pharmacy.
3. Classify the equipments used for mixing of solids with solids, liquids with solids, liquids with liquid and semi-solids with semi-solids with relevant examples.
4. Explain briefly the mechanism of mixing of solids with solids.
5. What do you know about how the liquids are mixed?
6. Write a note on the principle of twin shell blender.
7. What are the uses of twin shell blender and ribbon blender?
8. What are the advantages and disadvantages of twin shell blender and ribbon blender?
9. Write note on propeller mixer and turbine mixer.
10. Explain the features of Silverson emulsifier.

## Long Questions

1. 'Mixing is an important process in pharmaceutical manufacturing.' Justify the statement.
2. Explain how can you mix the liquids.

3. Explain the principle involved in mixing liquids and solids.
4. Explain the factors influencing mixing.
5. What is the mechanism of powder mixing? Explain the parameters involved in making homogeneous powder mixture.
6. Discuss the various parameters involved in mixing of semi-solids.
7. Explain the construction, working and uses of twin shell blender.
8. Explain with the help of a suitable diagram the principle, construction, working and uses of ribbon blender.
9. Explain with the help of a suitable diagram the principle, construction, and working of sigma blade mixer.
10. How the planetary mixer is constructed? How does it work? Write down its advantages.

# CHAPTER 5

# Crystallization

Objectives, Applications, and Theory of Crystallization. Solubility Curves, Principles, Construction, Working, Uses, Merits and Demerits of Agitated Batch Crystallizer, Swenson Walker Crystallizer, Krystal Crystallizer, Vacuum Crystallizer. Caking of Crystals, Factors Affecting Caking & Prevention of Caking.

## Objectives

Crystallization *is a process of separation of a solid from its solution in the form of crystal under certain conditions*. This process is widely used in the chemical and pharmaceutical industry. Crystal is a solid in which its constituents are arranged in a highly organized manner, so that the solid possesses a definite geometric structure. The principle of crystallization is based on the limited solubility of a compound in a solvent at a certain temperature, pressure, pH, etc. By changing these conditions to a limit where the solubility of the material becomes low, the dissolved solids will separate from its solution state in the form of crystals. For the production of salt and sugar, the technique of crystallization has been used during thousands of years. Many phenomena that occur during crystallization are not yet adequately understood. Particularly, the mechanisms of nucleation and crystal growth and the complex behavior of industrial crystallizers remain indescribable. The consistent quality of product such as purity, crystal size, etc. are increasing, thus creating a large interest in crystallization research.

The objective of this experiment is to demonstrate the problems and challenges commonly occur in crystallization. The equipments used for crystallization are classified as follows on the basis of the method used to bring about supersaturation:

1. Supersaturation brought about by cooling
   (a) Batch process
      - Tank crystallizer
      - Agitated batch crystallizer
   (b) Continuous process
      - Swenson-Walker process
      - Others
2. Supersaturation brought about by evaporating the solvent
   (a) Salting evaporators
   (b) Krystal evaporators

3. Supersaturation brought about by adiabatic evaporation (cooling and evaporation. simultaneously)
   (a) Vacuum crystallizer
      - With external classifying seed bed
      - Without external classifying seed bed
4. Salting out by adding a substance that can reduce the solubility of the solute to be crystallized.

## Applications

In pharmaceutical industry the crystallization technique is used for purification and separation for isolation and synthesis of pure drugs and other ingredients.

Drug molecules with limited micromeritic properties and aqueous solubility, about 90% of new APIs having low solubility in water, can be made suitable for dosage form development by an appropriate crystallization method using suitable solvent and temperature. The ability of a molecule to crystallize in different crystal forms is referred to as polymorphism. In the case of elements, this phenomenon is called allotropism. Hence, by using the crystallization technique, therapeutically active polymorph of a drug can be prepared.

When drugs and other excipients are synthesized, they are crystallized also. Because the crystallized drugs are expected to be pure. Hence, crystallization is an important process in pharmacy. The application of this process in pharmacy are listed below:

- **Purification:** After synthesis a drug is subjected to crystallization for its purification. That is, the impurities are removed. Sometimes, recrystallization becomes necessary for complete removal of impurities.
- **Modification of some physical properties:** For desired bioavailability and therapeutic efficacy, a drug must have proper micromeritics; that is, its particle size and size distribution should be within a required range. This is possible, if the drug is crystallized appropriately. Hence, the properties such as flow ability, compressibility, wet tability, and solubility, etc. can be improved.
- **Easy handling:** Materials are to be transported for different processes. Hence, transportation, storage, and overall handling of materials become easy through appropriate crystallization.
- Improved chemical stability: The stability of drugs and other substances can be improved by crystallization. For example, stability of crystalline penicillin G is much better than that of amorphous penicillin G.
- **Improved physical stability:** In case of emulsion, certain formulations such as suspension, the physical stability is a deciding factor for patient's acceptance. The physical properties including color and particle size of a drug are governed by the method of crystallization.
- Bioavailability: It is known that the bioavailability thereby therapeutic effectiveness of drugs depend principally on the solubility and crystalline characteristics. Some drugs are more effective and stable in their crystalline form. Hence, crystallization plays an important role in drug's performance.
- **Drug release characteristics:** To modify the duration of action of a drug the release characteristics of a drug is modified. For example, to sustain or extend the therapeutic action of a drug, the release characteristics, solubility and crystallinity of a drug is modified. Hence, crystallization demonstrate its role in formulation of a modified release dosage form.

## Theory of Crystallization

Before applying the process of crystallization, it is necessary to understand how the crystals are formed and how they grow. The over-all process of crystallization consists of two steps –

1. Formation of nucleus, and
2. Growth of crystals.

When the solution from which crystallization is supposed to occur contains any undissolved solid particles, the material may be crystallizing out.Then nucleus formation will start before the beginning of crystal growth. The formation of nuclei can continue and the nuclei already formed start growing. This can be better explained by Miers supersaturation theory.

### Miers Supersaturation Theory

Let us consider that the curve AB of the Fig 5.1 represents the normal solubility curve at equilibrium. It explains the maximum concentration of the solution. When the maximum amount of solute is dissolved in the solvent at equilibrium condition. That is, both solute and solvent are in equilibrium. However, this curve can represent the ultimate limit towards which crystallization from super saturated solution can occur. If a sample of such solution is cooled, it first crosses the solubility curve as shown by the arrow. At the point E the crystallization starts. When the solution is of pure solute, free from any solid particle (neither of the solute itself, nor any foreign matter) the solution will not start crystallizing until it is considerably supercooled. As per the Fig 5.1,the line CD represents the super solubility curve. It indicates the temperature limits at which nucleus will form spontaneously, and hence, the points where crystallization can occur. According to the Miers theory, at any point along the line EF, neither nuclei can form nor crystallization can start.

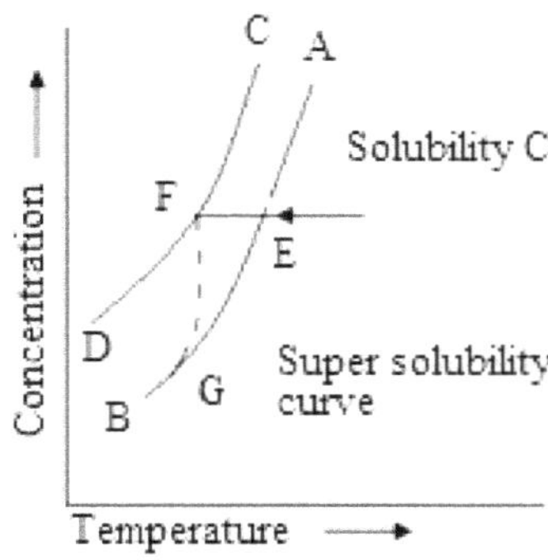


**Fig. 5.1** Miers supersaturation theory

### Nature of the Crystal Nucleus

The particles of both solute and solvent move in different molecular paths. Incidentally, a number of solute molecules come together and unite by mutual attraction. Of course, there may be some forces that act to separate these groups and such groups of molecules may be formed for very temporary period. If the extent of super-saturation is more, the formation of these groups would be less transitory; some of these groups orient well enough and these groups of solute molecules are called nuclei. These nuclei form the basis of crystal growth. When these groups acquire an appreciable size, their solubility becomes less than that of smaller transitory solute groups. Therefore, the small nuclei continue to grow and absorb solute molecules further from the surrounding solution.

### Short-comings of the Mier's Theory

- During long storage of a solution, nucleation may be observed well below the supersaturation, shown in the Fig 5.2.
- As per Mier's theory, crystallization starts at super-solubility curve. But this does not happen always; hence, crystallization may occur in any area.
- Because of accidental collisions, nucleation may occur well below the supersaturation.
- Larger the volume of the solution, more chance of such collision to form nuclei.
- Mier's theory is based on the assumption that the pure solute is dissolved in a pure solvent. But in practice this is very difficult to get this situation.
- According to the Mier's theory, a solution must be stored for very long time for crystallization to occur. But during such storage, there is a possibility of contamination of the solution with foreign particle (dust particles). These particles can act as seed and initiate nucleation.

## Solubility Curves

When a solute (solid) remains in its solution, it may dissolve if the solution is not saturated or can grow at the expense of the solution, if the solution is supersaturated. In any case, the solubility curve denotes equilibrium condition where the solute remains in the solution in dissolved state for a long period. Generally, the solubility of a substance depends mainly on temperature, slightly on the size of the material and pressure. In fact, pressure and particle size exert insignificant effect on solubility of substances. For this reason, the effect of temperature on solubility is considered in most of the solubility curves.

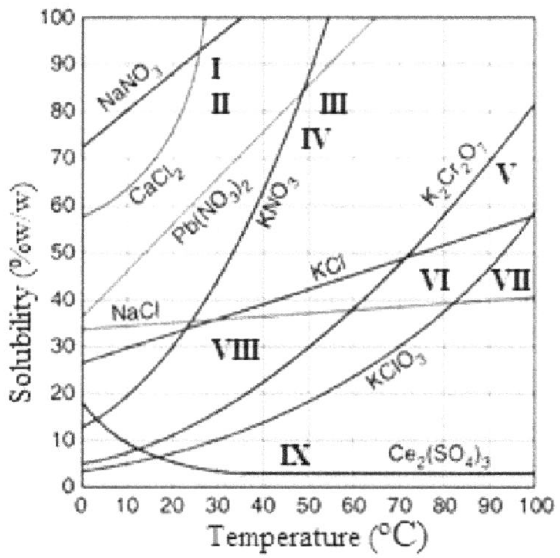


**Fig. 5.2** Solubility curve

Various experiments have also been conducted to determine the effect of temperature on solubility of various substances. When such data are used to plot the solubility curves, various types of curves are obtained as shown in Fig 5.2.

Crystallization of a dissolved solute requires certain definite experimental conditions. Solubility curve is useful in predicting these conditions such as the influence of temperature on the solubility of a substance. For example, by reducing the temperature, supersaturation of a solution can be achieved.

Generally, a substance (solute) dissolves in a solvent and an unsaturated solution is obtained first. By dissolving more of the solute, the solution is made saturated; at relatively higher temperature, further amounts of solute can be dissolved and the supersaturation is brought about. From this supersaturated solution crystallization occurs. Once the crystallization is over, the solution becomes saturated, this state is called *equilibrium state* and this condition is known as *stable equilibrium condition.* The Fig 5.2 represents the solubility curves of some common substances. The solubility curves of nine salts without their hydrates are mentioned below:

| Curve | Salt | Curve | Salt | Curve | Salt |
|---|---|---|---|---|---|
| I | $NaNO_3$ | II | $CaCl_2$ | III | $Pb(NO_3)_2$ |
| IV | $KNO_3$ | V | $K_2Cr_2O_7$ | VI | KCl |
| VII | $KClO_3$ | VIII | NaCl | IX | $Ce_2(SO_4)_3$ |

It is a common fact that the solubility of the solutes increases with increase of temperature. But there is exception; for example, in the Fig 2, the curve IX for cesium sulphate, the solubility decreases with increasing temperature. In case of other salts, the solubilities are increasing; however, the rate of increase in solubility is different for different solute. As per the Fig 5.2, the solubility of lead nitrate and sodium nitrate (ref. curve I and III) increase at a faster rate, whereas, the solubility of potassium nitrate (curve IV)increases sharply when the temperature is increased beyond 20°C. In case of sodium chloride (curve VII) its solubility can be increased by about 5% if the temperature is increased from 0°C to 100°C. Thus, the rate of increase in solubility is almost flat.The curve II indicates the effect of temperature on solubility of $CaCl_2$. The rate of change in solubility from about 57% at 0°C to 100% at 100°C taking a parabolic path. The rate of change of solubility of KCl (curve VI) with change of temperature is quite good. Similarly, the effect of temperature on change in solubilities of $KClO_3$ (curve VIII) and of $K_2Cr_2O_7$ (curve V) are noticeably high.

Thus, by increasing the temperature the solubility of a salt can be increased, but the extent and rate of increase of solubility would not be same.

## Agitated Batch Crystallizer

This is an old method used to grow the crystals. This method requires more labors and space, and material is also wasted. It requires artificial cooling. The equipment commonly used as agitated batch crystallization isschematically shown in Fig 5.3.

## Principles

This method is usually used only for those substances which showtheir solubility curves that decrease appreciably with temperature. For most of the substances, this is a normal type of solubility curve. For crystallization, probably this was the first method that has been used till this date. Supersaturation caused by evaporation of solvent has been used for production of common salt. Due to flatness of the solubility curve, the rate of production of common salt by cooling would be negligible. However, this method can be used for crystallization of substances other than sodium chloride provided that their solubility curve is not too steep. If the saturated solution contains a suspension of crystals, slight cooling of the evaporator will crystallize. Thus, the substances having steep solubility curves, it is desired to concentrate the solution in evaporators and cooled to crystallize from the supersaturated solutions.

## Construction

In industry, crystallization is carried out in crystallizers, commonly called *pans*. Pans can be batch or continuous, vacuum or atmospheric. In the pan, supersaturation of the solution (feed) is maintained by evaporation (evaporative crystallizers), using the method of cooling (cooling crystallizers) or both. Continuous pans are extensively used in modern, large-scale plants. Batch pans are used for the production of *seeds* (primary homogeneous nucleation) or for small-scale crystallization processes. Classically, crystallization pan is a vessel equipped with arrangements for heating or cooling and for agitation. The heat exchanger may be provided by a jacket or by a tubular heat exchange element. Agitation may be provided either by a mechanical stirrer or by recycling. Recycling pans with external heat exchangers are commonly used in the production of salt, citric acid, etc., but not in the sugar industry.

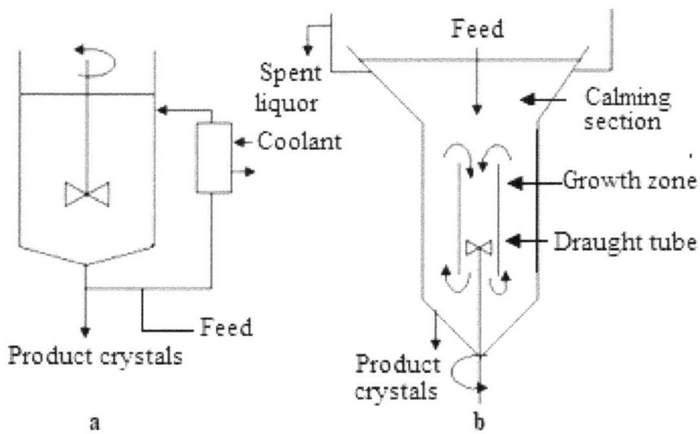


**Fig. 5.3** Schematic diagram of Agitated batch crystallizer (a) Internal circulation through tube (b) External circulation through heat exchanger

Because, the high viscosity of the material cannot follow the process mentioned above.

Agitation must be sufficiently vigorous to facilitate the transfer of mass and good mixing but can prevent crystal fracture, abrasion and secondary nucleation at mild rate. Vacuum is applied to carry out the process at lower temperature and to prevent degradation due to heat, such as inversion and caramelization/browning of sugar syrup.

### Working

Wateris circulated through the cooling coils and the solution is agitated by a suitable agitator (propeller) which is attached to the central shaft. For two reasons such agitation is done:

- Agitation increases the rate of heat transfer. The temperature of the solution becomes uniform and nearly to that of circulating water.
- Fine crystals present in suspended form in the solution can grow uniformly. Agitation does not allow them to form large aggregates; otherwise large crystals or aggregates would be formed.

  Thus, not only uniform, but also fine crystals are formed in this method.

### Uses

- Various solutes precipitate in their hydrate form at lower temperatures. This is useful, but it may be detrimental if, the mass of water of hydration produces a stable hydrated crystallization form which is more than the available water; a single block of hydrated solute will be formed– this happens in case of calcium chloride;
- Maximum supersaturation will take place in the coldest points. This may be achieved by the use of heat exchanger tubes which are sensitive to scaling, and heat exchange may be greatly reduced or discontinued, if sufficient scaling is formed;
- A decrease in temperature usually results in an increase in the viscosity of a solution. Too high a viscosity may give hydraulic problems, and the laminar flow may affect the crystallization dynamics.
- It is not applicable to compounds having *reverse* solubility. Reverse solubility indicates that solubility increases with decreasing temperature. For example, the solubility of sodium sulfate is reversed above 32.5 °C.

### Merits of Agitated Batch Crystallizer

- The crystals formed in agitated batch crystallizer are relatively more uniform and finer compared to tank crystallizer.

### Demerits of Agitated Batch Crystallizer

- Agitated batch crystallizer produces the crystals in batches, not in continuous form.
- At the surface of the cooling coil, the solubility of the solute is the minimum; hence, at this point, the crystals can grow at a faster rate.
- The crystals thus formed, may be deposited on the cooling coil surface. As a result, the rate of heat transfer may decrease.

## Swenson-Walker Crystallizer

This is one of the most commonly used continuous crystallizers. It utilizes cooling alone for crystallization. A schematic diagram of Swenson-Walker Crystallizer is shown in Fig 5.4.

### Principles

A hot concentrated solution flows in a direction opposite to the direction of flow of cold water. This causes the decrease of temperature of the solution and the solution becomes supersaturated. Due to supersaturation, the solution starts crystallizing at this state and the crystals deposit. Agitation or stirring of the solution does not allow the crystals to accumulate on the cooling surface. Hence, at regular intervals, the crystals deposited are removed from the mother liquor. Thus, the process can be used for continuous crystallization.

### Construction

It consists of an open trough of about 2 ft wide, with a semi-cylindrical bottom. A water jacket is welded to the outside of the trough. A slow-speed, long-pitch, spiral agitator is attached. The agitator is positioned at the position nearest to the bottom of the trough. The agitator rotates at about 7 – 8 rpm. To increase the capacity, the length of the equipment can bevaried from 10 ft to 40 ftby joining a number of units. Usually the length of single unit is about 10 ft and the maximum length of a single shaft that could be driven is 40 ft. Where more length with further increased capacity is required, several crystallizers are placed one above the other, instead of increasing the length of the unit. The solution (feed) is allowed to cascade from one bank to the other.

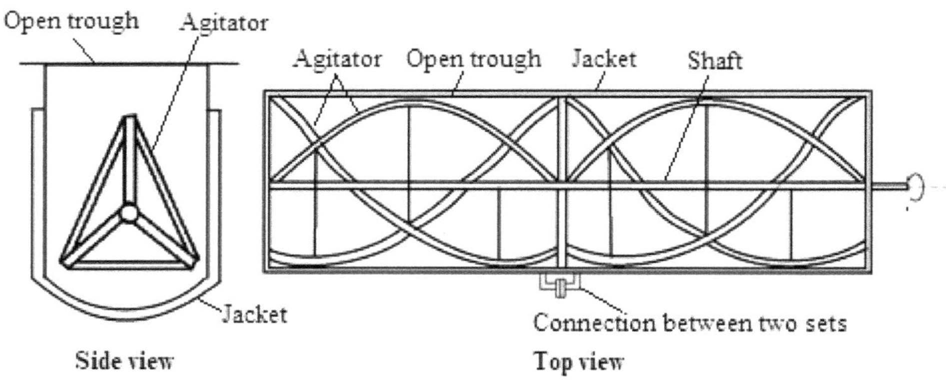


**Fig. 5.4** Schematic diagram of Swenson-Walker crystallizer

### Working

At the left side of the trough, the hot concentrated solution (feed) is introduced. The cooling water is fed at the right side of the jacket. The cooling water is circulated through the jacket in counter current to the solution. As the solution is cooled, supersaturation of the solution takes place and the crystals are formed. To control the size of the crystals, sometimes an extra amount of water is introduced into certain sections. The function of the spiral stirrer is not same as that of agitator. The spiral scrapper rotates along its own axis at a speed of about 7 revolutions per minute. The functions of the spiral stirrer are:

- Mix or stir the solution,
- Not to allow the crystals to accumulate on the cooling surface,
- To circulate the crystals that have already been formed within the bulk of the solution.

This allows the crystals to grow individually and uniformly, but at the same time does not allow to form aggregates. In this way, the excess growth of crystal is prevented; but the crystals can grow up to a desired size and they canremain suspended freely in the solution.Thus, the crystals obtained behave fairly as perfect units, almost uniform in size and free from inclusions or aggregation.

An overflow gate is provided at the end of the crystallizer where crystals and mother liquor together overflow to a drain box. The mother liquor is then sent back to the crystallizer and the wet crystals are taken to a centrifuge. In some cases, a short section of inclined-screw conveyer lifts the crystals out of the solution and transfers them to the centrifuge. At a convenient point the mother liquor overflows.

**Merits of Swenson Walker Crystallizer**

- It occupies less floor space; hence, saves the floor space.
- It is a continuous process and hence, less man power is required.
- Crystals produced are uniform in size and free from aggregates.

**Demerits of Swenson Walker Crystallizer**

- During stirring, the stirrer or agitator may break the crystals, may be to smaller extent.

## Krystal Crystallizer

Krystal crystallizer also called as Oslo crystallizer is another type of crystallizer. It is extensively used where large quantity of crystals of predetermined size is required.

### Principle

In this crystallizer, two operations– 1. concentration (super saturation) of solution and 2. crystallization occur in different chambers such as vapor head and crystallizing chamber respectively. The solution becomes concentrated to make super saturated solution by evaporation of the solvent with the help of vacuum pump attached to the vapor head. In crystallizing chamber, the super-saturated solution and the crystals are held in a fluidized state, so that uniform crystal growth takes place. Once the crystals attain desired size, they sediment by the gravitational force. The solution containing fine suspended crystals is recirculated for further crystallization. The crystals having desired size range are collected from the crystal growth chamber.

## Construction

Schematic diagram of a krystal crystallizer is shown in Fig 5.5. It consists of a vapor head and a crystallization chamber. The vapor head is a long tube, constricted towards lower end and extended almost to the bottom of the crystallization chamber. The upper end of the vapor head is connected to a vacuum pump. The other side-end of the vapor head is connected to a condenser and a circulating pump. The solution is fed into this pump which transfer the feed solution into the vapor head. During this movement, the solution passes through a heater.

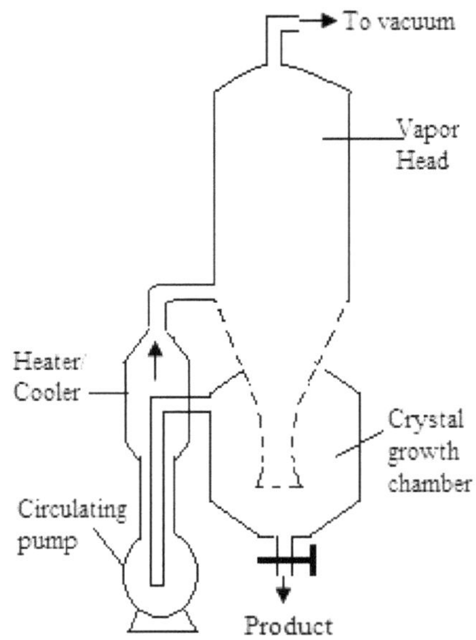


**Fig. 5.5** Schematic diagram of Krystal Crystallizer

## Working

The solution is pumped by a circulating pump and the solution enters into the vapor head through the heater. When the hot solution enters into the vapor head, it is subjected to vacuum and the vapor pressure is reduced, flashing of the hot solution occurs, the solvent vaporizes and the vapor is removed by the vacuum pump. As a result, the solution becomes supersaturated and passes through the long-tube below. The entire operation is controlled so that the crystallization does not occur in the vapor head. Crystallization occurs only in the crystallizing chamber.

In the crystallizing chamber the crystals remain suspended in the solution flowing upward. Supersaturated solution flows through the bed of crystals which remains in a fluidized state. Thus, a uniform temperature is maintained. In the chamber, a continuous grade of crystals as per the size range are present. As per the size, the larger crystals settle at the bottom and fines are above the coarse crystals. Very fine crystals, unable to settle, are carried over by the solution and enters into the circulating pump for recirculation. The solution is then mixed with fresh solution (feed). At the bottom of the crystallizing chamber there is an outlet through which the coarse crystals are collected regularly.

### Uses

This crystallizer is primarily used for crystallization of sodium chloride and magnesium sulphate.

### Merits

- Useful for preparation of crystals of desired size range.
- The crystallizer may be of very large size with a body of about 6 meter and diameter of about 4.5 meter.

## Vacuum Crystallizer

### Principle

In this crystallizer, super saturation of the solution occurs due to adiabatic cooling process. Because of high vacuum in the crystallizer, the hot saturated solution starts flashing. As a result, a portion of the solvent is evaporated, the temperature of the solution reduces, the solution becomes super saturated, and the crystallization occurs.

### Construction

Vacuum crystallizer is very simple, does not contain any moving parts. It can be made of acid resistant material such as lead or rubber-lined. A schematic diagram of vacuum crystallizer is shown in Fig 5.6. The vacuum crystallizer consists of a cylindrical body, the bottom portion of which is conical attached to a condenser, a vacuum pump, and a discharge tube. Two propellers are fixed above the discharge pipe. The propellers prevent short circuit of the feed.

### Working

For reduction of the boiling point of the solution, high vacuum is created by the vacuum pump attached to the crystallizer. However, the temperature maintained is lower than the feed temperature. The hot saturated solution is introduced into the crystallizer at any convenient point. Once the feed solution enters into it, undergoes flashing and the solvent starts evaporating. This process continues adiabatically resulting cooling of the crystallizer. Due to decrease in temperature (cooling), the solution becomes supersaturated and crystallization starts. The evaporation of solvent increases the rate of crystallization (the yield is increased). Evaporation of the solvent results a state of boiling (ebullition); as a result, the crystals produced remain suspended in the solution until they grow sufficiently. Once the crystals become large, they deposit in the discharge pipe. The propellers mix the solutions thoroughly as a result, the solution and suspended crystals cannot reach the discharge pipe without flashing. Through the discharge point the product (crystals) is collected with the help of a pump and to get the crystals only the collected product is filtered or centrifuged. The filtrate is again sent back to the crystallizer and mixed with fresh feed.

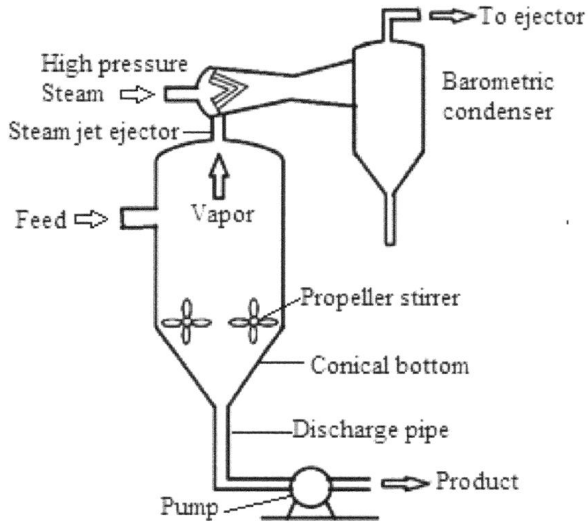


**Fig. 5.6** Schematic diagram of Vacuum crystallizer

### Application

As the crystallizer works at lower temperature, it is suitable for crystallization of thermolabile substances.

### Merits

- Construction of the crystallizer is very simple and does not contain any moving parts.
- Since the body is made of non-corrosive material, it can be used suitably for corrosive materials.
- The size and capacity of the crystallizer can be increased as per requirement.
- The operation of this crystallizer may be either batch-wise or continuous.

## Caking of Crystals

The crystals may have a tendency of binding together and forming a cake. It is a serious problem frequently occurs during handling of crystalline products. When the crystalline products are stored in bulk, or in barrels, sometimes it becomes troublesome; particularly when such a product is sold in small packages. The aggregation of crystals varies from loose to solid lump. The loose aggregates break easily and fall apart between the fingers; while solid lumps become difficult to break in form of powders by hand, a considerable force is required to break them. However, the consumers desire that the material should be free flowing and there should be no aggregate.

Generally, caking is produced by reduction of the crystal surfaces during storage. For free-flowing property the crystals should have a sufficient moisture content. The material should be stored under required atmospheric humidity. Because of inefficient drying or an increase in atmospheric humidity above some critical value aggregation or caking occurs. Caking of crystals depends on the substance and on the temperature change. If an impurity which is hygroscopic in nature is present in the crystals, the impurity can greatly influence the tendency to absorb atmospheric moisture. The moisture may be released, if the crystals fracture under the storage conditions. If later on, the moisture evaporates out from the crystal surface, the adjacent crystals form aggregates together with a cement of re-crystallized solute. Caking may be reduced or minimized effectively, if

- ➢ the crystals are dried adequately,
- ➢ packed in airtight containers, and
- ➢ stored under appropriate or recommended storage conditions.

Thus, compaction of crystals during storage can be avoided. In some cases, crystals are coated with an inert material that acts as a moisture barrier. Small crystals are more prone to form cake than large crystals, because of the greater number of contact points per unit mass.

## Factors Affecting Caking

From the discussion made above, the principal factors which influence the caking of soluble crystalline substances are:

1. Variation in moisture content
2. Impurity content and its nature
3. Particle size and shape
4. Humidity and temperature
5. Storage conditions

1. **Variation in humidity:** Caking of most of the crystalline substances such as common salt is influenced greatly by their moisture content. Crystals may be wet due to adhesion of mother liquor at the time of collection of crystals or due to subsequent absorption of moisture from the atmosphere. Thus, caking of crystals depends on the following parameters
   - ➢ Crystal size,
   - ➢ Shape of the crystals,
   - ➢ Size, shape and porosity of heap,
   - ➢ Relative humidity as well as temperature fluctuations, and
   - ➢ Period of drainage

   It is not the wetness of the crystals (salt), but subsequent drying out of moisture, that causes caking. The surface film of brine on individual adjacent particle is drawn to the loci of contact which can be anyone of the two points present at the edges or surfaces. Under favorable conditions, this film gets dried up and results in microcrystalline growth. Due to this growth of micro crystals in the bulk salt, particles of all sizes and shapes are cemented together and very hard mass is formed which is known as *cake* and the process by which cakes are formed is known as *caking*. For example, the common salt stored outdoor is exposed to severe conditions of humidity and temperature fluctuation; therefore, it forms cake. While refined salt stored indoor and packed with proper care does not form cake. However, aggregation cannot be avoided completely.

2. **Impurities:** This can be better explained by taking the example of sodium chloride. There are various sources and methods of preparing the salt. Solar salt is obtained from sea water, well brines, or lake brines. These salts contain 2 – 4% impurities. Such impurity contains mostly the salts of calcium and magnesium in form of chloride and sulphate; apart from certain amount of insoluble substances. Among sodium, calcium and magnesium salts, magnesium salt is the most hygroscopic. The pure and impure salts behave differently.
3. **Size of the crystals:** The size of the crystals should be large enough and contain much of voids. The smaller crystals have less voids but more points of contact. The rate of caking depends on the number of points of contact. Thus, smaller particles have more tendency to form cake than the larger crystals.
4. **Shape of the crystals:** Number of points of contact depends on the shape of the crystals. The spherical crystals contain a smaller number of points of contact; hence,the chance of bonding between the crystals is less. This does not happen if the crystals are broken. Thus, the broken crystals have more tendency to form cake.
5. **Duration of storage:** If the crystals are stored for longer period, the crystals may form cake.
6. **Melting point of crystals:** When the melting point of the crystal is less than or near to the room temperature, the crystals are likely to fuse. The solidified mass forms cake.
7. **Fluctuation of temperature:** If the storage temperature is high, the crystals start melting. Decrease in temperature causes solidification of the melt. Thus, too much of variation in temperature causes caking of crystals.

## Critical Humidity

The vapor pressure of water depends on the temperature. In fact, at a particular temperature the vapor pressure of any solution is normally little less than the vapor pressure of pure water. If a saturated solution or any crystal of a soluble salt is brought into contact with air, following observations can be made:

- If the partial pressure of water is less than the vapor pressure of the solution, the solution will evaporate out.
- If moisture content of air is more, the partial pressure of water would be more than the vapor pressure of the solution, the solution will not evaporate. The solution will absorb water until it is so dilute that its vapor pressure becomes equal to the partial pressure of water in the air with which the solution is in contact.
- If a crystal of a soluble salt is placed in air which contains less water than would be in equilibrium with the saturated solution, the crystal shall remain dry. Because the air will absorb moisture (water) from the crystal and thus, the crystal is covered by a layer of saturated solution, the air would have absorbed water from the solution resulting its evaporation.
- If a crystal of a soluble salt is placed in air which contains more water than would be in equilibrium with the saturated solution, the crystal becomes damp.In due course of time, the salt will completely dissolve and absorption of water from the air will continue until the vapor pressure of the solution becomes equal to the partial pressure of water present in air at the same temperature.

Within the ambient temperature range, the vapor of a given solution can vary with the temperature in such a way that almost constant percentage of vapor pressure of water would be observed till the temperature remains within the limit. For example, at about 21°C, the vapor pressure of a saturated solution of sodium chloride is 14.63 mm., and that of water is 18.76 mm. If a crystal of the salt is covered with a film of its saturated solution, the crystal cannot dry unless the partial pressure of water vapor in the prevailing air or in other words, unless the partial pressure of water vapor in the air is less than 14.63 mm; that is, $14.63\text{mm}/18.63\text{mm} \times 100 = 78\%$ of relative humidity. Thus, at about 21°C, the salt cannot be dried when the relative humidity remains at 78%. Because the partial pressure of water in the air is more than the vapor pressure of the saturated solution; hence, the moisture would be condensed over the salt.If the salt is exposed to air having relative humidity of about 78% for long period, the salt starts dissolving. This is generally observed, if the temperature does not change greatly. Thus, if pure sodium chloride is kept in air having relative humidity less than 78% even at 21°C, the air starts absorbing water from the salt and the salt becomes dry.

The above discussion brings about the concept of *critical humidity* of a solid salt. The critical humidity of a salt is the humidity above which the salt will become damp and below which it will remain in dry state. When a crystal is surrounded by its impurities derived from the mother liquor from which the salt has been obtained, the critical humidity of the salt would vary depending on the nature of the impurities present. The vapor pressure of solutions of the impurities may have either greater or less than that of the pure salt, accordingly the critical humidity of the impure salt will vary. For example, sodium chloride carries the chlorides of calcium and magnesium as impurities. The solutions of these salts have much lower vapor pressures than pure sodium chloride. Hence, the critical humidity of impure sodium chloride would be less than 78%. Actually, the critical humidity of commercial grade of sodium chloride is less than 78%.

## Prevention of Caking

Caking of crystals can take place when the crystals are fine with small number of voids (inter-particular space), have point of contact, stored in humid atmosphere for long time so that sufficient moisture is absorbed and the voids are filled entirely with saturated solution. When this water is evaporated, the crystals bind together, locked and form a solid mass. Briefly speaking, caking of crystals occurs due to bonding of crystals. Under the following circumstances crystals do not form cake:

- The crystals should be uniform in size with maximum number of voids so that they cannot attach together and bind.
- The shape of the crystals should be spherical and larger in size, but the size distribution should be narrow.
- The crystals should have minimum points of contact within these so that binding would not take place.
- The crystals should not be exposed to moist atmosphere for long time.
- Melting point of the crystal should be high enough.
- Storage temperature should not fluctuate too much.
- The crystals should be coated with inert powder which does not attract moisture.

## Short Questions

1. Define the term crystallization. Classify the equipments used for crystallization on the basis of method used.
2. Why crystallization is important in pharmacy? Write down its applications in pharmacy.
3. What are short-comings of Mier's theory?
4. Write down the principle of agitated batch crystallizer.
5. What are the applications, advantages and limitations of agitated batch crystallizer.
6. How does the krystal crystallizer function?
7. What is caking of crystals and how can it be prevented?

## Long Questions

1. Explain the theory of crystallization with respect to Mier.
2. Explain how solubility curve and crystallization are correlated.
3. Discuss with the help of a diagram the construction and working of agitated batch crystallizer.
4. Explain principle, construction and working of swenson-walker crystallizer with the help of a diagram.
5. Draw a neat diagram and label it properly. Write down the principle and construction of krystal crystallizer.
6. Draw a diagram of a vacuum crystallizer and label it properly. Explain the principle and construction of vacuum crystallizer.
7. How does a vacuum crystallizer works? What is meant by the term caking of crystal?
8. Discuss the factors that influence the caking of crystals.

# CHAPTER 6

# Evaporation

Objectives, Applications and Factors Influencing Evaporation, Differences between Evaporation and Other Heat Process. Principles, Construction, Working, Uses, Merits and Demerits of Steam Jacketed Kettle, Horizontal Tube Evaporator, Climbing Film Evaporator, Forced Circulation Evaporator, Multiple Effect Evaporator & Economy of Multiple Effect Evaporator.

## Objectives

Theoretically, evaporation refers to vaporization of liquid from its surface in which boiling of liquid is not essential. Evaporation takes place even at room temperature. The rate of vaporization depends on the diffusion of vapor through the boundary layers above the liquid surface. The partial vapor pressure works as the driving force.

Practically, the rate of vaporization (evaporation) is slow. The liquid is transformed into gaseous phase (vapor) from the liquid surface. Hence, the area of the liquid surface is important. The process of evaporation can be defined *as the removal of liquid from a solution contained in a container without boiling the solution, with drawing the vapor and leaving the concentrated liquid residue.*

Therefore, heat is required to provide the latent heat of vaporization and in general, the rate of evaporation depends on the rate of heat transfer and area of the liquid surface exposed to air. The evaporators are designed in such a way that maximum heat would be transferred for evaporation of the liquid. In pharmaceutical industries the process of evaporation is extensively used to prepare concentrated product. For example, the extracts of plants are evaporated to prepare the concentrated extract in the form of semisolid or solid extract.

## Applications

- Evaporation process is used in pharmaceutical and chemical industries for manufacture of bulk drugs.
- For the manufacture of biological products such as insulin, biochemical products such as penicillin and plant products, evaporation process is used. Evaporation is involved in the preparation of blood plasma, serum, enzymes, hormones, and antibiotic products.

## Factors Influencing Evaporation

There are various factors which influence the rate of evaporation:

1. Temperature
2. Heat sensitivity of the drug
3. Duration of evaporation
4. Moisture content in the circulating air
5. Type of product required
6. Concentration of the material being evaporated
7. Type of evaporator

1. **Effect of Temperature:** It has been mentioned earlier that the rate of evaporation depends on the temperature to which the liquid is subjected to evaporation. Usually, evaporation is carried out at the temperature of about 90° – 95°C; but many of the glycosides and alkaloids decompose even at a temperature below 100°C. Therefore, the temperature for evaporation depends on the thermal stability of the material in solution or type of volatility of the solvent.
2. **Heat sensitivity of the drug:** Hormones, enzymes, and some antibiotics are not heated even at 45° to 50°C or less. Because they cannot tolerate even this temperature. Due to their extreme heat sensitivity, the solution of these substances is dried under vacuum without any heat. Similarly, malt extract is evaporated under reduced pressure (freeze-drying)so that it does not lose any enzyme. On the other hand, most of the aqueous extracts of crude drugs (plant extracts) are concentrated by evaporating them at about 100°C. Hence, the temperature at which evaporation is to be conducted depends principally on the thermal sensitivity of the dissolved substances.
3. **Duration of evaporation:** There are various ways by which a drug can degrade such as hydrolysis, oxidation, etc. Thus, not even the duration of exposure to heat, also the solvent used has an effect both on the rate of evaporation as well as on the stability of the substance present in the solution. For example, some drug substances are very much susceptible to moisture than heat. The solutions of these substances can be evaporated at a moderate temperature for short duration. However, the final drying of the aqueous extract is conducted at a relatively higher temperature and for a higher duration.
4. **Moisture content in the circulating air:** When a drug is more sensitive to moisture than heat, it is better to avoid water during the preparation, purification, extraction of the drug. In general, the vapors produced during evaporation is absorbed by the circulating air. If the air does not contain much moisture, it can readily absorb the vapors and a concentration gradient would develop and the rate of evaporation will not be affected. But, if the air itself is saturated with moisture, it becomes difficult for the absorption of vapor produced during evaporation; hence, the rate of evaporation would be affected.
5. **Type of product required:** Sometimes, the type of product decides the type of method and type of equipment which would be required for evaporation. For example, evaporating pans are used to prepare liquid or dry products; whereas film evaporators are used for preparing liquid products.

6. **Concentration of the material being evaporated:** When the concentration of solid is increased, the boiling point of the solution also increases (elevation of the boiling point). Due to an increase in concentration, the boundary layer becomes thick and at the boundary, solids may deposit. At this point, the heat transfer process will be reduced. Moreover, thermolabile materials will be degraded quickly. Thus, the concentration of solid in a solution is an important factor to be considered.
7. **Type of evaporator:** Evaporation takes place from the surface of a liquid; that is, the liquid surface area exposed to air. This depends on the area of the mouth of evaporator used. Thus, wide mouth evaporator would be more efficient than a narrow mouth. Pan type evaporator has a wide mouth; hence, evaporation of a liquid placed in a pan would be more.

## Differences between Evaporation and Other Heat Transfer Processes

| Evaporation | Other heat transfer process |
|---|---|
| The residue obtained is a concentrated liquid. | The residue obtained is solid. The process used is called drying. |
| In most of the cases, evaporation refers to removal of a single liquid component at a time. | In this type of process, a mixture of components may be removed. The process used is called distillation. |
| The vapor mixture phase produced in evaporation cannot ordinarily be separated into its components. | It is compulsory to separate the components or it is possible to separate the components of a mixture. This is done by using a process called fractional distillation. |
| To concentrate a solution, that is, to remove water, evaporation is done. | A solution is concentrated to such as extent that crystals are obtained. The process used is usually called crystallization. |
| In evaporation the solvent molecules in liquid state is removed from the surface layer. | In other processes such distillation and drying, the liquid molecules are removed from surface as well as from the bulk. |

## Evaporators

The movement of heat is important for transformation of a liquid to its gaseous state and how the heat is moving is very important for efficient heat transfer. Hence, the efficiency of an evaporator depends on how the heat is being transferred. Accordingly, the evaporators can be classified mainly into three groups:

1. *Natural circulation evaporators:* In this category of the evaporator liquid moves due to the transfer of heat by convection method; for example, steam jacketed pan/kettle.
2. *Forced circulation evaporators:* The natural circulation evaporators with mechanical agitators can be called as forced circulation evaporators; for example, forced circulation evaporator.
3. *Film Evaporators:* In this type of evaporator, the vapor produced in evaporation process leaves the evaporator in the form of bubble and the concentrated solution is spread over the surface of hot tubes in the form of film; for example, climbing film evaporator.

Although there are different sources of heat, steam is most commonly used to heat the solution. Hence, the evaporators contain steam jacketed vessels.

1. **Natural Circulations Evaporators:** In this category of the evaporator liquid moves due to the transfer of heat by convection method and the evaporators usually used are steam jacketed pan/kettle,

## Steam Jacketed Kettle/Evaporating Pan

### Principle and Construction

The evaporating pan is the simplest form of natural circulating evaporator. It is a metallic, circular and shallow pan looks like a hemisphere. It is surrounded by a metal jacket. The pan may be made of copper or stainless steel and the jacket is made of stainless steel. The hemisphere gives the optimum surface/volume ratio for appropriate heating. It also provides the maximum surface area for evaporation. The pan may have a mounting system so that it can be tilted for easy removal of the product or an outlet may be provided at the bottom of the pan as shown in Fig 6.1, to remove the product. The jacket is attached to two valves – one for the supply of steam and other for removal of air from the jacket; so that pure steam can be made available for heating and proportionate temperature can be maintained by maintaining the steam pressure. One more outlet is also provided at the bottom of the jacket for removal of steam condensate.

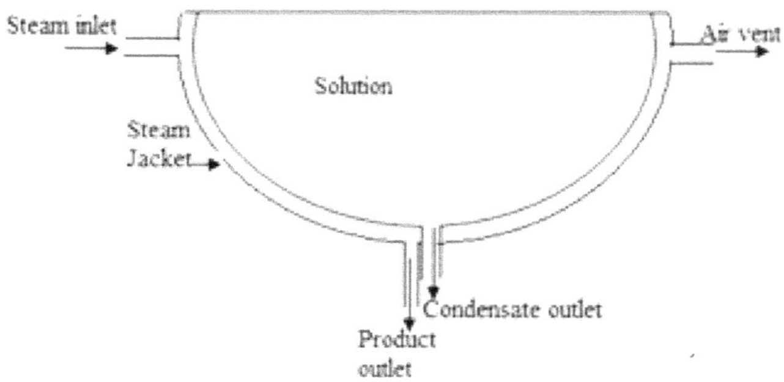


**Fig. 6.1** Evaporating pan

### Working

The aqueous solution or an extract is evaporated by placing the material in the kettle or pan. Steam is introduced through the inlet attached to the steam jacket at the upper side. Steam releases the heat which is subsequently transferred to the content (feed material) and steam condensate is removed through the steam condensate outlet placed at the bottom. The material inside the pan/kettle is agitated frequently by hand operated agitator, when the material is concentrated and of less volume. When the volume of the material is more and the material is thin, agitation can be done mechanically at lower speed by using a stirrer.

Initially, the rate of evaporation is more and gradually decreases as the liquid becomes concentrated. The amount of liquid in the material is less. The process of evaporation is carried out in a well-ventilated room or area, so that the vapor produced can be removed easily from the room. The fan hanging over the evaporating pan should be run to remove the vapor generated out of evaporation. This will increase the rate of evaporation. The exhaust fan attached to the room should also run during the process of evaporation.

The kettle or pan may be either fixed or tilting. With the tilting pan or kettle, it is easy to remove the product; but due to the heavy weight or any other reason, if it is fixed, an outlet is provided at the bottom of the pan or kettle for removal of product. The capacity of evaporating pan varies from 500ml to 100 lt.

### Advantages of Evaporating Pan

1. Simple to construct,
2. Economic,
3. Easy to use,
4. Easy to clean and maintain.

### Disadvantages

1. The overall coefficient of heat transfer is poor, because it provides only natural circulation. The solids can deposit on the surface. For this, the product may degrade.
2. Not convenient for the material produces foam on heating under natural convection.
3. May not be suitable for thermolabile material, because all the material is heated during the process.
4. With the increase in pan size, the heating surface decreases; heating efficiency is reduced.
5. With increasing concentration (during evaporation), the heat transfer reduces.
6. It is useful for aqueous preparations containing thermostable active constituents.
7. Not suitable for organic solvents.
8. Saturation of the local atmosphere may cause discomfort, since the pan is open.
9. Cannot work under reduced pressure, because it is open; hence, boiling temperature cannot be reduced.

Thus, evaporating kettle/pan is suitable for concentrating aqueous solutions which contains dissolved solids and they are stable at about 100°C.The rate of heat transfer varies from 50 – 300 Btu per sq. ft. per °F per hour.

## Horizontal Tube Evaporator

In 1843 Norbert Rillieux designed this type of evaporator. The design could not run for long time and it was replaced by vertical-tubes. In 1879, Wellner-Jelinek modified the horizontal-tube evaporator and it reappeared in the market after modification. This was widely accepted and has been recognized as the most modern horizontal-tube evaporator. The schematic diagram of the horizontal-tube evaporator is shown in Fig 6.2.

### Principles

Horizontal tube evaporator consists of horizontal tubes to pass the steam. The tubes are immersed within the liquid (feed). The tubes are horizontally placed for which it is called horizontal tube evaporator. It is shown in the Fig 6.2 that the tubes are attached to the evaporator body horizontally. When steam is passed through these tubes, heat is transported from the steam to the content of the evaporator. As a result, the temperature of the steam reduces and that of the content increases. The condensate passes through the outlet and the content becomes hot. The solvent starts evaporating. The vapor produced during evaporation leaves the evaporator through the outlet fixed at the top of the evaporator. This process continues till a thick liquid (desired consistency) is produced. The product is collected from the outlet attached to the bottom of the evaporator.

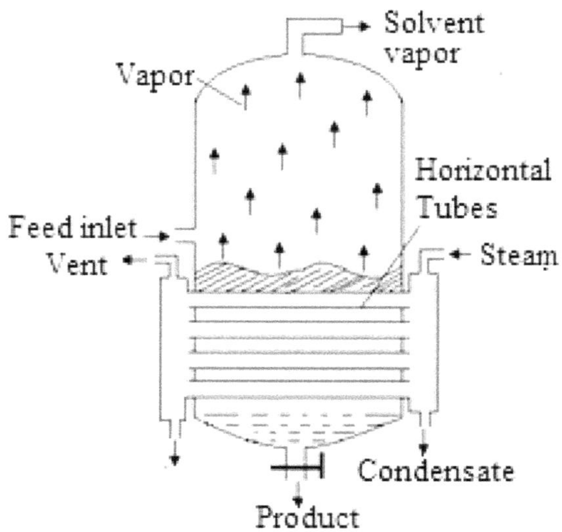


**Fig. 6.2** Schematic diagram of horizontal tube evaporator

## Construction

The body of this evaporator is cylindrical and is divided into two halves. A number of horizontal tubes are attached to the lower half. Within the body, the liquor or solution is placed. It can be closed at top and bottom with dished heads. However, the bottom may be conical. The steam compartments are attached to the lower parts of the body on opposite sides. The steam compartment can be closed by cover plates on the outside and on the inside, it is closed by tube sheets. In fact, the tubes are fixed with these tube sheets. Steam is introduced into a steam chest, attached to one side and flows through the tubes. During this flow, it removes or replaces non-condensed gases and condensate, which are then removed through the opposite steam chest. The liquid or solution is fed through the nozzle. The outlet at the bottom of the cylinder is provided to collect the concentrate (product). The evaporator stands on a suitable bracket. The sight glasses are provided to most of the evaporators. The vapor from boiling liquid escapes through the outlet at the top. The tubes are securely packed by a packing plate. The height of horizontal tube evaporator may vary from 8 – 12 ft and 6 – 8 ft in diameter; the outer diameter of the tubes may vary from 0.875 to 1.25 inch. The evaporators may be made of stainless steel; but usually are made of cast iron, because cast iron has a greater resistance and moderate corrosion. Space where the tubes are usually placed is shallower than their width. The ratio of width to the diameter of the evaporator should not be more than $\frac{1}{2}$. The level of the solution should be slightly above the tubes.

**Working**

The feed material is introduced through the feed-inlet valve till all the tubes are immersed completely. A sufficient amount of feed should remain above the tubes, (below the inlet valve as shown in the Fig. 6.2) so that heat can be transferred satisfactorily.

Steam is introduced into the tubes through steam inlet. Thus, the tubes become hot and heat is transferred from the tubes to the feed. Now, the feed becomes hot, evaporation of the solvent begins. When the steam becomes cold and condense, the steam condensate is removed through the steam-condensate valve, which is kept slightly open to drain out the condensate. The supply of steam is maintained at a required rate (pressure). The vapor produced during evaporation leaves the evaporator through an outlet placed at the top. The process of evaporation is continued until the content (liquid) acquires the required consistency. When the consistency of the feed reaches the desired level, the product is removed through the outlet attached to the bottom.

### Uses

This type of evaporator is of choice for the material which does not deposit scales or crystals after concentration. In fact, it is suitable for concentrating plant extract.

### Merits of Horizontal Tube Evaporator

1. Horizontal tube evaporator is suitable for aqueous as well as non-aqueous solutions,
2. It is cheaper than other evaporators.

### Demerits of Horizontal Tube Evaporator

1. Not suitable for viscous solutions,
2. Not suitable for making highly thick concentrate which cannot be removed through the outlet,
3. Cleaning of the evaporator is not very easy.

## Film Evaporators

This type of evaporators is operated by boiling the solution in a vessel. The vapor produced by evaporation process leaves the evaporator in the form of bubble and the concentrated solution is spread over the surface of hot tubes in the form of film.

## Climbing Film Evaporator

In this type of evaporator, steam-jacketed tubes are attached as a heating unit. For this reason, these evaporators are also called as *Long-tube evaporator*.

## Principles

When the solution to be evaporated is introduced into the bottom of the tube, the film of concentrated solution is formed over the inner surface of the upper part of the tube. The liquid during boiling go up along the tube and adheres to the surface in the form of film, on drying. In fact, the mixture of vapor and boiling liquid concentrate while going up, enters into a separator. The vapor leaves the separator and enters into the condenser, and the concentrated liquid remains in the separator; subsequently it comes down and exits through the outlet provided at the bottom of the separator. How the liquid (solution) climbs up within the tube while boiling without any mechanical assistance, is represented through a schematic diagram of climbing film evaporator shown in Fig 6.3.

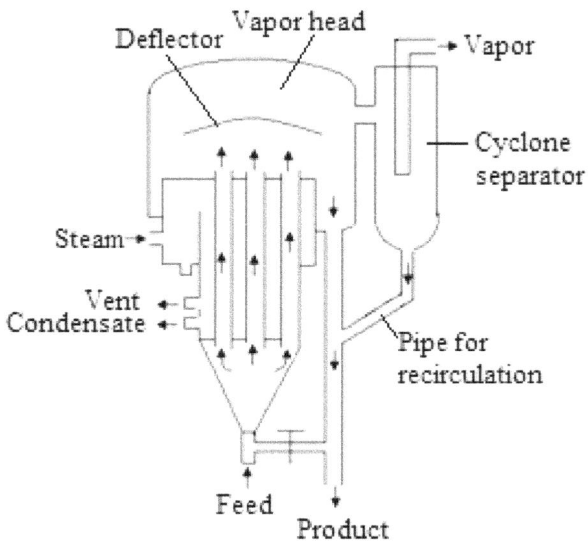


**Fig. 6.3** Schematic diagram of climbing film evaporator

## Construction

This type of evaporator consists of long, steam-jacketed tubes which have the length to diameter ratio of about 140, to provide a long surface area. Thus, if the evaporator contains 7 m long tube, the diameter of the tube would be around 50 mm.

## Working

The cold or pre-heated solution is introduced into the tube. Steam is passed and heat is transferred from the walls of the tubes to the solution and the solution starts boiling. Vapor forms smaller bubbles which join and form bigger according to the width of the tube. The bubble carries liquid above it and goes up along the tube. With the formation of more of vapors, the tubes become filled with vapor and liquid carried over by the bubbles, spreads as a film on the walls of the tubes. The film formed also continues to dry up rapidly. When the vapor goes up along the tube, friction occurs between the vapor and the liquid takes place. Due to this friction, the liquid film is dragged up the tube almost at a rate of 6.5metres/second.

This is why the solution travels up and reduced pressure does not affect the process of evaporation.

### Uses

1. The method requires less time for drying a liquid
2. Applicable for aqueous as well as for an organic solvent
3. Applicable for thermolabile as well as for thermostable material
4. The method works both in reduced and normal atmospheric pressure

### Merits of Climbing Film Evaporator

1. Heat transfer is efficient due to the minimum boundary layer which occurs as a result of very high film velocity.
2. Large area for heat transfer is available due to an increase in length and decrease in the diameter of the tubes.
3. Can work efficiently even with a small difference in temperature; this is due to efficient heat transfer.
4. Risk of deterioration of thermolabile drug even is less; hence the solution of thermolabile material can be dried.
5. Contact time between liquid and heating surface is less, maybe around 20 secs.
6. Rate of evaporation is very high, due to the large heating surface area provided to the unit volume of liquid.
7. The efficiency of separation of liquid concentrate and vapor is high, since the mixture of vapor and liquid enters into the separator at a very high velocity just like a cyclone.
8. The boiling point of the liquid does not increase due to hydrostatic effect; because the long tubes are not submerged, as is found in evaporators with short tubes.
9. Suitable for the materials that form a foam on heating.

### Demerits of Climbing Film Evaporator

1. The equipment is not economical,
2. Difficult to clean and maintain,
3. Rate of feeding has an influence on the effectiveness of drying.

## Forced Circulation Evaporator

In fact, the natural circulation evaporators with mechanical agitators can be called as forced circulation evaporators. For example, if an evaporating pan is attached to a stirring rod, it can be considered as forced circulation evaporator. In other words, when a mechanically operated propeller or paddle type is attached to an evaporator, it is called as forced circulation evaporator. A special form of forced circulation evaporator is shown in Fig 6.4.

## Principles

In this evaporator, the liquid to be evaporated is circulated at high pressure through the tubes placed vertically with the help of a pump. Steam passed through the inlet, circulates around the tubes and leaves the evaporator as condensate through the outlet. The heat is transferred from the steam to the liquid and the liquid becomes hot. The liquid does not boil due to elevation of its boiling point. When the liquid comes out of the tubes, enters into the vapor head. The vapor pressure falls due to sudden expansion of the liquid. As a result, flashing of super-heated liquid occurs. Hence, evaporation takes place and the vapor produced leaves through the vapor outlet. The tubes are slightly extended towards the vapor head, deflected by the deflector present over the tubes. The vapor head contains a return pipe through which the liquid return back to the bottom and again moves upward through the tubes at a force created by the pump.

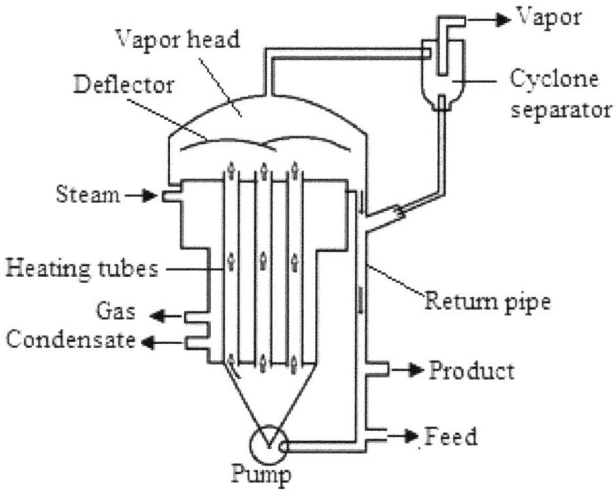


**Fig. 6.4** Schematic diagram of forced circulation evaporator

## Construction

The tubes are held between two metal sheets and the space between two tube acts as steam jacket. The length of each tube may be up to 2.5 metres and the internal diameter of the tube may be of about 0.1 metres. The tubes are partially projected into the vapor head. The vapor head contains deflectors which do not allow the liquid to go up further. The vapor head is connected to a return pipe which extends up to the bottom of the evaporator and enters into the inlet of a pump. A cyclone separator is connected to both vapor head and to the return pipe as shown in the Fig 6.4. The vapor moves from the vapor head to the cyclone separator from where it goes out.

## Working

Steam enters into the evaporator through the inlet valve and transfers the heat to the tubes. Then the heat is further transferred to the liquid passing through the tubes under pressure. Thus, the liquid gets heated and is about to boil. The mixture of vapor and liquid moves out of the tubes at a high velocity. This mixture hits the deflector, which throws the liquid downward. As a result, an effective separation of liquid and vapor takes place. The vapor moves towards the cyclone separator leaving the apparatus. The concentrated liquid returns to the pump for further evaporation. At last, the product is collected through the outlet valve attached to the bottom of the evaporator.

### Uses

- Forced circulation evaporator is suitable for thermolabile substances too, if the evaporation is conducted under reduced pressure.
- This method is useful for concentrating insulin and liver extracts.
- For preparation of crystals that can remain suspended in the liquid, this method is suitable.

### Merits of Forced Circulation Evaporator

- The evaporator provides increased heat transfer due to the rapid movement of the liquid.
- It is also suitable for a viscous solution.
- It is suitable for solutions that deposit solids or foam readily.
- The evaporator is suitable for evaporation under reduced pressure.
- It is suitable for processing of thermolabile materials, such as insulin, liver extracts, etc.

### Demerits of Forced Circulation Evaporator

- The liquid is held-up for long period.
- Power consumption is high.
- The equipment is expensive.

## Multiple Effect Evaporator

The single effect evaporators use steam as a source of heat and the steam provides the latent heat of vaporization. The vapor goes to the condenser where the latent heat is transferred to the cooling water. The simplest form of multiple effect evaporator contains two to three evaporators. The evaporators are connected together with piping.

### Principles

The vertical tube evaporators are interconnected in such a way that the steam is the heating medium for the first evaporator, while vapor from the first evaporator works as the heating medium for the next one. Let us assume that at the atmospheric pressure the system is cold and each unit is filled with the liquid to be evaporated to a predetermined level. The vacuum pump is switched on and the valves $C_1$, $C_2$, and $C_3$ (as shown in Fig 6.5) are opened. All other valves remain closed. Further, assume that the highest vacuum to be maintained is 66-cm referred to a 76-cm barometer. The vacuum pump is operated to produce this vacuum. Through the non-condensed gas lines and through the steam lines, the whole equipment is evacuated down to 26-in; if now the steam valve and the condensate valve $C_1$ are kept open until the desired pressure $P_o$ is build up in the steam space of the first evaporator. Let $t_o$is the temperature of the saturated steam at pressure $P_o$. The steam will first displace the residual air, if present, in the steam space of the first evaporator through the vent valve $C_1$. When all the air is displaced, $C_1$ will be almost closed. Since the liquid surrounding the tubes is closed, steam will condense. The trap removes the condensate immediately after collection. Thus, the liquid gains heat and becomes hotter until it boils under a vacuum of 66-cm; that is at about 52°C.in a similar way, the vapor comes from the first evaporator to the liquid present in the second evaporator; during this movement, some amount of steam/vapor condenses. The condensate leaves the second evaporator through the condensate valve $C_2$. The above process continues and the liquid in the second evaporator starts boiling at about 52°C. Accordingly, the liquid in the third evaporator boils at about 52°C.The heating surface in the first evaporator transmits the heat $q_1$ per hour can be given by

$$q_1 = A_1U_1\Delta t_1$$

If the heat consumed for boiling the liquid in the first evaporator is negligible, all the heat was used as latent heat of vaporization, and if the temperature of the vapor obtained due to boiling of liquid $t_1$is very close to the temperature of condensate, then all the heat is consumed for creating vapor in the first evaporator must be released during condensation of the same vapor in the second evaporator. Thus, the heat transferred $q_2$ to the second evaporator can be expressed as;

$$q_2 = A_2U_2\Delta t_2$$

Similarly, for third evaporator heat transmitted $q_3$ can be expressed as

$$q_3 = A_3U_3\Delta t_3$$

where A stands for the heating area of the evaporator.

U stands for over-all heat transfer coefficient, and

$\Delta t$ indicates the difference in temperature of vapor and the condensate.

Since, $q_1$, $q_2$, and $q_3$ are almost equal, and the heating surface in all the three evaporators are equal,

$$A_1U_1\Delta t_1 = A_2U_2\Delta t_2 = A_3U_3\Delta t_3$$

Or, $$U_1\Delta t_1 = U_2\Delta t_2 = U_3\Delta t_3$$

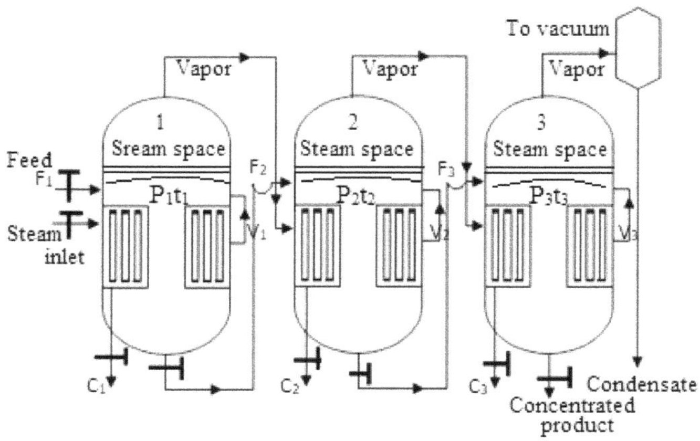


Fig. 6.5 Schematic diagram of multiple effect evaporator

Theoretically, a multiple effect evaporator may contain any number of evaporators; but in practice not more than three evaporators are connected due to the following reasons:

1. The evaporators operate at a lower temperature to provide the temperature gradient necessary for heat transfer in each evaporator. Say, the first evaporator works at atmospheric pressure, so that water boils at 100°C. If the steam of 120°C is used to heat the evaporator, the temperature gradient would be 20°C (120°C – 100°C). Since the vapor of the first evaporator is used to heat the second evaporator, water cannot boil unless the pressure is reduced. Hence, the evaporators must be operated under reduced pressure to maintain the desired temperature gradient. For example, the pressure is reduced to 0.5 bar, at this pressure water will boil at 80°C providing the temperature gradient of 20°C (100°C – 80°C); hence, there should be a limited number of evaporators to maintain the same temperature gradient.
2. If the number of evaporators is increased, the cost of the total process will also increase.

## Construction

The Fig 6.5 shows the construction of a triple effect evaporator. The vapor from evaporator-1 when enters into evaporator II, it works as the heating medium. Similarly, the vapor from evaporator-2 enters into the evaporator-3 as the heating medium. A vacuum pump is attached to the evaporator-3.

The multiple effect evaporator is fed with the material parallelly to each of the evaporators. A hot saturated solution, usually salt solution is fed directly to all the evaporators simultaneously. No material (feed) is transferred from one evaporator to another. The level of feed liquid remains just above the upper tube-sheets. The solute crystallizes when the solution become concentrated; however, the viscosity of the solution does not increase.

## Working

The vent valves $C_1$, $C_2$, and $C_3$ are opened and all other valves are closed. A high vacuum is created in the chambers of evaporators. The steam valve of evaporator-1, $S_1$ and the condensate valve, $C_1$ are opened. The steam when enters into the evaporator-1, it first completely replaces the air from steam-space and pipelines. This can be understood by observing the color of the vapors leaving from $C_1$. Saturated steam look like whitish. Heat is transferred from steam to feed and the feed gets heated. The heat is transferred to the feed, its temperature increases and subsequently starts boiling under vacuum. During this process, some amount of steam condenses and the steam condensate leaves through $C_1$. With boiling of the feed, water vapor (steam), in case of aqueous solution (feed), is produced.

The vapor or steam, so produced, enters into the evaporator-2, replaces the air from the steam space and pipe lines. The vent valve$C_3$ is opened. When air is completely removed, the vent valve is closed. The temperature of the feed in evaporator 2 is increased to its boiling temperature under vacuum and the feed solution starts boiling. The vapor produced due to evaporation of the liquid starts accumulating and moves towards the third evaporator. The feed becomes concentrated.

The vapor (steam) acts in the evaporator 3 a similar way as in evaporator 2.The feed liquid starts boiling and becomes concentrated. The vapor or steam

Thus, steam is required for first evaporator and thereafter very less or no stem would be required to make the feed concentrated.

### Uses

The multiple effect evaporator is usually useful for concentration of salt solution. The overall steam requirement is less compared to single effect evaporator. This type of evaporator is generally used for:

- Product concentration
- Reduction of volume of solvent of a solution
- Recovery of solvent/water
- Crystallization

### Advantages

Since the evaporation is conducted under reduced pressure, there are certain advantages.

- Evaporation takes place at a lower temperature,
- Low risk of degradation of heat-sensitive materials,
- Extra steam pressure/supply is not required since the operating temperature is low,
- Lower temperature requires low steam pressure. thus, the total amount of steam required for the process is low.

### Disadvantages

Since the operation is conducted at lower (under reduced pressure) it shows a definite disadvantage.

- With the reduction of pressure, the viscosity of water increases considerably affecting flowability of an aqueous solution. Thus, the pressure should be carefully reduced.

## Economy of Multiple Effect Evaporator

The economy of an evaporator refers to the amount of vapor produced per unit steam supplied. It can be calculated on the basis of following assumption:

When the feed material (liquid) is supplied at its boiling temperature, it does not require any heat to increase its temperature. Thus, the steam is condensed and the heat of condensation of steam is transferred completely to the liquid. The heat gained by the liquid is used as heat of vaporization and the liquid starts vaporizing. During this process let us assume that negligible heat is lost. Then the economy of the evaporator may be calculated as:

$$\text{Economy of an evaporator} = \frac{\text{Total amount of vapor produced}}{\text{Total amount of stream supplied}}$$

If in a single effect evaporator, let us assume that steam is supplied only once, then

$$\text{Economy of a single effect evaporator} = \frac{\text{n units of vapor produced}}{\text{n units of stream supplied}} = 1$$

In a multiple effect evaporator, one unit of steam produces *n* units of vapor; where *n* is the number of evaporators connected. Then,

$$\text{Economy of a multiple effect evaporator} = \frac{\text{n units of vapor produced}}{\text{1 unit of stream supplied}} = \text{n}$$

Hence, the economy of a multiple effect evaporator is 'n' times of that of a single effect evaporator. However, this economy 'n' depends on:

- Temperature of the feed material,
- Range of temperature prevailing in the evaporator,
- Ratio of feed weight to the product weight,
- Pressure difference, and
- Number of units (single effect evaporator) connected.

## Short Questions

1. What is the objective of evaporation? What are the applications of evaporation?
2. Differentiate evaporation process from other heat transfer processes.
3. What are advantages and limitations of a steam jacketed kettle?
4. How does a horizontal tube evaporator work. Draw a diagram of such evaporator and label it.
5. What are film evaporator and climbing film evaporator? Write down its applications, advantages and disadvantages.
6. How does a forced circulation evaporator work? What are its applications, advantages and limitations?
7. Write down the construction and working of a multiple effect evaporator.
8. What are the applications, advantages and limitations of a multiple effect evaporator?

## Long Questions

1. Explain the factors which influence the rate of evaporation.
2. What is natural circulation evaporator? Explain the principle, construction and working of steam jacketed kettle.
3. With the help of a diagram explain the principle and construction of a horizontal tube evaporator.
4. Explain the construction and working of a climbing film evaporator with the help of its diagram.

5. Draw the diagram of a forced circulation evaporator and label properly. Write down the principle and construction of forced circulation evaporator.
6. Explain the principle of a multiple effect evaporator.
7. How is a multiple effect evaporator constructed and how does it work?
8. Explain the economy of a multiple effect evaporator.

# CHAPTER 7

# Heat Transfer

Objectives, Applications and Heat Transfer Mechanisms. Fourier's Law, Heat Transfer by Conduction, Convection and Radiation. Heat Interchangers and Heat Exchangers.

## Objectives

Heat is used in the manufacture of many pharmaceutical formulations. Therefore, how the heat is transferred from one point to another must be clearly understood. It is also necessary to know what are various sources of heat. Many of the operations conducted in pharmaceutical industries use heat. These involve either in evolution (generation) or absorption of energy in the form of heat. For example, during the mixing of powders, a stirrer is rotated for which mechanical energy is utilized. But, during mixing heat may be generated due to friction between solid particles. Similarly, to prepare a solution, the solutes are dissolved in water, there may be generation or absorption of heat depending on the chemical property of the solutes. For example, heat is generated when sodium hydroxide is dissolved in water and heat is absorbed when ammonium acetate is dissolved in water. Therefore, the knowledge about the transfer of heat and how it is transferred is necessary.

## Applications

Heat transfer process has various applications in pharmaceutical industries. There are operations where heat is used during processing; in such cases, heat transfer takes place. Most common examples where heat transfer takes place are mentioned below:

- **Evaporation:** Evaporation is conducted to eliminate solvent from a solution (material) in form of vapor. Thus, a liquid phase is transformed into its vapor phase and the vapor is removed. Usually, the process of evaporation is conducted in pharmaceutical industries for preparation of concentrated plant extract or in crystallization. The construction of an evaporator is similar to that of shell-and-tube heater (heat exchanger). To determine the efficiency of the process of evaporation, heat flow is determined quantitatively.
- **Drying:** It is a very common process practiced in the pharmaceutical industries. For example, preparation of tablets, capsules, powders and granules, etc. Even for the preparation of some liquids this process is conducted. The process of drying can be conducted by various ways using various equipments. However, heat is transferred from the heating material to the feed material. The source of heat may be hot air, steam, etc. After drying, the heat shall be transferred from the product to the surroundings also, as in case of spray drying.

- **Distillation:** Heat is supplied either through steam or through electrical energy. For example, liquid (water) is heated to boiling either by an electrical heater or by steam for preparation of syrup or starch paste or for preparation of distilled water. Heat supplied during this period is consumed first to raise the temperature so that water starts boiling and the rate of evaporation becomes fast. Heat absorbed by water is spent as heat of vaporization. The liquid is converted into vapor, subsequently the vapor is condensed to form water. In case of steam distillation, steam is directly passed through feed (water), so that the volatile component (oil) is carried over and gets separated.
- **Sterilization:** Both dry heat and moist heat sterilization are conducted in pharmaceutical industry. The heating medium may be hot air (dry heat sterilization) or steam (moist heat sterilization) depending on the type of material being sterilized. Heat is transferred to water from the heating medium. Water starts boiling and the heat consumed during boiling is spent as latent heat of vaporization. The hot vapor is condensed, it forms liquid water and the heat is transferred to its surroundings.
- **Crystallization:** In this process the saturated solution is converted to supersaturated solution by applying heat to the solution. The solution absorbs heat from the heating medium and its temperature increases with the solubility. This is first phase.

  In second phase, the hot supersaturated solution is cooled and then the solute (dissolved solute) starts crystallizing. In this phase, the heat is released by the solution to cool down. Thus, in the first phase heat is absorbed by the solution and is released in the second phase. Therefore, heat is exchanged among the heating medium, solution, and the surroundings.

  There are other operations such as incubation, refrigeration, etc., usually performed in pharmaceutical industries where heat is exchanged.

## Mechanisms of Heat Transfer

When heat is applied to any material, there are three processes involved in the transfer of heat.

1. Conduction,
2. Convection, and
3. Radiation

**1. Conduction:** The mechanism of heat transfer by conduction can be expressed as;

$$\text{Rate of heat transfer} = \frac{\text{Driving force}}{\text{Resistance}}$$

The rate of heat transfer can be defined *as the heat passing in unit time from one face of a cube of unit side to the opposite face, the temperature difference is kept at one unit.*

Thus, if the rate of heat transfer $\frac{dQ}{d\theta}$ can be written as

$$\frac{dQ}{d\theta} = -\frac{k \times A \times dt}{dL} \quad .....(7.1)$$

The negative sign indicates that the temperature decreases in the direction of flow.

Where k is a proportionality constant which is characteristic of the material and is known as the *coefficient of thermal conductivity.*

Where, A is the area,

$dt = (t_1 - t_2)$ is the difference of temperature,

dL is the thickness, and

$\theta$ is the time.

If q is the amount of heat transferred in unit time, then $q = \dfrac{k \times A \times dt}{dL}$

If q is expressed as Btu, $\theta$ in hours, A in sq. ft, t is in °F, and L in ft; then the unit of k would be calculated as $\dfrac{\text{Btu} \times \text{ft}}{\text{hr} \times \text{Sq.ft} \times {}^{\circ}\text{F}}$ or $\dfrac{\text{Btu}}{\text{hr} \times \text{ft} \times {}^{\circ}\text{F}}$

Thermal conductivities vary widely. For example, metals have the largest thermal conductivities; while gases have the smallest. Table 7.1 shows the values of thermal conductivities of different types of materials. The thermal conductivities of liquids and gases are very small in comparison to those of mostof the solids. Silver has a thermal conductivity of 240 Btu. ft/hr. sq. ft. °F at 212°F; while water has 0.6Btu. ft/hr. sq. ft. °F at 212°F and air has only 0.017Btu. ft/hr. sq. ft. °F at 212°F.

**Table 7.1** Thermal conductivity of certain common materials

| Material | Type | Thermal conductivity |
|---|---|---|
| Air | Gas | 0.03 W/mK |
| Glass wool | solid | 0.06 W/mK |
| Boiler scale | Solid | 0.09 – 2.3 W/mK |
| Water | Liquid | 0.6 W/mK |
| Borosilicate glass | Solid | 1 W/mK |
| Stainless steel | Solid | 17 W/mK |
| Steel | Solid | 43 W/mK |
| Silver | Solid | 240 W/mK |
| Aluminium | Solid | 242 W/mK |
| Copper | Solid | 379 W/mK |

But, in case of a compound composed of more than two or three metals (alloys), it becomes difficult to measure its overall thermal conductivity. Thus, it becomes a problem to measure the rate of heat transfer through such material.

However, the overall thermal conductivity of such a compound can be calculated by using the reciprocal of the overall resistance.

$$\text{Resistance} = \frac{1}{k_1} + \frac{1}{k_2} + \frac{1}{k_3} + \ldots.. + \frac{1}{k_n} \qquad \ldots..(7.2)$$

This assumes that each layer is of unit thickness. This is not practically true. Hence, the resistance of each of the constituting materials can be written with respect to their respective thickness as

$$\text{Resistance} = \frac{L_1}{k_1} + \frac{L_2}{k_2} + \ldots\ldots + \frac{L_n}{k_n} \qquad \ldots..(7.3)$$

Where $L_1$, $L_2$, ……$L_n$ are the thickness of the materials.

This is called the *overall coefficient of heat transfer*, U.

$$U = \frac{1}{\frac{L_1}{k_1} + \frac{L_2}{k_2} + \ldots + \frac{L_n}{k_n}} \qquad \ldots..(7.4)$$

In place of k/L, U is used to calculate the heat transfer and equation 4 can be written as:

$$q = UA\,(t_1 - t_2) = UA\,\Delta t \qquad \ldots..(7.5)$$

**Heating of fluids**

In general, a liquid is heated in a steam-heated container. The temperature gradient exists through the wall between the steam jacket and the liquid. When a liquid or fluid comes in contact with a hot surface, a layer at the boundary behaves as a stationary layer to the bulk of the liquid. It is observed that heat passes through this layer to the bulk of liquid. During this process of heat transfer, some scale may be deposited on the surface of the metal wall, through which heat is transferred.

When steam releases its latent heat, water vapor condenses on the surface of the container. While heat needs to be conducted through this water film. Moreover, air remains present in the steam jacket. Although air is mostly removed even then a little amount of air may remain with the steam. No clearly defined film of air is formed; some air molecules remains adjacent to the surface. Let us assume that the air is present as a stagnant film through which heat is to be conducted. Presence of air film over the metal wall interferes greatly in the determination of thermal conductivity. Because an air film of 0.25mm thickness is same as of 36cm of steel, 2m of aluminum and more than 3m of copper.

2. **Convection:** When Reynold's number of fluids exceeds a certain value, the character of the flow changes from viscous to turbulent. Even in turbulent flow, at the boundary, a residual film persists in the viscous flow. When any type of stirrer or an agitator is used or a pump is used to flow a liquid through a pipe (forced convection), a natural convection currents is set up. When a body of liquid is heated, turbulence may be produced. When heat passes to the liquid through the retaining wall, the film remaining on the metal wall as stagnant layer plays an important role in determining the rate of transfer of heat. The heat to reach to the bulk of the liquid, must pass through this film by conduction. As such, the thermal conductivity of the liquid is less and the thickness of the stagnant film although is less, the thermal resistance of this film is large. On the other hand, rapid equalization of temperature takes place due to

turbulence beyond this film. In other words, the resistance to the flow of heat from the wall to the bulk of the liquid is observed due to the stagnant layer or film over the wall of metal at its boundary.

*Temperature gradients in forced convection:* In forced convection, the distribution of temperature across a column of liquid, hot or cool, depends on the velocity of distribution of heat across the same column of the liquid.

3. **Radiation:** Heat transfer by thermal radiation and heat transfer by conduction and convection takes place simultaneously. Compared to conduction and convection methods, heat transferred by radiation relatively depends on the temperature level. Heat transfer by radiation becomes more important when the temperature increases. Any solid radiates energy at any temperature above absolute zero degrees. This radiation is an electromagnetic phenomenon. It occurs even without the presence of a medium. Even across a perfect vacuum or interstellar space, it occurs. At ordinary temperature, it becomes effective through the layers of air. Various types of electromagnetic waves and their approximate wavelength have been given below:

| Type of radiation | Wavelengths, microns (μm) |
|---|---|
| Radio waves | $10 \times 10^7 - 3000 \times 10^7$ |
| Infrared or heat rays | 0.8 – 400 |
| Visible light rays | 0.4 – 0.8 |
| Ultraviolet rays | 0.014 – 0.4 |
| X rays | $6 \times 10^{-6} - 100000 \times 10^{-6}$ |
| Gamma rays | $1 \times 10^{-6} - 140 \times 10^{-6}$ |
| Cosmic rays | $1 \times 10^{-6}$ |

The term thermal radiation refers to the radiation that occurs at a wavelength of 0.8 – 400 microns(μm) (1 μm = $1 \times 10^{-6}$ metre). However, in most cases of industrial interest, the range is shortened to 0.8 to 25 microns. Both light and thermal radiation are electromagnetic radiation and follow the laws of light. That is, the thermal radiation travels in a straight line and can be reflected, refracted, and absorbed.

Amount and kind of thermal energy radiated by a surface, increases with the increase in temperature. It usually, depend on the radiant energy which is emitted from a solid surface and liquid continuously; if they are not in the form of a thin film. The energy emitted is also continuously distributed over all wavelength from zero to infinity. The major portion of the energy is concentrated within a relatively narrow range of wavelength. Compared to thermal radiation, the amount of energy in the range of visible radiation is insignificant.

## Black Body

All the substances do not radiate energy at the same rate at same temperature. Hence, there should be some specifications regarding the physical condition of a hot body emitting radiations. Theoretically, there is a special type of substance which radiates the maximum possible amount of

energy at a given temperature. Such a substance is called a *black body*. This is not related to the color of the body. If visible light rays are only considered, black matte substances behave like black bodies and light-colored substances deviate widely from it. However, in the case of thermal radiation, the color of the body has no role. For measurement of temperature inside of an enclosed space, a hole is necessary to insert the thermometer or to view or read. The size of the hole might be of any size, but some amount of negligible energy, will escape through the opening and will correspond to a black body. The black body is commonly prepared from a tube plugged with carbon at both ends and a small hole is made at the center of one end. The tube is kept in a furnace where a constant temperature is maintained. When viewed through the opening, it would be found that some amount of negligible energy is being escaped through the opening which corresponds to a black body. However, there is no physical substance which may be a perfect black body.
The total amount of radiation emitted by a black body can be expressed by the Stefan-Boltzmann equation as follows:

$$q = bAT^4 \qquad \text{.....(7.6)}$$

where, q is the amount of energy radiated per hour,

A is the area of the radiating surface,

T is the absolute temperature of the radiating surface, R

For black bodies the value of b is $0.174 \times 10^{-8}$ Btu/hr × sq ft × °F

No actual body radiates quite as much as the black body. The radiation by any actual body can be expressed as;

$$q = \epsilon bAT^4 \qquad \text{.....(7.7)}$$

Where, $\epsilon$ is the emissivity of the body. The emissivity is a fraction less than 1 and is the ratio of the energy emitted by the given body to that emitted by a black body at the same temperature.

## Fourier's Law

When conduction occurs through solids without convection, the mechanism of conduction can be easily understood. The basic law of heat transfer by conduction can be expressed as:

$$\text{Rate} = \frac{\text{Driving force}}{\text{Resistance}} \qquad \text{.....(7.8)}$$

The term 'resistance' in the above equation can be defined by Fourier's law. Let us assume that the area of a wall of thickness L, is A on its one face and uniform but slightly lesser than the same area on the opposite face. Then, the heat will flow at a right angle to the plane of A. According to Fourier's law *the rate of heat transfer through a uniform material is proportional to the area, the temperature drop, and inversely proportional to the length of the path of flow of heat.* If a thin section of thickness dL, parallel to the area A, is considered at some intermediate point in the wall, with a temperature difference dt across the layer, then the Fourier's law can be expressed as:

$$\frac{dQ}{d\theta} = -\frac{kAdt}{dL} \qquad \text{.....(7.9)}$$

Where $\frac{dQ}{d\theta}$ is the rate of flow of heat, k is a proportionality constant and other terms as have been mentioned earlier. If the temperature gradient, $\frac{dt}{dL}$ does not change with time; then the rate of heat flow would be constant with time, and

$$\frac{dQ}{d\theta} = \text{constant} = q = -\frac{kAdt}{dL} \qquad .....(7.10)$$

Generally, only the temperature at the two faces of the wall are known, not the intermediate temperature along the path of heat transfer. Ordinarily the Fourier's law requires that the differential equation should be integrated over the path, L = 0 to L = total length and k may be a function of temperature only, but independent on the length. However, the value of A may change with length L, but is independent of the temperature. Hence, by separating the variables,

$$\frac{q\ dL}{A} = -k\ dt \qquad .....(7.11)$$

The negative sign indicates that the temperature decreases in the direction of flow; hence, $\frac{dt}{dL}$ is negative.

Now, by integrating up to the higher temperature $t_2$

$$q\int_0^L \frac{dL}{A} = -\int_{t_1}^{t_2} k.dt = \int_{t_2}^{t_1} k.dt$$

since q is a constant, the variation of k with temperature may be considered as linear. Hence, the arithmetic mean value of k, $k_m$ can be considered a constant. If A does not change with L (flat wall) then the above equation may be integrated to

$$\frac{qL}{A} = k_m(t_1 - t_2) = k_m\Delta t$$

Or,

$$q = \frac{k_m \times A \times \Delta t}{L} \qquad .....(7.12)$$

Thus, by knowing Δt, the driving force, the resistance $\frac{L}{k_m A}$ can be calculated.

## Heat Transfer by Conduction

On heating, the atoms or molecules of a substance become energized and they start moving. When heat flows through a substance (body) by the transference of the momentum (mass × velocity) of the atoms or molecules without mixing, the process is called conduction.

For example, the transfer of heat through a brick wall or metal items. Thus, conduction of heat is limited to solids and fluids which are not in motion.

## Convection

When heat flows from a warmer portion to a cooler portion of the same material due to mixing or agitation, the process of propagation of heat (heat transfer) is called convection. Thus, the transfer of heat by convection occurs only in fluids. It is very rare that the flow of heat in a fluid takes place only by pure conduction or with some convection process. For example, heating of air in a room using a room heater, or heating of water by steam.

## Radiation

When a substance becomes hot, it starts emitting energy in the form of electromagnetic waves. This radiation proceeds in all directions. No energy is lost due to intervening atmosphere. If the waves fall on some body, some amount of radiation is transmitted, some amount is reflected and some amount is absorbed by the body. The actual amount of radiation absorbed, in other words, the extent of absorption depends on the properties of the body. In fact, a black body is the perfect emitter or absorber. However, all the bodies can emit or radiate to some extent. The quantity and quality of radiation depend on the temperature (in absolute scale). The radiation moves along a line.

For example, fused quartz transmits practically all the radiation that hit it, a polished opaque surface or mirror can reflect most of the radiations falling on it. A black or matte surface will absorb most of the radiations received by it and will transform such absorbed energy quantitatively into heat.

If E is the total energy and T is the absolute temperature, then

$$E \infty T^4 \qquad .....(7.13)$$

This emission of energy is distributed in the form of spectrum of wavelengths within 1 to 100μm. This wavelength is above the visible range, commonly called infrared. The useful wavelength is between 1 – 10μm.

The distribution of emitted energy is not uniform throughout the band of the spectrum. There is a peak wavelength, Z, at which the intensity of radiation is maximum. Thus,

$$Z \infty 1/T \qquad .....(7.14)$$

Moreover, the intensity of radiating energy, I, depends on the absolute temperature, T; hence, we can write

$$I \infty T^5 \qquad .....(7.15)$$

As the temperature of the emitting body increases, total radiated energy increases. The peak wavelength becomes shorter and radiation at peak wavelength is of maximum intensity.

### Steam as a Source of Heat

Among various methods of heating used for different operations such as drying of granules, distillation, sterilization, etc. steam is used. The few reasons for which steam is used to heat are:

- Steam has high heat content,
- Heat is released at constant temperature,

- Raw material used for producing steam is water which is cheapest,
- Steam is clean, odorless and tasteless.
- Steam can be used at high pressure to produce electric power,
- Steam is easy to produce, distribute and control.
- Steam contains heat in two forms – sensible heat and latent heat.

Sensible heat can be sensed. Due to release or receipt of heat, the temperature changes. While, latent heat is not visible or cannot be detected in form of temperature. The latent heat is consumed by the substance during the change of its state; that is, to change from the solid to liquid (melting), to change from the liquid to vapor (boiling) and to change from the vapor to solid (freezing). Hence, consumption of latent heat cannot be expressed by the change in temperature, but can be calculated. Both sensible and latent heat contents are very important properties of steam.

When steam does not contain any water, it is called dry steam and it exerts its full saturated vapor pressure. Steam at this state is called saturated steam.

If an additional amount of heat is added to the steam, the heat is not consumed as latent heat of vaporization. All the heat added will increase the sensible heat in the steam and the temperature of the steam will increase. At this state, the steam becomes *superheated.*

## Heat Exchangers and Heat Interchangers

Chemical and pharmaceutical industries use various types of heat transfer equipments. The liquids, gases and sometimes solids are heated. The heating media may be a hot fluid or steam. In pharmacy, there are some processes in which heat is transferred, such as

- Wet granulation, for preparation of binder paste,
- Crystallization of salts,
- Evaporation for preparation of plant extract,
- Lyophilization for drying of thermolabile materials,
- Distillation for preparation of water for injection, etc.

*Heat exchangers are the equipments or devices used to transfer heat from one substance (hot gas or steam) to another substance (liquid) through a metal wall. Some of the heat exchangers are;*

- Tubular heater (shell-and-tube heater),
- Multi-pass heater,
- Two pass floating head heater

In case of heat exchanger, the film coefficient on the steam side is usually much larger than that on the cold liquid side. Thus, the overall heat transfer coefficient will be nearer to the cold liquid side and total heat transfer would be less. However, the efficiency can be improved by passing the liquid at a high speed, because the thickness and resistance of the liquid film decrease. Usually, the space outside the tubes is large, but the speed of steam is low. Since, the values of steam film coefficients are high, these are still used.

*Heat interchangers are the devices used to transfer heat from one liquid to another liquid or from one gas to another gas through a metal wall. Both heat exchanger and heat interchanger transfer heat.*

## Heat Interchangers

Heat interchanger has been defined earlier. This type of devices is used for transferring heat from one liquid to another liquid or from one gas to another gas through a metal surface.

Heat interchanger utilizes a hot liquid as the heating medium. The feed is a cold liquid. In this type of heat interchanger, the film coefficient at outside and inside the tubes are of almost same magnitude. The value of overall heat transfer coefficient, U will be similar to the minimum value of two film coefficients. Hence, efficient heat transfer will not be achieved.

However, by increasing the speed of flow, the film coefficient can be increased. From construction point of view, although it is difficult to increase the speed of flow of hot liquid outside the tubes by fixing the baffles, the surface area of contact can be increased. As a result, film coefficient would be increased and the rate of heat transfer would also increase.

### Liquid-to-liquid Heat Interchanger

The basic constructions and working principles of all heat transfer devices are almost similar. In particular, the device may be modified to certain extent. The schematic diagram of this interchanger is shown in Fig 7.1. It contains tube sheets, spacer rods and baffles are assembled and installed. The baffles are arranged with required spacing using short sections. Baffles have perforations through which tubes are inserted. The ends of the tubes are expanded into the tube sheets. The whole assembly is enclosed in a shell.

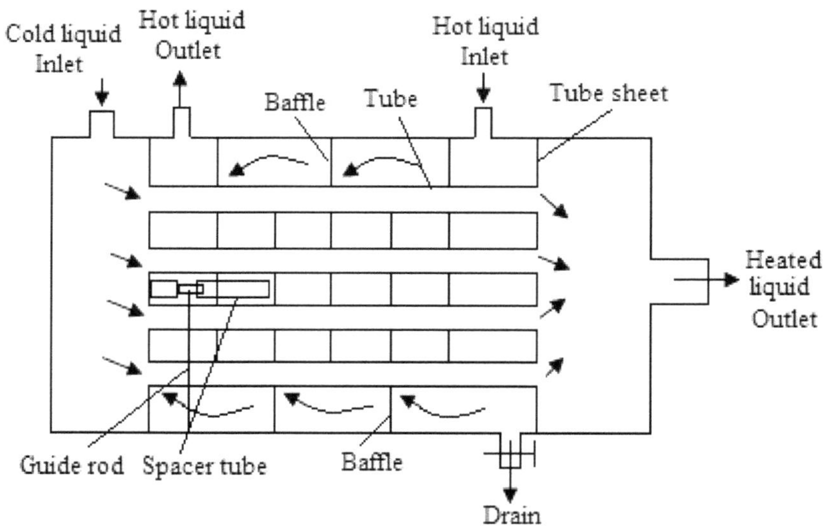


**Fig. 7.1** Schematic diagram of liquid-liquid heat interchanger

The shell has two inlets– one for cold liquid and the other one for hot liquid; two outlets– one for hot liquid and the other one for heated liquid. There is one more outlet to drain off the condensate. The hot liquid(heating medium) is pumped into the outside-space of the tubes from the top-inlet. The hot liquid flows down to the bottom of the shell, then moves up. This up-down movement is repeated and finally the hot liquid leaves the shell through the outlet. Baffles attached to the shell increase the speed of the liquid outside the tubes. Due to the presence of these baffles, liquid flows almost right angles to the tubes, which creates more turbulence. The cold liquid is introduced into the shell through the inlet, it moves around the space within the tubes. It becomes hot due to heat transferred from hot liquid to cold liquid. Finally, when the cold liquid becomes heated liquid, it leaves the shell through the outlet.

In a liquid-to-liquid heat interchanger, the heat transfer is rapid since the speed of the liquid passing at high speed outside the tubes and it flows more or less at right angles to the tubes.

## Double-pipe Heat Interchanger

In the double-pipe heat interchanger, efficient heat transfer does not take place. The number of tubes should be more than one is desired, for this reason, double-pipe heat interchanger is used. Generally, in this type of heat interchanger two tubes are there – one is inserted into the other. The cold liquid (to be heated) is introduced into the inner tube by a pump. The outer tube acts as a jacket in which the hot water is circulated.

As shown in the Fig 7.2 all the outer tubes are interconnected. In this heat interchanger, the length of the tube is less and the number of tubes may be adjusted as per requirement.

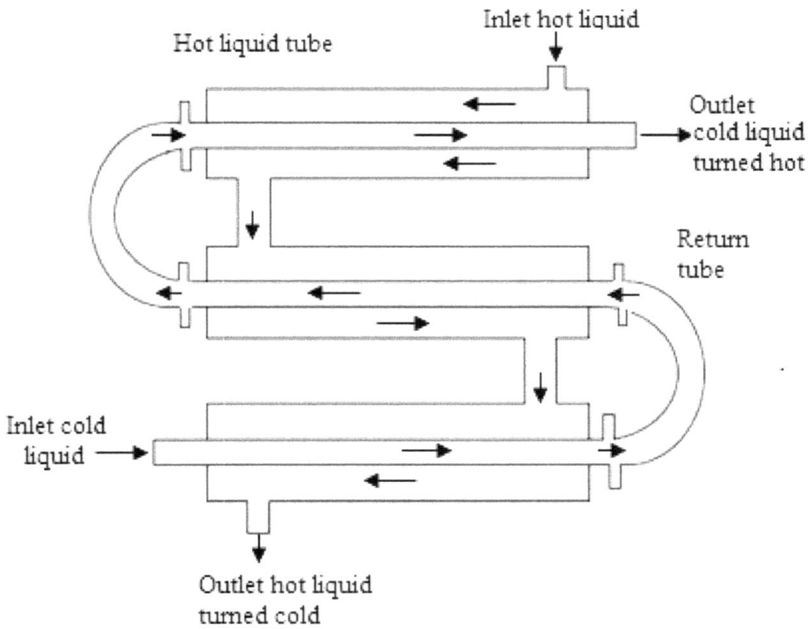


**Fig. 7.2** Schematic diagram of double-pipe heat interchanger

The heating medium (hot liquid) is pumped into the jacket and circulated throughout the annular space. After complete circulation, the hot liquid leaves the jacket. During circulation of the hot liquid, the tubes are heated. This heat is subsequently transferred to the cold liquid which after complete circulation leaves through the outlet.

## Heat Exchangers

### Tubular Heater (Shell-and-tube heater)

Shell-and-tube heater is the simplest form of tubular heater. It is a single-pass heater. A simple tubular heater consists of almost parallel tubes expanded between two tube sheets. The tube sheets containing the parallel tubes are fitted to a cylindrical body called shell. In some heaters the shells are made of cast iron. The shell contains two distribution chambers at two ends. One chamber contains feed inlet at its cover. The shell also contains steam inlet, vent outlet in one side and in other side it contains condensate outlet.

Steam is introduced through steam inlet into the space between the tubes and steam distributes into the entire space. The tubes become hot quickly due to high steam film coefficient. The condensed vapor leaves through the condensate outlet. The non-condensable vapor or gases leave through the vent. The liquid to be heated is introduced through the cold liquid inlet with the help of a pump. The liquid flows inside the hot tubes. Thus, liquid and steam are separated physically by the tube walls. The heat is transferred by conduction through the metal wall and the liquid gets heated. The heat transferred by conduction is followed by stagnant layer and finally by convection. Total heat is transferred to a single pass of liquid. The hot liquid enters into the distribution chamber and leaves the heater through the outlet made for it. Since, the width of the tubes of this type of heater is more, the velocity of the liquid is less.

### Multi-pass Heater

The speed of the liquid can be increased in a multi-pass heater. Thus, heat transfer coefficient would be more. The name of heater indicates that the liquid to be heated pas through the tube many times before leaving the heater. As a result, an effective heat transfer takes place. Thus, a multi-pass heater is more efficient than a single-pass heater.

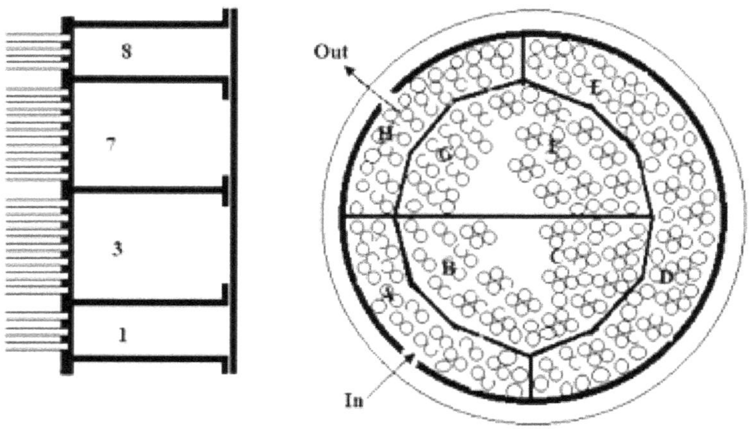


**Fig. 7.3** Schematic diagram of multi-pass heater

Construction of both the heaters is almost same. The difference in construction of multi-pass heater is that it contains several inlets for feed liquid because the liquid flows through several tubes at a time and the movement is 'to and fro'. To make this process convenient the baffles are attached. The baffles partition the distribution chambers. In the same distribution chamber both inlet and outlet provisions are there.

Steam is introduced into the space surrounding the tubes to make the tubes hot. When the steam flows down the tubes become hot and steam the heater through condensate outlet. The liquid to be heated is pumped at the high speed into the right distribution chamber through the compartment made. Due to the high speed of the liquid, heat transfer takes place from the metal surface (hot tubes) to the flowing liquid effectively.

The construction of this type of heater is such that the liquid is allowed to enter only a fraction of the tubes through the baffles fixed to the distribution chamber. The liquid flows from right to left and then, from left to right, and so on. During this movement of liquid, the liquid gets heated due to the heat transfer from the hot metal surface to the liquid. Heat transfer process follows both conduction and convection as in single-pass heater. In this case, the rate of heat transfer is high. The speed of the liquid depends on the power of the pump and increases the cost of the pump. However, by reducing the diameter of the tubes, the speed of the liquid can be increased.

## Floating Head Two-pass Heater

The construction of a floating head two-pass heater is similar to that of tubular heater; however, some modifications are there.

The floating head two-pass heater consists of horizontal tubes parallelly placed inside a shell. In the right side of the distribution chamber there is a partition which does not allow to mix the cold fluid entered with hot fluid ready to be removed and in both sides of the partition the same number of tubes are present. On the left side, the assembly of tubes is not structurally connected to the distribution chamber. For this reason, it is called floating head. As shown in the Fig 7.4, the outer end of the tubes is connected to a floating head. The steam is introduced into the system through steam inlet valve. There are three outlets – one is vent to remove the air and the other is for removal of the hot fluid and the last one is for removal of steam condensate.

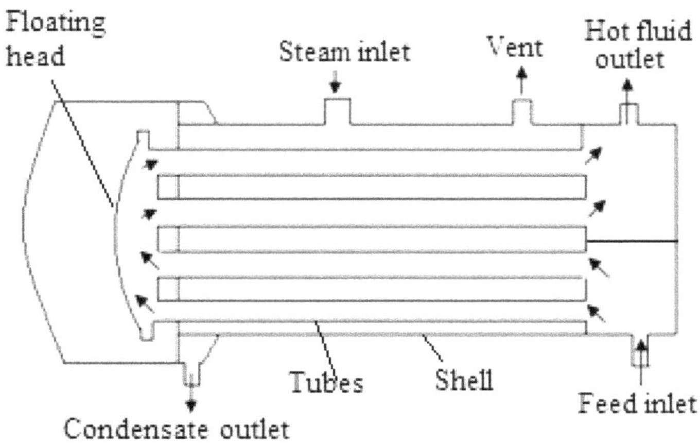


**Fig. 7.4** Schematic diagram of floating head two-pass heater

Steam is introduced through the steam inlet valve, it replaces the air present in the pipe line and in the equipment, air leaves through the vent. During downward movement of the steam, the tubes are heated. The fluid to be heated is then introduced through fluid inlet valve. The fluid while moving through the hot tubes heated the partitioned area. The hot fluid after reaching the floating head changes its direction. It moves through the tubes present in other part of the partition chamber. Thus, the fluid passes through the tubes twice before going out. That is why it is called 'two-pass'. During this movement, the fluids get heated and the solvent vaporizes. Heat transfer takes place by two methods– conduction and by convection. When the fluid comes in contact with hot metal wall, heat is transferred by conduction. In the distribution chamber, the fluid remains in form of stagnant layer, the heat is transferred by convection. Finally, the hot fluid leaves through the outlet valve.

In a shell-tube heat exchanger, the tubes and shell may expand due to the temperature difference. Similarly, these may contract when switched off. Since, the tubes are not directly in contact with shell, both contraction and expansion cannot influence the performance of a floating-head two-pass heater.

## Short Questions

1. Define the terms, evaporation, drying and distillation
2. Distinguish between evaporation and crystallization
3. What are three mechanisms by which heat is transferred?
4. What is a black body?
5. Explain the method by which the sun rays can heat a substance.
6. What are heat exchanger and heat interchanger?
7. What is the Fourier's law?
8. Write a note on double-pipe heat interchanger.
9. Write a note on how a shell-and-tube heater is the simplest form of tubular heater.
10. What is coefficient of thermal conductivity and explain it.

## Long Questions

1. Write a note on how the heat is transferred through conduction.
2. Explain the basic constructions and working principles of a heat interchanger used for heat transfer between two liquids.
3. Explain how heat is transferred through convection and radiation.
4. Write a note on the substance that can radiate the maximum possible amount of energy at a given temperature.
5. Explain single-pass heater and multi-pass heater with the help of diagrams.
6. With the help of a neat diagram explain floating head two-pass heater.
7. Explain how a multi-pass heater is more efficient than a single-pass heater.
8. Explain the Fourier's law.

# CHAPTER 8

# Drying

Objectives, Applications & Mechanism of Drying Process, Measurements & Applications of Equilibrium Moisture Content, Rate of Drying Curve. Principles, Construction, Working, Uses, Merits and Demerits of Tray Dryer, Drum Dryer Spray Dryer, Fluidized Bed Dryer, Vacuum Dryer, Freeze Dryer.

## Objectives

Drying is a process of elimination of water, usually small amount, from solid or almost solid material. While evaporation is the process of removal of a large amount of water from a solution. It is an important operation in pharmaceutical industries. Commonly before packaging, it is the last operation of a manufacturing process. The property of the product can be affected by the drying process used. Proper drying can ensure the desired flow property or the solubility of the product, prevention of deterioration of the constituent of the product. Most of the drying processes are related to the properties of the product.

In drying processes, the major importance is usually on the solid product. Generally, in drying, water is removed at a temperature below the boiling point of water; while in case of evaporation water is removed by heating the substance at the boiling point of water. During drying hot air or some other gas is circulated over the material and water is removed as water vapor mixed with circulating air or gas. When a solution is sprayed into a current of superheated steam, the process is called drying, although it complies with all the requirements of evaporation.

The materials that are normally present as solids are subjected to drying. When a solid is in equilibrium with atmosphere with which it is in contact, the condition is called 'dry' condition and the material is called dry solid.

There are various types of equipments called dryers used for drying the materials. Based on the type of materials to be dried, appropriate dryer is used. Thus, based on the physical state of the material the dryers can be classified as:

1. Granular or loose materials
    - (a) Rotary dryers
        - (i) Standard rotary
        - (ii) Roto-Louvre
    - (b) Turbo dryers
    - (c) Conveyor dryer
    - (d) Filter-dryer combination

2. Materials in sheet or carried through conveyors or trays
   (a) Batch dryers
      (i) Atmospheric-compartment dryers
      (ii) Vacuum tray dryers
   (b) Continuous dryers
      (i) Tunnel dryers
3. Materials in continuous sheets
   (a) Cylinder dryers
   (b) Festoon dryers
4. Materials in form of pastes, sludges or cakes
   (a) Agitator dryers
      (i) Atmospheric
      (ii) Vacuum
5. Materials in form of solution
   (a) Drum dryers
      (i) Atmospheric
      (ii) Vacuum
   (b) Spray dryers
6. Special method
   (a) Infrared radiations
   (b) Dielectric heating
   (c) Sublimation or Lyophilization (Vaporization from ice)

## Applications of Drying

Drying operation is a very common operation and is performed for many processes, in pharmaceutical and chemical and other industries. Few examples related to its application in pharmaceutical manufacturing are mentioned below:

- *Preparation of bulk drugs:* Drugs and excipients are usually synthesized, precipitated and purified. After purification, it is dried to make powder. Depending on the thermostability and other properties, the actual method of drying is selected. Even for preparation plant extractives, drying is conducted.
- *Preparation of dosage form:* When a drug product is prepared, drying is a common operation performed. For example, for manufacturing of tablets, capsules or powders or granules must have required characteristics such as moisture content, flow property, compressibility, stability, etc. The moisture content of a material can be controlled by appropriate drying. Similarly, for preparation of injection, solutions, the containers are dried. For preparation of powder of injections, the powders are dried.
- *Improvement of properties:* Appropriate moisture content is necessary for producing desired size and shape of the substance, to achieve the desired rate of solubilization, etc. Control of moisture content is related to the drying of the substances. Hence, drying can modify the characteristics of a substance, drug and excipient.

- *Handling of materials:* Excess of moisture in a substance makes it difficult to be handled. A hygroscopic material becomes sticky and viscous materials when they absorb moisture. Hence, proper drying of these materials makes them suitable for handling.

These are few examples among many others of pharmaceutical applications of drying. In other industries, even in our daily lives drying is an essential operation.

## Mechanism of Drying

The mechanism of drying can be explained from two points of views:

1. The equilibrium relationships, and
2. The rate relationship.

During drying, the heat transfer to the material ways takes place in different ways. Drying is a complex operation; it involves momentary transfer of heat and mass. Various rate processes, such as physical or chemical transformations occur. Consequently, this may cause changes in quality of product. Physical changes such as shrinkage, puffing, crystallization, glass transitions occur. In some cases, desirable or undesirable chemical or biochemical reactions such as changes in color, texture, odor or other properties of the solid product may also occur. For example, in the manufacture of catalysts, drying conditions can produce significant changes in the activity of the catalyst, if the internal surface area is changed.

When heat is supplied to the wet feedstock, vaporization of liquid or solvent takes place. Heat may be supplied by

- Convection (direct dryers),
- Conduction (contact or indirect dryers),
- Radiation or volumetrically
- Placing the wet material in a microwave or radio frequency electromagnetic field.

More than 85 percent of industrial dryers are of the convective type and use hot air or direct combustion gases as the drying medium; more than 99 percent of the processes remove water. In most of the processes except the dielectric (microwave and radio frequency) oven, heat is supplied at the boundaries of the material (drying object) so that the heat can diffuse into the solid mainly by conduction. The liquid moves to the boundary of the material. Then the liquid is transported away by the carrier gas (or by application of vacuum for non-convective dryers).Transport of moisture within the solid may occur by any one or more of the following mechanisms of mass transfer:

- Diffusion of liquid, if the wet solid is at a temperature below the boiling point of the liquid.
- Diffusion of vapor, if the liquid vaporizes within material.
- Knudsen diffusion, if drying takes place at very low temperatures and pressure, such as in freeze drying.
- Surface diffusion (possibly)because of hydrostatic pressure differences, the internal rate of vaporization is more than the rate of vapor transport through the solid to the surroundings.

Since the physical structure of the solid is likely to change during drying, the mechanisms of moisture transfer may also change with time of drying.

## Equilibrium Moisture Content

The equilibrium moisture content (EMC) is defined as *the moisture content of a wet solid in equilibrium with air of given humidity and temperature*. Hence, equilibrium moisture content of a material depends on both temperature and humidity. The plot of equilibrium moisture content of the solid vs. relative humidity at a particular temperature is shown in Fig 8.1. Such a plot is known as *sorption isotherm*. Similarly, the solid is exposed to decreasing relative humidity and the equilibrium moisture content is measured and plotted against relative humidity, the curve obtained is called *desorption* isotherm. The Fig 8.1 shows the same. During drying the desorption isotherm is important because the moisture content of the solid decreases gradually. In most drying cases, the materials show the two isotherms which are not identical. There are three typical zones A, B, and C which indicate different water binding mechanisms at different sites on the solid matrix. In region A, water is tightly bound with the sites and is unavailable for reaction. In this region, there is basically monolayer adsorption of water vapor occurs and no distinction of water vapor exists between the adsorption and desorption isotherms. In region B, the water is more loosely bound. The vapor pressure depression below the equilibrium vapor pressure of water at a given temperature is due to its confinement in smaller capillaries. In region C water is even more loosely held in larger capillaries. The water is available for reaction and also as solvent. To explain the hysteresis, many investigators have proposed many hypotheses. Figure 8.2 shows schematically the shapes of the equilibrium moisture curves for various types of solids. The definitions of different types of moistures have been shown in Fig 8.3. Desorption isotherms also depend on external pressure. Although this effect is neglected in all practical cases of interest.
According to Keey, the temperature dependence of the equilibrium moisture content can be expressed by:

$$\left[\frac{\Delta X}{\Delta T}\right]_{\Psi=\text{const}} = -\alpha X$$

Where X is the equilibrium moisture content on dried basis, T is the temperature and $\psi$ is the relative humidity of air. The parameter $\alpha$ ranges from 0.005 to 0.01 $K^{-1}$. If no data are available, this expression can be used to measure the temperature dependence of X.

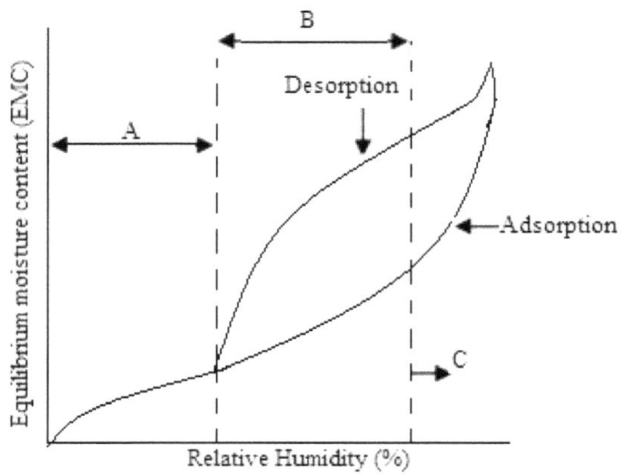


**Fig. 8.1** Typical sorption isotherm

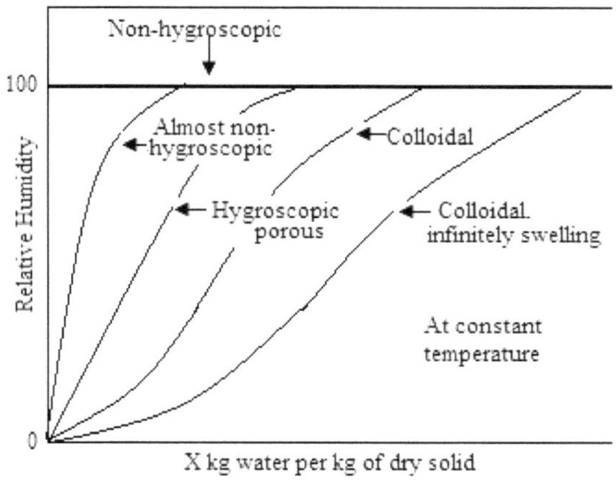


**Fig. 8.2** Equilibrium moisture content curves for various types of solids

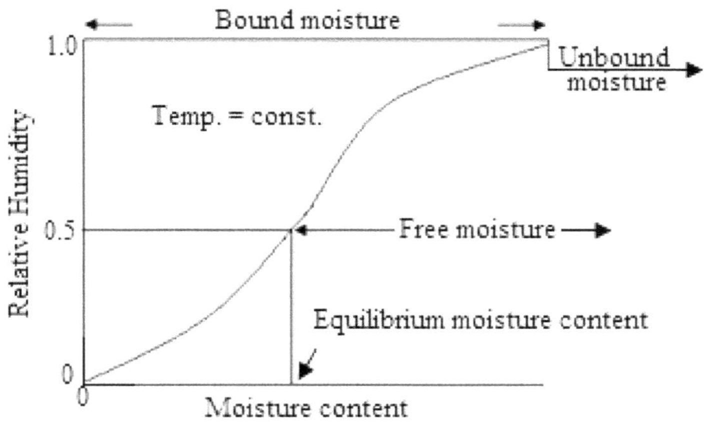


**Fig. 8.3** Various types of moisture content

For hygroscopic solid materials the enthalpy of the moisture attached is less than the enthalpy of pure water by an amount equal to the binding energy. According to Keey, this binding energy can also be termed as the enthalpy of wetting, $\Delta H_w$. It includes the heat of sorption, hydration and solution and may be estimated from the following equation:

$$\left[\frac{d(\ln \Psi)}{d\left(\frac{1}{T}\right)}\right]_{X=\text{const}} = -\frac{\Delta H_w}{R_g T}$$

A plot of ln(Ψ) against 1/T would be linear with a slope of $\frac{\Delta H_w}{R_g}$ where $R_g$ is the universal gas constant ($R_g = 8.314 \times 10^3$kg kgmol$^{-1}$ K$^{-1}$). The total heat required to evaporate the bound water is the sum of the latent heat of vaporization and the heat of wetting. The latent heat of vaporization is a function of the moisture content X. For unbound water the heat of wetting is zero and it increases with decreasing X. Since the lowering of the vapor pressure of bound water depends on $\Delta H_w$, at the same relative humidity, $\Delta H_w$, is almost same for all the materials.

When a material is taken out of the dryer, it may or may not be *bone-dry*; that is the material is completely from moisture. It depends on the temperature and humidity at the dryer outlet. The dried material if exposed to atmosphere can regain certain amount of moisture even after bone-drying.

Generally, over-drying should be avoided. That is, the *drying should be discontinued when the moisture content of the material is reached to its equivalent level under the conditions to which material would be exposed.*

For most of the materials, the energy required for binding with moisture is positive. Generally, it is amonotonically decreasing function of the moisture content, having a value of zero for unbound moisture. For hydrophobic food materials (e.g., peanut oil, starches at lower temperatures) the binding energy can be negative.

Generally, water sorption data is determined experimentally. According to different theories, there are some 80 correlations; most of these are purely empirical. Apart from temperature, the physical structure and the composition of the material also can influence water sorption. The pore structure and size, physical or chemical transformations during drying can produce significant variations in the moisture binding ability of the solid.

**Moisture content**

In a solid the moisture may be present in more than one physical condition. The moisture content may be determined by drying the material. However, the moisture present in a solid may be in bound, unbound or free form depending on the characteristics of the solid material.

**Bound moisture**

In a solid the *bound moisture* refers to the liquid (water) whose vapor pressure is less than that of the pure liquid (water) at the same temperature and atmospheric pressure.

This happens because the liquid remains within the small capillaries, or in solution, or in crystals or particles, or in a combined form by adsorption.

**Unbound moisture**

Unbound moisture exerts its vapor pressure equivalent to that of the free liquid. Hence, the moisture present in a non-hygroscopic material as unbound moisture. In a hygroscopic material the unbound moisture refers to the amount over and above its equilibrium moisture content. This depends on the saturation humidity.

**Free moisture**

It refers to the amount of moisture present in excess of the equilibrium moisture content of a material at a particular temperature and humidity. When saturation humidity persists at a particular temperature, the free moisture and unbound moisture become same. While in other circumstances, the free moisture is the sum of bound and unbound moistures. Thus, free moisture content refers to the moisture free to evaporate from the solid surface.

Free moisture content = Total moisture content – Equilibrium moisture content

The difference between free moisture content and equilibrium moisture content depends on the drying conditions.

## Measurements of Equilibrium Moisture Content

According to the International Energy Agency Annex 24 Report on material properties, there are three definitions for "moisture content" in building materials. These are:

1. Mass of moisture per unit volume of the dry material,
2. Mass of moisture per unit mass of the dry material, and
3. Volume of condensed moisture per unit volume of the dry material.

A material attains the equilibrium moisture content (EMC) when the moisture content of the material does not change with change of time under the combined effect of water vapor pressure and air temperature.

The definition of EMC seems to be relatively simple. But the experimental determination of EMC is not so simple because many factors play important roles in a reliable determination of EMC. The major factors are:

- Hysteresis (Adsorption-desorption as shown in Fig 8.1),
- The reference dry state,
- The initial moisture content,
- The history of the test specimen,
- The size of the test specimen,
- The drying technique and
- Drying temperature

When the moisture content of a material does not change with time for a given combination of humidity and air temperature, the material is then said that it has reached the equilibrium moisture content (EMC) at that humidity and temperature. In other words, when left undisturbed, the natural end of any adsorption or desorption process is the attainment of EMC. Determining sorption isotherms, the method primarily depends on its accuracy, simplicity, reproducubuluty, stability, range of data obtained, the type of material, time required for measurement and cost. Relatively fast and simple method to determine equilibrium moisture content in food and pharmaceutical substances is to determine the convective drying kinetics. The experiments are conducted on a convective laboratory dryer with representative samples, in a wide range of drying air temperature changes (30, 40, 50, 60 and 70°C) and drying air velocity changes (1, 1.5 and 2 m/s), under particular humidity. The typical graphs of adsorption-desorption isotherm are shown in Fig 8.4 and 8.5. The most preferred experimental methods for determining adsorption-desorption isotherm are:

- Colligative properties method,
- Gravimetric method,
- Manometric method,
- Hygrometric method, and
- Other methods.

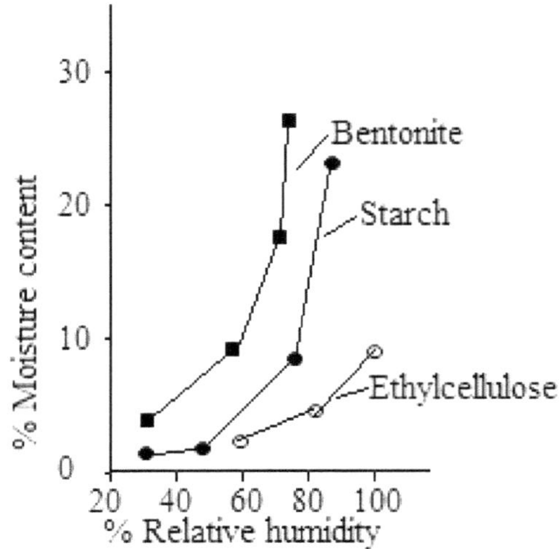


**Fig. 8.4** Equilibrium moisture content curve

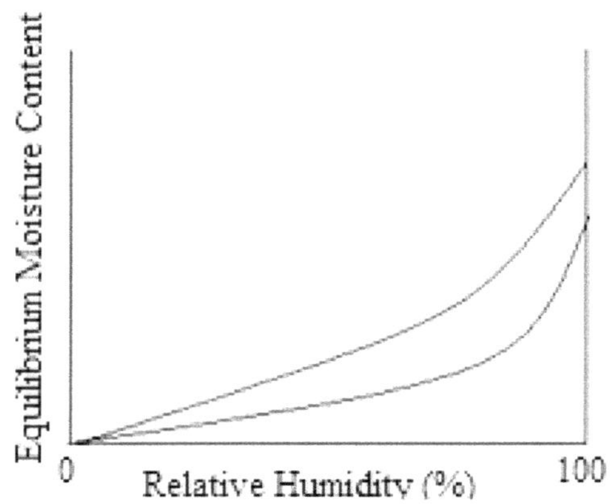


**Fig. 8.5** Sorption-desorption isotherm for porous materials, the upper curve represents desorption and the lower one is sorption

Gravimetric method is based on achieving equilibrium state of samples with the atmosphere of known humidity. There are two types of gravimetric methods:

1. Method with continuous registration of mass sample changes (static systems – isopiestic method, dynamic and evacuated systems), and
2. Method with discontinuous registration of mass sample changes (static, dynamic and evacuated systems).

**Method**

The weighed samples of a solid are placed in a series of closed chambers such as desiccators. Within each desiccator different relative humidity is maintained. Each desiccator contains different and appropriate desiccant. Thus, the samples are exposed to different humid condition at ambient temperature. The samples are kept in the desiccators till the weight of each sample becomes constant. Such condition is called equilibrium condition. The final weight of each sample is determined and the moisture content of each sample is calculated as;

$$\text{The moisture content per g of sample} = \frac{\text{Initial final weight of sample} - \text{Final weight of sample}}{\text{Initial weight}}$$

## Applications of Equilibrium Moisture Content

The EMC graph (Fig 8.4) can indicate

- How can be a material dried (drying conditions)?
- When the drying should be stopped?
- What would be the equilibrium moisture content of a material?
- What would be storage conditions for a material?
- To reduce the moisture content the material should be exposed to reduced humidity.

## Drying Rate Curve

When a material is dried, practically in various phases the drying of a material occurs. The change in moisture content during drying of a solid with respect to time is shown in Fig 8.6. As shown in the figure, the moisture content decreases linearly from A to B. This is called *constant rate period*. The moisture content at point B is known as *critical moisture content*. On further drying the moisture content decreases from B to C, not in a linear manner, the moisture content at the point C is called *equilibrium moisture content*.

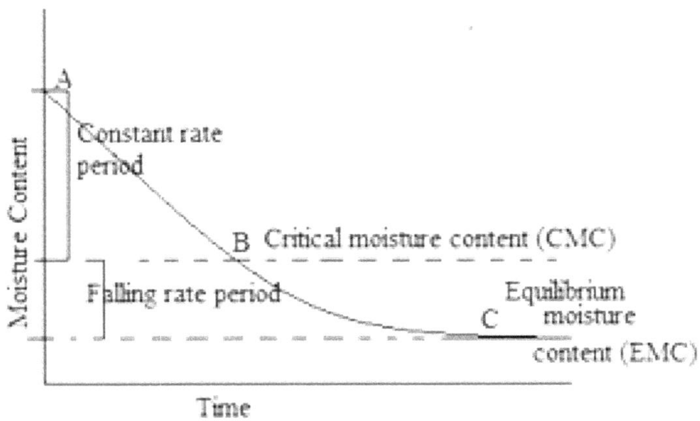


**Fig. 8.6** Drying curve

The effect of external conditions on drying rate of a material has been studied extensively. The external conditions include air, temperature, humidity, and pressure. The plot of the drying rate per unit area of drying surface vs. free moisture content of a solid indicates how the moisture content is reduced due to circulating air as a function of time. Thus, the decrease of moisture content per unit area per unit time is known as *drying rate*. The Fig 8.5 illustrates such a curve called *rate of drying curve*. The term constant drying conditions refers to the following both at air inlet and outlet:

- Constant velocity of air,
- Temperature of circulating air,
- Relative humidity of air,
- Atmospheric pressure.

The material is put in a tray in form of layer. The bottom and sides of the tray are insulated. Air at a particular temperature and humidity is blown over the surface of the tray at a definite rate. At various time intervals the losses in weight of the material are determined and the time required for a predetermined loss in weight is calculated. The experiment is repeated at least for three times to determine an average actual rate of drying.

The drying rate curve (Fig 8.6) indicates two stages– (1) the portion AB of the curve is known as *constant-drying rate and period*, and (2) the portion BC is called *falling-rate and period*. The free moisture content of the material at point B is known as *critical moisture content* (CMC). Since during drying operation, the actual local moisture content of the material is not uniform throughout the layer in the tray, the moisture content of the solid varies with location. In each case the drying period as described above may not take place uniformly. The constant rate period will occur, if the desired moisture content is more than the critical moisture content. This is not true for all cases. For example, the initial moisture content of soap is less than the equilibrium moisture content and the entire drying operation occurs in the falling period. The Fig 5 represents only one type of material composed of non-porous solid particles. But the solid may be porous and hygroscopic also. The Fig 8.7 shows other types of typical drying-rate curve. These curves represent how the slab of solid are dried by air (air drying process). The air flows past both the surfaces of the slab.

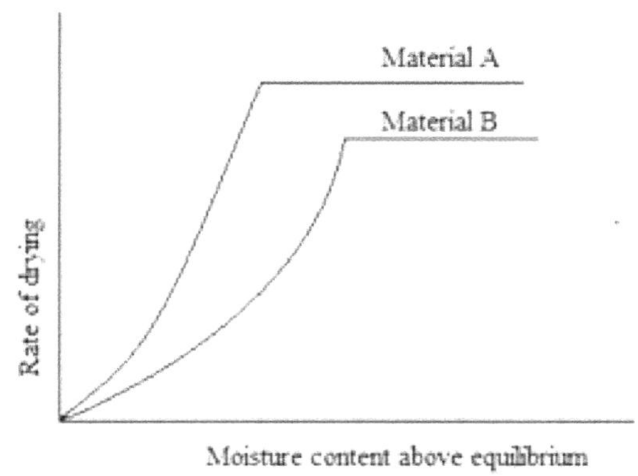


**Fig 8.7** Rate of drying curve

The rate and form of drying-rate curves depend on – 1. structure and composition of solid, and 2. mechanism of drying. Alternatively, this can be explained as shown in Fig 8.6 which explains how the drying rate changes with the change in moisture content. The figure also shows 1. how the behavior of different materials varies considerably, 2. variation in critical moisture content.

When drying rate is plotted against free moisture content, a graph shown in Fig 8.8 would be obtained. Where AB shows the initial adjustment period. During this period the solid material absorbs heat and the temperature increases. Similarly, the moisture present in the solid starts evaporating. The time corresponding to BC indicates the constant rate period. at this zone, the temperature remains constant and the drying rate remains constant. The period CD represents the first falling rate period. The rate of drying gradually during this period. The point C is called the critical moisture content and the point D is called second critical point. At this point D the film of surface water is completely evaporated. The period DE represents the second falling rate period. During this period the drying falls at a faster rate than during the previous period. In this period, the rate of drying depends on the rate of diffusion of vapor of moisture to the surface. The moisture content at the point E is called equilibrium moisture content.

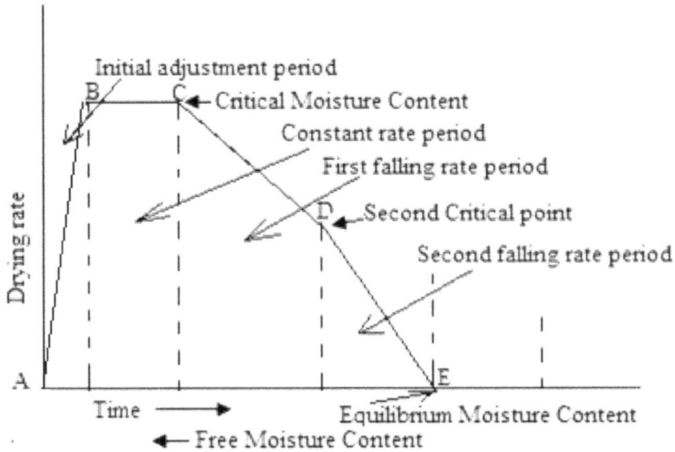


**Fig. 8.8** Free moisture curve

## Mechanism of Drying

There are two processes involved in drying of solid materials:

- *Heat transfer process:* In this process heat is transferred from the heating medium (hot air) to the solid material.
- *Mass transfer process:* In this process mass of water (moisture) is transferred from the surface of material to the environment (surrounding air).

This can be explained by various theories:

(a) Diffusion theory,

(b) Capillary theory,

(c) Pressure gradient theory,

(d) Gravity flow theory, and

(e) Vaporization and condensation theory.

Among these five theories the first three are important and briefly discussed here.

1. *Diffusion theory:* According to this theory the effects of capillary, gravity and frictional forces are not important. The rate of flow of water is proportional to the moisture gradient. That is, the difference between the moisture content of the material and that of the circulating air. The movement of water (moisture) takes place when
   - Water diffuses out from the bulk to the surface of the solid and then evaporates out into the surrounding atmosphere.
   - At an intermediate zone quite below the surface of the solid evaporation takes place. The vapor produced diffuses through the solid into the air.

   However, this theory fails to explain (i) the drying rate at various ranges of moisture gradients, (ii) decrease in diffusivity with decreasing moisture content and humidity, (iii) increase in diffusivity with increasing pressure.
2. *Capillary theory:* This theory is applicable to porous granular material. A material is called porous when it contains a network of inter-connected pores and channels. These capillaries form pores of different sizes at the surface of the solid material. With the start of drying process, meniscuses are formed in the capillaries and a force is exerted. This force works as the driving force for the movement of the water from the bulk to the surface through the channels. The strength of the capillary force depends on the size of the pores. Small pores exert greater capillary force. The small pores draw more water from the larger ones and thus, the larger pores get emptied relatively faster and the moisture content increases at the surface. Air enters into the vacant spaces of the larger capillaries. However, this theory is applicable when the material contains free water. In fact, the liquid/water moves in pores of the granules as well as in the intergranular void spaces. When the diameter of the pores decreases and the pores become small inside the granules than the surrounding granules, water can be removed first from the surrounding granules. Thereafter, the water present in the pores of centrally placed granules get vaporized. This theory is applicable to the hygroscopic porous materials.
3. *Pressure gradient theory:* This theory can explain the process when a material is dried by radiation energy not by normal heating. Radiation interacts with the polarized molecules and ions. As a result, heat is generated internally and the molecules are aligned in an orderly manner instead of random. When the field is reversed, the molecules tend to return to their original orientation. During such orderly orientation, the molecules release kinetic energy (heat) to the internal surface of the solid. Thus, inside the solid particles, the liquid (water) present in the solids, is vaporized. Thus, a vapor pressure gradient is produced and it acts as the driving force for the movement of vapor to the surface. If the rays can penetrate deeply inside the solid mass, the drying process will follow this mechanism.

## Constant-drying-rate Period

The term constant-drying conditions refers to the constant maintenance of velocity of air, temperature, humidity, pressure and position of the material during drying. It also means that the conditions of air inlet and outlet would remain almost same. Usually, the results of the studies on drying rate are plotted either against time or free moisture content. The Fig 8.9 illustrates a typical drying rate curve.

Now during constant-rate-drying-period, it is accepted that the surface of the particles/ granules of a material which are in contact with air, would remain completely wetted. In fact, under any set of air conditions, the rate of evaporation does not depend on the type of material. It is similar to the rate of evaporation from a free liquid surface under same air conditions. However, the rate of evaporation depends on the smoothness of the particle surface. If the surface of the particles is rough, the rate of evaporation will increase. Moreover, the rate of evaporation does not depend on the mechanism of mass (water) transport from lower layer to the particle surface, till the particle surface remain wetted. Even at this period the rate of mass (mass of water) transport from the solid surface to circulating air, and heat transfer from air to the solid surface are reduced, if the heat transfer does not follow insignificantly radiation and conduction.

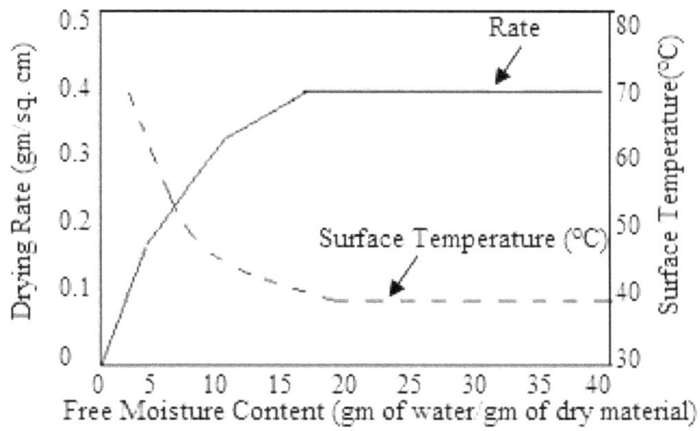


**Fig. 8.9** Typical drying rate curve

The rate of heat transfer and mass transfer can be expressed as under adiabatic condition and under steady-state condition,

The rate of heat transfer, $q = h_G A (t_G - t_i)$ .....(8.1)

and the rate of evaporation from wetted surface into air, $N_a = k_G A (p_i - p_G)$ .....(8.2)

Where,

$q$ = Rate of heat transfer, Btu/hr

$h_G$ = Heat transfer coefficient from air to wetted solid surface, Btu/hr × sq ft × °F

$A$ = Area of the wetted surface of the solid which is in contact with air stream, sq ft

$t_G$ = Bulk temperature of air, °F

$t_i$ = Temperature of wetted surface, °F

$N_a$ = Rate of evaporation from wetted surface into air, lb mole/ hr

$k_G$ = Coefficient of mass transfer from wetted surface to air, lb mole/ hr × sq ft × atm

$p_i$ = Partial pressure of water vapor in gas phase at interface, atm, and

$p_G$ = Partial pressure of water vapor in main body of the gas, atm

Practically, the heat is transferred to the wetted surface by radiation and by conduction, and the actual surface temperature would be slightly more than the wet bulb temperature. In general, it has been observed that during constant-rate drying period the surface temperature is about 2°C higher than the wet bulb temperature of the air. The drying rate per unit area of wetted surface may be derived from eqns. 8.1 and 8.2, and expressed as:

$$\frac{dw}{Ad\theta} = \frac{h(t_G - t_i)}{\lambda} = 18k_G\,(p_i - p_G) \qquad .....(8.3)$$

Where, $\frac{dw}{Ad\theta}$ is the drying rate per unit area, lb/ hr×sq ft

h is the total heat-transfer coefficient, including radiation, etc.

$\lambda$ is the latent heat of vaporization of water at temperature, $t_i$, Btu/lb

The eqn. 8.3 can be used to determine the drying rate. However, in the determination of interface temperature, $t_i$ can influence the driving force, $(t_G - t_i)$ more than $(p_i - p_G)$.

Factors affecting the constant drying rate are:

- Temperature of air,
- Humidity of the air, and
- Velocity of air.

## Tray Dryer

Tray dryer is the most commonly and widely used dryer in various industries, pharmaceutical, chemical and other industries.

### Principles

In this dryer heat transfer takes place by forced convection. The hot air is circulated continuously over the layers of the material to be dried, placed in trays. The wet material present in trays gives up (releases) the moisture to the hot circulating air, and the surface becomes dried. Then the moisture moves up to the surface from the inner layers and is again given up to the air. The process is continued till the material put in the trays is completely dried. The process duration may be reduced, if the material is redistributed in the trays intermittently. According to the Fig 8.10, it consists of two rectangular chambers– one is placed inside the other. Two chambers are separated by a suitable insulating material, such as glass wool, so that the heat cannot move outside or heat cannot come inside from outer environment.

### Construction

Construction of a tray dryer is simple. As shown in the Fig 8.10 and as the name indicates, the inner chamber holds a number of trays. Thus, the inner chamber consists of various racks on its three sides so that the trays can be held horizontally. The number of racks present in the chamber depends primarily on– 1. the capacity or size of the dryer, 2. the gap between two vertically placed trays to be maintained, and 3. capacity of the heater and fan. However, there should be a minimum gap of 4 cm between two vertical trays. The dryers commonly used in the laboratories contain 2 – 3 racks; while dryers used for commercial production may contain more than 20 racks. Although tray dryers are rectangular in shape, but may be square also. The material to be dried is placed in the trays in form of layers of about 1 to 7 cm in deep. In industries, the trays may be placed in trucks on wheels which is subsequently put inside the chamber of the dryer for drying. This type of arrangement becomes convenient when lot size is very large.

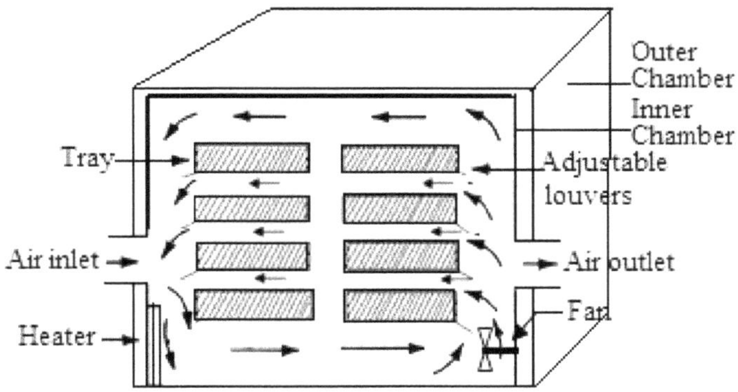


**Fig. 8.10** Schematic diagram of tray dryer

A fan for circulation of hot air over the trays is fitted to the dryer at one side. On the other side, opposite to fan a heater is attached. When the fan runs the hot air moves within the dryer. There is inlet for fresh air and outlet for hot and moist air.

## Working

Wet solid material is spreaded uniformly in the trays in layer. The trays are placed over the racks horizontally inside the chamber. The door of the dryer is closed, the heater and fan are switched on. A thermometer attached to the dryer is used to set and read the temperature. The hot air moves inside the dryer at a speed of about 3.5 m/sec. If the flow of air becomes turbulent, the partial vapor pressure in the atmosphere and also the thickness of the air layer reduces in the boundary area. During circulation, the hot air picks up the moisture from the material surface in the trays through evaporation. Thus, the surface layer gets dried with increase temperature also. On reduction of the moisture content of the surface layer, a pressure gradient is developed which pulls out the water from the inner layer through capillary action and this process continues till drying is completed. During this process of drying about 80% of the discharged air is recirculated within the dryer.

## Uses

Tray dryer is commonly used to dry the sticky materials, granular, crystalline materials, pastes and plastic materials. Thus, tray dryer is used for drying various types of materials prepared in pharmaceutical, chemical and other industries.

## Merits of Tray Dryer

There are various advantages of the tray dryer. Important advantages are mentioned below:

- During drying, loss due to loading and unloading is generally a matter of concern. But, loss of material during handling is negligible.

- Costly materials can also be dried efficiently.
- This dryer can be used for drying various types of materials.
- Tray dryer is used for batch wise drying. Hence, it is very suitable for use in pharmaceutical industries where batch-wise production is conducted and it provides easy identification of problems, if taken place during drying.

In pharmaceutical industries the lot/batch size is relatively small. It amounts to about 250 kg or less; while the lot/batch size goes up to 1000 kg or more per hour in chemical industries.

The same equipment can be used with small modifications or without modification for drying of different types of materials.

### Demerits of Tray Dryer

- For loading and unloading of the dryer more man power is required.
- Cost of drying becomes more.
- Time required for drying is more. However, by re-spreading the material in the tray at least twice the drying time can be reduced.

## Drum Dryer

Drum dryer is alternatively known as *Roller dryer* or *Film Drum dryer*. The roller dryer may consist of a single roll or double rolls.

There are many materials such as colloids which cannot be precipitated from its solution. Hence, the solvent is removed in two steps– one, evaporation till the solution/suspension becomes paste like consistency and second is the drying of the paste to make powder. If the material is very hygroscopic, vacuum shelf dryer is used, otherwise roller or drum dryer is used.

### Principles

A hallow metal drum is dipped partially in the solution to be dried. The drum is heated electrically or by steam. It rotates on its horizontal axis.

When the drum rotates, some amount of the material is adhered and spreaded over the hot surface of the drum and gets dried. The speed and temperature of the rolling drum are adjusted in such a way that the material adhered to the rolling surface is dried within the time required for a complete revolution. In fact, within this time the dried material is removed by a doctor knife, attached to the drum as shown in the Fig 8.11. The scrapped dried material is removed through a chute attached to the knife. A schematic diagram of a drum dryer is shown in Fig 8.11.

### Construction

As shown in Fig 8.11 a single drum dryer consists of a metallic, stainless steel, drum or roller fixed horizontally. The diameter of the drum may vary from 0.6 to 3.0 metres and the length varies from 0.6 to 4.0 metres. The external surface of the drum is smooth and polished. The drum is placed partially within a pan containing the material to be dried. A spreader is attached to one side of the drum and the doctor's knife on the other side. The function of the spreader is to spread the material to be dried over the outer surface of the drum in form of a film. When the drum rotates, it carries a film of the material which is subsequently dried in contact with the hot metallic surface. Before completion of full rotation, the film is dried and then scrapped out by the doctor's knife and the dried material is collected into a suitable container placed below the knife or carried through conveyor to suitable storage tank.

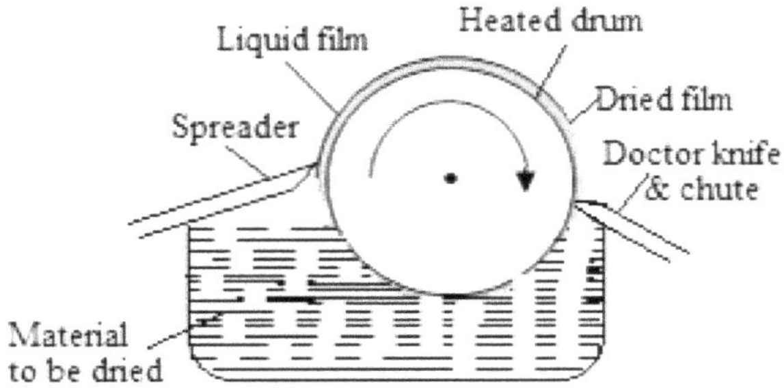


**Fig. 8.11** Schematic diagram of a single drum dryer

## Working

Steam is introduced inside the drum. The heat is transferred from the steam to the surface of the drum and the drum-surface is heated. The heat transfer coefficient of metal being high, the metal is quickly heated. When the drum starts rolling over the material kept in the pan, some amount of material is adhered over the surface of the drum. The spreader spreads the adhered material in form of a layer. The heat is transferred from the metal to the adhered layer through conduction and the material becomes dried. Once the drum reaches the knife, the knife scratches the dried material from the surface. The material is removed and falls down to storage tank or is transported through a conveyor. Usually, the drum rotates at a speed of 1 – 10 revolutions per minute and thus, the film of material remains in contact with the hot metal for a period from 6 – 15 seconds. The processing parameters are:

- Thickness of the film or layer of the material,
- Temperature of steam,
- Rate at which steam to be introduced into the drum, and
- Speed of drum (rpm)

## Uses

For drying the solutions, slurries, suspensions, etc, commonly this dryer is used. For example, solutions of ferrous salts, milk, slurry of starch, suspension of kaolin, zinc oxide, etc. are dried by using drum dryer.

## Merits of Drum Dryer

- In this method, the material for drying remains in contact only for few seconds and becomes dry.

- Since the contact period between the material and heat is too short, the method can be used to dry the heat sensitive materials.
- The dryer being compact like a spray dryer, requires lessspace. Hence, the less working area is required.
- The rate of heat and mass transfers are high enough, since the material remains as a thin film over the drum-surface.
- The final product obtained is completely dried.

### Demerits of Drum Dryer

- Compared to a spray dryer its maintenance cost is more.
- To control the processing parameters such as the feeding rate, thickness of the film, speed of rotation of the drum (rpm), and drying temperature (temperature of the steam) skilled operator is required.
- This method is not suitable for drying poorly soluble salt solutions.

## Spray Dryer

Spray drying is a method that converts a liquid substance to dried powder or particles. A hot gas is used as the drying medium. In 1860, Samuel Percy patented this method in the United States. With respect to its design and application, spray method has been developed a lot. For production of microcapsules and microparticles this method is usually used in pharmaceutical industries. The microparticles and microcapsules are used for delivery of drug. The method is a popular one not in pharmaceutical industries but in food industries. This method is commonly used to prepare milk powder from liquid milk. Drying of thermolabile materials can be done by this method.

### Principles

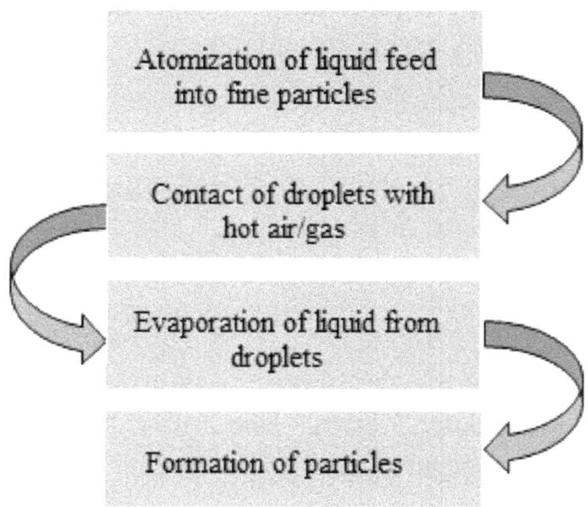


Two main operations are involved in this technology– spray drying and spray congealing. In spray drying the liquid is atomized in form of droplets. The liquid is evaporated out and form the soft particles. In spray congealing, changing of phase takes place. Both the processes are similar except for the flow of energy. In the first operation (spray drying), energy is applied to the droplets, so that the solvent or medium is evaporated out; thus, both energy and mas transfer take place through the droplets. While in spray congealing, the energy is removed from the droplets and the soft mass is solidified. This method is the most suitable and ideal for continuous production of dry solids in form of granules, particles or agglomerates of uniform particle size and size distribution. Even their residual moisture content, bulk density and shape are same or similar.

In spray drying there are three primary steps –

(a) Atomization of the liquid or solution or suspension into fine droplets.
(b) Mixing of the droplets with hot gas stream, evaporation of the liquid, and formation of dried particles.
(c) Separation of dried particles from the gas (heating medium) and collection.

That is, in a chamber containing hot air or gas, the whole process takes place. The sprays are produced by either rotary or nozzle atomizer. The atomizing devices is the *heart* of the spray drying process. Atomizer breaks the liquid into small droplets or sprays.
The primary objectives of an atomizer are:

- To break the liquid in such a way that high ratio of surface to mass is produced to achieve high rate of evaporation.
- To produce particles of desired size, shape and density.

To achieve these objectives, it is necessary to select an appropriate atomizer. Commercially five types of atomizers are there:

1. Rotary atomizer that atomizes by centrifugal energy,
2. Pressure nozzle that atomizes by pressure energy, and
3. Spinning-disk atomizer that atomizes by using kinetic energy.
4. Electrohydrodynamic atomizers
5. Ultrasonic atomizers

Recently, ultrasonic energy is being used in place of centrifugal energy and pressure energy to form the droplets. In this method, a liquid is placed over a rapidly vibrating surface at ultrasonic frequencies. As a result, the liquid spreads, becomes unstable and collapses, and produces very fine droplets of desired size range and shape. A schematic diagram of a spray dryer is shown in Fig 8.12.

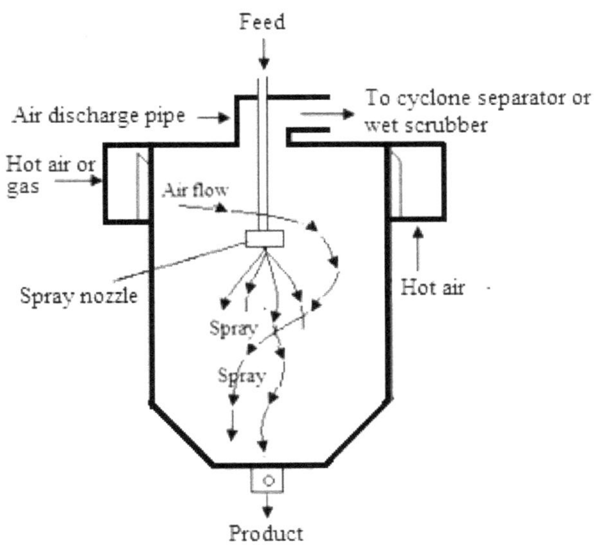


**Fig. 8.12** Schematic diagram of spray dryer

## Guidelines for Selection of Atomizer

1. The inlet temperature must be high enough to obtain a final product with low residual moisture and a higher thermal efficiency.
2. If the feed-flow rate is increased, the outlet temperature is reduced and if the feed-flow rate is decreased, the outlet temperature increases. Thus, the feed-flow rate is to be optimized for required temperature difference between inlet and outlet.
3. High speed of aspirator results higher degree of separation in the cyclone.
4. Residual moisture content is reduced, if the aspirator speed is lowered.
5. Thesize of the particles in the final product becomes larger, when the feed-flow rate is larger.
6. If the feed concentration is increased, the moisture content of the particles also increases; hence, the possibility of agglomeration increases and the irregular particle shapes occurs.
7. The drying air temperature should be below the glass transition temperature to prevent product from collapsing and stickiness in the spray chamber.
8. The Tg of the feed material can be increased by the addition of high molecular weight components such as maltodextrin to makethe spray drying operation convenient.
9. The percentage of moisture content in the feed is also a significant parameter in controlling the Tg, since water depresses Tg considerably.
10. 10.A shorter residence time (RT) (10–15 sec) is recommended for fine particles containing a sufficient amount of free surface moisture content. This enables easy evaporation. A medium RT (25–35 sec) should be applied for fine to semi-coarse sprays that needs to be dried to low residual moisture content. A longer RT is required for drying coarser sprays to obtain lower residual moisture content.

## Construction

The construction of a typical spray dryer is shown in Fig 8.12; it consists of a large cylindrical drying chamber. The bottom of the chamber is short and conical in shape. It is made of stainless-steel. The diameter of the chamber varies according to the need and the height may also vary. The size of the dryer should be as per the lot size or production requirement. At the top of the cylindrical chamber there is an inlet for hot air. Another inlet is provided at the roof of the chamber for carrying spray disk atomizer; through this inlet a cyclone separator is connected.
The diameter of the disk is about 30 cm. The atomizer can rotate at a speed varying from 3000 to 50000 revolutions per minute.

## Working

In a spray dryer the material is dried in three stages:

- The liquid to be dried is atomized first in the form of droplets,
- The liquid/solvent of the droplets is dried due to evaporation,
- Finally, the dried particles are separated from the hot air/gas and collected.

The feed (liquid) is introduced into the drying chamber through the atomizer either by gravity or with the help of a suitable pump. The property such as size and shape of the dried particles depend mainly on the size and shape of the droplets formed. Again, the type of droplets formed depends on the type of atomizer used. Hence, selection of an appropriate atomizer is most important. The rate of introducing feed is adjusted so that the droplets formed are completely dried before reaching the walls of the drying chamber and particles (product) is not overheated.

Hot air or suitable hot gas is introduced through the respective inlet. The pressure of hot air is so adjusted that the droplets formed remain suspended, the surfaces of the droplets are dried immediately and form hard shell. During surface drying the liquid must diffuse out from the bulk of the drops. For quick drying heat must be transferred from outer layer to inner layer at a rate greater than the rate at which the water/liquid diffuses out from the bulk to surface. This will ensure the evaporation of inner liquid at a faster rate and heating of the droplets will be faster. As a result, the internal pressure may increase and the droplets may swell up, the thickness of the shell decreases resulting the increase of permeability of vapor. Under this condition, the shell of the particles will rupture to release the internal pressure, if the shell is neither elastic nor porous (permeable).

Due to the centrifugal force of atomizer, the droplets follow the helical path. The droplets become dried and fall at the bottom of the dryer. All these processes are completed within few seconds. The size of the dried particles ranges from 2 – 500 mm. Factors that control the particle size are:

- Content of solid in the liquid,
- Viscosity of feed material,
- Rate at which feed material is introduced, and
- Speed of atomizer

About 2000 kg of material can be evaporated in an hour by a spray dryer.

## Uses

For the following reasons a spray dryer can be used;

1. Compared to other processes or equipments, spray dryer can produce better form of particles.
2. It has larger capacity; that is, larger amount of material can be dried by this method.
3. Spray dryer can be used to dry the thermolabile materials.
4. This dryer can be used to dry hygroscopic materials.
5. The dryer is used for drying food and pharmaceutical substances.

## Merits of Spray Dryer

1. Spray drying can be used for continuous as well as batch drying.
2. It is a rapid method, within 3 – 30 secs the drying process can be completed.
3. Particles of desired size range can be prepared by this method using a suitable atomizer.
4. Fine droplets provide large surface area and the product exhibits greater solubility.
5. In a single step a solution, suspension or thin paste can be dried and the product becomes ready for package.
6. The method is suitable for drying a sterile solution.
7. Reconstituted product appears to be similar to the fresh material.

8. When an emulsion is dried, the disperse phase remain inside the particle and the continuous phase form the shell.
9. It can be operated in absence of oxygen.
10. It can be operated under closed condition and the solvent can be recovered.
11. It can be used for encapsulation of drug within the base material.

### Demerits of Spray Dryer

1. The dryer occupies large space for its greater size.
2. It is more expensive.
3. Cannot be operated easily because of its large size.
4. Thermal efficiency is low because much of heat is lost in the discharged gases.

## Fluidized Bed Dryer

### Principles

If air is allowed to flow through a bed of solid powder material in the upward direction and if its flow rate is greater than the settling rate of the particles, the particles will remain suspended in the air stream. At this stage the powder bed will be looked like a boiling liquid. This stage is called fluidized. If hot air is used to fluidize the bed, the rate of drying would be increased.

### Construction

The fluid bed dryer contains a stainless-steel chamber having a detachable perforated bottom, known as *bowl*. The material to be dried is taken in the bowl. The top of the bowl is covered by air filter bags. The bowl is fitted to body of the dryer and tightened, so that no powder can go to the outside or can come into the inside. Air is introduced from the bottom of the bowl, heated at required temperature by the heater attached. The hot air is first filtered and then, passed through powder bed. At the top of the equipment, a fan is provided to generate air-flow. The rate of air-flow and temperature are controlled by the regulators provided to the control panel. With the increase of air velocity, the bags present in the dryer start expanding. As a result, the particles undergo turbulent motion. Since, the powders remain in contact with hot air constantly, the powder becomes dried. The Fig 8.13 shows the schematic diagram of a fluidized bed dryer (FBD).

### Working

The wet material to be dried is put in the bowl. The bowl is pushed into the dryer. Fresh air is passed through a prefilter, then through a heater. The air gets heated. The hot air is allowed to pass through the bottom of the bowl. At the same time, the fan is allowed to run. The velocity of air is gradually increased. If the velocity of the air is greater than the settling velocity of the granules, the granules remain suspended in the air stream. After some time, at a particular pressure the frictional drag on the particles becomes equal to the force of gravity. The granules rise in the container due to high velocity of the air, about 3 – 13cm per sec. After some time, the granules fall down in a boiling motion. This state of granules at which they fall back is called *fluidized state*. Each granule is surrounded by hot air/gas for drying. The hot air leaves the chamber after passing through the bag filter. The entrained particles adhere to the inner surfaces of the bags. Entrainment is caused by increase of air velocity. For this reason, the bags are shaken at regular intervals to detach the adhered particle from the bags.

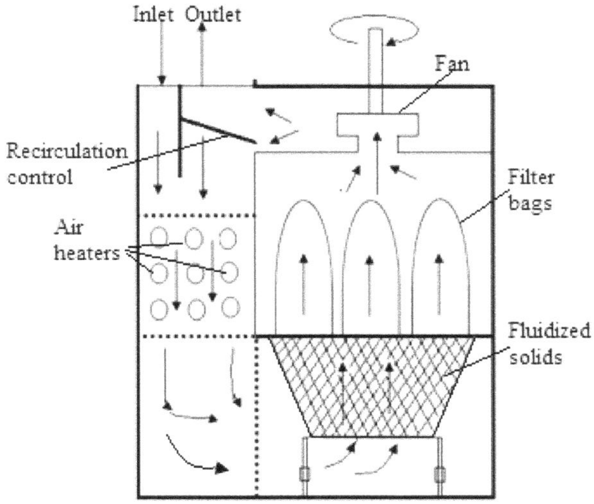


**Fig. 8.13** Schematic diagram of fluidized bed dryer

Since the particles or granules and hot air or gas remain in intimate contact, uniformity in temperature, composition and particle size distribution could be maintained. The rate of drying is constant and the rate of falling is short. In this method about 40 minutes would be required for drying. After completion of drying the material should be left in the dryer for some time for attainment of room temperature. Then the bowl is detached, taken outside for unloading the dried granules.

## Uses

In pharmaceutical industries fluidized bed dryer (FBD) is extensively used for drying the powders and granules for manufacture of capsules, powders and tablets.

Fluidized bed dryer is generally used for three purposes such as mixing, granulation and drying. With some modification it can also be for coating of powders or granules.

### Merits of Fluidized Bed Dryer

1. It requires relatively less time about 20 – 40mins, for complete drying. Compared to tray dryer it is about 15 times faster.
2. It is available in different sizes and thus, capacities; so that during formulation development the method can be optimized for use in commercial production. The capacity may vary from 1 – 200 kg.

3. Since the bowl is moveable, it is convenient for handling and relatively less man power is required.
4. Its thermal efficiency is about 2 – 6 times greater than the traditional tray dryer.
5. Due to its higher mixing and drying efficiency, it has replaced tray dryerin many cases.
6. Compared to tray dryer the drying can be done at low and high temperature with lesser time and more satisfactorily.
7. For both batch drying and continuous drying, it can be used.
8. It requires relatively less floor place, almost similar to a tray dryer.
9. Its output is high.
10. Since it requires less time, FBD can be used for drying thermolabile materials.
11. Since it is a dynamic process, during drying in FBD, every particle remains in motion, the soluble substance cannot migrate as seen in a static process such as tray drying.

### Demerits of Fluidized Bed Dryer

1. During drying some organic substances may acquire electrostatic charges which is not desirable. Efficient electrical earthing of the dryer can avoid this problem.
2. Due to the turbulent motion of fluidized particles, the particles collide each other and produce fines. This problem can be solved by using suitable binding agent.
3. The entrained fine particles should be regularly collected by shaking the filter bags.

## Vacuum Dryer

In pharmaceutical industries vacuum dryer is also widely used. The Fig 8.14 shows the schematic diagram of a vacuum dryer. Vacuum dryer may be of two types– vacuum drum dryer and vacuum oven. Modifications of drum dryer and tray dryer have been combined in such a way that vacuum can be applied and drying can be done at a lower temperature. Construction wise these are strong enough to withstand vacuum within the heating chamber and steam pressure.

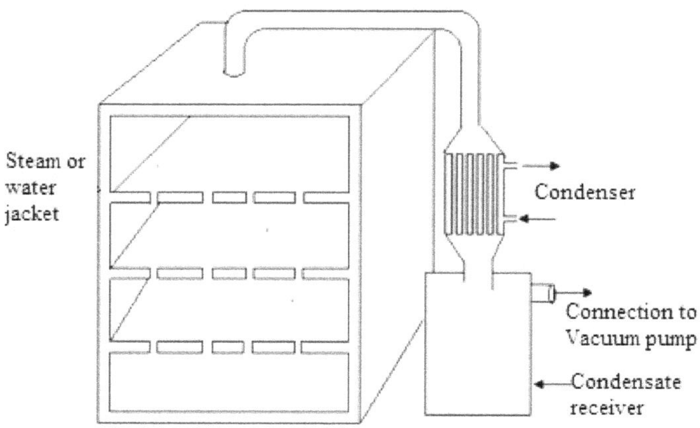


**Fig. 8.14** Schematic diagram of vacuum pump

## Principles

At the outer side of the walls of the dryer, a steam jacket is attached to supply the steam for heating the material. These are primarily used for drying the materials which cannot be dried at boiling temperature (100°C) under normal atmospheric pressure (thermolabile materials). A vacuum pump is connected through a condenser and receiver. If water and water vapor are to be removed from the material, condenser and receiver are not be connected to the vacuum pump. Generally, the drying operation is done under a pressure of 2.3 to 4.6 mm of Hg. Under this pressure the boiling point of water is reduced to 25°C to 35°C. The vacuum ovens used in laboratory or in small industry may be attached to heater to heat the material. The heater must be thermostatically controlled to set the temperature at required level.

There is an alternative design of vacuum oven containing various compartments instead of single one. The advantage of such oven is that the compartments can be closed individually. A large heavy door is not required. If the compartments are sequentially used, the load of vacuum pump would be spreaded and a semi-continuous operation could be achieved.

## Construction

The vacuum oven is basically a jacketed square or rectangular container or vessel. The supports for holding trays are parts of the jacket as shown in Fig 8.14. These supports provide large surface area for transfer of heat through conduction. The oven can be closed by a strong door that can lock the oven air-tight. The oven is connected to a vacuum pump through a condenser and receiver. Some ovens are large in size and can be operated in continuous mode. In pharmaceutical industries the oven may be of 1.5 metres cube having capacity of holding 20 shelves. These ovens are commonly used for commercial production. Such large ovens provide an area of about 45 – 50 sq metres for heating.

## Working

The wet material or the material to be dried is spreaded on the trays in form of layers. The trays are put over the shelves. The door is tightly closed. The vacuum pump is switched on. The pressure inside the oven is reduced gradually up to a desired level. If the material can withstand a temperature of about 35°C; steam is introduced into the oven, so that the inside temperature does not exceed 35°C; water present in the material starts boiling and water vapor produced is removed through the vacuum. After completion of drying the vacuum pump is switched off and steam line is closed. The oven is opened and the dried material is collected from the trays.

## Uses

Typical applications for vacuum dryer include drying of heat-sensitive products, semiconductors, and electronic components such as connectors, switches, and relays after cleaning.

1. Chemical process industries
2. Food processing
3. Pharmaceutical
4. Plastic
5. Timber
6. Paper and other industries

### Merits of Vacuum Dryer

1. For drying of unstable materials this method is suitable.
2. It dries the materials at lower temperature; thus, thermolabile materials are comparatively less damaged.
3. During vacuum drying, contact with oxygen in the air remains absent; hence, oxidative degradation of material cannot take place.
4. A dry extract is prepared by this method, because the extract pass through a viscous fluid stage, under reduced pressure, formation of vapor bubble is increased appreciably and on dryingthe product becomes porous and friable. Thus, this method is very useful for manufacturing of granules for tablet.
5. This method allows the recovery of solvent, which is sometimes very useful particularly for the expensive solvent. For this purpose, condenser is to be used.

### Demerits of Vacuum Dryer

1. In this method the heat transfer coefficient is low. Heating takes place mostly by conduction; particularly from walls and from the shelf, heating takes place through radiation. Thus, there should be close contact between the material and shelf and the shelves should be closely placed.
2. It has limited capacity; for larger amounts *agitated vacuum dryer* is more suitable. The agitated vacuum dryer is similar to agitated vacuum evaporating pan. In place of pan, cylindrical vessel is used to facilitate agitation.

## Freeze Dryer

Freeze drying or lyophilization is a *process in which water is frozen, followed by the removal of frozen water from the sample.* This process is basically used to manufacture certain pharmaceuticals and biologicals that are thermolabile or unstable in aqueous solutions when stored for prolonged periods. But these substances are stable in the dry state. The term 'lyophilization' refers to a process to produce a product that 'favors the dry state'.

### Principles

The freeze drying is a phenomenon called *sublimation drying or lyophilization*, where water transforms directly from solid state (ice) to the vapor state with out being transformed into liquid state. Sublimation of water can take place at pressures and temperature below the triple point; that is, 4.579 mm of Hg and at a temperature of 0.0099°C. The material to be dried is first frozen and then exposed to a high vacuum with or without heat (by conduction or radiation or by both) so that frozen liquid (ice-water) sublimes leaving only the solid. The temperature must be maintained below the triple point temperature; that is, within – 10° to – 30°C. Similarly, the pressure must be maintained below the triple point within 10 to 30 N/m$^2$. This is very difficult, because the vapor must be removed. Otherwise, the vapor pressure will immediately exceed the required value.

The material to be dried is frozen first and the vapor sublimes from the surface of the material. The ice is withdrawn in form of the material in a similar way of drying, during second falling rate in the normal drying process. For this phenomenon to occur, a large area is required. For this reason, a thin layer of the material is exposed to reduce the distance over which the ice must depart through the solid.

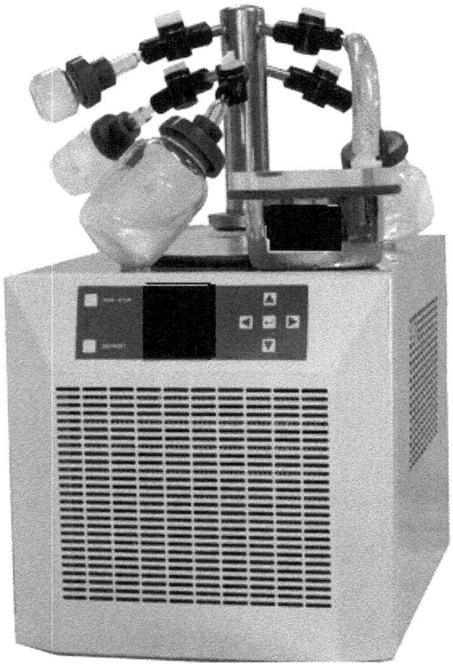

**Fig. 8.15** Bench-top freeze dryer

Finally, to reduce the moisture content of the dried product further, the product must be kept away from the atmosphere. This is possible when the material is taken into the final container and dried. After drying, the container is sealed immediately before removing from the dryer.

## Construction

The Fig 8.15A shows the construction of a typical freeze dryer. Generally, it consists of a drying chamber similar to a tray dryer, heating coils which can radiate heat, a system for condensation of the vapor produced, and a suitable vacuum pump or a steam ejector.

Since the chamber made for vacuum drying allows the trays to be held, it works as a batch wise operation. Thus, it has shelves for holding the material to be dried in trays. The trays should be placed close to the condenser, so that the rate of drying can be increased as much as possible. The condenser contains a coolant of solid carbon dioxide dispersed in acetone or ethyl alcohol. The temperature of the condenser is maintained much below the temperature of the surface of the frozen material.

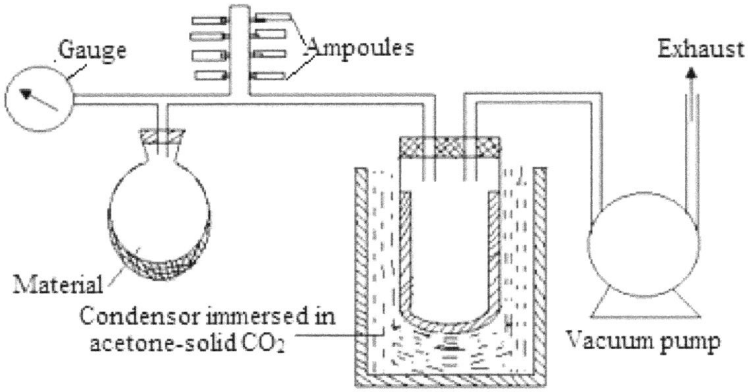


**Fig. 8.15A** Schematic diagram of laboratory scale freeze dryer

## Working

The drying process takes place in different stages as mentioned above. Before applying vacuum, the material is frozen, so that foaming is avoided. In primary drying phase, drying takes place through sublimation and the moisture content is reduced to 0.5 – 1.0%. Further reduction of moisture content below this range, can be done in the second phase of drying. The moisture can be removed below this range by increasing the temperature and applying vacuum (vacuum drying) or by using a suitable desiccant. The process of drying takes place in four stages as shown in the figure 8.16:

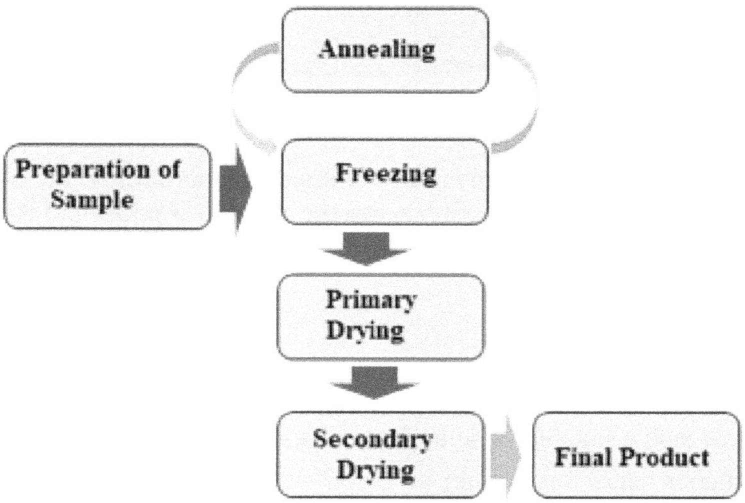


**Fig. 8.16** Processes involved in freeze drying

- Freezing
- Application of vacuum
- Primary drying, and
- Secondary drying

- **Freezing**

This involves pre-freezing and shelf-freezing.

***Pre-freezing:*** Before starting the starting the drying process the solution is pre-frozen. In general, this is done when the larger amount of solution is put in the container, such as whole human blood.

***Shelf-freezing:*** This is done when the containers are partly filled with the solution to be dried. The containers are rotated slowly and almost horizontally in a refrigerated bath. The material freezes in form of a layer around the inner walls of the container as shown in Fig 8.17. As a result, a thin layer with larger surface area is obtained. This helps rapid sublimation and quicker drying. With slower freezing large ice crystals are formed and these large crystals have some adverse effects on some biological products.

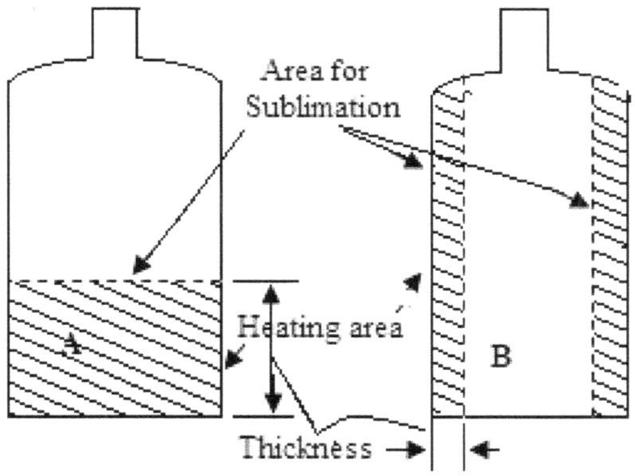


**Fig. 8.17** Freeze drying (a) Before freezing (b) Frozen layer

Sometimes, vertical spin freezing is done which produces small crystals of ice. In this method, the bottles are initially chilled and then spun individually holding the bottle in a vertical position in a stream of very cold air. This makes the content supercooled and freezing occurs very rapidly. In case of blood and blood plasma, production of small crystals of ice is preferred.

Generally, the solution taken in small antibiotic vials is frozen in the dryer or the bulk solution is taken in trays and is frozen. If the solution is taken in small antibiotic vials of squat design, it provides a reasonable surface area and a thin layer is formed.

***Centrifugal evaporative freezing:*** In this method, the liquid or solution is filled in small containers to freeze without refrigeration. Vacuum is applied when boiling occurs. Foaming is avoided by spinning the containers in a centrifuge head. Under the low-pressure rapid vaporization removes the latent heat of vaporization to the extent that the liquid freezes. In fact, before freeze drying about 20% of water is removed from the material. The major advantage of this method is that the primary drying is shortened and no refrigeration is required. In this manner generally the ampoules are spun vertically so that the content is thrown outwards and freezes in a slice shape.

- **Vacuum**

  Vacuum is applied to reduce the pressure sufficiently. Hence, an efficient vacuum pump is required. For small scale operation, usually two-stage rotary vacuum pump is required and for large operation an ejection pump is necessary.

- **Primary drying**

  This step of drying requires two activities – 1. supply of adequate latent heat of sublimation, 2. removal of vapor. Either a vacuum oven or the containers can be attached individually to the outlet can be used for this purpose.

- **Heat transfer**

  This is a critical step because insufficient heat can prolong the drying process and excess heat can cause melting. For example, bottles containing pre-frozen blood are placed in individually heated cylinders or are connected manifold and heat is absorbed from atmosphere.

  Shelf-frozen materials are heated in the shelves of a dryer while ampoules are attached to the centrifuge head or are placed together. In both the cases heat received from the atmosphere would be sufficient. How the material is placed is immaterial, heat must be transferred in a controlled manner, because only about $5W/m^2K$ would be required and overheating will cause melting.

  ***Vapor removal:*** The vapor formed must be removed continuously otherwise vapor pressure will increase and sublimation will stop. In case of small-scale operation, the vapor is absorbed by the desiccant used. Usually, phosphorous pentoxide is used as the desiccant. In large scale operation, condensation is used for removal of vapor. In general, mechanically refrigerated condensers are used. heat transfer is reduced if ice is accumulated. In case of very large-scale operation, the condenser can be scraped and the ice compressed to a solid block is ejected through a special pressure lock.

  In large-scale production, the vapor is usually removed by pump of larger capacity. The pumps should not be affected by moisture. Usually, 1g of ice can produce 1000 lt of vapor.

  ***Rate of drying:*** In freeze drying the rate of drying is low, the ice is removed at a rate of about 1mm depth per hour. A typical drying curve is shown in Fig 8.18. As such, this curve is almost similar to that obtained in normal drying curve. During most of the time the rate of drying is almost constant. The mechanism of freeze drying is similar to the falling rate period of normal drying process. The constancy in the rate is seen because the slow rate of sublimation acts as the rate control factor. In case of normal drying process, the vapor diffuses through the pores and the rate of diffusion behaves as the rate limiting factor. By increasing the heat transfer coefficient, the rate of sublimation can be increased, but it causes melting of the substance (product).

  ***Secondary drying:*** During primary drying process, the moisture content of the product is usually reduced to 0.5%; this can be further reduced in secondary drying process. Usually, the drying temperature is increased to 50 – 60°C under vacuum. The risk of hydrolysis does not exist; if exists, it is negligible.

  In some cases, the secondary drying is started when the moisture content of the product is reduced to 2 – 5% in primary drying phase. This is done because of the slower rate of drying at end phase of primary drying process.

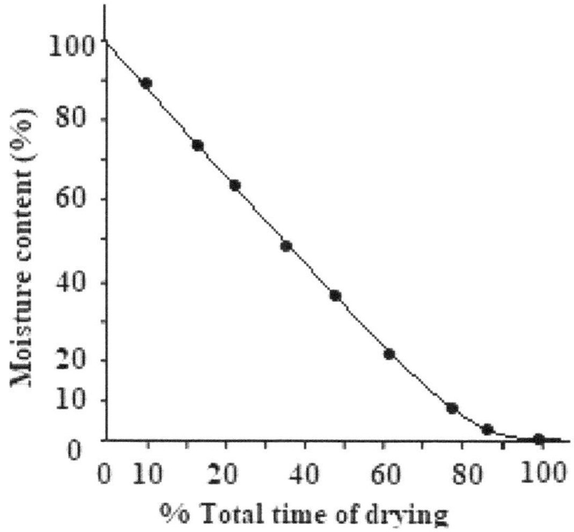


**Fig. 8.18** Rate of drying curve (sublimation)

The freeze-dried product should be packed very carefully so that the product is not exposed to external atmosphere to absorb moisture.

## Uses

- Freeze drier is used in pharmaceutical industries to increase the shelf life of products, such as vaccines and other injectables. The water is removed from the material and the material is filled in a vial and sealed. Thus, the material can be easily stored, shipped, and reconstituted to its original volume for injection.
- In food industry freeze drying is used to preserve food and to make it very lightweight. For example, freeze-dried ice cream, food for astronaut, etc.
- In chemical industries, synthesized products are often freeze-dried to make them more stable, or easier to dissolve in water for subsequent use.
- In bioseparations, freeze-drying can be used also as a late-stage purification procedure, because it removes solvents effectively. Further, it is capable of concentrating substances with low molecular weights that are too small to be removed by a filtration membrane.
- In bacteriology freeze-drying is used to conserve special strains.

## Merits of Freeze Dryer

- Chemical decomposition can be minimized.
- Water can be removed without excessive heating.
- In a dry state the stability of the product can be improved.
- Processing of a liquid can be done easily; hence, aseptic materials can be safely handled.
- The method is more suitable for sterile operations than dry powder filling.

### Demerits of Freeze Dryer

- Handling and processing time are increased.
- Volatile compounds may be removed by vacuum.
- For reconstitution, sterile diluents are required.

## Short Questions

1. Define the term drying. Classify the dryers on the basis of physical state of the material.
2. What are the applications of drying in pharmacy?
3. What is equilibrium moisture content? Define the terms bound and unbound moisture.
4. What does the equilibrium content graph can indicate? What is meant by the 'term rate of drying'?
5. What is principle of tray drying? Draw a diagram of tray dryer.
6. What is a drum dryer? Write down the principle and working of a drum dryer.
7. What are the components present in a spray dryer? What are the points to be considered during selection of an atomizer?
8. Write down how is a fluidized bed dryer work constructed. What are its limitations?
9. Write down the principle of a vacuum dryer. What are the advantages of a vacuum dryer?
10. Briefly mention the principle of freeze-drying process. What is meant by primary drying?

### Long Questions

1. Explain the mechanism of drying on the basis of the equilibrium and rate relationships.
2. Explain the term equilibrium moisture content with the help of a graph.
3. How can the moisture content of a material be defined? What are the factors involved in the determination of equilibrium moisture content?
4. What are various methods that can be utilized for experimental determination of adsorption-desorption isotherm? What are two types of gravimetric methods used in determination of adsorption-desorption isotherm?
5. With the help of a typical drying curve explain the rate of drying. What does a 'drying curve' indicate?
6. Explain the term 'constant-drying-rate' period with the help of a suitable graph.
7. What are the advantages and disadvantages of a tray dryer? Write down the construction of a tray dryer.
8. Write down the principle of a drum dryer and how does it work? What are the advantages and disadvantages of a drum dryer?
9. Write down the principle and working of a spray dryer. Why a spray is used?
10. How does a fluidized bed dryer work? What are its applications and advantages?

# CHAPTER 9

# Distillation

Objectives, Applications and Types of Distillation. Principles, Construction, Working, Uses, Merits and Demerits of (Lab Scale and Industrial Scale). Simple Distillation, Preparation of Purified Water and Water for Injection BP by Distillation, Flash Distillation, Fractional Distillation, Distillation under Reduced Pressure, Steam Distillation and Molecular Distillation.

## Objectives

Distillation can be defined as a process where a single component or constituent of a solution is vaporized from its solution and collection of the vapor of the component separately in pure state as condensed form. For example, distilled water is produced by boiling (distillation) of water and water vapor produced is condensed as water and collected. The process of separation (distillation) includes:

- Separation of one liquid component from non-volatile solute components which may be considered as impurities of the mixture; for example, separation of alcohol from a liquid extract containing plant actives present in a mixture of water and alcohol.
- Separation of one liquid from one or more liquids which are non-volatile in nature and may be miscible, partially miscible or immiscible with the separated component liquid; for example, separation of ether from a mixture of water, ether and alcohol.

In fact, it is difficult to distinguish distillation from evaporation, and from drying. These processes can be defined as;

1. Distillation is the process where the vapor of a liquid is condensed and collected.
2. Evaporation is the process of removal of the solvent and the residue of the solution is collected; however, in some cases the solvent is also collected along with the residue.
3. Drying is the process of removal of the solvent or water and to obtain a solid free from moisture (water) or solvent.

Distillation process occurs in two steps: (i) transformation of a liquid into vapor phase by boiling a solution or mixture, and (ii) transfer of the vapor phase and conversion of the vapor into the liquid by condensation.

The liquid to be distilled is called *distill and* and the condensed vapor is known as *distillate or condensate*.

If one component of the mixture is volatile and other one is non-volatile, the volatile component can be separated by distillation. Similarly, the mixture may contain two volatile liquids, one is more volatile than the other. In such cases, the liquid which is more volatile, would be distilled first after heating of the mixture. Such a distillation process is said to be *partial separation method*. Thus, distillation may be considered as a process of purification. The extent of separation is controlled by the properties of the components.

## Applications

The process of distillation is used for different purposes.

1. Separation of volatile oils from the extract of cloves, anise seeds and eucalyptus leaves by steam distillation.
2. Purification of organic solvents can be done by simple distillation, when the mixture contains only one solvent as a major fraction.
3. Determination of boiling range can be done by simple distillation. This method is used to determine the purity of a solvent.
4. Purification of petroleum products in the petroleum industry is done by flash distillation. The crude oil is refined into different fractions; each fraction is a multi component system. Petroleum ether 60 and 80, etc. are examples of such fractions.
5. Official preparations such as Spirit of nitrous ether, Aromatic Spirit of Ammonia are prepared by simple distillation. As per the Pharmacopoeial specifications, Distilled water and Water for injection are prepared by simple and double distillation methods respectively.
6. Solvent from extracts of drugs of plant origin or from synthetic reaction mixture can be separated by distillation. To prevent environmental contamination, these solvents need to be recovered and the recovered solvent may be recycled for further use.
7. Determination of alcohol content in pharmaceutical preparations is done by distilling the preparation such as Elixirs containing alcohol. For determination of water content in an hydroalcoholic mixture by azeotropic distillation using toluene.

## Types of Distillation

Distillation methods can be classified as mentioned below:

- Simple distillation
- Flash distillation
- Fractional distillation
- Azeotropic distillation
- Vacuum distillation
- Steam distillation
- Molecular distillation
- Destructive distillation
- Compression distillation

## Principles

This has already been mentioned that distillation is a process of separation and purification of components in a liquid mixture. To understand or solve any distillation problem, it is necessary to understand the vapor-liquid equilibria between the liquid and vapor phases of a system. Distillation methods depend on the relative volatilities of the components of the mixture.

Two liquids may be miscible in all proportions. The mixture of such two liquids is called binary mixture. For example, water and alcohol, water and acetone, carbon tetrachloride and benzene, etc. Before understanding the principle or theory of distillation, it is necessary to understand theories of ideal and real (non-ideal) solutions. All the discussions mentioned here shall be limited to the binary systems only.

## Ideal Solutions

Ideal solution is defined as a system in which the properties of the components do not change on mixing, other than dilution.

During preparation of an ideal solution, neither heat is evolvednor absorbed. The final volume of such mixture may increase or decrease when two liquids are mixed. For example, water and alcohol have similar properties and can form an ideal solution. The ideal solutions are characterized by an important physicochemical property such as vapor pressure.

## Raoult's Law

This law speaks about a quantitative relationship between the concentration and vapor pressure of a solution. According to the Raoult's law, *the partial vapor pressure of each volatile component of a solution is equal to the vapor pressure of the pure component multiplied by its mole fraction in the solution at a particular temperature.*

Solution is a homogeneous system; it contains solute in dissolved state in a solvent. The solute may be single component or a mixture of components. Similarly, solvent maybe one liquid or a mixture of liquids. Thus, a solution may be simple system or multiple system where number of solutes are more than one. The solute may be a solid or liquid. The numbers of components present in the solution are expressed on mole fraction scale. For example, $n_A$ represents the mole of solute present in the solution. To explain the Raoult's law, let us consider the example of a mixture of benzene and toluene. At 100°C, toluene has a vapor pressure of 556mm. If partial pressure is plotted against composition as shown in Fig 9.1, the partial pressure of toluene at various compositions will fall along a straight line from 556 mm for pure toluene to zero for pure benzene.

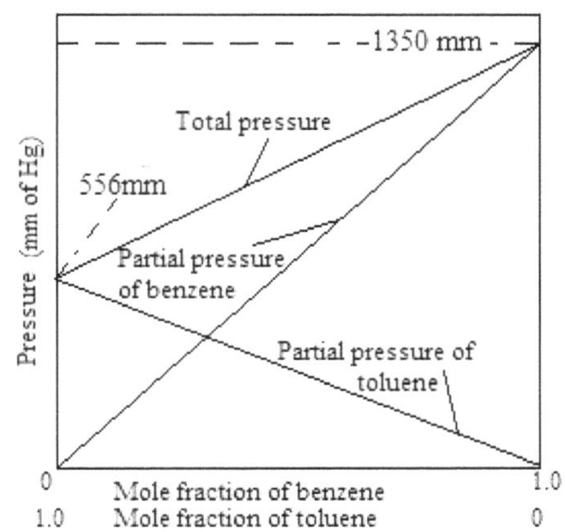


**Fig. 9.1** Plot of pressure against mole fraction (Vapor composition curve)

When the temperature is 100°C, the vapor pressure of pure benzene is 1350 mm. The total pressure for any composition will be the sum of the partial pressures of the two solvents at that composition and temperature.

It is observed graphically that the composition of the liquid becomes 0.26 mole fraction of benzene and 0.74 mole fraction of toluene at the point where total pressure is 760 mm. The composition of vapor is calculated from the partial pressure by using Dalton's law. In this case, $P_A$ = 351 mm and total pressure = 760 mm. Thus, the composition of vapor = $\frac{351}{760}$ = 0.46 (mole fraction of benzene). Similarly, at 100°C as per the plot, the abscissa of the point on the liquid curve is 0.263 and on vapor curve is 0.462. This calculation can be done by using Raoult's law for component A (more volatile) as;

$$p_A = P_A . x \quad .....(9.1)$$

Where, $p_A$ is the partial pressure of component A in the vapor phase (above the solution),

The mole fraction of A is $x$, and

$P_A$ is the vapor pressure of A in pure state at the experimental temperature of the solution.

Similarly, for component B,

$$p_B = P_B(1 - x) \quad .....(9.2)$$

Where, $p_B$ is the partial pressure of the component B in the vapor phase (above the solute),

$p_B$ is the vapor pressure of pure B at the same temperature.

If P is the total pressure, then

$$P = p_A + p_B$$

$$= P_A . x + P_B (1 - x) \quad .....(9.3)$$

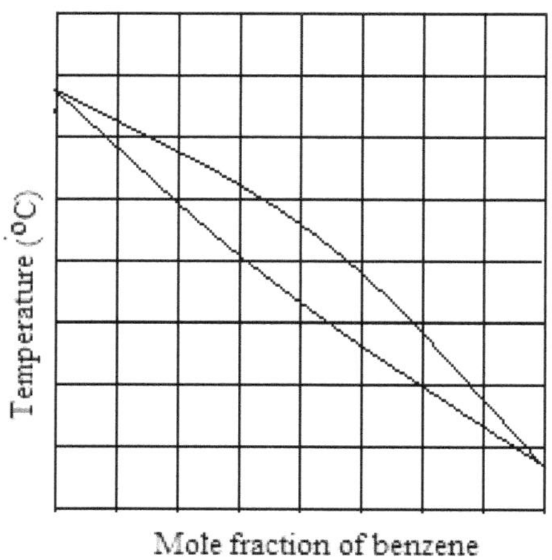


**Fig. 9.1A** Boiling point diagram for benzene-toluene system at 1 atm.

The mole fraction of component A in the vapor, is the ratio of partial pressure of A to the total pressure,

Thus, the mole fraction of A = $\dfrac{p_A}{p_A + p_B}$

$$= \frac{P_A x}{P_A + P_B(1 - x)} \quad .....(9.4)$$

At a series of temperatures in between boiling points of the two pure components, the points can be calculated on both the vapor and liquid curves of the boiling points diagram for a particular pressure, provided that the mixture of the two components obeys Raoult's law throughout the entire range of compositions.

Raoult's law is applicable only to the mixtures in which the components may be chemically similar and they do not react each other. Hence, mixtures of benzene and toluene obeys the Raoult's law; while the mixtures of alcohol and water, acetic acid and water, methanol and acetone do not. In practice, most of the combinations deviate more or less from this law.

## Volatility

When a substance is present in a solution, it vaporizes and the vapor remains present in the vapor phase above the liquid phase. The volatility of the substance can be defined as the ratio of the concentration (mole fraction) of the substance in the vapor phase to its concentration in the solution in terms of mole fraction.

Let us assume that a solution contains a substance A whose concentration in the vapor phase is $Y_A$ and its concentration in the liquid mixture is $X_A$in terms of mole fraction. Then the volatility of A ($v_A$) may be mathematically expressed as:

Volatility of component A, $v_A = \dfrac{\text{Mole fraction of A in vapor phase}}{\text{Mole fraction of A in liquid phase}}$

$$= \frac{Y_A}{X_A}$$

## Relative Volatility

Say, the vapors of two components A and B of a mixture are in equilibrium with the liquid phase; then the relative volatility of component A (more volatile) with respect to the component B can be expressed as;

$$\alpha_{AB} = \frac{Y_A / X_A}{Y_B / X_B} \quad .....(9.5)$$

Where, $\alpha_{AB}$ is the relative volatility of component A with respect to the component B,

Y is the mole fraction of components in vapor phase and

X is the mole fraction of components in liquid phase.

In case of a binary system, $Y_B = 1 - Y_A$ and $X_B = 1 - X_A$.

By substituting the above and eliminating A and B in the equation 9.5, we can write the equation 9.5 in a general form as follows;

$$\alpha = \left(\frac{Y}{1-Y}\right)\left(\frac{1-X}{X}\right) \qquad .....(9.6)$$

When the liquid mixture obeys the Raoult's law and its vapor phase obeys the Dalton's law, then

$$Y = \frac{P_A.x}{P} \text{ and } 1 - Y = \frac{P_B(1-x)}{P}$$

or

$$\alpha = \frac{p_A}{p_B} \qquad .....(9.7)$$

## Dalton's Law

According to the Dalton's law, *the total pressure of a mixture of gases is equal to the sum of the partial pressures of the components of the mixture.*

Assuming that two components A and B of a liquid mixture are in equilibrium.

Thus, the total vapor pressure = partial pressure of A + partial pressure of B

$$P = P_A + P_B$$

Or,

$$P = p_A.x + p_B(1-x) \qquad .....(9.8)$$

The properties of the components are additive in nature; that is, the total vapor pressure of the mixture is the weighted average of the vapor pressures of pure components.

The Fig 9.1 shows the ideal behavior of the liquid mixture as per the Raoult's law.

## Henry's Law

Henry's law is similar to Raoult's law under certain conditions. Henry's law states that *the partial pressure of a component above a solution is proportional to its mole fraction in the liquid.* The law can be expressed as:

$$p_A = C.x \qquad .....(9.9)$$

Where, pA is the partial pressure of A above the liquid mixture; $x$ is the mole fraction of A in the liquid mixture and C is a constant only at constant temperature. If the equation 9.1 is compared with equation 9.9, it can be said that Raoult's law is primarily a special case of Henry's law wherein the constant C in equation 9.9 is vapor pressure of the pure component.

## Real Solution

It has been stated earlier that most of the practical systems show variation from Raoult's law. The deviation from Raoult's law may either be positive or negative as shown in the Fig 9.2.

Such deviation depends on the nature of the liquids and the temperature. These solutions are called real solutions. Deviation from Raoult's law takes place due to solute-solute, solute-solvent or solvent-solvent interactions.

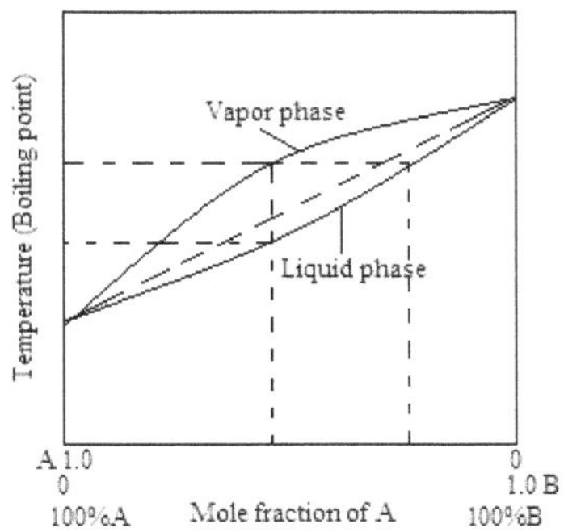


**Fig. 9.2** Boiling point diagram of a real binary system (Positive deviation)

## Positive Deviation

When the vapor pressure of a component is greater than the sum of the partial pressures of the individual components, it is called positive deviation. This is observed in mixture of carbon tetrachloride and cyclohexane, benzene and ethanol. The Fig 9.2 shows such deviation. The positive deviation takes place when the components have different polarities, degrees of association, and lengths of hydrocarbon chain. The degree of deviation from Raoult's law decreases with increase in temperature. The difference in the nature of the components are reduced at higher temperature. On the other hand, the miscibility of the two components decreases with decrease in temperature and finally phase separation takes place.

## Negative Deviation

When *the vapor pressure is lower than that of the sum of the partial pressures of the individual components*, it is called negative deviation shown in Fig 9.3. Such behavior is observed in mixture of chloroform and acetone, water and nitric acid, etc. Negative deviation takes place when hydrogen bond, salt and hydration take place between two components of the solution. Thus, the vapor pressure of each component is lowered with respect to the behavior of an ideal solution.

Raoult's law does not hold good throughout the entire range of concentrations of a non-ideal solution. Only in very dilute solutions the Raoult's law holds good.

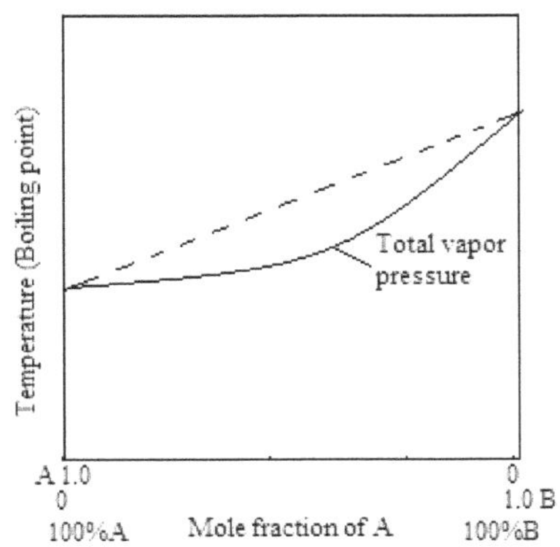


**Fig. 9.3** Boiling point diagram of a real binary system (Negative deviation)

## Distillation

As such there are various methods of distillation and all these methods are based on the particular use of the distillate. Primarily, in one method, the vapor of the boiling liquid is collected and condensed. No part of the condensate is returned to the still. This type of distillation is classified into two important types–

1. simple or differential distillation, and
2. equilibrium or flash distillation.

In another method, a part of the condensate is returned to the still, so that the liquid comes in direct and closed contact with the vapor moving towards the condenser. Such type of distillation is called rectification or fractional distillation.

Before discussing about the various methods, some information about the equipments used for the purpose are mentioned below. Generally, three types of equipments are used – 1. distilling still, 2. condenser, and 3. receiver.

### Still

This is a container or vessel in which the liquid to be distilled is taken. The still is also called as vaporizing chamber, because the liquid is boiled inside this container and vapor is produced. The size of the still varies from small to large and the material for construction may be glass or metal. The material used for construction of still must not react with any of the components of the liquid to be distilled. The size of the still depends on the particular use of the condensate. For example, round bottom glass still of varying capacity such as from 500 ml to 5 lt are used in the laboratories; while in production the size of the still may go up to few thousands of liters. Normally, these stills are made of stainless steel, copper, or any other suitable material.

The mouth of the still is called neck. There may be single-neck, double or triple-neck still. The central neck is used for attaching the condenser in such a way that air-tight fitting becomes possible. If the still contains one or two more necks, out of remaining necks one is used to insert a thermometer and through the third one, the feed material is introduced into the still.

Some liquids can bump or froth on heating. The froth may carry the liquid with the vapor, so that the froth along with vapor can enter into the condenser. This can be prevented by inserting a trap between the still and condenser. Heating of the still may be done by steam or by electric means or directly by burner(flame).

### Condenser

Primary function of a condenser is to facilitate condensation of vapor on the way to receiver. The condenser is surrounded by a water jacket to circulate cold water; so that, the hot vapor is cooled and condensed into its liquid state. Heat gained by the vapor during boiling of the liquid is transferred to the circulating water through the glass-jacket and the vapor is condensed.

The selection of a condenser depends on the boiling point of the liquid and volatility of the component. The component which is more volatile, shall be condensed first and fast. There are different types of condensers. Whatever may be the type, a condenser should have following characteristics:

- It should be easily cleaned.
- It should provide maximum cooling surface; so that the vapors moving inside the condenser can be cooled fast. The rate of condensation depends on the area of the condensing surface and the rate of transfer of heat.
- The condensing surface should be a good conductor of heat. The rate of condensation depends on the rate of heat transfer. The metal condenser is better than the glass condenser, because metal is better conductor of heat.
- The inner surface of the condenser should be such that it should not adhere the condensed liquid film formed on the surface. The liquid film should immediately be removed, otherwise the efficiency of the condenser will decrease. For this reason, a condenser is fitted in an inclined direction.
- The cold water is circulated almost in opposite direction to provide better cooling of the condensing surface. The warm water should immediately be replaced by cold water. For this reason, the inlet for cold water is provided to the lower end of the condenser and warm water is removed through the outlet provided near the top of the condenser.

The lower end of the condenser is connected to the receiver through an appropriate adaptor, if the mouth of the receiver and the end of the condenser do not match each other.

In case of vacuum distillation, the adaptor should have a provision to connect with the vacuum pump. There are three types of condensers:

1. Single-surface condenser can again be classified into categories – plain tube condenser and spiral condenser as shown in Fig 9.4.
2. Double-surface condenser is another type of condenser having greater efficiency of condensation.
3. Multi-tubular condensers are usually used for commercial production of distilled water. Such condensers are usually made of metal.

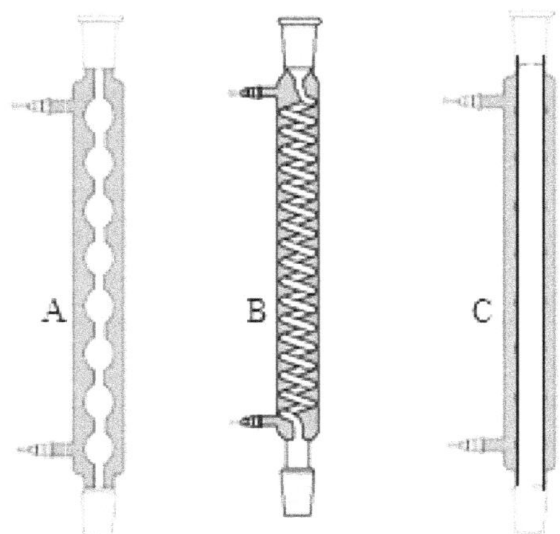


A-Bulb condenser, B- Spiral condenser
C- Plain condenser

**Fig. 9.4** Different types of condensers

4. When the liquid boils at a temperature more than 130°C, water-cooled-condensers are not suitable. In such cases, air condensers can be used. Air condensers are 1 – 2 metres long tubes which can be fitted to the distilling flask or still either through a rubber bung or through standard joint.

### Receiver

These are used to collect the distillate. It may be a simple round bottom flask, may be full flat bottom or of partly flat bottom. Sometimes the receiver is immersed in an ice-bath or any other freezing mixture, so that the volatile component is not lost.

The receiver can be used to separate component heavier than or lighter than water. Such receivers have two taps – 1. one for removal of oil (lighter than water and is collected above the water layer) and the tap is attached above the water layer; 2. second tap for removal of heavier layer (the component is heavier than water and is collected below the water layer, at the bottom); that is, at the bottom.

When the oil is lighter than water, the oil accumulates at the top of the receiver and is removed from the tap attached to the upper side of the receiver. Another tap attached to the lower side is used to remove the aqueous layer for returning to the still.

When the oil is heavier than water, the upper tap is used to remove overflown aqueous layer for returning to the still and the tap present in the lower end of the receiver is used to remove the oil accumulated at the bottom.

## Simple Distillation

Simple distillation process is used to purify many organic liquids. The process requires one distillation flask, one condenser, and one receiver. If necessary, the process can be carried out under reduced pressure by connecting a vacuum pump to lower end of the condenser. This process is also called *differential distillation*, because on the basis of the differences in volatilities and vapor pressure of the components of the liquid, the distillation process is carried out. Source of heat may be steam, electricity, or flame (Bunsen burner). When steam is used as a source of heat, the flask should be jacketed. If electricity is used as the source of heat, there should be a heating coil inside the flask. In case of Bunsen burner, flame through a wire-gauge is used to heat the flask as shown in Fig 9.5. The condenser has one inlet and one outlet. The inlet provided at the lower end is used for introducing cold water and the outlet provided at the upper part of the condenser is for removal of warm water. The lower part of the condenser is inserted into the receiver through a suitable adaptor. In this method the vapor produced by the boiling liquid is immediately separated from the liquid and condensed. In case of binary system, a simple, batch distillation occurs. This simple batch distillation process is governed by the Rayleigh's equation which is expressed as:

$$\ln \frac{W_o}{W_1} = \int_{x_1}^{x_0} \frac{dx}{y - x} \qquad \text{.....(9.10)}$$

Where,

$W_o$= the total number of moles of the liquid in the still before distillation,

$W_1$ = the total number of moles of the liquid in the still after distillation for some time,

$x_o$ = the mole fraction of the more volatile component in $W_o$,

$x_1$ = the mole fraction of the more volatile component in $W_1$,

x and y are the liquid-vapor composition relationships obtained from equilibrium diagram obtained by plotting x vs $\frac{x}{y-x'}$. The plot can be drawn and the integrated value of $\int_{x_1}^{x_0} \frac{dx}{y-x}$ can be calculated by measuring the area under the curve between the limits of $\mathbf{x_o}$ and $x_1$. The equation 10 remains valid even when W and x are expressed in terms of weight fraction respectively.

## Principle

A liquid will boil when its vapor pressure becomes equal to the atmospheric pressure surrounding it. Thus, if the volatility of the components is well different, their separation would be better by simple distillation. When the liquid is gradually heated, more and more vapor of the component (more volatile) will be produced and when the vapor pressure becomes equal to surrounding atmospheric pressure, the liquid starts boiling. The vapor so produced, if condensed will be converted into liquid and the condensed liquid is collected in the receiver.

## Construction

The equipment used in simple distillation is also simple. One distillation flask, one condenser and one receiver are required. The flask is to contain the liquid to be distilled. The condenser is attached to the flask using a suitable adaptor to introduce a thermometer. The condenser is connected to two pipes through two inlets – one at the lower part of the condenser to supply cold water and the other one at the upper part of the condenser pipe for removal of warm water. The condenser is attached to the distillation still, air-tight. The lower end of the condenser is introduced into a receiver. The flask is heated electrically or through steam supplied through a steam-jacket.

## Working

If the steam is used as the source of heat, the steam jacket is made free from air present in the jacket. Steam replaces the air through the vent. When steam is introduced into the jacket, initially no smoke is removed from the vent. When the air is completely replaced, almost white stream of steam is being removed through the vent, the vent is slightly opened and steam is introduced to maintain a required pressure. Supply of cold water is started. Once the liquid starts boiling, the vapor will be formed rapidly and pass through the condenser. Due to circulation of cold water, the surface of the condenser becomes cool. When the vapor comes in contact with cool surface of the condenser, the heat is transferred from the vapor to water. As a result, the vapor will condense and is converted to liquid which will be collected in the receiver.

### Uses

- Simple distillation is used in pharmaceutical industries to prepare distilled water for analysis in laboratory.
- To prepare aromatic waters.
- To purify organic solvents.
- To eliminate the non-volatile solids from volatile liquids
- After re-distillation, the distillate is used as Water for injection.

## Laboratory Scale Simple Distillation

For distillation in laboratories, simple distillation unit as shown in Fig 9.5 is used. The apparatus consists of a distillation flask fitted to a condenser in an inclined position and the lower end of the condenser is inserted into a receiver through an adaptor. Generally, the distillation unit used in the laboratories is made of all glass. A straight or spiral condenser is used for condensing the vapor. The inlet at the lower end of the condenser is connected to a water tap through a pipe to supply the cold water. At the upper end of the condenser there is an outlet to remove the warm water. The outlet is connected to a drain-pipe. The liquid to be distilled is introduced into the still up to its two-third volume. The distillation flask is heated by a Bunsen burner. The cold water is circulated through the jacket and the condensed water is collected in the receiver.

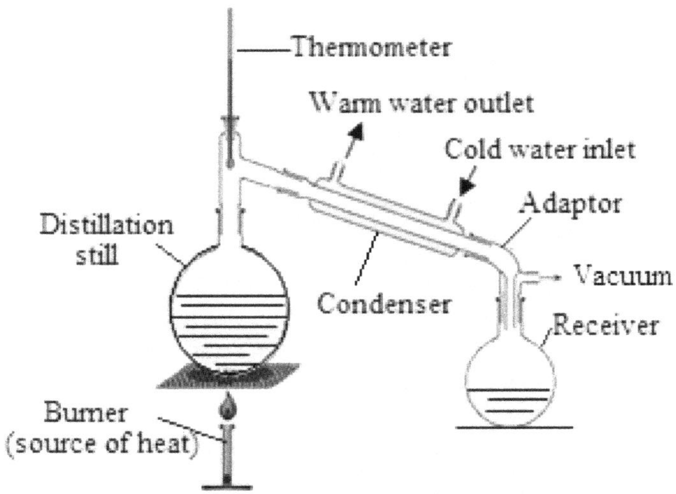


**Fig. 9.5** Schematic diagram of simple distillation unit

### Merits of Simple Distillation

- A simple distillation process requires only one cycle in order to obtain the required product.
- The equipment required is simple
- Rate of distillation is fast
- Less energy is required

### Demerits of Simple Distillation

- The difference in boiling points of the components in a liquid must be high.
- Separation of fractions is poor
- Requires pure liquid

## Industrial Scale Simple Distillation

### Construction

An equipment shown in Fig 9.6 can be used in industrial scale for simple distillation. The still is made of stainless steel, copper, suitable metal. The still is surrounded by a jacket for introduction of steam. Thus, steam is the source of heat. The distillation still is fitted to a bent condenser. Near the neck, a sight glass is provided to see the level of the liquid inside the still. At the bottom of the jacket there is an inlet for introduction of steam and an outlet for removal of steam condensate. The bent tube is attached to a spiral condenser immersed in a water bath. The cold water is introduced at the bottom and the warm water is removed at the top. The lower end of the condenser is inserted into a receiver to collect the condensed component.

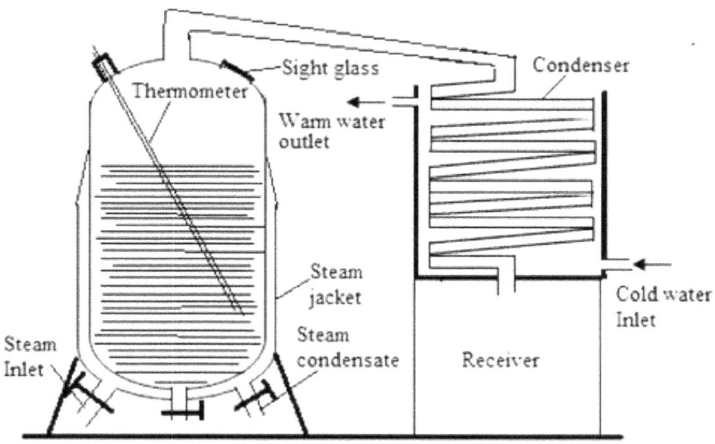


**Fig. 9.6** Schematic diagram of large scale simple distillation

### Working

The liquid to be distilled is introduced into the still up to its two-third volume. Small pieces of porcelain are introduced into the still, to avoid bumping. One thermometer of 0 – 300°C is inserted into the still through a hole made for the purpose and for reading the temperature. The bulb of the thermometer should remain immersed into the liquid. Steam is introduced into the jacket, air in the jacket is replaced completely by the steam and heating of the still is continued. Cold water is circulated. The receiver attached firmly starts collecting the condensed liquid. As discussed earlier, distillation is continued till the liquid is not concentrated; that is, when a small volume of the liquid is left, the distillation should be stopped. For preparation of distilled water, potable water (drinking water) is used as the liquid to be distilled.

## Preparation of Purified Water or Water for Injection BP By Distillation

Ina laboratory, the purified or distilled water is produced by special technique, because:

- Water contains dissolved gases which must be removed before distillation and the distilled water produced should not be contaminated with those gases.
- The solids (residue) present in water should not be allowed to hydrolyze. Hence, distillation should not be continued with concentrated or residual water. The distillation process should be discontinued when the water becomes concentrated.

This is possible, if in a batch distillation, the middle fraction is collected. But, in pharmaceutical industries, the distillation is being done continuously. In such cases, certain precautions are to be taken:

- The feed water is heated before distillation, to remove the dissolved gas (de-gassing). This can be done by feeding the water warmed after condensation. This has another advantage also; it gives the thermal efficiency.
- Moreover, baffles are provided in the path of the vapor; that is, between the still and the condenser jacket to prevent entrapment of liquid droplet by the vapor.
- A device is attached to the still (boiler) to maintain a constant level of water, so that, excessive concentration of salt can be avoided.
- Depending on the hardness of water, solids (scales) are deposited in the still (boiler); hence, on regular basis the de-scaling should be done.

A typical distillation unit is shown in Fig 9.6. The still (boiler) may be made of cast iron, but the baffles and condenser tubes are made of stainless steel, copper, or any other suitable metal.

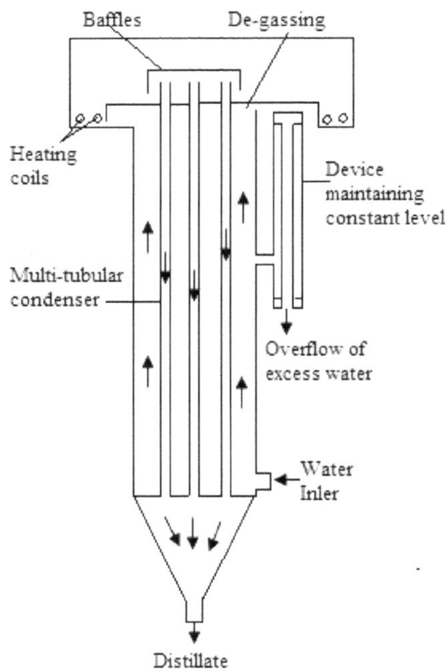


**Fig. 9.7** Distillation unit for preparation of water for injection

## Flash Distillation

In this process the entire mixture is suddenly vaporized (flash) by passing the feed (liquid) from a high-pressure zone to a low-pressure zone.

### Principle

A hot liquid mixture is allowed to enter from a high-pressure zone into a low-pressure zone, the entire liquid mixture is suddenly vaporized. This process is called *flash vaporization.* When such process takes place in a chamber, the chamber becomes cool. The vapor phase is a mixture of molecules of high boiling fraction as well as low boiling fraction. The molecules of high boiling fraction condense first and the molecules of low boiling fraction remains as vapor. Thus, the liquid and vapor remain in intimate contact till an equilibrium is attained. The vapor is separated from the liquid and vapor mixture; the liquid is collected separately and the vapor is allowed to condense.

### Construction

It consists of a pump connected to a feed receiver. The pump sends the feed into the heating chamber containing a suitable heating system. The other end of the pipe is directly introduced into the vapor-liquid separator through a reducing valve. At the top of the separator, an outlet is provided for the vapor to exit and at the bottom there is an outlet for the liquid to be collected.

### Working

The feed is introduced into the chamber through a heater at a particular pressure. The liquid becomes hot and enters into a vapor-liquid separator through the pressure reducing valve. Since, the pressure drops, flashing of hot liquid occurs. This increases the vaporization process. Due to sudden vaporization, cooling takes place. As a result, the molecules of high boiling fraction condense; while the molecules of low boiling fraction remain as vapor. The mixture is allowed to remain as such for a sufficient period of time; the vapor and liquid phases come to a stage of equilibrium and separate. The separated liquid is removed through the outlet provided at the bottom. The schematic diagram of the equipment is shown in Fig 9.8. If feed is introduced continuously into the still, a continuous flashing takes place and continuous flash distillation occurs. The operating conditions are regulated in such a way that the rate of feeding becomes equal to the rate of removal of the product and the ratio of concentration of vapor to liquid remains constant.

### Uses

- The method is very useful for separating the components having widely different boiling points.
- For refining crude oil in petroleum industry.

### Advantages

- Flash distillation is a continuous process.

➢ The method is used for preparing multicomponent system of narrow boiling range; for example, petroleum ether 60, 80, etc. obtained in oil refinery.

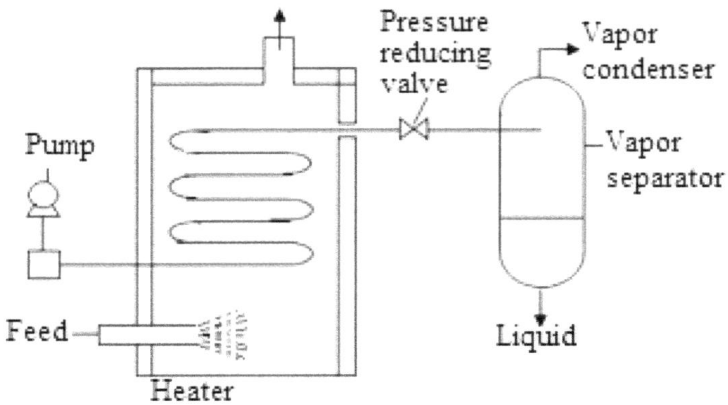


**Fig. 9.8** Schematic diagram of flash distillation equipment

### Disadvantages

➢ The method is not effective for separating components of almost similar volatility.
➢ The method is not suitable for two-component systems.
➢ The method fails to produce almost pure components efficiently, because the condensed vapor and residual liquid are not pure.

## Fractional Distillation

### Principle

For separation of miscible liquids, the fractional distillation process is used. The fractional distillation depends on heating of the mixture, repeated condensation of the vapor, and reheating of the liquid. At each stage, equilibrium between the liquid and vapor is established. This can be done by using fractionating column. Fractional distillation is a mass transfer process, involves counter-current diffusion of the components at each stage of equilibrium. The fractionating column is represented diagrammatically in the Fig 9.9. The concentration gradient acts as the driving force in fractional distillation. The less volatile component (LVC) diffuses through the boundary layers from the vapor to the liquid phase. The more volatile component (MVC) diffuses in the opposite direction. Thus, a counter-current diffusion occurs. The vapor becomes richer in MVC and the liquid becomes richer in LVC, until equilibrium is reached. This is repeated in sufficient number of equilibrium stages till the vapor contains only MVC and the liquid contains only the LVC.

The mass transfer by molecular diffusion can be expressed by an equation similar to heat transfer by conduction.

$$X = \frac{DA(C_1 - C_2)t}{L} \quad \text{and} \quad X = \frac{DA(C_1 - C_2)}{L}$$

Where, X is the amount of solute diffusing,

*x* is the amount of solute diffusing in unit time,

D is the diffusion coefficient,

A is the area,

t is the time duration,

$C_1$ is the concentration of solute at the interface,

$C_2$ is the concentration of solute in the bulk, and

L is thickness of the film.

The fractionating column must have certain characteristics to meet these requirements.

- Heat must be supplied to the bottom of the column to re-vaporize the liquid so that the temperature gradient is set up through the column.
- A condenser is attached to the top of the column to return liquid refluxed in sufficient quantity to effect condensation of the rising vapor.
- The column must have devices to provide conditions for mass transfer between the vapor moving upward and the liquid flowing downward.
- The column should have a low pressure-drop; that is, the contacting devices should not obstruct vapor flow.
- The liquid should be held by the column for a minimum period.

The Fig 9.9 indicates the construction of a fractional distillation unit. The mixture of liquids to be distilled is introduced into the boiler and heated, usually by steam coil. The broken lines in the column indicates a sufficient number of the contacting devices to provide the appropriate 'steps' (theoretical plates) on the vapor/ liquid equilibrium. The vapor is taken to a condenser at the top of the column and the condensed liquid is split in a reflux divider. A suitable quantity is returned to the column as reflux and the remainder is taken off as the product. The ratio of reflux to product is known as the *reflux ratio*. Distillation will continue until all the MVC has been distilled off and form the top product, and the LVC is left in the boiler to give the bottom product.

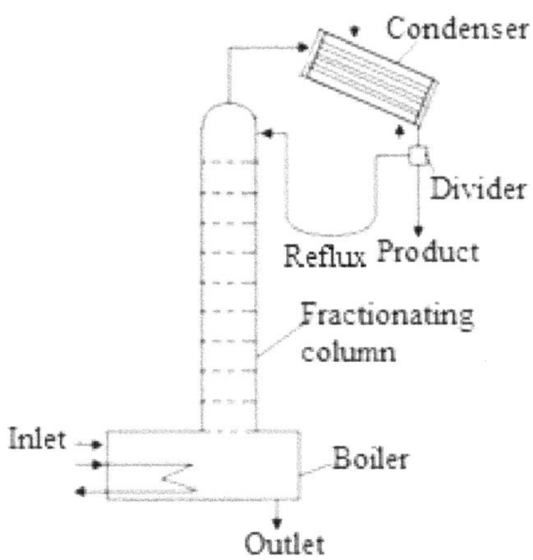


**Fig. 9.9** Fractional distillation column

## Fractionating Columns

The fractionating columns are broadly divided into two categories –

1. Packed column containing some type of packing within it to effect necessary liquid/vapor contact and a certain height of the packing is equivalent to one theoretical plate.
2. Plate column is divided into a number of sections by suitably designed 'plates', the liquid and vapor are brought into contact on each plate.

## Packed Column

It consists of a tower containing a packing that is wetted with a film of the liquid which subsequently comes in contact with the vapor in the intervening spaces.

In small scale columns *Dixon gauze rings* having high efficiency are used. The rings are made of 100 mesh stainless steel gauze. The shape of the rings is cylindrical with the size of 1.5 × 1.5 mm. The rings are placed upwards.

In case of large columns, the rings used are made of either metal or ceramic. The rings may be of different sizes. For example, *Raschig rings* are simple, open-ended cylinders; while *Lessing rings*, similar to Raschig rings, have a septum across their diameters. In both the types, the rings of smaller sizes are usually dumped in the column, and the rings of larger sizes are stacked.

The size of the rings is very important because the available surface area depends on their sizes. The smaller rings provide larger surface area. However, smaller rings give smaller column height per theoretical plate, but provide greater pressure-drop.

There may be other types of packings that include different shapes of expanded metal. However, in any case, the packing must be uniform; otherwise the flow will be irregular and channels will be formed. As a result, the mass transfer process will not be effective.

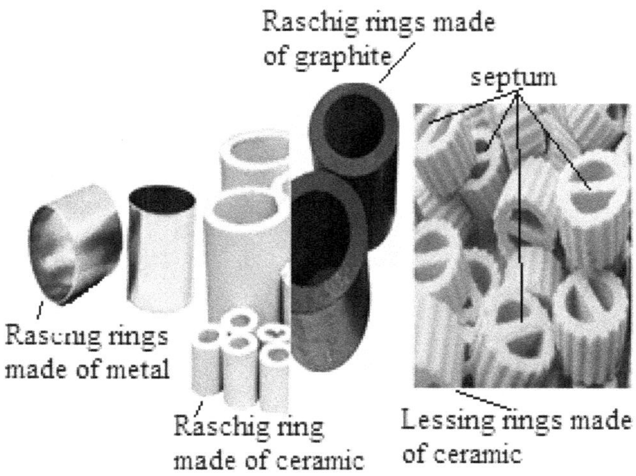


**Fig. 9.9A** Diagrams of Raschig rings and lessing rings

## Plate Columns

There are various forms of plate which are used in distillation columns. In pharmaceutical industries, two types of plates are commonly used;

1. Bubble cap plate, and
2. Turbogrid-plate.

## Bubble Cap Plate

This is the most commonly used contacting device. The schematic diagram of such plate is shown in Fig 9.9B.It consists of a plate across the column with a barrage (weir) that leads to down-comer. As a result, a layer of liquid is formed on the plate and the liquid overflows to the plate below. The end of the down-comer is sealed by the liquid on the lower plate. Vapor from below passes through the vapor riser which are covered by caps. The edges of these caps seal into the liquid layer. Thus, the vapor can only escape by bubbling through the liquid. The edge of the cap is usually slotted to facilitate uniform bubble formation.

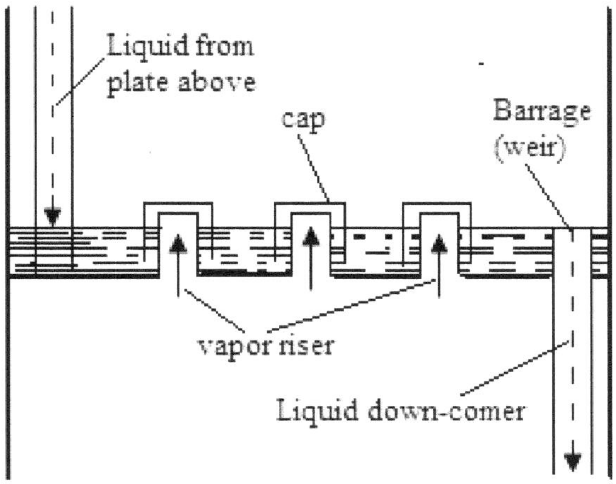


**Fig. 9.9B** Schematic diagram of bubble cap plate

With a single cap small plate can be used, but the columns with wide diameter ranging from 5 – 6 m are also available and used with various caps. In such units about 1000 caps are fitted and the diameter of each such cap is about 10 cm.

## Advantages

- The contact between liquid and vapor is excellent; since the vapor bubbles through the liquid.
- It is very effective for a wide range of proportions between vapor and liquid and also with different velocities.

## Disadvantages

- Throughout the column hold-up of liquid layer on each plate is for considerable time.

- To remove the vapor from the cap, the liquid has to exert a force; as a result, large pressure drop takes place throughout the column.
- When the column is not used, the column fails to drain off the liquid.
- The structure of the column is complicated; the construction and maintenance are expensive.

## Turbogrid Plate

Turbogrid plate is simple in construction, if compared with bubble cap plate. It consists of a flat grid having parallel slots that extend throughout the whole plate. As a result, no down-comer or vapor riser are there. During operation, the liquid is held on the plate due to the vapor rising through the slots. This results circulation.

**Fig. 9.9C** Diagram of turbogrid plate

## Advantages

- Construction wise it is very simple and easy to maintain.
- The plates are very economical to manufacture.
- Liquid hold-up is much less.
- Pressure-drop is also low.
- When not in use the column can drain itself.

## Disadvantages

- Limited range of operations can be done. Excessive liquid goes down the plate and insufficient quantity of liquid will make the contact with vapor.
- If the velocity of vapor is increased, it will blow the liquid off the plate and the vapor with low velocity would not be able to hold the liquid on the plate.
- The proportion and velocities of the liquid and vapor need to be optimized to ensure the necessary contact for required mass transfer.

## Distillation under Reduced Pressure

The method is defined *as a distillation method carried out at a temperature below the boiling point under vacuum*. To reduce the pressure on the liquid surface, vacuum pump or suction pump is used. Thus, vacuum distillation or distillation under reduced pressure is a type of simple distillation with certain modification.

### Principle

When the vapor pressure above the liquid becomes equal to the atmospheric pressure, the liquid starts boiling. By applying vacuum if the external pressure is reduced, the boiling point of the liquid would be reduced. Hence, the liquid boils at a lower temperature. For example, at 1.013 atm (760 mm Hg) water boils at 100°C. On reducing the atmospheric pressure to 70 mm Hg, water starts boiling at 40°C; As a result, the rate of mass transfer into vapor is increased.

In case of evaporation, mass of vapor formed $\infty \frac{\text{Vapor pressure of evaorating liquid}}{\text{External pressure}}$

As per this formula, if water boils at 40°C at 760 mm Hg pressure, then the mass of vapor formed in unit time would be $\frac{760}{70} = 11$ times (for water).

### Construction

It consists of a double-neck distillation flask known as Claisen flask. For vacuum distillation a thick-walled glass apparatus having interchangeable standard joints are used for vacuum distillation. Through one neck of the Claisen flask, a thermometer is inserted almost up to the bottom of the flask. As shown in the Fig 9.10, a fine capillary tube is inserted through the second neck of the flask. In vacuum distillation bumping occurs, the capillary tube prevents such bumping. Through this tube, a stream of air bubbles is drawn out. For heating, water bath or oil bath is used.

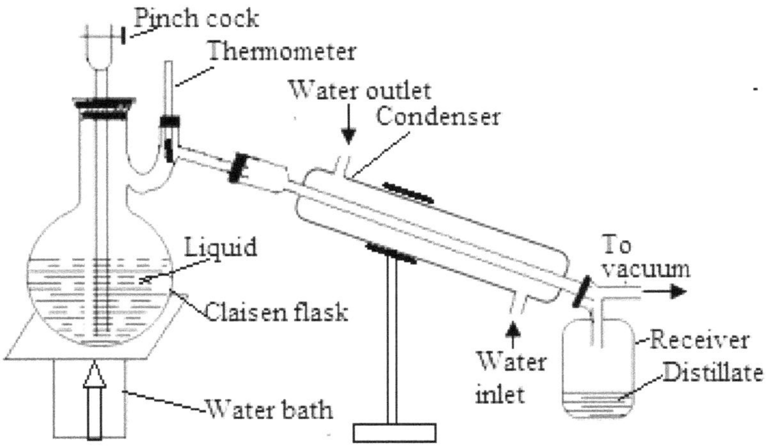


**Fig. 9.10** Schematic diagram of vacuum distillation unit

The flask is connected to a receiver through a condenser. The vacuum pump is attached through an adapter to the receiver.

### Working

The liquid to be distilled is introduced up to one-half or two-third of the volume of the flask. To avoid bumping few porcelain beads are placed inside the flask. The flask is connected to upper end of the condenser and the receiver is connected to the lower end of the condenser. There should not be any leakage in both the joints. The vacuum is applied to achieve the required pressure. The liquid becomes heated gradually and starts vaporizing quickly because of the applied vacuum. The vapor passing through the condenser starts condensing and the condensate is collected in the receiver. The temperature of the liquid, if recorded, it would be found to be less than the normal boiling point of the pure liquid.

When large volume of the liquid is to be distilled, it is better to take the flask of larger capacity and the operation should be carried out repeatedly.

### Uses

- It can prevent or avoid degradation of active component. The active substance may degrade when processed at higher temperature. Hence, by vacuum distillation their activity can be protected. For example, ascorbic acid, thiamine, pancreatin, etc. are liable to degrade, if processed at a temperature more than about 50°C.
- The method can be suitably used for making a product suitable for further processing. For example, the granular extract of crude drug is sometimes required for compression and this is possible if the extract is distilled under vacuumto remove the solvent.

### Advantages

- Liquids of high boiling point at atmospheric pressure can be purified by vacuum distillation because in this method thermolabile, potent active constituents can be obtained.
- When active principle present in a liquid may decompose at higher temperature, should be separated by vacuum distillation because the method is conducted at relatively lower temperature.

### Limitation

- The method is not suitable for making semisolid or solid extract of some component which produces foam during distillation.

## Steam Distillation

When a liquid X, immiscible with water, is to be separated from other non-volatile components, it is frequently distilled with steam. The process of steam distillation becomes useful particularly when the substance X has high boiling point and can decompose near its normal boiling temperature, for example, phenylamine, iodobenzene, etc. A liquid starts boiling when the vapor pressure above the liquid surface becomes equal to the atmospheric pressure. Steam distillation is an example of *differential distillation.* In steam distillation, the substance is distilled with steam at near about 100°C.

## Principle

As mentioned above, a mixture of immiscible liquids boils when the sum of vapor pressures ($p_1$+---+$p_n$) becomes equal to the atmospheric pressure, P. Say, there are two liquids A and B are present in the mixture. Their partial vapor pressures are $p_1^A$ and $p_2^B$; say $n_1$ moles of A and $n_2$ moles of B are present in the mixture, then as per above discussion, we can write as:

$$P = p_1^A + p_2^B$$

In general, the above equation can be written as:

$$P = p_1 + p_2$$

$$p_1 = \frac{n_1}{n_1 + n_2} \times P \quad \text{and} \quad p_2 = \frac{n_2}{n_1 + n_2} \times P$$

$$\frac{p_1}{p_2} = \frac{w_1/M_1}{w_2/M_2}$$

Where, $M_1$ and $M_2$ are the molecular weights of component A and B respectively;

$w_1$ and $w_2$ are the amounts of components A and B present in the vapor phase, that is in the distillate. For example, iodobenzene having its boiling point of 188°C is purified by steam distillation at about 98°C. At this temperature, the partial vapor pressure of water $p_{water}$ is 712 mm Hg and the partial vapor pressure of iodobenzene, $p_{iodobenzene}$ is 48 mm Hg.

So, the total vapor pressure = 712 + 48 = 760 mm Hg = 1 atm.

Thus, steam distillation is suitable for purification of organic liquids which are not miscible with water.

## Laboratory Scale Steam Distillation

The equipment used for laboratory scale steam distillation is shown in Fig 9.11. It consists of a metallic or glass flask. The mouth of the flask is fitted with a cork. The cork has two holes. Through one hole a long glass tube is inserted almost up to the bottom of the flask. Due to continuous heating, if the vapor pressure inside the flask is high, the boiling water comes outside the flask through this tube and the vapor pressure inside the flask comes down. For this reason, this long tube is called '*safety tube*'. Through another hole of the cork a bent tube is inserted to pass the water vapor (steam) to sample distillation flask as shown in the Fig 9.11. The other end of the bent tube is inserted into a flask containing the liquid to be distilled (sample). The length of this tube should be such that it can dip into the liquid. Through the other hole of the cork fitted to the distilling flask, one bent tube is inserted and the other end of the bent tube is fitted to a condenser through a cork. The lower end of the condenser is connected to a receiver through a suitable adaptor to collect the distillate.

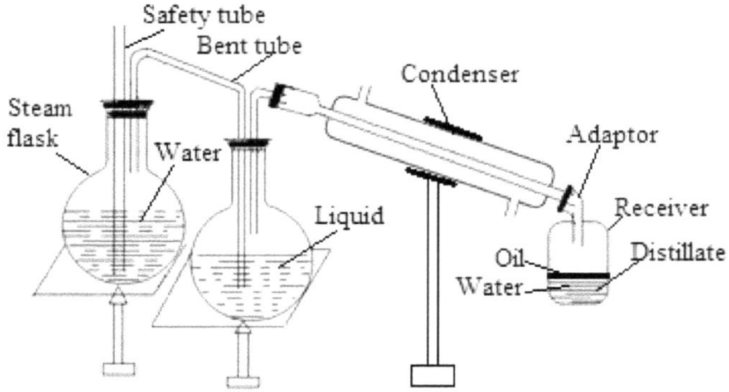


**Fig. 9.11** Schematic diagram of laboratory scale steam distillation equipment

## Procedure

Water is introduced into the water-boiling flask, two tubes are fitted firmly to the flask. The non-aqueous liquid is taken to another flask and joined through a bent tube. Safety tube is inserted into the water boiling flask and the flask containing the liquid to be distilled is connected with the condenser through a bent tube. Cold water is circulated outside the condenser. Both the flasks are heated, the steam is produced in the first flask is passed into the second flask containing the liquid. The steam starts carrying the volatile component present in the liquid. When the steam carrying the component passes through the condenser becomes cool and deposited into receiver. Distillation should be continued till all the component is isolated. In the receiver, the distillate has two layers– at the top there is volatile component and lower layer is of water. The layers are separated by a separating funnel. The volatile substance which is miscible with water, can be separated by using fractional distillation method.

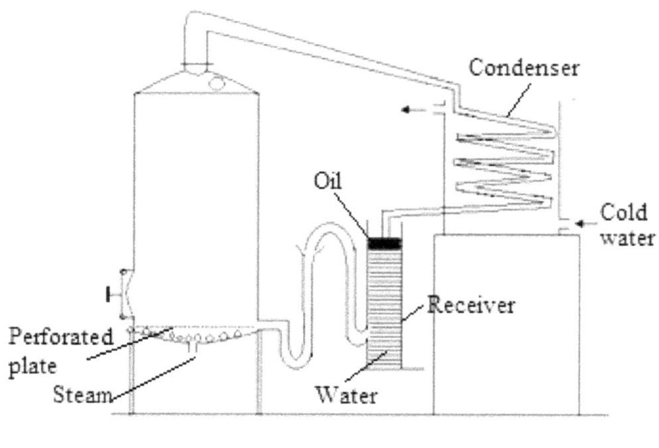


**Fig. 9.12** Schematic diagram of steam distillation unit used in industry

### Industrial Scale Steam Distillation

The Fig 9.12 shows the equipment for steam distillation used in industries. It consists of a jacketed still. The still has a perforated plate which forms a false bottom. Holes are provided at the top and side used for charging the sill with liquid and removal of waste. A receiver is placed between the sill and condenser. The condenser is cooled by circulating cold water.

The material from which the volatile oil is to be extracted is introduced into the still above level of perforated plate. Steam is introduced into the jacket to boil the water in the still. The steam produced carries the volatile oil and passes through the condenser. In the condenser the vapor becomes cool, condenses and the condensate is collected in the receiver. Since the volatile oils are generally lighter than water, the oil remains in the form of separate layer at the top (upper layer) and water accumulates at the bottom (lower layer).

### Uses

- For separation of immiscible liquids steam distillation is used.
- For extracting most of the volatile oils such as clove oil, anise oil, etc. this method is used.
- For purification of liquid with high boiling point such as almond oil, it is used.
- For preparing aromatic water, this method is used.

### Advantages

➢ This method can be used to separate or extract volatile oils without decomposition and loss of aroma.

➢ Substance having low volatility but molecular weight higher than water can be separated.

### Disadvantages

➢ The method is not suitable for material immiscible with water and the material that reacts with water.

## Molecular Distillation

It is a special application of simple distillation process. It is alternatively called *evaporative distillation* or *short path distillation.*

### Principle

*The average distance through which a molecule can move without any collision with another molecule is called mean free path.* The mean free path is expressed as:

$$\lambda = \eta\sqrt{\frac{3}{p.\rho}}$$

Where,

$\lambda$ is the mean free path,

η is the viscosity,

ρ is the density of the material, and

p is the pressure.

**Note:**

- The mean free path of the molecules of a material is long, if the viscosity and density of the material are low. The distillation becomes simple.
- The mean free path of the molecules of a material is short, if the viscosity of the material and pressure are high.
- The mean free path of the molecules of a material is long, if the viscosity of the material decreases at higher temperature and under the reduced pressure.

Accordingly, under normal temperature and pressure the non-volatile substances can be made volatile. This has been found that the mean free path of heavy molecules such as butyl phthalate and olive oil are about 30 mm and 20 mm respectively at a pressure of $1 \times 10^{-6}$ bar.

Therefore, under these conditions such substances can be distilled when their evaporating surface become close to the condensing surface. There are three characteristics of molecular distillation:

1. To reduce the number of collisions between the molecules, the distillation process should be conducted under vacuum of $1 \times 10^{-6}$ to $10 \times 10^{-6}$ bar. Hence, the pumping system should be strong and efficient enough to create such vacuum, there should be no leakage, and before distillation the liquid should be de-gassed.
2. The surface area of the liquid should be as large as possible. There should be no boiling, only from the surface the vapor should be produced. For this reason, this process is called *evaporative distillation.*
3. The evaporative surface and condensing surface must be closed to each other. For this reason, the process is called *short-path distillation.* Although this distance is similar to mean free path of the molecules; the distance between the two surfaces should be at least slightly lesser than the mean free path. It has been seen that sometimes the molecules can withstand few collisions without noticeable deflection.

This is the major difference between the simple distillation and molecular distillation. In simple distillation, baffles are required for arresting the volatile components carried by the vapor; while molecular distillation does not require the baffles.

## Construction

The industrially used molecular distillation can be broadly classified into two categories on the basis of the type of still being used –

1. Falling film molecular still, and
2. Centrifugal molecular still

1. **Falling film molecular still:** This works according to the same principle of falling film evaporator. In the falling film evaporator, the feed enters over a barrage (weir) made at the top of the tubes. The concentrated liquid (product) and vapor leave from the bottom. Here, the vaporization takes place from the film of the liquid flowing down over a hot surface. When the

fluid flows down, heat transfer takes place. The heat transfer can be improved mechanically by wiping the film. The Fig 9.13 shows a schematic diagram of a wiped film molecular distillation still. The vessel has a diameter of about 1 m and the walls are heated either by steam or electrical means. The liquid (distill and) flows down the walls of the condensers and is spreaded over the walls by the polytetrafluoroethylene (PTFE) wipers. The speed of wiping is about 3 m/s and the film is produced at a rate of 1.5 m/s. The residue (un-spreaded liquid) is collected at the bottom and is recirculated. The distillate is collected in the receiver at the bottom. The entire process is conducted under vacuum. Thus, a vacuum pump is connected at the centre through a large diameter pipe. Capacity of such still is quite high, about 1000 lt/h.

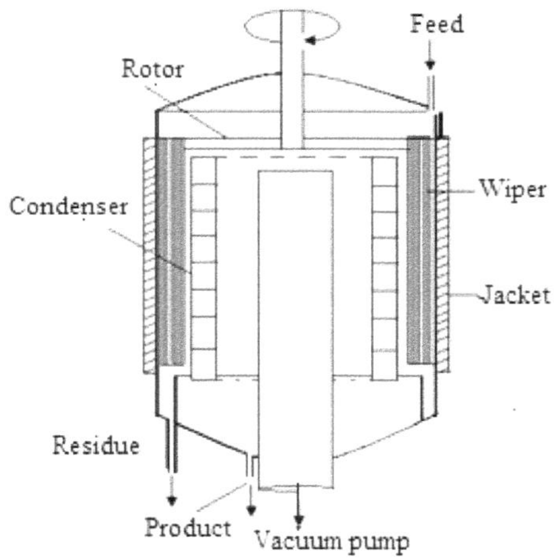


**Fig. 9.13** Schematic diagram of wiped film molecular still

2. **Centrifugal molecular still:** In this method a thin liquid film is produced by a centrifugal force. The liquid is fed into the centre of a bucket shaped vessel having diameter of about 1.0 – 1.5 m. The vessel rotates at a high speed. The film of liquid formed moves outwards over the surface of the vessel which is heated externally by radiant heaters. The condensers and a collection apparatus are placed closed to the inner surface of the rotor. The Fig 9.14 shows a typical diagram of centrifugal molecular still.

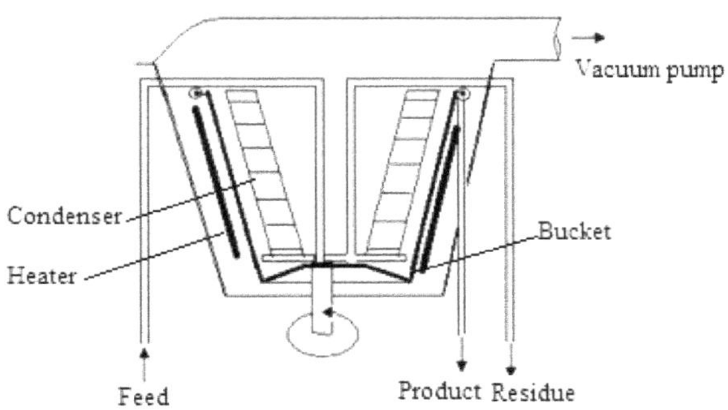


**Fig. 9.14** Centrifugal molecular still

### Uses

- Purification of chemicals of low vapor pressure such as tricresyl phosphate, dibutyl phthalate, dimethyl phthalate, etc.
- Refining of fixed oils and separating vitamins. Free fatty acids are distilled off at about 100°C, vitamins and sterols at a temperature between 100° and 200°C, triglycerides at a temperature at 200°C and above. Proteins, gums and similar materials remain as a non-volatile residue.

### Disadvantages

- The construction and operation are more complicated due to high speed of rotation.
- The centrifugal still has a similar throughput to the wiped film still.

## Short Questions

1. What are distill and distillate? 'Distillation is a process of separation'– how can you explain?
2. What are the applications of distillation?
3. What are different types of distillation processes? What is molecular distillation?
4. What is meant by 'relative volatility'?
5. How the Dalton's law and Henry's law are related to distillation?
6. What are ideal solution and real solution?
7. What is a flash distillation equipment? What are its applications?
8. What are different types of fractionating columns used for fractional distillation?
9. Write down the principle of steam distillation.
10. Write a note on 'laboratory steam distillation'.

## Long Questions

1. Explain the principle involved in distillation.
2. Discuss the characteristics of real solutions with respect to Raoult's law.
3. Explain the characteristics and types of condenser. What is importance of still and condenser in distillation?
4. With the help of a diagram write down the principle, construction and application of simple distillation.
5. Draw the diagram of a typical distillation unit used for preparation of water for injection and explain its functions.
6. With the help of a schematic diagram write down the principle and construction of a flash distillation equipment.
7. Explain the principle of fractional distillation.
8. Write down the principle and purpose of distillation under reduced pressure.
9. Write down working, applications and advantages of vacuum distillation.
10. Explain the concept of molecular distillation, classify the equipments on the basis of still, and application of centrifugal molecular still.

# CHAPTER 10

# Filtration

Objectives, Applications, Theories & Factors Influencing Filtration, Filter Aids, Filter Medias. Principle, Construction, Working, Uses, Merits and Demerits of Plate & Frame Filter, Filter Leaf, Rotary Drum Filter, Meta Filter & Cartridge Filter, Membrane Filters and Seidtz Filter.

## Objectives

Filtration is a technique used for separation of unwanted, undissolved solids from a solution or from a liquid to obtain a clear solution or liquid. Filtration is done when the number of solid particles to be separated is quite less than the volume of the liquid. Separation of undissolved solids from liquids can generally be done in various ways. The selection of an appropriate method depends mainly on;

- The size of solid particles,
- Nature of the solid to be separated, and
- The volume of liquid.
- The ultimate use of the liquid.

Filtration can be defined as *the process of separating the solids from a fluid using a porous medium that retains the solid but allows the fluid to pass through. The fluid may be a gas or liquid.* The fluid obtained after filtration is called filtrate, and through which it is filtered is called filter media.

## Applications

Filtration is a physical method of purification. Application of filtration process can be summarized as below:

- *Production of oral solutions:* After preparation of a bulk solution, it is necessary to filter the solution to make it free from visible foreign particle. This is done by filtering the solution through an appropriate filter.
- *Production of sterile solutions:* Depending on the ultimate application of a product, environmental conditions during manufacturing are maintained. Similarly, the product is manufactured. For example, the air circulated in manufacturing area is filtered through HEPA filter and circulated in a streamline manner. The bulk solution once prepared is filtered through suitable filter medium before filling into container.

- *Production of bulk drugs:* When a drug is manufactured by synthetic process, the drug or its intermediate is necessary to be separated from its solution to purify. For this reason, the solution is required to be filtered through appropriate filter medium. Hence, filtration technique is used to remove the dissolved impurities.
- *Crystallization:* The solution used for crystallization should be free from undissolved or suspended foreign particles (impurities). For this purpose, the solution used to feed a crystallizer should be filtered through suitable filter medium.
- *Disposal of waste material:* The waste material or effluent of an industry contains undissolved solid as well as liquid. Before disposal of the effluent, the solids are separated from the liquid by filtering. Hence, filtration is a common process which is used in chemical, biochemical, pharmaceutical and other industries.

## Theories

During filtration, the fluid flows through a porous filter medium which offers resistance to flow. Thus, the rate at which the filtered liquid will flow can be expressed as:

$$\text{Rate} = \frac{\text{Driving force}}{\text{Resistance}} = \frac{dV}{dt} = \frac{\text{Volume of filtrate}}{\text{Time}} \text{ (cubic cm per time)}$$

The driving force = pressure above the filter – pressure below the filter.

In other words, the difference between the pressure at upstream and downstream of the filter medium would be responsible for flow of liquid through the filter medium. Both pressure difference and resistance changes with time but not in a same rate. Initially, the resistance will be very less; but with passage of time, after formation of cake over the filter, the resistance will increase. Thus, the resistance depends on the thickness and nature of the cake deposited over the filter. The resistance can be calculated as:

$$\text{Resistance} = \frac{\text{Upstream pressure-Downstream pressure}}{\text{Length of capillaries}}$$

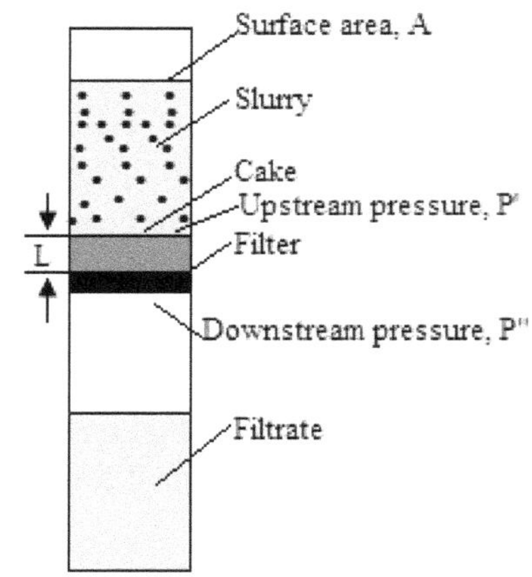

Schematic diagram of batch filtration system

The process of filtration is shown here.

The rate of filtration has been explained by different scientists at different times; for example, Poiseuille, Darcy, and Kozeny-Carman.

### Poiseuille's Equation

According to Poiseuille, in filtration the movement of the liquid under pressure is of streamline or laminar; just similar to the movement of a liquid through capillaries. Accordingly, the equation developed by Poiseuille is known as Poiseuille's equation which is expressed as:

$$V = \frac{\pi.\Delta P.r^4}{8L.\eta}$$

Where, V is the rate at which the liquid flows through the cake ($m^3/S$)

$\Delta P$ is the pressure difference across the filter bed (Pa)

r is radius of the capillary in the filter bed (m)

L is thickness of the filter cake; that is, the length of the capillary (m)

$\eta$ is viscosity of the filtrate (Pa.S)

The above equation is applicable when the cake is made up of bulky material and the liquid flows through the capillaries formed by the particles of the cake.

## Darcy's Equation

The Poiseuille's law is based on the assumption that the material forming the cake over the filter cake is composed of the particles of irregular size and shape, and is highly nonuniform also. Thus, they form capillaries whose length is considered as the thickness of the cake. In this case, for radius of the capillaries a correction factor should be taken into consideration so that the rate equation become relatively more accurate and also become simplified. Darcy in his equation to express the flow rate included the factors that influence the rate of filtration. Darcy's equation can be written as:

$$V = \frac{K.\Delta P.A}{\eta.L}$$

Where, V is the rate of filtration ($m^2/S$)

K is the permeability coefficient of the cake ($m^2$)

A is the specific surface area of the filter medium through which filtration takes place ($m^2$)

$\Delta P$ is the pressure difference across the filter (Pa)

$\eta$ is the viscosity of the filtrate (Pa.S), and

L is thickness or depth of the filter cake (m)

The permeability coefficient, K is the rate of flow of a liquid of unit viscosity across a unit area of the cake having unit thickness under a unit pressure gradient. The value of K depends on the porosity, specific surface area and compressibility of the cake.

In fact, this equation can be applied to flow or passage of the liquid through a bed of sand, glass beads and other porous materials. Kozeny-Carman modified the equation developed by Darcy, and also modified the characteristics of permeability coefficient, K.

## Kozeny-Carman Equation

Poiseuille's equation was modified by Darcy to make it applicable to porous bed having capillaries or capillary type structure. Thereafter, Kozeny and Carman modified the Darcy's equation by including other additional parameters and now, the Kozeny-Carman equation has gained well acceptance and has been commonly and widely used to determine the rate of filtration.

Kozeny-Carman equation can be expressed as:

$$V = \frac{A}{\eta S^2} \times \frac{\Delta P}{K.L} \times \frac{\varepsilon^2}{(1-\varepsilon)^2}$$

Where, V is the rate of filtration ($m^3/S$)

ε is porosity of the bed (cake)

S is the specific surface area of the filter medium through which filtration takes place ($m^2$)

K is the Kozeny constant

ΔP is the pressure difference across the filter (Pa)

η is the viscosity of the filtrate (Pa.S), and

L is thickness or depth of the filter cake (m)

The value of K (Kozeny constant) is commonly considered as 5. The Poiseuille's equation considers the effect of compressibility of the cake on the rate of flow of liquid. However, in Kozeny-Carman equation, a factor $\frac{\varepsilon^3}{(1-\varepsilon)^2}$ has been included which is proportional to the rate of flow. According to this equation, if the porosity ε changes up to 10%, the flow rate will change to about 3 times.

Although the Kozeny-Carman equation is widely used but it fails to explain the rate of filtration through a granular bed (cake). The actual path is not straight, but for the shake of convenience it is considered as the thickness or depth of the cake.

## Factors Influencing Filtration

The rate of filtration is affected by the following factors:

1. The physical properties of liquid such as viscosity, density, corrosiveness.
2. The physical properties of solid such as particle size and shape, particle size distribution, rigidity or compressibility of the particles.
3. The number of solid particles present in the fluid.
4. Purpose of filtration – whether the solids are to be collected or thrown.
5. Whether the solids are to washed after filtration.
6. Whether the fluid is to be collected and retained after filtration.
7. The ultimate application of filtrate.
8. Type of filter medium used.

## Types of Filtration

Filtration can be classified into two types

1. *Depth filtration:* Solids are removed within a bed of porous material, such as rapid granular bed filters. The filter layer being deep, solid particles are retained. For example, for clarification of drinking water, sand filters are used whichcan retain the particles even up to the colloidal sizes. In this type of filtration, the small particles are adheredon to the grains of the filter layer. The big particles are retained by the screening effect.

2. *Cake filtration:* Removal of particle occurs mainly at the surface of the media through formation of a filter cake, such as pre-coat filtration, diatomaceous earth, etc. is the most frequently used model. It is assumed that the solids are deposited on the upstream side of the filter medium as a homogeneous porous layer with a constant permeability. As soon as the first layer of cake is formed, the subsequent filtration takes place at the top of the cake and the medium provides only a supporting function. If the flow rate dV/dt is kept constant, the pressure drop would increase linearly and would be proportional to the quantity of solid deposited. This model can be applied particularly for all hard, particulate solids.

## Classification of Filters

Filters can be classified into different categories based on different criteria.

1. On the basis of type of granular medium used
   - *Single medium* such as sand or anthracite
   - *Dual media* such as anthracite and sand, these are better, suitable for filtration for longer period and the pore size is maximum at the top but gradually decreases to minimum at the bottom.
   - *Multimedia* such as anthracite, sand and garnet.
2. According to the flow through the medium
   - *Gravity filters:* These are open to atmosphere and filtration takes place due to the gravitational force. The fluid flow from the cylinder into the conical flask is driven by gravity; that is, the hydrostatic pressure of the slurry above the filter.
   - *Pressure filters:* The filter medium is placed within a pressure vessel and water is delivered under pressure. A vacuum pump is attached to the conical flask and is used to create a constant vacuum pressure inside the flask. Under this condition, the difference between the atmospheric pressure and the pressure in the flask works as the driving force for the filtration to occur. While the hydrostatic pressure still contributes to the driving force, it is usually much smaller than the vacuum pressure generated by the pump.
3. According to the rate of filtration
   - *Rapid sand filter*, and
   - *Slow sand filter*
4. According to the filter flow control
   - *Constant rate*, and
   - *Declining rate*

## Type of Filter

The filter medium acts as a mechanical support for the filter cake and it is responsible for the collection of solids. Different types of materials used as filter media are presented in Table below.

| Type of filter media | Characteristics | Applications |
|---|---|---|
| Metal fiber media (non-woven metal fiber) | Excellent durability with corrosion and abrasion resistance | In polymer and gas industry |
| Multilayer sintered mesh | It can be reused | In gas industry |
| Stainless steel (plain and Dutch type) | Water proof inside and plastic woven cloth outside | Inoil, chemical, food, pharmaceutical and in aviation industry |
| Anthracite filter media | It has high efficiency | For purification of water |
| Filter media treated by graphite | Made up of fibre glass | Used in cement and steel industry. Used as filter cloth for air filter |
| Activated carbon fabric (non-woven type) | Little air current resistance, strong strength | Used in air conditioner as auto air filter or carbon air filter |
| Biocell | High biological activity | Sanitary sewage and industrial waste processing |
| Aramide filter fabric | Easiness of cake peeling, high stability, anti-distortion | Used in ore dressing, chemical and brewing industry, equipped in filter presses, vacuum filters, etc. |
| Autoroll filter media | It has metal structure, saves energy and work stably | Used in air filtrate |
| Laminating PTFE membrane | Felt type of filter | Used in cement company and incineration fields |
| Air filter | Pocket type of filter | Air conditioner and electronic industry, food industry, applied to the pre-filtration of coarse efficiency |

## Filter Aids

In general, the filter medium does not resist the liquid to flow and some of the fine particles may pass through the pores of the filter medium. For this reason, the process is repeated until a clear filtrate is obtained. During recirculation of the filtrate or repeat filtration, the pores of the filter medium are blocked partly and the insoluble particles cannot pass through and are retained over the filter medium. But, the layer of the particles retained over the medium does not provide the required porosity. As a result, the filter medium becomes chocked and the rate of filtration reduces.

To overcome this problem, filter aid is mixed with the fluid to be filtered and then filtered. Sometimes, the clarity of the filtrate does not come in the first filtrate, in such cases thefiltrate is recirculated till a clear is obtained. The filter aid powder deposit over the filter but, after deposition of sufficient filter aid over the medium, a layer is formed which can produce clear filtrate. The filter aid is capable of forming a porous layer over the filter medium and facilitate the filtration. Thus, the filter aid powder is used to(1) improve the clarity of filtrate, and (2) facilitate the filtration process. Therefore, the filter aids are light in weight, porous and inert solid and can be used in two ways:

1. A suspension of sufficient amount of filter aid is filtered through the filter medium to form a pre-coat over the medium; so that a coating up to 0.5kg/$m^2$ is formed. As a result of this coating, the fluid can be filtered at the required rate.
2. Sufficient amount of suitable filter aid is added to a small amount of fluid to prepare 0.1 to 0.5% of suspension, this suspension is filtered and recirculated till the filtrate becomes clear. The purpose of recirculation is to develop the layer of filter aid powder over the medium so that filtration of the fluid can take place easily withrequired clarity.

Selection of filter aid is an important activity; the characteristics of a suitable filter aid powder are;

- It should not adsorb the solute,
- Should not interact with the solute and with the medium,
- It should be capable of forming a porous layer that
- Can facilitate the filtration rate, and
- Should improve the clarity of the filtrate.

Materials used as filter aid are talcum powder, kieselguhr, etc. In some cases, kieselguhr has been found to effective at a concentration of only about 0.1% and it improves the filtration rate of a solution containing 20% dissolved solute to about 5 times. Filter aid powder should be used where filtrate is of use and solids are not. However, filter aids are sometimes used when the solids are of use.

## Filter Medias

Filter media is primarily used to retain the undissolved solids present in a solution or slurry being filtered. It should allow the dissolved molecules of a solution to pass through but not the undissolved (suspended) ones. The filter medium should have a minimum strength to withstand the pressure developed during filtration; as well it should be made of porous material so that it can strain out the solution as filtrate. There are particles of different size ranges, similarly there are filter medias having different porosity. Depending on the ultimate use of the product, the specific type of filter media is selected and used. Hence, there are various types of filter media based on 1. the porosity such as G3, G4, etc.,

1. the material of construction of the filter media, such as filter paper, sintered filter, asbestos filter, etc.,
2. how do they work, such as plate and frame filter, filter leaf, vacuum filter, etc.

## Plate & Frame Filter

Filter presses are pressure filters used for de-watering the chemicals generally on batch basis using mechanically applied pressure to obtain satisfactory rate of filtration. As such there are different types of filters presses –

1. Plate filter presses
2. Chamber Filter Presses
3. Membrane Filter Presses

4. Plate & Frame Filter Presses –Sheet Filters
5. Tubular Filter presses

Here we shall discuss on plate and frame filter press which consists of a series of parallel plates, each is covered with a suitable filter cloth and firmly held together within a structured frame. The fluid flows through a filter medium by virtue of a pressure difference across the filter.

## Principle

The mechanism of filtration through filter press is surface filtration. It provides more satisfactory and more adaptable type of filter. Sometimes, it is called *flush plate*, simply *filter press*. The press filter consists of plates with slightly raised edges, and hollow frames, as shown in Fig 10.1. These are assembled alternately in similar way as is done in case of chamber press.

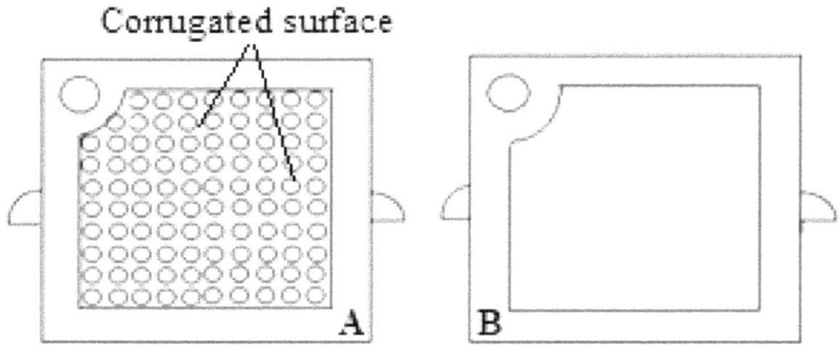


**Fig. 10.1** Schematic diagram of plate and frame filter press A; Frame, B: Plate

While assembling the plate and frame, a suitable filter cloth is placed over each plate. A number of plates and frames are assembled together and each plate holds a filter cloth. Each filter cloth has hole similar to that present in each plate, so that after assembly, these holes can make a continuous channel for movement of liquid. This type of fitting of plates and frames is called fitting *eyes* to the plates and frames. The filtrate which is likely to be contaminated, the contamination can be avoided. During filtration the solids present in the liquid gets deposited in the frames in form of cake. The thickness of the cake can be changed by changing the thickness of the frame. However, depending on solid, there is an optimum thickness of the filter cake. During filtration, the resistance of the cake increases and the rate of filtration decreases gradually. At a certain point, based on the rate of filtration, the filtration process is stopped. The plates and frames are then washed, re-assembled and thereafter, the filtration is continued.

## Construction

The frame is open, with an inlet for slurry (liquid to be filtered). The plate has a corrugated surface to support the filter cloth and an outlet for exit of the filtrate. The Fig 10.2 shows diagrammatically how the slurry enters into the frame (marked by 2 dots) from the feed channel. The filtrate passes through the filter medium on to the surface of the plate (marked by 1 dot). On the frame the solids form the cake.

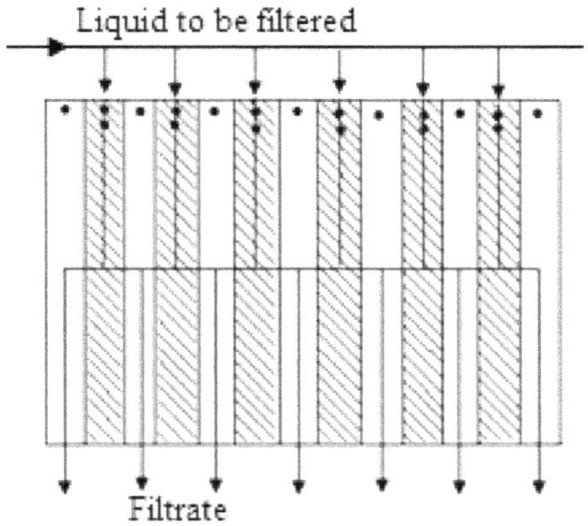


**Fig. 10.2** Schematic diagram of operation of filter press

Then, the filtrate drains down the surface of the plate between the projections on the surface and goes out through the outlet. Initially, the filtrate obtained may not be perfectly clear; in that case, the filtrate is recycled with the slurry until a clear filtrate is obtained. Filtration is continued until the frame is filled with filter cake, and the filtration process is stopped or about to be stopped.

Plate and frame may be made of different metals such as aluminium, stainless steel, etc. The metal used to make the plate and frame must be completely inert; that is, free from corrosion and erosion. Reinforced plastics are completely inert and light in weight. Certain woods can also be used to make plate and frame. However, the wooden plates and frames need to be kept wet all the time, otherwise they will shrink.

The size of the plates and frames may vary widely from 0.16 sq. m to 1 sq. m. The plates and frames having 1 sq. m in size can provide about 120 sq. m filtration area. If the frames of 4 cm thick are used, the press can hold about 2.5cubic m. Such a filter press will be 6 – 7 m long. The Fig 10.3 shows how the plates and frames are assembled.

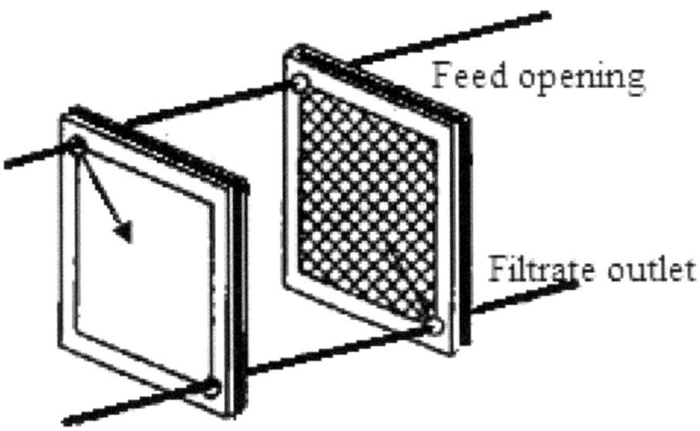


**Fig. 10.3** Assembly of plate and frame

## Working

Working of a filter press includes two activities – 1. filtration operation, and 2. washing of the cake, if required.

The slurry enters the frames (marked by 2 dots)through the feed channel and passes through the filter medium on to the surface of the plate (marked by 1 dot). The solids form a filter cake which remains in the frame.

Filtration takes place on both sides of each frame. The thickness of the cake occupies 50% of the frame thickness. The filter cakes formed initially, then accumulate in the centre of the frame. However, there is an optimum thickness of the cake for each slurry. This thickness depends on the solid content of the slurry and the resistance offered by the cake formed. The filtrate drains between the corrugations on the surface of the plate and exit from the outlet. During filtration, at a certain point the resistance of the cake becomes maximum which subsequently reduces the rate of filtration. At this point, the filtration is stopped. Then the press is emptied, washed and the filtration is re-started.

## Washing

When the thickness of the cake becomes thick and accumulate in the middle of the frame, the filtration becomes almost ceased. Hence, washing with water is required; but it is not possible to wash using the same channel of the filtrate. As a result, the design of the plate and frame is modified by providing an additional channel to some plate called wash water plate. These wash plates are identified by 3 dots. Thus, the plates and frames are modified accordingly. The principle of washing the cake is shown in Fig 10.4, 10.5 and 10.6. In half of the plates there is a connection from the wash water channel to the surface of the plate and special plates having 3 dots. Two varieties of plates are alternately connected with the frames. In general, the plates and frames are connected as per the sequence: 1. 2. 3. 2. 1. 2. 3. 2. 1.2. 3. 2. 1., etc.

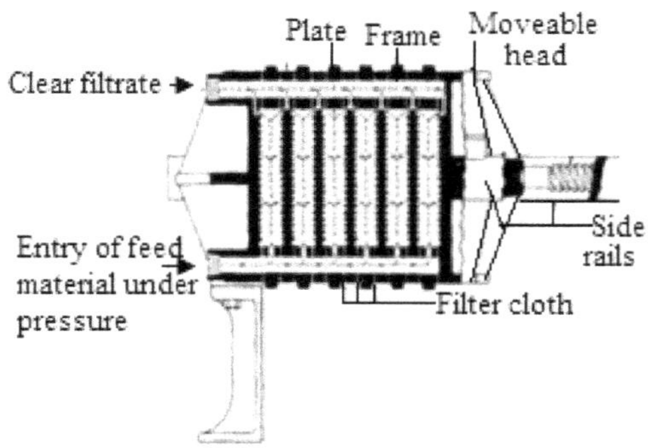


**Fig. 10.4** Plate and frame filter press

For washing the filter cake, the outlets on the washing (3 dots) are closed, and wash water is pumped into the washing channel. The water enters the inlets on to the surface of the washing plates and passes through the filter cloth on that plate from behind, through the filter cake, through the filter cloth on the ordinary (1 dot) plate, down the surface of the plate and finally escape from the outlet on that plate.

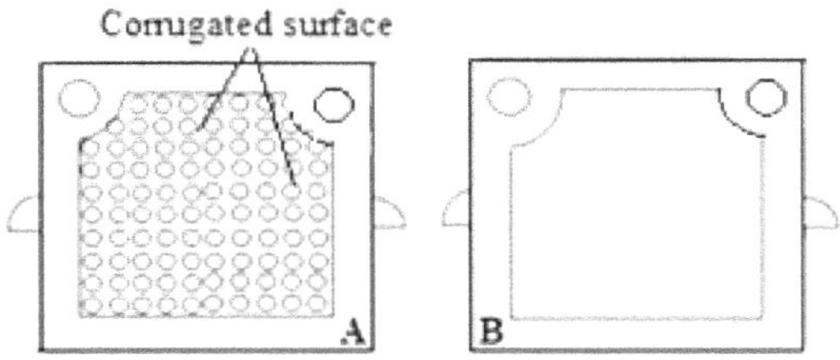


Modified form of Plate (A) and modified frame (B)

**Fig. 10.5** Modified plate and frame for washing

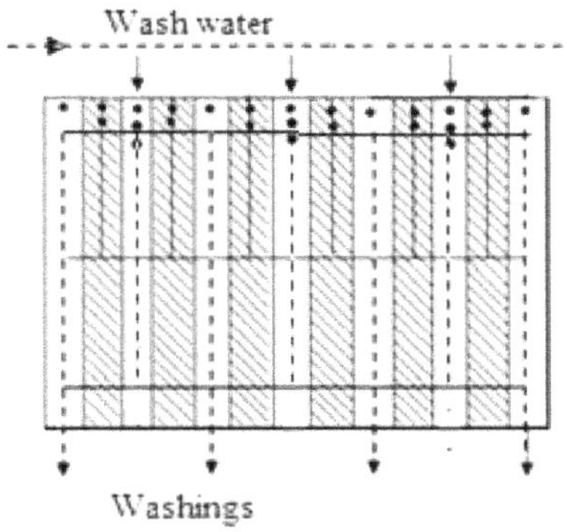


**Fig. 10.6** Plate and frame washing operation (cross sectional view)

Washing of cake on the frames of filter press can be summarized as follows:

- The outlets of the washing plates (3 dots) are to be closed.
- Water for washing is to be pumped into the washing channel. Through the inlets water reaches to the surface of washing plates.
- Inside the filter press water passes through the cloth and wash the frame (2 dots) wherein the cake is present. Then, the water washes the cake, exit through the filter cloth and thereafter enters into the plates (1 dot), drains down the surface and is removed through the outlet of that plate.
- If the frames are filled with cake fully, the water wash would be effective. If the frame is not completely filled with cake, during washing the water may break the cake and washing would not be so effective.

## Uses

If pre-sterilized filter press and filter medium are used, it can produce sterile filtrate. Generally, cellulose acetate or nitrate filters are used to filter the bacteria and the porosity (less than 0.2μ) filter medium will be such that it can retain bacteria.

## Merits of Plate & Frame Filter

- Construction of filter press is very simple and widely used for removal of water.

- It gives large surface area, but requires less space.
- It can be used for various slurries.
- Its capacity can be changed on the basis of thickness of the frames and on the number of plates and frames assembled.
- The heavy construction of the filter press can withstand wide pressure difference, normally up to 20 atms.
- The rate of filtration can be improved by washing the cake efficiently and effectively.
- Maintenance of filter press is also easy.

### Demerits of Plate & Frame Filter

- It can filter batch wise. Hence, it has a 'down-time'.
- It requires filter cloth which cannot be reused. Hence, the method is expensive. For change over labor is required.
- The operation of the equipment is not easy; since, the frames are filled with solids.
- If the washing is not effective, it would be difficult to remove the water from the feed.
- Filter press is suitable when the slurry contains less than 5% solids. Due to high labor cost, it is not suitable for low cost materials.

## Filter Leaf

Although the filter press is well accepted and has been used widely, it is not so economical for filtering large quantities of slurries. It cannot be effectively and efficiently washed with small amount of wash water. The leaf filter was first developed in metallurgical industries and is more suitable for handling different types of materials.

### Principle

Filter leaf is suitable where an ordinary filter press is found difficult or inconvenient. The leaf filter requires relatively less labor. The initial cost of such filter is more. The mechanism of filtration through the leaf filter is surface filtration. If vacuum or pressure is applied, the rate of filtration will increase.

### Construction

The Fig 10.7 shows the general construction of a filter leaf. The leaf may be rectangular or round. The core of the leaf is a piece of heavy, coarse-mesh double-crimped wire screen.

Sometimes, core of the screen, there is finer screen, as shown in the Fig 10.7. Although called finer, the screen cannot function as filter medium. Around the outside edge of this assembly there is a light piece of metal of U-shaped cross section, that holds the edges nipple is attached to this binding and works to remove the filtrate as well as to suspend the leaf. A sack of filter cloth is fixed tightly around the edge of the leaf and is hung under a collar around the nipple.

In the filter leaf, weir filter cloth is used. In fact, a simple wire screen cannot be woven so fine that can work as a filter medium. Only if fine wires are used to make the screen, it might have fine pores, suitable for use as filter cloth; but the strength of the screen would be less. A fairly compact and strong filter medium can be prepared, if the metal cloth is rolled after weaving and the strands of the meshes spread out for each filter leaf. The nipple passes through a collar on the body of the filter and is tightened by the cap nut.

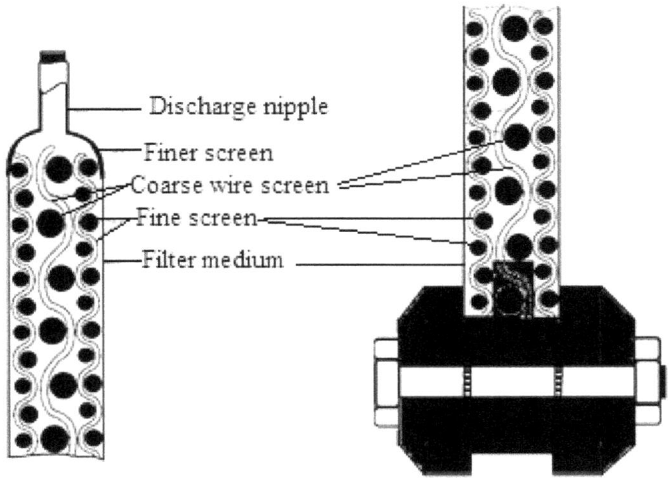


**Fig. 10.7** Schematic diagram of filter leaf

### Working

The filter leaf is immersed into the slurry, the filtrate outlet is connected to the vacuum. The slurry starts passing through the filter cloth. The filtrate enters into the drainage canal and exits through the filtrate outlet to the receiver. In opposite direction, air is passed to facilitate the removal of cake.

### Uses

If the slurry is a dilute dispersion containing about 5% of solid, filtration through a filter leaf equipment is satisfactory.

Filter leaf can be used where enormous volumes of waste solids must be filtered per unit of volume recovered.

### Merits of Filter Leaf

- This equipment is widely used for batch filtration.
- To increase the surface area for filtration a number of units can be connected in parallel.
- The rate of filtration can be increased by filtering under vacuum or by increasing the pressure up to 800 kilopascals. As a result, the pressure difference is increased.
- From any type of container, the slurry can be filtered. Just by immersing the filter leaf in water, the cake can be washed.

## Rotary Drum Filter

Filter leaf and filter press are batch operated and can handle dilute suspensions only. In large scale industrial operations, sometimes continuous operation is required. Besides, the solutions containing high proportion of solid is also required to be filtered. It is also necessary that the method should be economical and easy to perform.

The rotary drum filter can filter continuously. It has a system for removing the cake which is formed during filtration. Moreover, it is suitable for use with concentrated slurries.

### Principle

The mechanism followed by the rotary drum filter is sieve-like filtration on a rotating drum surface under reduced pressure (vacuum). Moreover, compression and drying can be done by this method by using hot air.

The equipment can remove the filter cake by using a knife.

### Construction

The Fig 10.8 shows the construction of a rotary drum filter. It consists of a metallic drum (metal cylinder) mounted horizontally. The length of a drum is around 3.5 m and the diameter of the drum may be up to 3 m. It provides a surface area of about 20 sq metres. The curved surface of the drum is a perforated plate that supports a filter cloth. The filter units have the shape of longitudinal segments of the periphery of a cylinder. Thus, each filter unit is rectangular in shape with a curved profile so that a number of such units can be joined to form a drum. Appropriate connections are again made from each unit through a rotating valve at the centre of the drum. During operation, the drum rotates at low speed, so that each unit passes through the various zones of the slurry present in the vessel. Special attachments such as pre-coat filter and cake compression rollers can be fitted with the drum. The drum is radially partitioned into separate compartments. Each compartment and the centre of the drum are connected by an internal pipe through a rotating valve.

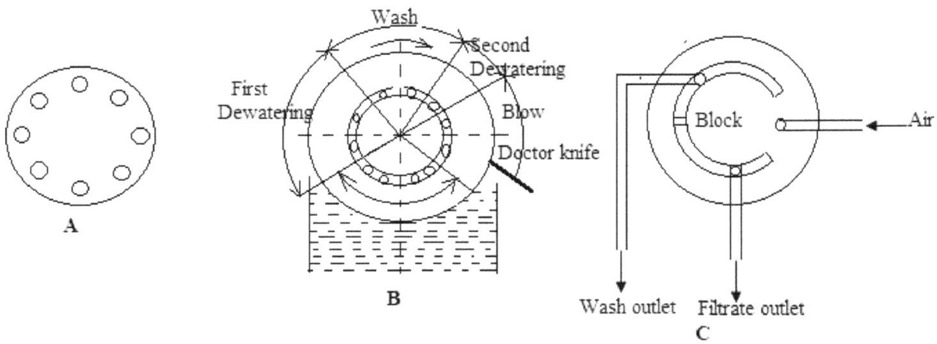


**Fig. 10.8** Rotary drum filter A: Valve seat, B: Single cycle of a rotary drum filter, C: Stationary plate of a rotary drum filter

### Working

The speed of the drum is usually less than 1 rpm. That is, for one revolution it takes more than one minute. The drum enters into the slurry contained in a trough. When the drum dips, the vacuum is applied and deposition of the solids is gradually built up on the surface of the drum. With slow rotation of the drum, the liquid passes through the filter cloth and moves into an internal pipe through a valve. At last, the filtrate moves to the receiver.

When the drum leaves the slurry, it enters the drainage zone. The excess of liquid is sucked inside. At this stage, if a cake compression roller is attached to the drum, the solids can be compressed in form of a cake. This increases the efficiency of washing and drying process. Hot air is supplied after this stage to dry the cake formed. Thereafter, the drum reaches the cake removal zone where the scrapper knife removes the cake. The drum again reaches the slurry. Vacuum is applied on the panel separately to suck the wash water. Wash water is removed through the filter into a separate collecting tank. The above steps are repeated.

### Uses

- For continuous filtration the rotary drum filter can be used.
- It can filter the slurries containing 15 – 30% solids. For example, during preparation of penicillin the extract is separated from mycelium (cell-mass) by rotary drum filter. Such filter can be used for preparing calcium carbonate, starch, etc.

### Merits of Rotary Drum Filter

- The rotary drum filter works automatically and can also be operated continuously.
- For running the operation, the labor cost is low.
- The capacity of the filter is high and the rate of filtration is high.
- The thickness of the cake formed can be varied by altering the speed of rotation of the drum filter. For example, the thickness of impermeable cake should not exceed 5mm. If the solids are coarse powder and can form porous cake, the thickness may be more than 10cm.

### Demerits of Rotary Drum Filter

- The rotary drum filter is not a simple equipment, it requires many spares.
- It requires ancillary equipments such as vacuum pump, slurry pump, agitator, etc.
- It is not relatively cheaper.
- The washing and drying operations may not be efficient; since the cake may crack due to air drawn through the vacuum pump.
- It is being a vacuum filter; its efficiency depends on the pressure difference which is limited to 1 atm.
- Hot filtrate may boil.
- If the solids form impermeable cake, the filter cannot work satisfactorily.
- If the cake does not separate perfectly from the filter cloth, the filter is found less satisfactory.
- The filter is suitable for the solids that form porous cake.

## Meta Filter

In these filters the stainless-steel discs of about 1inch diameter are stamped on one face only. Their heights are accurately controlled on the basis of requirement. Usually the height is maintained at less than 0.001 to 0.005inch.

### Principle

It works as a strainer; that is, the surface filtration for separation of particles. In this filter, metal rings have semicircular projections. These are arranged in the form of nest to form channels on the edges. This channel resists straining to the flow of solids (coarse particles). Into a receiver, the clear filtrate is collected from the top.

### Construction

The construction of a meta filter is shown in Fig 10.9. A meta filter consists of a number of metal rings. The rings are threadedto form a channel on the edges. These rings are usually of stainless steel and have about 15 mm inside diameter and their outside diameter is about 22mm with 0.8mm thickness. As shown in Fig 10.9, on one surface semicircular projections are there. The height of the projection ranges from about 25μm to 250μm.

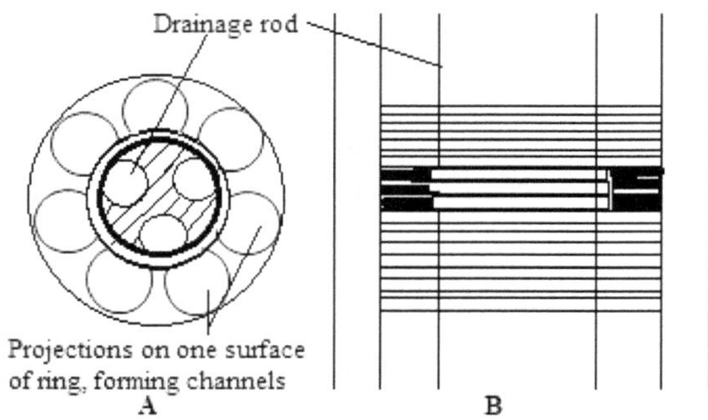


**Fig. 10.9** Meta filter A; Top view, B: Side view

When the rings are packed together, all the same way up, and tightened on the drainage rod with a nut channels form a taper shape as shown in Fig 9B. In a vessel, one or more of such rings are mounted. The filter may be operated by pumping in the slurry under pressure. Reduced pressure may be applied to the outlet side also.

The meta filter may be used as a strainer for coarse particles. For finer particles, a bed of a suitable filter aid material such as kieselguhr is first built up. The pack of rings works as a base on which the true filter medium is supported.

### Working

The meta filters are placed in a vessel and the slurry is pumped under pressure. In some cases, vacuum is applied at the outlet side. The slurry moves through the channels formed on the edges between the rings as shown in Fig 10.9B. The clear liquid goes up and collected from the outlet into the receiver.

For separation of fine particles, a bed of suitable material such as kieselguhr is first built up. The pack of rings acts as a base to support the true filter medium.

### Uses

- It can be used for filtration of syrup,
- It can filter the solutions for injection,
- Filtration of insulin liquors,
- By applying pressure, the viscous liquids can also be filtered by meta filter.

### Merits of Meta Filter

- The meta filter has considerable strength and thus, can withstand high pressure, if applied.
- The running cost is less, since there is no filter medium as such.
- It is an economical filter.
- The slurries containing most sensitive material can be filtered through meta filter, if the filter is prepared from such material that are resistant to corrosion and can prevent contamination.
- It is possible to filter the slurry containing very fine particles by using an appropriate filter aid material for forming the filtering bed. In fact, it has been observed that a solution can be sterilized by filtration using a suitable filter bed.
- The cake can be washed or removed effectively by back-flushing with water.
- It is easy to change over from one batch to another or one product to another.

### Demerits of Meta Filter

- The small surface area of the meta filter limits the amount of solid that can be separated.

## Cartridge Filter

### Principle

By combining a prefilter and a membrane filter into a single unit, a cartridge filter can be formed. The mechanism of filtration in a cartridge filter is sieve penetration or sieve filtration. That is, the slurry containing the particles whose size is less than the pore size of the membrane (undersize particles)can pass through; while the particles of oversize cannot. Just similar to sieve separation. The porous membrane retains the particles of oversize on its surface.

### Construction

The Fig 10.10 indicates rough estimate of construction of a cartridge filter. The cartridge filter looks like cylinder. It is made up of disposable filter media. The material used for construction of a cartridge filter is either a plastic or metal. It consists of a prefilter and a membrane filter combined together. Usually, the filters made with polypropylene is used in cartridge filter. The membrane filter is surrounded by a protective layer. The cartridge is housed in a holder. In the same housing a number of cartridges can be put together. There is a lid to close the housing or cartridge holder. The housing is provided with one inlet for entry of slurry and an outlet for exit of filtrate.

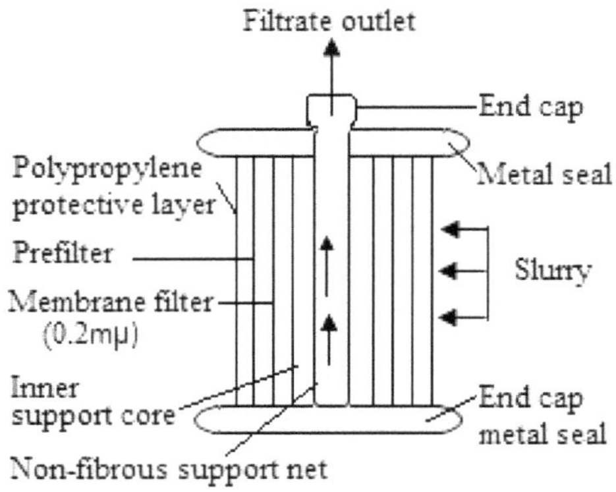


**Fig. 10.10** Schematic diagram of cartridge filter

## Working

When the slurry is pumped into the cartridge holder, it moves towards the filter unit, passes through the filter membrane, after filtration the clear filtrate moves towards the centre of the holder and goes up to where it is collected through the outlet.

## Uses

- For preparation of solutions for ophthalmic and parenteral dosage forms, the cartridge filter can be used.
- It makes the solution free from particulate matter.
- This filter can be used to prepare about 1500 lt of sterile solution in an hour.

## Merits of Cartridge Filter

- It can be sterilized, if it is made of stainless steel or any sterilizable material.
- If it has self-cleaning ability, it would be more beneficial.
- It can be easily assembled and disassembled also.
- The cartridge is not brittle in dry condition.
- It can be used for in-line or continuous filtration. Thus, handling time can be saved.
- It reduces the chance of contamination.

## Demerits of Cartridge Filter

- The cost of filter is relatively high.
- The spares of the filter manufactured by different manufacturers are not equal and interchangeable between the manufacturers.

## Membrane Filters

Membrane filters were first used in the 1920s.A membrane is a thin layer of material that allows only certain materials to pass through it. Membrane filtration depends on the size of the material and the chemical characteristics of the membrane and the material to be filtered.

Membrane filters are made of cellulose acetate, cellulose nitrate, polytetra- fluoroethylene, nylon, etc. Each type is used for its own properties, suitable advantages.

Membrane filters or 'membranes' are microporous plastic films with specific pore size. These are also known as screen, sieve or microporous filters. Membranes retain particles or microorganisms larger than their pore size primarily by surface capture. Some particles smaller than the stated pore size may be retained by other mechanisms also.

### Principle

Membranes are produced frommixed cellulose esters, such as cellulose acetate, cellulose nitrate and nylon, etc. These form the porous structure. Both hydrophilic and hydrophobic polytetrafluoroethylene (PTFE)is a patented one where the membranes are stretched biaxially to form the porous structure. Membrane filtration is a mechanical filtration technique. The pore size of the membranes varies from 0.01 to 0.1mμ. These membranes can remove the particles of bacteria, bacterial spores, fungi, and sometimes even certain viruses from air or water. Membranes with pore size ranging from 0.2 to 0.45mμcan remove all bacteria and fungi from a solution; while membranes having the pore size ranging from 0.8 to 3.0mμ are used for filtration of aerosol, radioactive substances for their particle sizing. Since the membrane filters are very thin, they require some support during filtration. For this reason, a suitable prefilter is placed over a perforated metallic sheet and over the prefilter the membrane filter is placed. Over the membrane filter another sheet is placed. The prefilter is used for three reasons – 1. reducing the load of large particles on the membrane filter, 2. providing the support to the membrane filter, and 3. to maintain a steady rate of filtration.

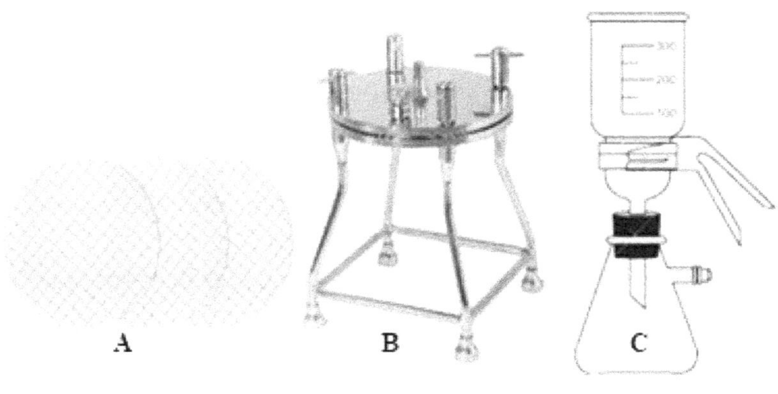


**Fig. 10.11** Membrane filter, A: Membrance filter, B: Assembled membrane filter for commercial use, C: Laboratory scale membrane filter assembly

## Construction

A membrane filtration requires a holder. The holder consists of a frame with three or four legs, one base plate, one cover plate, and two perforated sheets. The cover plate or lid is provided with an outlet, the lid must be tightly fitted to base. The holder and metallic sheets are made of stainless steel. The lower base is provided with an inlet for introducing the solution to be filtered. Generally, the filter is round in shape, the diameter of the filter may be 13, 25, 37 and 47mm.

## Working

The feed water is pumped into membrane through the inlet provided at the lower end of the membrane filter holder. The filtered water is collected through the outlet provided at the upper part of the filter holder. The membrane filtration can be used for manufacturing sterile product or to assess whether the product manufactured is sterile or not, 'the test for sterility'. The method described below is for the test for sterility.

- The sample is either directly filtered in or necessary dilution is made before filtration.
- The appropriate nutrient or culture medium is selected. The broth is dispensed into a sterile petri dish, evenly saturating the absorbent pad.
- Flame the forceps, and remove the membrane from the sterile package.
- Place the membrane filter into the funnel assembly.
- Flame the pouring lip of the sample container and pour the sample into the funnel.
- Turn on the vacuum and allow the sample to draw completely through the filter.
- Rinse funnel with sterile buffered water. Turn on vacuum and allow the liquid to draw completely through the filter.
- Flame the forceps and remove the membrane filter from the funnel.
- Place the membrane filter into the prepared Petri dish.
- Incubate at the proper temperature and for the appropriate time period.
- Count and confirm the colonies and report the results.

## Uses

- Membrane filters are used extensively in the laboratory and in industry to sterilize heat labile fluid materials.
- Effective and acceptable technique to monitor drinking water.
- Useful for monitoring the bacterial contamination in the pharmaceutical, cosmetics, electronics, and food and beverage industries.
- Allows the removal of bacteriostatic or bactericidal agents that would not be removed in pour plate, spread plate, or MPN techniques.

## Merits of Membrane Filters

- Permits testing of large sample volumes. Theoretically almost any volumes of non-turbid water could be filtered through the disk, the organisms from any given volume being deposited in the disk.

- The membrane can be transferred from one medium to another for purposes of selection or differentiation of organisms, thus allowing isolation and enumeration of discrete colonies of bacteria.
- Results can be obtained more rapidly than by the conventional MPN standard methods. It provides presence or absence information within 24 hours.

## Seidtz Filter

This type of filter was first developed in Germany; subsequently in many countries this is being made and used. The filtering medium is relatively thick mat made of fibrous materials. It is generally prepared from asbestos which is not a pure mineral compound. It is a general term or trade name used to describe a category of silicate compounds which may be hydrous magnesium silicate, calcium-magnesium silicate, calcium-magnesium-iron silicate, or sodium-iron silicate, etc. For this reason,the pH of a solution changes after filtration through seitz filter.

### Principle

Seitz filters are almost similar to other depth filters. The actual spacing between the individual fibres may be greater than the size of the particles to be removed. The surface charge and electrostatic attraction can have significant effect when these filters are used for filtering air. The Fig 10.12 shows the diagrams of typical seitz filters. Usually, these filters are of 2mm thick and can be used for filtering the particles of different size ranges, such as the particles of micro size range to even further fine particles of virus size range. When aqueous suspensions are filtered through seitz filters, the effects of surface charging and electrostatic attraction are much less but their effect is increased by the permittivity of the solution. Moreover, the ions and charged micelles present in most of the biological fluids are adsorbed on to the fibre surfaces.

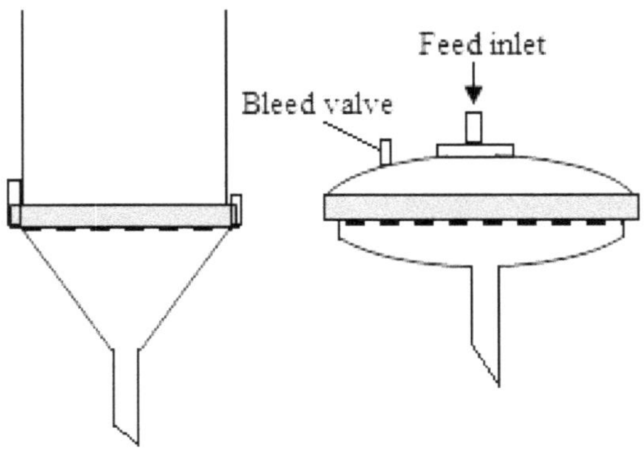


**Fig. 10.12** Schematic diagram of Seitz filters

### Construction

Usually, for industrial application 103 sq cm in size and 0.635 cm thick filter pads are fitted in filter press. A filter press can hold about 100 such filter pads(sheets) and can provide about 13.9

sq.m of filtering area. Finely spreaded asbestos may be used to make seitz filter. Such asbestos filter provides the highest adsorption of microorganisms and other particles. The seitz filters may be of different porosities.

The press filter packed with seitz filters with graded porosity can filter the liquids containing particles of heterogenous sizes. The filter pads with open texture (largely porous) are fitted near the inlet of the feed material, thereafter the pads with graded porosity are fitted in such a way that the pads with very fine porosity remains present near the outlet for filtrate. With such orderly arrangement of filter pads, there are few advantages, such as

- Suspending particles can be distributed uniformly throughout the pads according to their size range,
- The filtration process can run for longer period,
- Choking of filter rarely take place,
- The rate of filtration is quite high.

Recently, instead of using several pads of graded porosities, a single pad is being made with layers of graded porosities, so that one side of the filter has open texture and other side has very fine porosity.

### Working

The fibrous filter pad either alone or in combination are used to filter the liquids. If a filter press is used, it contains number of pads with graded porosities. The feed liquid is introduced through its feed inlet valve. A pump is connected with required pressure and the filtrate is collected from the filtrate outlet.

If a single filter pad is used, the open texture of the pad is kept upside and the side having finest porosity remains facing the bottom. The feed liquid is fed from the top and the bottom of the filter is fitted with a receiver to collect the filtrate. Vacuum is also kept on. The rate of filtration and the rate of feeding are adjusted accordingly. If there is any decrease in rate of filtration, filtration assembly is checked for choking of the filter pad.

### Uses

- Seitz filter may have different porosities from large to very fine,
- It can be used for preparing sterile solution,
- Seitz filters are useful for filtration of both air and water.

### Merits of Seidtz Filter

- If the filter used is a closed system, there is no risk of contamination of the filtrate.
- The equipment is very simple to use.
- It is very suitable for filtration of viscous liquids.

### Demerits of Seidtz Filter

- Since the filter is made of asbestos, shedding of loose asbestos fibre may be observed,
- The filter pad may absorb sufficient amount of drug substances.

- ➢ Re-use of the filter pad is not possible.
- ➢ The asbestos being carcinogenic, use of pad made of asbestos is not safe.

## Mechanisms of Filtration

The mechanisms involved in retention of particles by a filter are of significance only in the early stages of filtration. Once the particles retained from the cake, the filter medium becomes a support only. However, the mechanisms involved in filtration are briefly described below:

- **Straining:** This is the simplest mechanism of filtration. Just like sieving mechanism, the particles having sizes larger than the pore size of the filter, are retained over the filter. However, the particles having sizes smaller than that of filter pass through.
- **Impingement:** When a liquid containing undissolved solids is flowing in streamline, approaches a cylindrical object, the flow pattern changes. Some solids having momentum are expected to cross the streamlines and hit the object, and some will not. Among the solids hitting the object, some solids will deposit over the surface of the object. Thus, the particles in that zone will be collected in the form of a roughly triangular shape. Other particles will re-enter the zone and the layer of deposit will go on increasing.
- **Entanglement:** When the filter medium is made of a cloth with a nap or a porous felt, the particles become entangled in the form of a mass of fibres. In this case, the particles are usually smaller than the pores, so that impingement becomes possible.
- **Attractive forces:** In some cases, the particles may deposit on a filter medium due to the attractive forces. This happens as a result of electrostatic precipitation. For example, the large potential differences are used to remove particles from air stream.

In practice, this process may combine different mechanisms. The removal of solids practically takes place by a straining mechanism. Once the initial layer of solids is formed, cake formation starts.

## Short Questions

1. What is filtration? Write down the applications of filtration in pharmacy.
2. Write down the theory of filtration. What are the factors that affect the filtration process?
3. How can the frames of a plate and frame filter is washed?
4. Write down the advantages and disadvantages of plate and frame filter.
5. Write down the applications, advantages and disadvantages of rotary drum filter.
6. What is a meta filter? How does it work?
7. What is a cartridge filter? Write down its principle of working.
8. What are the advantages of a membrane filter? How can it be constructed?
9. What are the applications, advantages and limitations of a seidtz filter.
10. Writea note on filter aids.

## Long Questions

1. Write notes on filter aids and filter media.
2. Write down the principle of plate and frame filter. How is the plate and frame filter constructed?
3. Discuss the principle and construction of a filter leaf. Draw a schematic diagram of filter leaf.
4. Describe the principle and construction of a rotary drum filter with the help of a diagram.
5. How can a meta filter be constructed? What are its advantages and limitations?
6. Write down the principle and working of a membrane filter.
7. What is seidtz filter? Write down its principle of working.
8. How can a seidtz filter be constructed? Write down how does it work.
9. Discuss the applications of filtration and the factors that influence the rate of filtration.
10. How does a plate and frame filter work? What are its applications?

# CHAPTER 11

# Centrifugation

Objectives, Principle and Applications of Centrifugation, Principles, Construction, Working, Uses, Merits and Demerits of Perforated Basket Centrifuge, Non-perforated Basket Centrifuge, Semi Continuous Centrifuge & Super Centrifuge.

## Objectives

In the filtration process, it is necessary to create or to maintain a driving force for facilitating the process. For example, in normal filtration, the gravitational force acts as the driving force. According to Darcy the centrifugal force is a force that provides the driving force that creates a pressure difference in the filtration process. *The process of developing the centrifugal force within a sample by rotating it at a high speed is called centrifugation.* In some cases, the gravitational force is either not effective or slowly effective to separate certain particles from their suspension medium/solvent. In those cases, centrifugation finds its application. For example, separation of finely divided solids from their dispersion (very slow sedimentation takes place) or separation of proteins as per their molecular weight through centrifugation, or separation of two phases of a stable emulsion under normal conditions. Sometimes, the process is considered or described as an 'accelerated gravitational process'; but care should be taken not to describe the process accordingly.

It is well known that if a substance is rotated about a centre point at a particular radial distance from the point, it creates a force which acts on the rotating substance. Centrifugation has been developed on the basis of this principle.

## Principle

According to the Darcy's law the rate of filtration (volume of filtrate produced per unit time) is directly related to the area of filter medium, pressure drop across the filter and filter cake, and inversely related to the viscosity of the filtrate and thickness of the cake. The law can be expressed as;

$$\frac{dV}{dt} = \frac{K \times A \times \Delta P}{\mu \times 1} \qquad .....(11.1)$$

Where,

V is the volume of the filtrate,

t is the time of filtration,

K is the constant for the filter medium,

ΔP is the pressure drop across the filter medium and filter cake,

μ is the viscosity of the filtrate, and

l is the thickness of the cake.

This represents the rate of flow of filtrate through capillaries of the filter medium and filter cake; it is almost similar to the Poiseuille's law for flow of liquid through a single tube.

The centrifugal force can be measured in terms of the ratio of the centrifugal force to the gravitational force, this is termed as centrifugal effect, C. This ratio indicates the number of times the centrifugal force is greater than the gravitational force. The centrifugal effect is then put into an appropriate equation with gravitational force. The centrifugal effect can be calculated as follows:

Let us assume that a body of mass 'm'g is rotating in a circular path of radius r cm at a velocity v cm/sec as shown in Fig 11.1. Then the force acting on the body in a radial direction is given by:

$$F = \frac{m \times v^2}{r} \quad .....(11.2)$$

Where, F is the centrifugal force,

m is the mass of the body,

r is the radius of circle of rotation, and

v is the velocity of the body.

The gravitational force will also act on the same body. The gravitational force acting on the same body can be calculated as:

$$G = m \times g$$

Where, G is the gravitational force,

m is the mass of the body and

g is the gravitational constant.

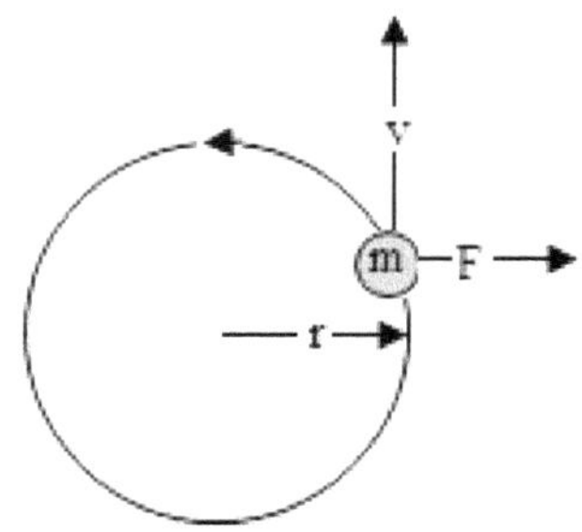


**Fig. 11.1** Principle of centrifugation

If the centrifugal effect, C is expressed as,

$$C = \frac{F}{G} \quad .....(11.3)$$

$$= \frac{m \times v^2}{m \times g \times r}$$

$$= \frac{v^2}{g \times r}$$

$$= \frac{(2\pi \times r \times n)^2}{g \times r} \quad [v = 2\pi \times r \times n, \text{ where n (s–1) is the speed of rotation}]$$

$$= \frac{4\pi^2 r^2 n^2}{gr} = \frac{2d \times \pi^2 \times n^2}{g} \quad .....(11.4)$$

[where d (in meter), the diameter of rotation = 2r]

The value of gravitational force, g is 9.807m/s$^2$, and the value of $\pi = 3.14$ which are when put in the eqn. 4is reduced to

$$C = \frac{2d \times n^2 \times \pi^2}{g} = \frac{2d \times n^2 \times (3.14)^2}{9.807} = 2.013n2d \qquad .....(11.5)$$

For example, if a centrifuge having diameter of 1 m rotates at a frequency of 10 s–1; its centrifugal effect would be 2.013 × (10)2 × 1 = 201.3.

From the above discussion it is understood that the centrifugal effect is directly proportional to the diameter of rotation as well as to the square of the speed of rotation. Thus, the speed of rotation (rpm) of a centrifuge is more important for centrifugal effect.

## Applications of Centrifugation

- **Isolating suspensions:** Simple centrifuges are used in chemistry, biology, and biochemistry for isolation and separation of suspensions. These centrifuges vary widely in speed and capacity. They usually comprise a rotor containing two, four, six, or many more numbers of wells (in centrifuge tubes) within which the samples are put.
- **Isotope separation:** Centrifuges used in nuclear power and nuclear weapon programs are of different types. The first being the Zippe-type centrifuge which separates isotopes. Gas centrifuges are used in uranium enrichment. The heavier isotope of uranium (uranium-238) in the uranium hexafluoride gas tends to concentrate at the walls of the centrifuge as it spins, the desired uranium-235 isotope is extracted and concentrated with a scoop selectively placed inside the centrifuge. It takes many thousands of centrifugations to enrich uranium for use in a nuclear reactor (around 3.5% enrichment), and many thousands more to enrich it to make it weapon-grade (above 90% enrichment).
- **Aeronautics and astronautics:** The centrifuges used in a**eronautics and astronautics** are exceptionally large to test the reactions and tolerance of pilots and to assess the astronaut's reaction at the acceleration above those experienced in the earth's gravity. For this reason, these centrifuges are also called as *human centrifuges*.

  The centrifuge is operated by the aerospace physiology department for the purpose of training and evaluation of prospective fighter pilots in the Air Force fighter aircraft. Exposure to this simulated gravity would prevent or reduce the bone decalcification and muscle atrophy that affect the individuals exposed to long periods of freefall. The first centrifuges used for human research were used by Erasmus Darwin, the grandfather of Charles Darwin. The first large scale human centrifuge designed for Aeronautical training was created in Germany in 1933.
- **Geotechnical centrifuge modeling:** A geotechnical centrifuge is used to perform the model tests to study geotechnical problems such as the strength, stiffness and capacity of foundations for bridges and buildings, settlement of embankments, stability of slopes, earth retaining structures, stability of tunnel and seawalls. Other applications include explosive cratering, contaminant migration in ground water, frost motion and sea ice. The centrifuge may be useful for scale modeling of any large-scale nonlinear problem for which gravity is a primary driving force. The scale model is typically constructed in the laboratory and then loaded onto the end of the centrifuge, which is typically between 0.2 and 10 metres (0.7 and 32.8 ft) in radius. The

purpose of spinning the models on the centrifuge is to increase the gravitational forces on the model so that stresses in the model are equal to the stresses in the prototype. For example, the stress beneath a 0.1-metre-deep (0.3 ft) layer of model soil spun at a centrifugal acceleration of 50 g produces stresses equivalent to those beneath a 5-metre-deep (16 ft) prototype layer of soil in earth's gravity.

- **Commercial application:** Some centrifuges such as sugar centrifuges are used to separate sugar crystals from the crystallized syrup or mother liquor. Centrifuges with a batch weight of up to 2200 kg per lot (charge) are used in the sugar industry to separate the sugar crystals from the mother liquor.
  - Standalone centrifuges for drying (hand-washed) clothes – usually with a water outlet.
  - Washing machines
  - Centrifuges are used in the space mission. This type of centrifuge propels the riders using a combination of a centrifuge and a motion simulator to simulate the feeling of going into space.
  - In soil mechanics, the centrifuges utilize centrifugal acceleration to match soil stresses in a scale model to those found in reality.
  - Large industrial centrifuges are commonly used in water and wastewater treatment to dry sludges. The resulting dry product is called *cake*, and the water leaving a centrifuge, after removal of most of the solids, is called *concentrate*.
  - Large industrial centrifuges are also used in the oil industry to remove solids from the drilling fluid.
  - Disc-stack centrifuges are used in oil sands industry to separate small amounts of water and solids from bitumen.
  - Centrifuges are used to separate cream (remove fat) from milk.

## Difference between Centrifugation and Vacuum Filtration

Generally vacuum filtration and centrifugation are used for the same sludge treatment purpose. But these processes are different. The difference between these processes are mentioned below.

| Centrifugation | Vacuum filtration |
|---|---|
| • Lower capital cost.<br>• Space requirement is less<br>• Capacity of treating suspension with poor filtration capacity. | • Higher solid concentration in the cake<br>• Solid concentration in the effluent is less. |

## Process variables Affecting Centrifugation

The following are the process variables that affect the centrifugation:

- Liquid viscosity
- Liquid density
- Solids concentration
- Particle size distribution

- Surface charge of particles
- Type and/or shape or particles
- Feed rate of slurry
- Agitation speed
- Size of centrifuge (distance from rotation axis)
- Height of cake
- Allowable pressure-drop across the cake
- Mode of operation (batch vs. continuous)
- Time at full speed
- Depth of skimming

## General Application of Centrifuge

1. **Production of bulk drugs:** After crystallization, the drugs are separated from the mother liquor by centrifugation. For example, traces of mother liquor are separated from potassium penicillin G crystals by centrifugation method.
2. **Production of biological products:** Most of the biological products are either protein aceous or macromolecules. During manufacturing, they remain in colloidal dispersion in water. It is difficult to separate the colloid particles by normal methods of filtration. For such cases, the centrifugal methods are used. For example, Insulin is purified from other precipitates of protein materials by centrifugation. Blood cells are separated from plasma by centrifugal method. Bacterial enzymes are separated from bacterial culture medium by sedimenting the bacterial cells by centrifugation. Dirt and water are separated from olive oil and fish-liver oils by centrifugation.
3. **Evaluation of suspensions and emulsions:** Sedimentation is one of the major stability problems of suspensions and creaming is one of the major stability problems of emulsions. These problems may not occur immediately after the preparation of a suspension or emulsion. To evaluate the stability or to assess whether the preparations may likely show such instability, the rate of sedimentation is increased for assessment of creaming, the suspension or emulsion is transferred into a centrifuge and rotated at a rpm of 200 to 3000. If any problem does not occur, then the suspension or emulsion can be considered as stable formulation.
4. **Determination of molecular weight of colloids:** Polymers, proteins and such other macromolecules can form colloidal dispersions. The molecular weights of those molecules can be determined by ultracentrifugation. The larger molecules will be arranged at the periphery while the lighter molecules will accumulate near the center.

## Basket Centrifuge

The basket centrifuges have been used in the pharmaceutical industry for many years and for many purposes during production of intermediate and final filtration steps.

For production of chemicals this type of equipment has been used widely. There are two types of centrifuges which belong to the group of basket centrifuge –

1. Perforated basket centrifuge, performs the works similar to filtration, and
2. Non-perforated basket centrifuge having a solid-walled vessel in which the particles sediment to the wall under the influence of centrifugal force.

## Perforated Basket Centrifuge

### Principle

Perforated basket centrifuge is alternatively called as *centrifugal filter*. It contains a perforated basket which rotates and allows the cake of solid to accumulate within the basket. The clarified liquid is also removed continuously through the cylindrical wall of the basket because of centrifugal filtration. The solid is intermittently removed with the help of a knife, which is placed within the basket but not rotating with the basket. The solid is collected in a vertical chute. Thus, with this type of centrifuge, drier cakes are produced and are collected. This does not happen with other types of centrifuges. Hence, most suitably the solids can be recovered from this type of basket centrifuge.

### Construction

The Fig 11.2 shows the schematic diagram of perforated basket centrifuge. The construction of this type of centrifuge is similar to that of a domestic spin dryer. An industrial centrifuge of this category contains a vessel, usually about 1m in diameter has an outer perforated wall which is attached to a vertical shaft so that it can be rotated at a frequency of 20 to 25 $S^{-1}$. The perforated basket throws the liquid out by the centrifugal force. An outer casing with an outlet collects this liquid. For safety, the casing is closed by a cover. The cover is usually interlocked with the drive motor so that the centrifuge cannot be operated when the cover is raised.

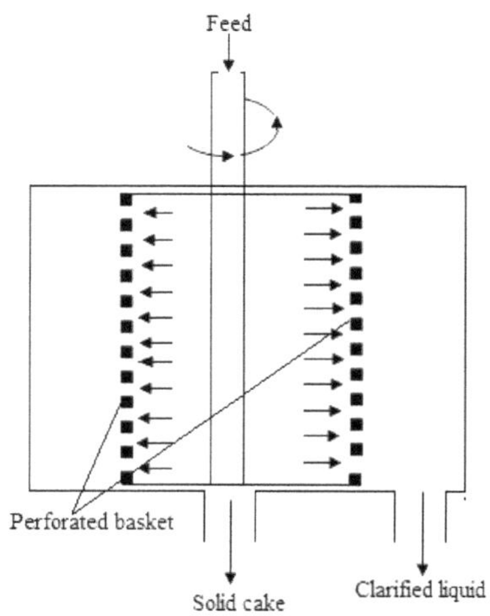


**Fig. 11.2** Schematic diagram of perforated basket centrifuge

The centrifuge used in pharmaceutical industries are generally made of either stainless steel or rubber coated mild steel, so that rusting does not take place. The drive motor may be at below the basket or above the basket. If the motor drive is attached to the below the basket, it is called *under-driven* and if the motor drive is attached to above the basket, it is called *over-driven* centrifuge. The Fig 11.2 is an example of over-driven centrifuge.

## Working

It contains perforated bowls with a filter bag of nylon or cotton. Liquid may be fed in a continuous mode or batch wise. It is operated at below 4000 rpm. Solid mass can be washed before removing the bowls. Rate of feeding may vary from 50-300 $dm^3$(lt) per min and have a solid holding capacity of maximum 500 $dm^3$(lt).It is primarily used for the separation of mycelial mass, moulds and crystalline compounds.

## Uses

- For removing unwanted solids from a liquid, a centrifuge can be used. For example, precipitated protein is to be separated from the product such as insulin.
- Centrifugation method can recover maximum amount of the liquid than the filtration. The cake requires little or no fresh liquid for washing; thus, reduces the time of evaporation and drying.
- For separating and drying the solids particularly of crystallized substances, centrifuge is very useful. Because the mother liquor can be removed from the surface rapidly and the process avoids efflorescence and free flowing product is produced.
- Centrifuge can remove the impurities relatively to higher extent compared to filtration and subsequent drying.
- This method is useful for retention of water of crystallization of crystallized substances.

## Merits of Perforated Basket Centrifuge

- Centrifugal methods can handle slurries containing high proportion of solid, even like a paste.
- The centrifuge is very compact, occupies very little floor space compared with filters of similar capacity.
- Moisture content of the final product is less than that of a product obtained in filtration (filter cake).
- Liquid is removed from the cake by centrifugal force; as a result, a dry product can be obtained and dissolved solid is separated from the cake. This is different from the solids obtained by thermal drying process. In the latter case, the dissolved solid is not separated from the cake.
- The processes of charging, separation of phases, washing, drying, and removal of cake are rapid. A centrifuge having diameter of about 1 m can process about 200kg of slurry.

## Demerits of Perforated Basket Centrifuge

- The process is expensive because of high labor cost involved in cycle of operation.
- Usually the process is intermittent and is done on batch wise.
- In case of continuous operation, the wear and tear of the machine becomes high because of removal of hard, abrasive cake by using knife. The wall of the basket erodes quickly.

## Non-Perforated Basket Centrifuge

### Principle

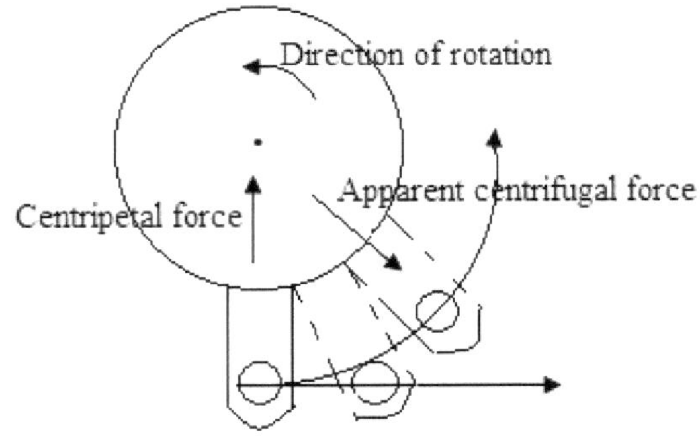


In a solution, there may be particles whose density is higher than that of the solvent and is called *sink*(sediment). Particles which are lighter than that of solvent, *floats* on the top. Thus, the movement of particles towards the bottom of the container depends on the difference in densities. If there is no difference indensities (isopyknic conditions), the particles stay steady. The advantage of even tiny differences in density may be used to separate various particles in a solution. C*entrifugal force* provided by a centrifuge is much more powerful than gravity. High centrifugal effects can be achieved by using a centrifuge of small diameter rotating at high speed. This is the principle of the tubular (tube like)bowl centrifuge that can separate the solids of small particle size from liquids.

The method is alternatively called *sedimentation centrifuge*. If F is the relative centrifugal force, m is the mass of the particle, r is radius of rotation (cm) i.e., the distance of particle from the axis of rotation, and ω is the average angular velocity (radians/sec); then

$$F = m\omega^2 r$$

Where, the average angular velocity, $\omega = \frac{2\pi \times (\text{rev./min})}{60}$ [1 revolution = 2π radians = 360]

So, $$\omega^2 = \frac{4\pi^2 (\text{rev./min})^2}{3600} = \frac{4\pi^2 (\text{rev./min})^2}{3600}$$

Therefore, the applied centrifugal field, G for the particle of unit mass

$$= \omega^2 r = \frac{4\pi^2 (\text{rev./min})^2}{3600} \times r$$

At a point equivalent to 4 cm from the centre of rotation and if the angular velocity is 2500 rad $S^{-1}$, then the value of centrifugal field, G would be: $G = (2500)^2 \times 4\text{cms}^{-2} = 25000000 = 2.5 \times 10^7 \text{cm.S}^{-2}$.

Similarly, if an ultracentrifuge is run at a speed of 37500r.p.m. the angular velocity, ω can be calculated as:

$$\omega = \frac{2\pi \times (\text{rev./min})}{60} = \frac{2 \times 3.1416 \times 37500}{600} \text{rad.S}^{-1}$$

$$= 3927 \text{ rad.S}^{-1}$$

The non-perforated basket centrifuge is used when the solid content of the suspension is more. It consists of a simple drum-shaped basket or bowl which rotates around a vertical axis. The solids accumulate and form cake due to the effect of the centrifugal force, but they are not dewatered. The residual liquid is drained out when the rotation of the bowl is stopped. Then the solid layer (cake) is removed manually by scraping or scooping. Unloading of the centrifuge can be done semi-automatic methods – (1) by use of a skimmer pipe to remove the residual liquid, and (2) by lowering a knife blade into the solid and cutting or scraping it out from the bowl.

This does not require switching off of the machine.

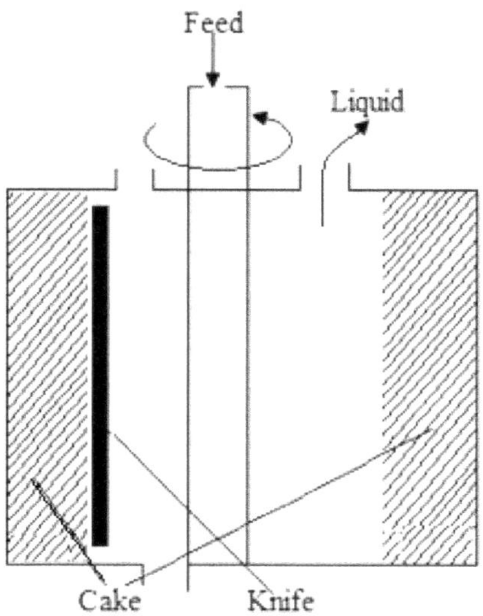


**Fig. 11.3** Schematic diagram of non-perforated basket centrifuge

## Construction

A cylindrical bowl of about 10 cm diameter and 1 m in length is mounted in such a way that it can be rotated about its longitudinal axis at high speed (rpm). The speed varies from 300 $S^{-1}$ to 1000 per sec.

## Working

The feed may be introduced into the centrifuge continuously or in batches through the rotating shaft. Similarly, the liquid, after clarification, is also continuously removed from the centrifuge through overflow weir inside the centrifuge. During centrifugation solids form the cake which is periodically removed. Once the basket is filled with the cake the centrifuge slows down and the soft cake layer is removed (skimming). About 5 – 15% of the bowl solid volume is removed by skimming. The bulk of the cake is removed by tilling with a knife which moves slowly with the rotating cake (basket). The solid cake is discharged centrally at the bottom of the centrifuge. Depending on the depth of the basket, the solid cake can accumulate from 60 – 85% of the total volume of the basket. The cycle of unloading the cake can be made through automated system also. In this system, unloading of cake takes only 10% of the cycle time. This type of centrifuge is typically operated at low centrifugal force and generally possesses a low solid handling capacity. The non-perforated basket centrifuge is usually used for typical sludge dewatering purpose. However, high solid recovery can be achieved with this type of centrifuge even without using any chemical additive.

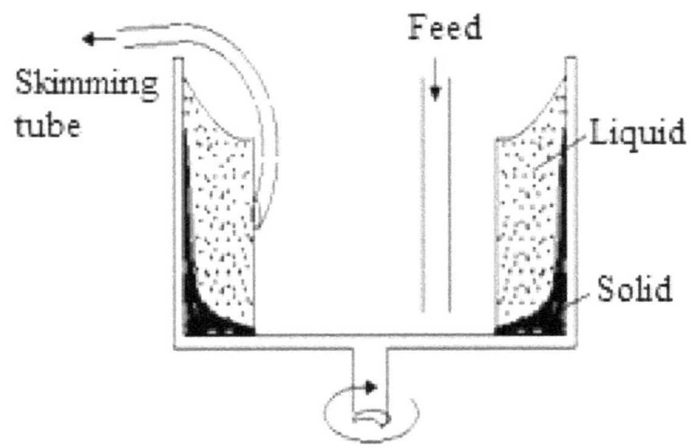


**Fig. 11.4** Schematic diagram of non-perforated centrifuge

### Uses

Non-perforated basket centrifuge is used when deposited solids resist the liquid to flow through it.

### Merits of Non-Perforated Basket Centrifuge

- Removes the solid particles from a liquid,
- Causes separation of particles on the basis of density difference between two phases,
- Can be used as continuous centrifugation.

### Demerits of Non-Perforated Basket Centrifuge

- If the densities of the two phases are same, the centrifuge cannot work.

## Semicontinuous Centrifuge

For operation of a batch centrifugation labor is required and such centrifuge consumes high power. The basket has an inertia. Larger quantity of material (suspension) is required to run the machine at a desired speed. More power is required and the power is required to maintain the speed. For this reason, semi continuous and continuous centrifuges have been developed.

### Principle

Semi continuous centrifuge acts as a filtration centrifuge. The extent of separation of solid from the liquid depends on the difference in densities of solid and that of liquid. The side walls of basket are perforated. During centrifugation, the liquid passes through the perforated walls and the solid remains within the basket. The solids deposit in form of cake. The cake is washed with water. Centrifugation is continued till the moisture content is reduced to 2 – 4%. With the help of a knife the major portion of the cake is removed and collected through the chute attached.

## Construction

A semi continuous centrifuge consists of a perforated basket. The basket rotates continuously on horizontal axis. As shown in the Fig 11.5, the suspension to be filtered is continuously fed until a cake of about 3 mm thick is formed. With the help of a feeler, feeding is discontinued. The cake formed in the basket is washed with water and washing is removed completely.

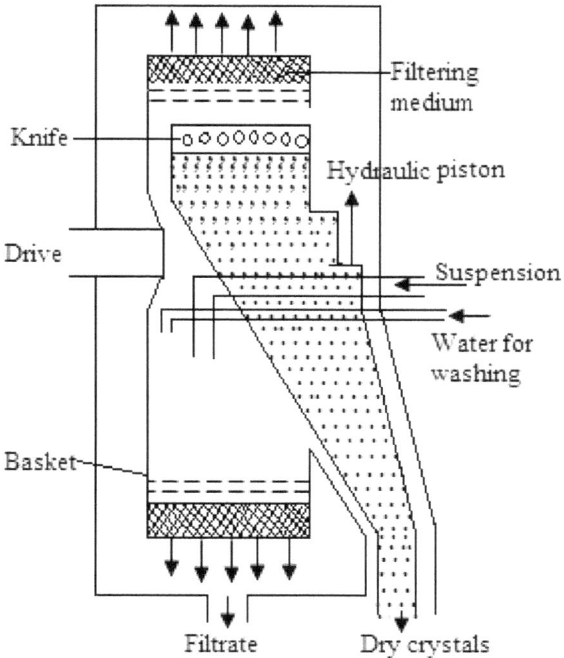


**Fig. 11.5** Schematic diagram of semicontinuous centrifuge

## Working

The perforated basket is rotated and the suspension is fed from the side tube. During centrifugation the medium passes through the perforations and solid is retained within the basket. The filtrate or medium is collected at the specific outlet. The solids retained in the basket is deposited in the form of cake which is washed thoroughly with water. The washings leave the basket through the perforations and is removed through the filtrate outlet. When the cake becomes 5 – 7 cm thick, the feeler cuts off the air supply to the diaphragm valve and entry of the feed material is then automatically stopped. The hydraulic cylinder is then activated and the knife along with the chute is lifted. The knife scrapes out the cake leaving a thin layer of about 3 mm. The scrapped cake leaves the basket through the chute and is collected at the product outlet. The cake remains in form of a thin layer and acts as the filtering medium for next cycle. Before starting the next cycle, the residual layer of the cake can be washed with small amount of water.

A suitable timer can be used to control the air supply system. However, all the steps are controlled through the diaphragm valve. For this reason, this centrifuge can be called semi-automatic also. The product (solids) contains about 2 – 4% of moisture.

### Uses

- The semi continuous centrifuge is used when sufficient labor is not available,
- It is used to reduce the power consumption.

### Merits of Semi Continuous Centrifuge

- Requires less labor,
- Power consumption is relatively less,
- Able to maintain required revolutions per unit time,
- Requires relatively less time for completion of a cycle.

### Demerits of Semi Continuous Centrifuge

- Crystals may break during discharge,
- Moving parts of the equipment are many,
- Function of the equipment is complicated.

## Super Centrifuge

It is alternatively called as tubular bowl centrifuge. In equation, $F = \frac{Wu^2}{R}$, it can be observed that for any particular peripheral velocity, the centrifugal force exerted on a particle is inversely proportional to the radius of the basket, but it is proportional to the square of the speed. On the other hand, the strain developed on the basket is proportional to its linear speed (peripheral velocity). If the radius of the basket is reduced by 50%, the speed (rpm) is doubled. The linear speed of the basket remains unchanged. But the centrifugal force becomes double.

These centrifuges are widely used in food, biochemical and pharmaceutical industries. The Fig 11.6 refers to this type of centrifuge and is known as *Sharples Super-centrifuge*. It is used for continuous separation of the two phases of an emulsion.

### Principle

It is a sedimentation centrifuge. The separation of the phases depends on the difference between the densities of two immiscible liquids. Centrifugation is done in the bowl of small centrifuge. During centrifugation, the heavier liquid is thrown against the wall and the liquid of lesser density remains in the inner layer. The two layers are separated at the same time using modified barriers (weirs).

### Construction

It consists of a solid vertical, cylindrical bowl. The diameter of the bowl varies from 1.75 inch to 5 inches. The centrifuge used in the laboratories contains the bowl having diameter of about 1.75 inch; while in the commercial centrifuges, the bowl-diameter is about 5 inches. Similarly, the length of the bowl varies from 9 inches to 30 inches respectively.

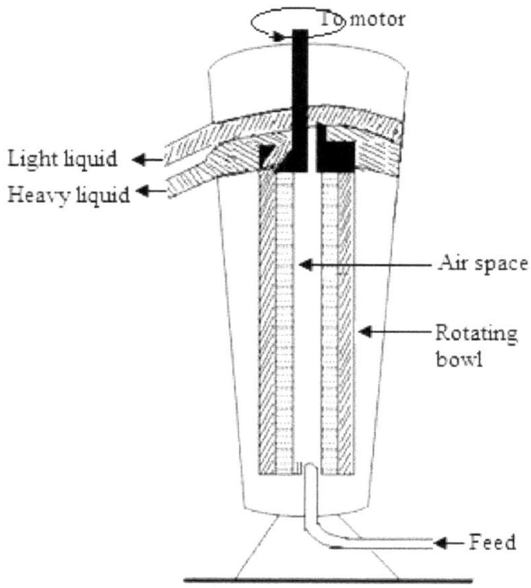


**Fig. 11.6** Schematic diagram of supercentrifuge (Tubular bowl centrifuge)

In laboratory centrifuges, the rotation varies from 1500 to 2000 rpm; while in case of commercial centrifuges, the rotation varies from 22000 to 50000 rpm. The bowl is suspended from an upper bearing and the drive assembly is suspended through a flexible drive spindle. This spindle hangs freely with only a loose guide in a controlled damping assembly at the bottom. Thus, it can find its natural axis of rotation, if it becomes slightly unbalanced. The unbalancing occurs due to the load during processing. Feed is introduced at the bottom of the bowl through a stationary feed nozzle under pressure. The liquid after introduction starts moving with same acceleration as the rotor moves. The liquid moves up through the bowl as an annulus and discharges at the top. The solid materials move upward with the liquid. The materials going up experience a radial motion depending on their size and weights. A particle can be separated from the liquid, if its path intersects the internal surface of the bowl wall. Otherwise, it remains in the effluent and flows out through the outlet at the top of the bowl. It is then caught and delivered in the form of a jet.

If two liquid-outlets are provided at the top of the bowl of different radii and at different elevations, continuous separation of two immiscible liquids of different densities become possible. The solids of any phase are collected on the internal surface of the bowl. Tubular bowl centrifuges are available with different casings and covers so that noxious, volatile vapors and flammable liquids can be used for centrifugation. Solids sedimented against the bowl-wall are generally removed manually, so that the quantity of solid separated cannot spoil the clarity of the liquid overflown.

## Working

With the help of a drive-assembly the centrifuge is rotated on its horizontal axis at a high speed of about 2000 rpm. The feed material is introduced at the bottom of the centrifuge with the help of a suitable pump system. Based on the difference in the densities, the two liquid phases can separate during centrifugation. The liquid of lower density forms an inner layer, while the liquid of higher density is thrown against the wall. Both the liquids move up to the top of the vertical bowl. With the help of a hydraulic balance the liquid-liquid interface (neutral zone) is maintained. Both the layers are removed at the same time when they rise different heights through modified weirs due to their different densities. Thus, continuous separation of immiscible liquid phases becomes possible.

### Uses

- Super centrifuge is mainly used in food and pharmaceutical industries to separate liquid phases of emulsions.
- Solids can be separated by this centrifuge; for example, tubular bowl centrifuge.
- It is used to separate two immiscible liquid phases of an emulsion.
- It is used for continuous separation of phases.

### Merits of Super Centrifuge

- Super centrifuge is used for separation of two immiscible liquid phases of emulsions.
- Super centrifuge can be used for separation of solids from liquid.
- For continuous centrifugation super centrifuge is used.

## Short Questions

1. Define the term centrifugation. What is the objective of centrifugation?
2. What are the applications of centrifugation?
3. Write down the principle of basket centrifuge. Draw a schematic diagram of basket centrifuge.
4. What are advantages and limitations of basket centrifuge?
5. What are the applications, benefits and limitations of a semi-continuous centrifuge?
6. What is super centrifuge? On which principle it works?
7. What are the applications, advantages and limitations of super centrifuge?
8. What are commercial applications of centrifugation?
9. How does centrifugation differ from vacuum filtration?
10. What are the process variables that can influence the process of centrifugation?

## Long Questions

1. Explain the principle of centrifugation.
2. How is a basket centrifuge constructed? What are the applications of a basket centrifuge?
3. Explain the principle of a non-perforated basket centrifuge with the help of a schematic diagram of it.
4. How does a non-perforated basket centrifuge work? What are its benefits?

5. What is the principle of semi-continuous centrifuge? Explain its principle.
6. Write down the working of a semi-continuous centrifuge.
7. How is a super centrifuge constructed? How does it work?
8. Write down the general applications of centrifugation.
9. What is a basket centrifuge? What are different types of basket centrifuge and how do they work differently?
10. With the help of a diagram discuss the principle of non-perforated basket centrifuge.

# CHAPTER 12

# Plant Location, Industrial Hazards and Plant Safety

Plant Layout, Utilities and Services, Mechanical Hazards, Chemical Hazards, Fire Hazards, Explosive Hazards and their Safety.

## Introduction

The geographical location of a pharmaceutical plant can have strong influence on the success of an industrial venture. Considerable care must be given while selecting the plant site, and many different factors must be considered. Primarily, the plant should be located where the cost of production would be minimum and distribution can be done easily. But other factors, such as scope for expansion and safe living conditions for plant operators as well as the surrounding community, are also equally important. The major factors in the selection of most plant sites are:

- Marketing area
- Raw materials
- Transportation facilities
- Availability of labor
- Water supply
- Availability of power and fuel
- Climate

In fact, before plant layout, site layout must be made. Both can be done simultaneously. The process units and ancillary buildings should be laid out to give the most economical flow of materials and personnel around the site. Hazardous processes must be located at a safe distance from other buildings. Consideration must also be given to the future expansion of the site. The ancillary buildings and services required on a site, in addition to the main processing units(buildings), include

1. Storage for raw materials and products: tank, farms, and warehouses;
2. Maintenance workshops;
3. Stores, for maintenance and operating supplies;
4. Laboratories for process quality control activities;
5. Fire stations and other emergency services;
6. Utilities;

7. Effluent disposal plant: waste water treatment, solid and or liquid waste collection;
8. Offices for general administration;
9. Canteens and other amenity centres, such as medical centers;
10. Parking areas.

When the preliminary site layout is roughly made, the process units are sited first and arranged to give a smooth flow of materials through the various processing steps, from raw material to final product storage. Process units are normally spaced at least 30 ma part; greater spacing maybe needed for hazardous processes. The location of the principal ancillary buildings should then be decided. They should be arranged in such a way that the time spent by personnel in traveling between buildings can be minimized. Administration offices and laboratories, in which a relatively large number of people will be working, should be located well away from potentially hazardous processes. Control rooms are normally located adjacent to the processing units, but those with potentially hazardous processes may have to be sited at a safer distance. The sitting of the main process units determines the layout of the plant roads, arrangement of pipes, and drains. Access roads to each building are required for construction and for operation and maintenance.

## Objectives of Industrial Safety

- To prevent accidents in the plant by reducing the hazard to as minimum as possible.
- To eliminate chance of accident that may stop the work and cause loss of production.
- To achieve lower workmen's compensation, insurance rates and reduce all other direct and indirect costs of accidents.
- To prevent loss of life, permanent disability and the loss of income of worker by eliminating causes of accidents.
- To evaluate the employees' morale by providing safe workplace and good working environment.
- To educate all members of the organization in continuous state of safety mindness and to make supervision competent.
- A safety programmes includes mainly following four E's.

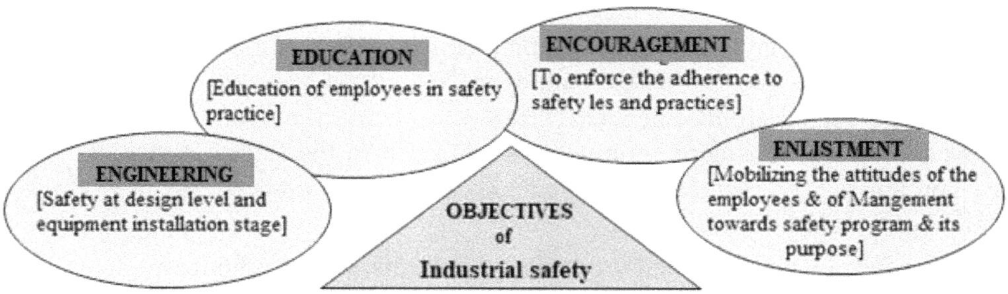


## Some Rules about the Site Layout

- ➢ Utility buildings should be located at a place so that the most economical run of pipes to and from the process units become possible.

- Cooling towers should be sited so that, under the prevailing wind, the column of condensate spray can run away from the plant and adjacent areas.
- The main storage areas should be placed between the loading and unloading facilities and the process units they serve.
- Storage tanks containing hazardous materials should be located at a place at least 70 m (200 ft) away from the site boundary.

The arrangement of the major items of equipment should follow the sequence on the process flow sheet. The columns and vessels should be arranged in rows with the ancillary equipments, such as heat exchangers and pumps, are placed along the outside. The principal factors to be considered in making plant layout are:

1. Construction and operating costs;
2. The process requirements;
3. Convenience of operation;
4. Convenience of maintenance;
5. Safety;
6. Future expansion;

## Plant Layout

The plant layout indicates the physical arrangement of production facilities. It refers to the configuration of departments, work centres and equipments to be used in the processes of conversion. It is a floor plan of the physical facilities, which are used in production.

According to Moore "*Plant layout is a plan of an optimum arrangement of facilities including personnel, operating equipment, storage space, material handling equipment and all other supporting services along with the design of best structure to contain all these facilities*".

A good layout is one that integrates man power, materials, machines and supporting services and others, to achieve the optimum utilization of resources and maximum effectiveness. The Fig 12.1 shows a typical plant layout.

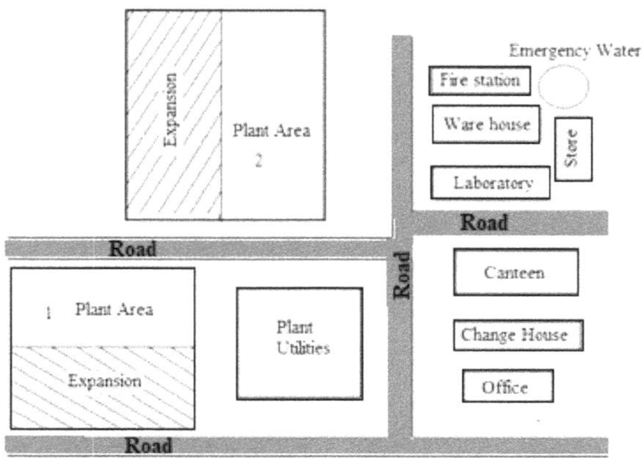


**Fig. 12.1** A typical layout

## Purpose of Plant Layout

Primarily the reason for the plant layout is to maximize the profit by arrangement of all the plant facilities to the best advantage of total manufacturing of the product.

The objectives or purposes of plant layout are:

1. The flow of materials should be streamlined throughout the plant.
2. To facilitate the manufacturing processes.
3. To maintain high turnover of in-process inventory.
4. For effective utilization of man power, equipment and space.
5. To make effective utilization of cubic space.
6. To make the manufacturing operations and arrangements flexible.
7. To provide better convenience, safety and comfort to the workmen (employees).
8. To reduce the investment in equipments.
9. To reduce the overall production time.
10. To facilitate the organizational structure.

### Classification of Plant Layout

As shown in Fig 12.2, the plant layout can be classified intothe following five categories:

1. Process layout
2. Product layout
3. Combination layout
4. Fixed position layout
5. Group layout

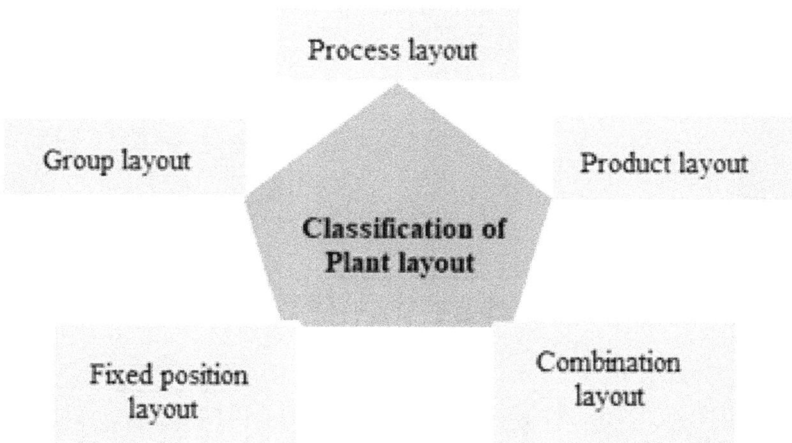


**Fig. 12.2** Classification of plant layout

## Utilities

The word utility is used for the ancillary services required for the operation of any production process. These services are normally supplied from a central facility and include:

1. Electricity;
2. Steam, for heating;
3. Cooling water;
4. Water for general use;
5. Demineralized water;
6. Refrigeration;
7. Compressed air;
8. Inert-gas supplies;

1. **Electricity:** The power is essential for any kind of activity such as electrochemical processes, driving the motors, for lighting, cleaning, operating a machine, and for general use. Power may be generated on site, but usually, is purchased from the local supply company.
2. **Steam:** The steam is necessary for heating process. It is usually generated in water tube boilers, using the most economical fuel available.
3. **Cooling Water:** The source of cooling water may either be natural or forced-draft cooling towers. The cooling towers work by evaporation of a part of the circulating water by ambient air and hence, the remaining water becomes cool. Water can be drawn from a convenient river or lake in sufficient quantity. Sea water, or brackish water, can be used at coastal sites; but if used directly, it is necessary to use more expensive materials of construction for exchange of heat and non-corrosion. The minimum temperature that can be maintained with cooling water depends on the local climate. If the room temperature and humidity are high, then a cooling water system would be less effective and air coolers or refrigeration would be required for this purpose.
4. **Demineralized Water:** Demineralized water should be used where pure water is required for use during processing and as boiler feed water. For this purpose, mixed and multiple-bed ion-exchange units are used. One resin converts the cations to hydrogen and the other removes the anions. Water with less than 1 part per million of dissolved solids can be produced.

1. **Refrigeration:** Refrigeration is required for the processes that require temperatures below those that can be economically obtained with cooling water. Usually, vapor compression refrigeration machines are used for this purpose.
2. **Compressed Air (instrument air):** Compressed air is required for general use and for the pneumatic controllers (usually used for chemical plant control). Rotary and reciprocating single-stage or two-stage compressors are used. Air used for instruments must be dry and clean (free from oil and dust).
3. **Inert Gases:** A large quantity of inert gas may be required for the processes where air may react with the constituent/intermediate/drug product; that is, for inert blanketing of tanks

and for purging. It is usually supplied from a central facility. Nitrogen is normally used for the same and can be manufactured on site in an air liquefaction plant (membrane system) or purchased as liquid in tankers.

4. **Storage:** Storage facilities are required for storing different types of materials used for manufacturing the products. The materials to be stored can be categorized into different categories on the basis of their nature as well as practical application. For example, the materials are of following types on the basis of their nature–
   - Inflammable, and
   - Non-inflammable
   - Toxic, and
   - Non-toxic.

   On the basis of their application
   - Raw materials – drugs and excipients,
   - Intermediate products,
   - Recycle materials,
   - Off-grade materials,
   - Final products

For storage, different types of container would be required; also, the different conditions for storage. For example, a storage tank is required for holding liquids which may be glycerin or liquified nitrogen, (gas tanks for compressed gases).Storage tanks are available in many shapes: vertical and horizontal cylindrical; open top and closed top; flat bottom, cone bottom. Large tanks tend to be vertical cylindrical, or to have rounded corners (transition from vertical side wall to bottom profile, to easier withstand hydraulic hydrostatically induced pressure of contained liquid. The material of construction of tank is a matter of consideration. For example, for storing liquor of caustic soda, hydrochloric acid, and polyethylene glycol would not be same. Similarly, a hygroscopic drug or gelatin capsules requires a controlled temperature and humidity.

## Services

The major factors considered for service providers are–

- Impact of location on sales, and
- Customer satisfaction.

Usually, the customers consider how close a service facility is available, particularly if, the process requires considerable customer contact. Hence, the layouts for service facility should provide easy access to these facilities. Most importantly some of the requirements of service facility layout are:

- Well-organized packing areas,
- Easily accessible facilities,
- Well-designed walkways and
- Parking areas.

Service facility layout should be designed on the basis of number of customers contacting per hour or per day and the type of service to be provided to a customer or by a customer. These service layouts follow conventional layouts as required. Probably, hospital service is the best example for adaptation of process layout, where the service required for a customer requires an independent path.

## Industrial Hazards

Industrial hazards may be defined *as a condition produced by industries that may cause injury or death to personnel working or loss of product or property*. The accidents in various types of industries like manufacturing, power production, etc. and in storage and transportation of various hazardous materials used in these industries. The risk involved in this category is defined *as the chances of death or injury per person or per number of hours exposed*. The major disaster threats occur in the chemical and nuclear industries. The manufacturing, processing, transportation, distribution/storage and the application or use of many products of these two areas are hazardous.

### Types of Industrial Hazards

- **Physical** hazards include noise, vibration, heat, cold, pressure, radiation, fibres.
- **Chemical** hazards include handling of flammable or explosive materials, toxic materials, sensitizing agents, etc.
- **Biological** hazards refer to dust, pathogens which either damage or change the normal functions of life.
- **Psychological** hazards refer to those related to the practices in work place, systems, and payment systems, etc. that may affect the psychology of the employees.

### General Hazards in Industries

- Fire hazards
- Mechanical hazards
- Electrical hazards
- Chemical hazards
- Pharmaceutical hazards
- Radiation hazards
- Dust explosion

## Classification of Hazards

In accordance with National Fire Protection Association (NFPA), areas are typically classified as being light (low) hazard, ordinary (moderate) hazard, or extra (high) hazard.

**Light or low hazard** areas are related to locations where the quantity and combustibility of Class A combustibles and Class B flammable materials present are low. In these areas, expected fires have relatively low rates of heat release. Light hazard areas may include offices, classrooms, meeting rooms etc.

**Ordinary (moderate) hazard** areas are the locations where the quantity and combustibility of Class A combustible materials and Class B flammables are moderate. Fires with moderate rates of heat release are expected in these areas. Ordinary hazard locations could be offices, malls, light manufacturing or research operations, parking garages, workshops, or maintenance/service areas.

**High or extra hazard** areas refers to the locations where the quantity and combustibility of Class A combustible material are high or where high amounts of Class B flammables are present. Quickly developing fires with high rates of heat release are expected. These locations could be the sites for car-repairing, aircraft and boat-servicing, painting, and coating, storage areas (tanks, containers etc). Types of hazardous materials have given in Table 12.1.

## National Fire Protection Association (NFPA)

The Standard System (NFPA 704) designed for the identification of the hazards of materials for emergency response refers to the standards maintained by the U.S. based National Fire Protection Association. In 1960 the first 'tentatively adopted as a guide', and it has been revised several times. It defines the colloquial 'fire diamond' used by emergency personnel to quickly and easily identify the risks likely to be brought about by hazardous materials. This helps to determine what, if any, special equipment should be used, procedures to be followed, or precautions to be taken during the initial stages of an emergency response. There are a number of sources of hazards in the pharmaceuticals industry, such as:

- Installation of equipments and machineries for manufacturing and their performance during formulation.
- Handling and storage of hazardous chemicals including warehouses, go-downs, tank in ports/fuel depots/docks, transportation (road, rail, air, water, pipelines),and
- Emission of pollutants.

The air pollutants include carbon monoxide (CO), nitrogen dioxide ($NO_2$), sulphur dioxide ($SO_2$), and volatile organic compounds (VOCs), particulate matter of 10 microns or less (PM10), total suspended particulate matter (SPM). The most common volatile organic compounds include methanol, dichloromethane, toluene, ethylene glycol, N, N Dimethylformamide, and acetonitrile. Effluents, especially those are not easily biodegraded and those are toxic in nature. The effluent-releases can go directly to river streams, lakes, oceans, or other water-bodies. The release of toxins due to runoff, including storm water runoff, can also be a potential hazard.

## Hazardous Wastes

These may be in the form of liquids, solids, contained gases or sludges. As a general measure, about 200kg of waste is generated per metric ton of active ingredient manufactured by the pharmaceutical industry. This waste, containing spent solvents and other toxic organic substances present in significant amounts, requires treatment before its safe disposal. The toxin released from the pharmaceuticals industry includes on-site discharge of a toxic chemical to the environment. This includes emissions to the air, discharges to water-bodies, releases at the land, as well as contained disposal into underground injection wells.

## Mechanical Hazards

There are several mechanical systems in the accelerator complex that could have potential hazards associated with them if they were to fail. Failure of any mechanical systems, could lead to collapse (in vacuum chamber) or explosion (in gas or liquid filled pipes). Other mechanical hazards may exist from machine shop tools, metal grinding, industrial vehicles, etc.

- Mechanical hazards is caused due to:
  - Impact force
  - Collision
  - Falls from height
  - Struck by objects
  - Confined space
  - Slips and trips
- Falling on a pointed object may be caused due to
  - Compressed air/ high pressure fluids (such as cutting fluid)
  - Entanglement
  - Equipment related injury
- Based on the type of damage, following can occur:
  - Crushing and cutting
  - Friction and abrasion
  - Shearing
  - Stabbing and puncture
  - Poor maintenance or house keeping

**Preventive measures:** Occurrence of hazards may be prevented by taking the following measures which includes:

- **Proper planning of the building,** that is,
  - Making the floors non-slippery,
  - There should enough space for easy and smooth movement,
  - Providing easy access of workers to safety switches.
- **Safe material handling**
  - All material handling equipments should be repaired and maintained properly.
- **Personnel protective devices**
  - Protection of head by using hard hats and helmets,
  - Protection of ears by using ear muffs and plugs,
  - Face may be protected by using face masks.

## Chemical Hazards

Chemical hazards may be toxic, corrosive, irritant, carcinogenic, flammable and mutagenic. According to WHMIS (Workplace Hazardous Materials Information) chemical hazards are classified as shown below in the Table 12.1.

**Table 12.1** Types of hazardous materials and their descriptions

| Type | Description |
|---|---|
| Class A | Compressed gas |
| Class B | Dissolved gas or liquified gas:<br>1. Flammable gas<br>2. Flammable and combustible gas<br>3. Flammable solids<br>4. Flammable aerosols |
| Class C | Reactive flammable materials:<br>1. Oxidizing materials, oxidizer such as chlorates, nitric oxide, peroxides, permanganates, per chlorates, nitrites, and<br>2. Organic peroxide such as tetra hydro furan, diethyl ether, dioxane, methyl iso butyl ether. |
| Class D | Poisonous and infectious materials: cyanides, tea salts, asbestos. |
| Class E | Corrosive materials: inorganic acids and bases, hydrogen fluoride |
| Class F | 1. Dangerous reactive materials: ethylene dioxide, organic azides, Na, Li, Ca<br>2. Pyrophosphoric material: white phosphorous, diethyl aluminium chloride, lithium |

Effects of chemical exposures on the body

- Skin burn
- Ache
- Anthrax
- Ulcer in hand, nose etc
- Cancer
- Irritation on wind pipe
- Many chemicals can cause severe burns, if they come in contact with living tissues such as concentrated sulphuric acid, raw sodium hydroxide, sodium metal.
- Living tissue may be destroyed/damaged by following chemical reactions:
  - Dehydration by strong dehydrating agents
  - Digestion by strong acids and bases
  - Oxidation by strong oxidizing agents

**Table 12.2** Some clinical symptoms and hazard caused by chemicals

| Organ | Symptoms | Chemicals |
|---|---|---|
| Eyes | Corneal and conjunctival disturbances | Sulphur dioxide, Hydrogen sulphide |
| Nervous System | Drowsiness | CNS depressants |
| Mouth and Throat | Green tongue salivation | Vanadium mercury |

**Table 12.3** Additives and their effects on health

| Additives | Health hazards |
|---|---|
| Azo dyes | Bladder cancer |
| Benzene | Leukemia |
| Caustic soda | Blindness and respiratory damage |
| Zinc salts | Skin and eye damage |
| Chlorine ions | Lung and skin damage |
| Lead | Lead poisoning |

### Preventive Measures

- Solvents other than water used in extraction, purification of synthetic drugs and chemical analysis should be handled with care.
- Flammable and explosive chemicals should be kept at proper distance.
- Tolerance levels for toxic chemicals set by federal regulation have to be followed.
- Suitable label should be attached to the chemicals for proper handling.
- Personnel protective cloth should be provided.
- Suitable cream should be applied before commencement of work.
- Goggles should be used.

## Fire Hazards

Fire causes an exothermic chemical reaction between oxygen and fuel. This happens most frequently. The effect of fire on people usually is observed in the form of skin burns. Its intensity and consequence usually depend on

- ➢ The duration of exposure to the body,
- ➢ The intensity of the heat.
- ➢ Which part of the body has been exposed to heat?

Toxic fumes such asacrolein, carbon monoxide and cyanides can be produced due to fire. Due to greater intensity of the heat or combustion, the physical structures can be damaged. It may also have an adverse effect on the essential services in the premises like power and instrumentation which can subsequently result an aggravation of the incident.

### Sources of Fire Hazards

There may be various sources of fire hazards in a premise. The most commonly observed sources are:

- Hot surfaces
- Combustible and flammable materials
- Overheating of equipments
- Chemical process equipments

- Lightening
- Gas cylinders
- Ovens and furnaces
- Reactor
- Welding and cutting
- Spark from metal to metal contact
- Carelessness

## Types of Fire

The National Fire Protection Association (NFPA) have categorized fires in terms of different classes. The NFPA have also specified the standard for portable fire extinguishers.

**Table 12.4** Type of fire and its consequence

| Type of fire | Consequences |
|---|---|
| Class A | *Involving solid material:* solid materials of an organic nature such as wood, paper, cloth, rubber and plastics that do not melt. |
| Class B | *Involving liquid material:* petrol, diesel, thinners, oils, paints, wax, cooking fat and plastic that melts. |
| Class C | Involving electric connections |
| Class D | Involving flammable metals such as aluminium, titanium, magnesium, sodium, potassium, etc. Cooking media such as vegetable or animal fats and oils |

## Flammable and Combustible Liquids

For fire flammable and combustible liquids can work as potential fuel. These are present in almost every work place. The vapor created by flammable and combustible liquids ignites and burns. The flash point of flammable liquids is less than 537.8°C. This means that flammable liquids can burn easily at normal working temperatures. Combustible liquids, having a flash point 537.8°C or more, are less hazardous than flammable liquids, but still represent a risk. The volatility of flammable and combustible liquids requires special storage and handling requirements.

## Storage of Flammable and Combustible Liquids

The flammable liquids must be stored away from ignition sources in cool, well ventilated areas. These materials should be kept away from incompatible materials. The amount of these liquids is to be minimized. In general, not more than 10 gallons of flammable materials should be kept outside the approved flammable liquid storage cabinets or approved storage rooms.

## Sources of Fire

The fire triangle or combustion triangle, as shown in Fig 12.3 illustrates the three elements a fire needs to ignite:

Usually, a fire occurs when three elements are present and combined in the right mixture. A fire can be prevented or extinguished, if any of the elements in the fire triangle can be removed. For example, a fire can be extinguished by covering a fire with a blanket. This blanket does not allow the oxygen of the air to participate in the combustion. Oxygen is one of three elements in the fire triangle. This does not allow the fire to take place.

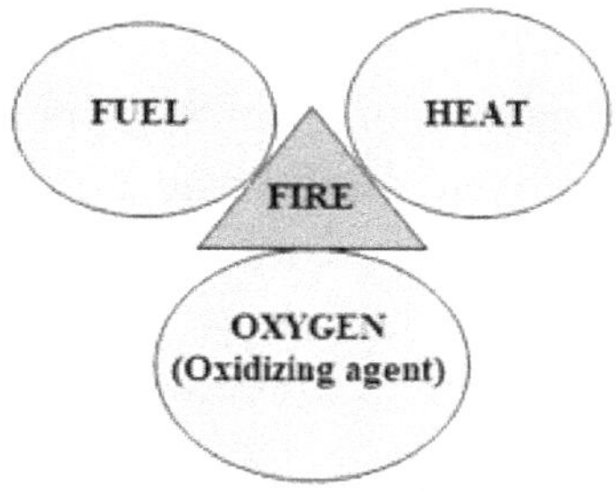


**Fig. 12.3** Factors responsible for fire hazards

## Preventive Measures

By taking the measures indicated below, fire can be prevented.

- Solvents used in extraction, purification of synthetic drugs and chemical analysis should be handled with care.
- Flammable and explosive chemicals should be kept at proper distance.
- Tolerance levels for toxic chemicals set by federal regulation have to be followed.
- Suitable label has to be placed for each chemical for proper handling.
- Personal protective cloth should be used.
- Before performing the work, a cream should be applied.
- Goggles should be used.

## Pharmaceutical Hazards

Some general health hazards in the manufacture of pharmaceuticals due to:

- Exposure to dust and noise.
- Exposure to UV radiation.
- Exposure to formaldehyde.
- Repetitive motion disorders.
- Formaldehyde may cause lung cancer, prostate cancer. Acute exposure may cause pulmonary edema and pneumonia leading to death. Also causes allergic dermatitis.
- Repetitive motion disorder associated with packing and filling could lead to carpal tunnel syndrome ortendonitis.
- Hazards from handling crude drugs and its extracts such as ipecacunha.
- Solvents such as benzene.
- Alkaloids such as scopolamine, emetine.
- Toxic intermediate.

- Final product such as local anesthetic.
- Miscellaneous hazards such as radiant energy, bacteria and viruses.

## Explosive Hazards

### Dust Explosion

A dust refers to a particle of maximum size of about 5 cm. In a mixture of solid particles, if a dust particle is found to be present, the mixture can become a problem for civic life. The dust particle may be combustible or can burn or oxidize. Dust explosion occurs due to combustion of dust particles or oxidization of an oxidizable particle of metals. A rapid combustion of such dust particles may cause dust explosion. During this process, heat and reaction products are produced. If there is proper mixture for rapid combustion, the mixture is considered to be within explosive range. Of course, such mixture may contain different amounts of dust and air. Air may be less or high. No flame would be produced, if air is less. If air is present in slightly more than this lower limit, burning will take place.

Usually, the moisture content and degree of fineness of the particles can control the degree of flammability. The movement of flame in a confined space is visible. For combustion, oxygen is required and air is the source of oxygen. Presence of dry and fine particles in the mixture increases the flammability.

In pharmaceutical industries, various grinding operations are conducted. During grinding of iron or stone, sparks may be emitted and this may cause explosion with some easily combustible materials. Hence, adequate preventive measures should be taken so that dust is not accumulated in the premises. Apart from this, the dust of starch, dextrin, and other organic substances are present in pharmaceutical and ancillary industries. These dusts are very hazardous. The Fig 12.3, the hazard triangle indicates three resources responsible for explosion.

The Fig 12.3 also indicates how the dust explosion can be avoided:

- **Prevention of the development of explosive mixture:** This is possible, if the dust particles do not accumulate, then explosion can be avoided or prevented. Hence, the dust accumulated, if any, should be removed regularly.
- **Inerting:** This is done by replacing the atmospheric oxygen by a suitable inert gas. The working environment should be vacuum or the dust produced should be inert. This process is known as *inerting*. Explosive dust can be made inactive by adding inert dust such as rock salt and sodium sulphate so that the dust is diluted to a level below the explosive range.
- **Effective ignition source should not occur:** Welding, smoking, sparks, cutting, etc. are the sources for ignition. Brush discharge, bulk surface discharge, spark discharge, etc. come under electric discharges. Thus, the premises must be kept very clean and kept free from any explosive substances and all sources of ignition. Sometimes, explosive substances can be handled by using remote control system within the machine.

## Control of Dust Explosion

The generation of dust is avoided or dusts are not allowed to propagate, it is controlled in pharmaceutical industries. The methods used for this purpose are:

- Filtration,
- Inertial separation, and
- Electrostatic precipitation.

## Filtration

Filters are fibrous and porous. They work as mechanical barrier. Filters are available as pads or panels fitted to the walls and windows in a manufacturing premises. Bag filters are attached to the machine which produces dust. Air containing dust is sucked or blown through a filter. The pore size of the filter should be smaller than that of the particles floating in the air, so that the filters used can retain the particles as shown in the Fig 12.4.

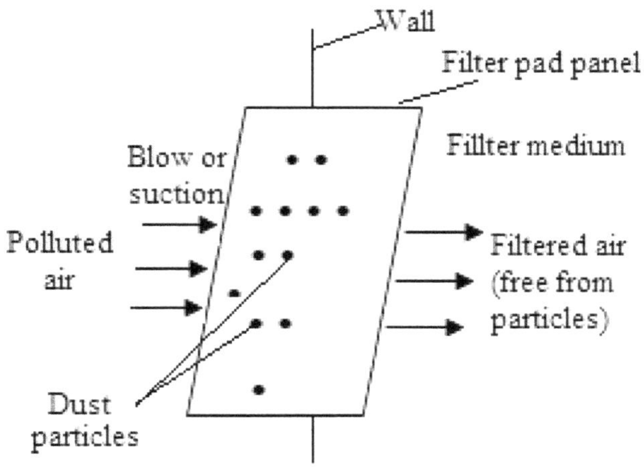


**Fig. 12.4** Filter used for filtration of air

## Inertial Separation

Cyclone separator can be used to separate the particles floating in the air. Air containing the particles of different size ranges, is exposed to centrifugal force developed in a cyclone separator. The particles get precipitated by the combined action of centrifugal force and the gravitational force. The particles deposit at the bottom of the separator according to their size. The larger particles deposit first and the finest ones at the last. The deposited particles are collected from the bottom of the separator and the dust free air goes out from the top as shown in the Fig 12.5. Thus, the circulating air inside the premises can be made free from floating dust and explosion due to dust can be avoided.

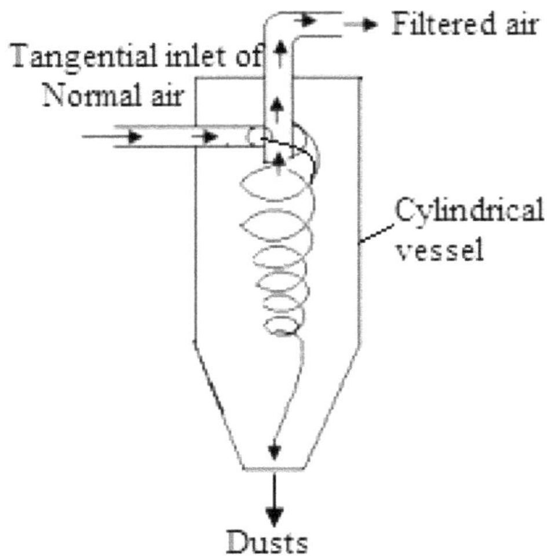


**Fig. 12.5** Cyclone separation for air filtration

## Electrostatic precipitation

In this method, fine metal wires are stretched between the tubes. The entire assembly is then earthed and a current of high voltage is passed through the wires. As a result, a high potential difference is generated between the tubes and wires. When the dust particles pass through the electrified wires, the dust particles become ionized. The ionic dust particles get deposited on the metal plates and from where these are removed or collected on regular basis. This method is generally used to prevent pollution of air in production area. The schematic diagram of the equipment used for this purpose is shown in Fig 12.6.

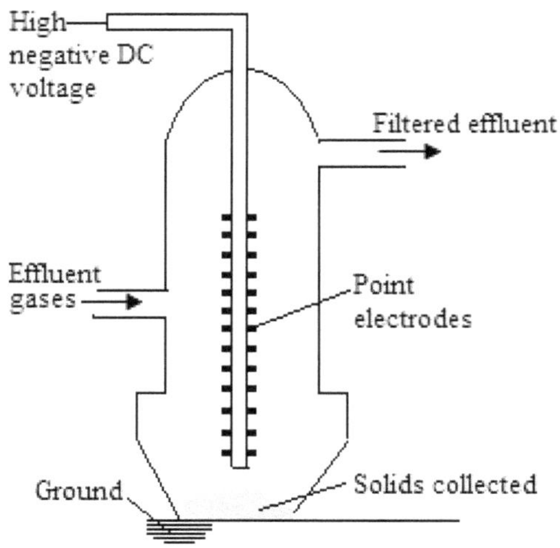


**Fig. 12.6** Electrostatic precipitator

## Fire and Explosion Hazards

Fire set on in the buildings and in industries. The occurrence of fire is more than that of explosion and release or leak the toxic substances. The loss of life or permanent disability are also less. Generally, the electrical equipments and electrical connections have been found responsible for such fire. The people trapped in the fire generally suffer from skin burns. The severity of the burns depends on the intensity of the fire, location of the body and duration of exposure. Thus, fire is less hazardous than other explosions such as chemical explosions. Materials such as wood, fabrics, papers and flammable plastics are very susceptible to fire. The building containing such flammable materials should be carefully maintained and regular checkup of the electrical connections should be done.

## Control of Fire and Explosion

Good house-keeping can protect the building from fire. In fact, good house-keeping does not allow the fire to occur and if occurs, does not allow to spread. In bulk drug manufacturing units, inflammable solvents and organic substances are commonly used. For this reason, suitable measures are necessary to be taken to control or prevent fire. Government regulations are there for safety and protection from fire. These are to be strictly followed. Following measures should be taken to prevent fire:

- The plant must be suitably laid out and appropriate materials used for construction should be selected and used. It is better to avoid flammable materials in construction.
- If possible, the hazardous operations should be done separately in places where human movement is very less. Preferably, such operations should be done in separate building.
- Fire resistant brick-walls or reinforced concrete-walls can control the occurrence of fire explosion.
- It is necessary to reduce the possible sources of fire; for example, flames, sparks, heated materials, match boxes, smoking, welding, gas cutting, and generation of static electricity should not be done where movement of people is much, better should be avoided.
- There should be a regular checkup of electrical connections.
- Fire alarms, fire extinguishers, temperature alarms, and water-sprinkling systems should be installed in many places of the industries and buildings and these should be checked for their efficient performance on regular basis.

## Industrial Safety

Industrial safety is primarily a management activity, concerned with reducing, controlling and eliminating hazards from the industries or industrial units. Industrial safety is the ability to manage the risks related to the operations or related to the environment. Industrial safety does not mean disliking of risks, rather it is a commitment to clearly identify them in relation to production operations, assess them in terms of quality and quantity, and taking appropriate measures to prevent or control them. In total, practically, it refers to regular observation of how risk management is controlled at the company's facilities and how much progress the company has made in its action plans to reduce them.

### Safety Measures for Mechanical Hazards

- All machinery must be fenced or mechanical inter locking or photocell.
- Machine should be fitted with emergency shutdown system.
- Control system override should be monitored.
- Turnkey system for cleaning and for repairing
- Operator must have a safe distance from the machine
- Strictly following the standard operating procedure (SOP)
- Stop and lock button for machines

As a whole there are three types of risk:

- Risks related to the products that we use or prepare,
- Risks related to the processes and equipment used in the operations, and
- Transportation risks related to the operations.

### Importance of Industrial Safety

The danger of human life is being increasing with advancement of scientific development in different fields. The importance of industrial safety has been realized because, in every millions of industrial accidents occur, at least one faces either death or disablement, may be temporary or permanent, of workmen along with huge losses. The losses include the danger to the properties, waste of man hours and human lives.

From the management perspective the importance of industrial safety in any organization include monitoring of the following actions:

- **Treatment:** Industrial safety management provides treatment for injuries and illness at the work places.
- **Medical Examination**: Carries out medical examination of staff joining the organization or returning to work after sickness or accident.
- **Hazards identification**: Providing provision of protective devices.
- **Consultancy:** It provides medical advised on other condition potentially affecting health such as works, canteen etc.
- **Education:** It makes the people concern about safety and health training.

## Short Questions

1. What is meant by 'plant layout'? What are the purposes of plant layout?
2. What are different categories of plant layout? What are ancillary buildings and services required on a site, in addition to the main processing building?
3. What do you understand by 'services and hazards'?
4. What happens when the body is exposed to chemical?

5. What are fire hazards? What are the sources of fire hazards?
6. How can the fire be prevented? How are flammable and combustible liquids stored?
7. Enlist the pharmaceutical hazards?
8. How can the dust pollution be controlled?
9. What is meant by 'industrial safety'?

## Long Questions

1. Explain the ancillary services to be supplied from a central facility.
2. What is meant by 'hazards'? What are different types of hazards?
3. Discuss mechanical hazards. How can the mechanical hazards be prevented?
4. Explain chemical hazards with suitable examples. What are the preventive measures to be taken for chemical hazards?
5. Classify the fire as per National Fire Protection Association and what are the consequences of each type?
6. Explain the term 'dust'. How can the dust pollution be prevented?
7. What is the importance of industrial safety?

# CHAPTER 13

# Material of Pharmaceutical Plant Construction, Corrosion, and its Prevention

Factors affecting during materials selected for pharmaceutical plant construction. Theories of corrosion, types of corrosion and their prevention. Ferrous and nonferrous metals, inorganic and organic nonmetals.

## Factors Affecting During Materials Selected for Pharmaceutical Plant Construction

For construction of pharmaceutical plant, selection of material is an important activity; because chemical reactions are involved in many processes, contamination with other materials or particles are also common. However, economic consideration is the most common everywhere. Therefore, the factors to be considered during construction of pharmaceutical plant may be categorized into three classes:

- Physical,
- Chemical, and
- Economic

## Physical Factors

Physical factors include:

1. Strength of the material to be used for construction,
2. Weight of the material,
3. Wearing qualities,
4. Ease of fabrication,
5. Thermal expansion,
6. Thermal conductivity,
7. Ease of cleaning,
8. Sterilization, and
9. Transparency.

In fact, the factors 1 to 6 are common; in some cases, additional factors 7 to 9 are to be considered. For this reason, the factors 7 to 9 are called subsidiary factors.

1. **Strength:** The strength should be according to the size of the plant and as per the stress to which the material would be subjected.
2. **Weight:** In general, the weight of the material is kept as minimum as possible, sufficient to serve the purpose and also durable. Behind reduction of weight there are two reasons: 1. the material cost would be less, 2. the plant can be shifted from one place to another. In fact, many pharmaceutical industries shift their location after few years.
3. **Wearing qualities:** This is an important factor because there are materials which abrade during processing. Due to the continuous friction, if the surface materials come out, these will contaminate the product. For example, during tableting the punches regularly enter into and exit from the die, if this continuous friction releases particles, the particulate matter would be found in the tablets being compressed. Similarly, during grinding the surfaces of the grinding mill should not release any material into the drug substance.
4. **Ease of fabrication:** To fabricate the various units of the plant, it is necessary to process the materials before construction such as casting, welding, etc. The properties of the materials should be such that these can be casted, welded, forged, and machined without any problem.
5. **Thermal expansion:** If the materials used to make pharmaceutical plant have a high coefficient of thermal expansion, the design of plant becomes complicated and the stress is increased. As a result, with change in temperature there is a risk of fracture. The plant should be operated within a restricted temperature.
6. **Thermal conductivity:** A good thermal conductivity is necessary for the plant of distillation still and evaporators. However, this must be kept in mind that the formation of scales or films can greatly affect the heat transfer which is essential for such type of plant. On the other hand, the metal used to prepare die and punches used for tableting, or the vessels used for preparation of bulk solutions should have minimal thermal conductivity.
7. **Cleaning:** Pharmaceutical products must not contain any foreign particles. For this reason, the surfaces of walls, roof, working table, and surfaces of all machineries used in pharmaceutical plant should be smooth enough to facilitate easy and regular cleaning.
8. **Sterilization:** Some of pharmaceutical products are sterile and the areas wherein these products are manufactured should be kept sterile. To make sterile products, sterilization is an essential operation. Hence, the materials used should be capable of withstanding the necessary treatment, usually steam under pressure. To maintain the sterility the equipments and machines used for manufacture should be easily cleaned because without cleanliness it is not possible to maintain sterility.
9. **Transparency:** Transparency of material is another useful property that allows observation or detection of presence of foreign particles in the product. Most commonly glass is the material of concern. Glass is used as container which can withstand high temperature of sterilization. Borosilicate glass is most suitable for this purpose.

## Chemical Factors

These consider two aspects of chemical action:

1. Contamination of the product by the material of the plant,
2. The effect of the drug and chemical substance being processed on the material of the plant.

The first aspect becomes important when the impurities or contaminants of the product possess some physiological effects that may be of therapeutic in nature or may be unwanted (side effect). Moreover, the impurities, even in traces, may be responsible for decomposition of the product. For example, heavy metals in traces, if present, penicillin can decompose. In addition to these effects, the physical appearance of the product, such as change in color, may also be affected by the contamination from the material of the plant.

It is also important to note that the contamination from some materials may be harmless; although the product remains non-toxic, it is desirable to ingest such contaminated material into the human body. There is no guarantee that such contaminants may be apparently found non-toxic, but later on, they may have some action or they may interact with any physiological constituent in the body and show some undesired effect.

The knowledge about the materials used for construction of plant has been increasing gradually. The plant can be constructed with such materials that are resistant to attack of acids, alkalis, oxidizing agents, tannins, etc. and the pharmaceutical products can be prepared safely without any type deterioration or contamination. New alloys with required physical and chemical properties have been developed. Plastics are generally resistant to such deterioration. Nowadays, wherever possible suitable plastics have been used in place of metal for construction of pharmaceutical plants.

## Economic Factors

From the above discussion it is understood how the materials used for pharmaceutical plant construction is important with respect to physical, chemical and therapeutic safety of product. Of course, during designing, the cost and maintenance of the plant becomes most important factor, relatively lesser costly material is usually used. However, in some cases, higher initial cost becomes more economical in long run, if the materials are found to have better wearing qualities and require low maintenance.

The Fig 13.1 shows the classification of the materials commonly used for construction of pharmaceutical plant and machineries, equipments and apparatuses.

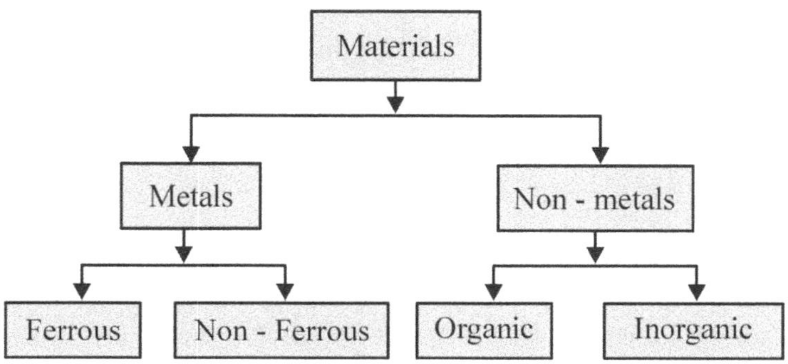


**Fig. 13.1** Classification of materials

## Corrosion

Metals and alloys are most commonly used as material for fabrication or construction of plants. Thus, the metals or alloy structures should be properly maintained, otherwise they deteriorate slowly by the action of atmospheric gases, moisture and other chemicals. This phenomenon of destruction of metals and alloys is known as *corrosion*. Corrosion is a destructive electrochemical phenomenon. Besides its economic effects, it can damage the appearance of metals and in some cases can cause the equipment/structural component failure. In all environments it may take place. Corrosion may be defined as *the process of unwanted attack by the environment on a metal*.

According to Shreir *corrosion is the reaction of a solid with environment*. Commonly observed examples of corrosion are rusting of iron and steel, tarnishing of silver, copper, zinc, and nickel etc.

Briefly, the corrosion of metals is defined as the spontaneous destruction of metals in the course of their chemical, electrochemical or biochemical interactions with the environment. Thus, it is exactly the reverse of extraction of metals from ores. The cost of replacement of materials and equipments lost through corrosion is unlimited.

The most common example of corrosion of metal is rusting of iron and formation of green color on copper.

(i) Rusting of iron: Due to the reaction between Fe (iron) and $O_2$(oxygen) of air in presence of water, as a result, a layer of reddish scale or powder of iron oxide ($F_3O_4$) is formed on the surface of iron.

(ii) Corrosion of copper: This indicates the formation of green color film of basic copper carbonate [$CuCO_3$+$Cu(OH)_2$] on the surface of copper. Copper carbonate is formed due to chemical interaction between copper, carbon dioxide and water in presence of air.

Corrosion of metals should be studied in detail so that appropriate action for prevention and maintenance can be done in time. The needs of corrosion studies are:

- In all fields of technology, the use of metals has been increasing gradually.
- Rare and expensive metals are also used; hence, special preventive measures are required for their protection.
- High strength alloys which are susceptible to certain types of corrosion, are also being used.
- More corrosive environment is being produced due to increasing pollution of air and water.
- According to the type and extent of corrosion, a strict safety standard of operation with respect to the equipment must be developed.

### Effect of Corrosion

The consequences of corrosion include:

(i) Due to formation of corrosion product over the machinery, the efficiency of the machine is reduced resulting in ultimate shut down of the plant.

(ii) The products may be contaminated which subsequently results the loss of products due to corrosion.

(iii) The corroded equipment must be replaced.

(iv) Preventive maintenance like metallic coating or organic coating would be required.

(v) Health hazards may occur such as pollution due to a corrosion of product or due to the escaping chemical from a corroded equipment.
(vi) Corrosion can release the toxic products.

### Factors Influencing Corrosion

The nature and extent of corrosion depends mainly on the metal and the environment. Thus, to understand corrosion thoroughly, the factors like structural features of the metal, nature of the environment and the type of reaction that occurs at the metal-environment interface must be considered. The important factors which may influence the corrosion process are:

(a) Nature of the metal,
(b) Nature of the environment,
(c) Electrode potential,
(d) Temperature,
(e) Concentration of the solution,
(f) Aeration,
(g) Agitation,
(h) pH of the solution,
(i) Nature of corrosion products.

Generally high temperature (more than 100°C) produces more intense corrosion.

## Theories of Corrosion

There are primarily two theories of corrosion: 1. homogeneous, and 2. heterogeneous.

1. **Homogeneous theory:** According to Wagner and Traud the impurities or any other heterogeneous substance present on the surface are not solely responsible for corrosion process. As per this theory, the metals become unstable because of different electronic charge transfer reactions that occur simultaneously in opposite direction at the surface. Thus, as per Wagner-Traud mechanism, the necessary condition for corrosion is the dissolution reaction of the metal and some electronation reaction; this reaction continues simultaneously at the metal/environment interface. Therefore, it is necessary that the potential difference across the interface should be more positive than the equilibrium potential of metal dissolution reaction and /or more negative than the equilibrium potential of the electronation reaction.
2. **Heterogeneous theory:** According to this theory, the impurities present on the surface of a metal are responsible for corrosion.

   Thus, between the anodic and cathodic parts of the corroding surface, a local cell is developed and electrochemical reaction takes place. As a result of this electrochemical reactions at the interface of the metal and ionically conducting moisture films or actual solution, the metal becomes unstable and corrosion occurs. Thus, it is clear that a corroding metal consists of

   (i) an electronsink area at which a de-electronation reaction occurs(metal dissolution),and an electron source area where electronation reaction occurs,
   (ii) an electronic conductor to carry the electrons to the electron source area, and

(iii) an ionic conductor to keep the current flowing and to functionas a medium for the electrodic reaction.

This model is generally termed as *'Local cell theory of corrosion'.*

## Corrosion Rates

According to the literature, corrosion rates can be expressed in a number of ways. The following are the major systems of corrosion units. Usually, corrosion rates are expressed in two basic units– 'mpy' and 'mdd'. The corrosion rates in 'mpy' and 'mdd'scales can be directly calculated using the following expressions:

1. $$\text{mpy} = \frac{534 \times W}{a \times t \times d}$$

2. $$\text{mdd} = \frac{53.5 \times W}{a \times t}$$

Where, W is the weight loss (grams),

a is the area of the specimen (sq. in)

t is the time (hrs.), and

d is the density of the specimen (g/cm$^3$)

If the area of the specimen is calculated in square centimeter (sq.cm), then the corrosion rate in 'mpy' units can be calculated as:

$$\text{mpy} = \frac{82.75 \times W}{a \times t \times d}$$

## Types of Corrosion

Uniform corrosion is also known as general corrosion. The surface effect is produced mostly by direct chemical attacks such as by an acid. It is a uniform engraving of the metal. The use of chemical-resistant protective coatings or more resistant materials will control this type of corrosion. Based on the usual environment, corrosion can be of two types:

1. Dry or Chemical corrosion,
2. Wet or Electrochemical corrosion

1. **Dry or Chemical corrosion:** When the chemical such as oxygen, halogen, hydrogen sulphide, sulphur dioxide, nitrogen or anhydrous inorganic liquid, etc. of atmosphere directly attacks the surface of a metal this type of corrosion takes place. Thus, the chemical corrosion can be defined as the direct chemical attack on metal-surface by the atmospheric gases present in the environment. For example:
   (i) Silver undergoes chemical corrosion by atmospheric $H_2S$ gas.
   (ii) Iron undergoes chemical corrosion by HCl gas.

Types of dry or chemical corrosion

1. Corrosion by Oxygen or Oxidation corrosion
2. Corrosion by Hydrogen
3. Liquid Metal Corrosion

- **Oxidation Corrosion** occurs due to the direct attack of oxygen at low or high temperature on metal surfaces in the absence of moisture. Alkali metals such as Li, Na, K etc., and alkaline earth metals such as Mg, Ca, Sn, etc. are rapidly oxidized at low temperature. At high temperature, almost all metals, except Ag, Au and Pt are oxidized.

  The reactions of oxidation corrosion are as follows:

  $$\text{Metal} + \text{oxygen} \rightarrow \text{Metal oxide (corrosion product)}$$

  (i) Oxidation takes place at the surface of the metal forming metal ions, $M^{2+}$ $M \rightarrow M^{2+} + 2e^{-2}$

  (ii) Oxygen is converted to oxide ion, $O^{2-}$ due to the transfer of electrons from metal.

  $$\frac{n}{2}O_2 + 2n\,e^- \rightarrow n\,O^{2-}$$

  (iii) The overall reaction is of oxide ion reacts with the metal ions to form metal oxide film.

  $$2M + \frac{n}{2}O_2 \rightarrow 2M^{n+} + n\,O^{2-}$$

  In oxidation corrosion processes, the nature of oxide formed plays an important role. When oxidation starts, a thin layer of oxide is formed on the metal surface and the nature of this film decides the further action.

- **Hydrogen embrittlement:** Loss in ductility of a material in the presence of hydrogen is, known as *hydrogen embrittlement*. This type of corrosion occurs when a metal is exposed to hydrogen environment. Iron liberates atomic hydrogen when reacts with hydrogen sulphide in the following way:

  $$Fe + H_2S \rightarrow FeS + 2H$$

  Hydrogen gas diffuses into the metal matrix in this atomic form and gets collected in the voids present inside the metal. Further, atomic hydrogen diffuses and combine with each other and forms hydrogen gas.

  $$H + H \rightarrow H_2\uparrow$$

  Collection of these gases in the voids develops very high pressure and produces cracks or blisters in the metal.

  All metals above hydrogen in the electrochemical series have a tendency to get dissolved in acidic solution with simultaneous evolution of hydrogen. This occurs in acidic environment. Let us consider the example of iron.

  At anode: $Fe \rightarrow Fe^{2+} + 2e^-$

  These electrons flow through the metal, from anode to cathode; where $H^+$ ions of acidic solution are eliminated as hydrogen gas as shown in Fig 13.2.

  At cathode: $2\,H^+ + 2\,e^- \rightarrow H_2\uparrow$

  The overall reaction is: $Fe + 2H^+ \rightarrow Fe^{2+} + H_2\uparrow$

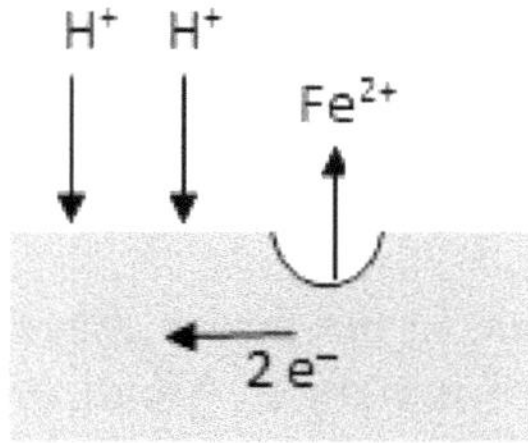


**Fig. 13.2** Corrosion of iron

- **Decarburization:** Carbon present in steel makes the steel sufficiently strong. But when steel is exposed to an environment containing hydrogen at high temperature, atomic hydrogen is formed.

$$H_2 \xrightarrow{\text{Heat}} 2H$$

Atomic hydrogen reacts with carbon of the steel and forms methane gas.

$$C + 4H \rightarrow CH_4$$

Therefore, the carbon content in steel decreases. The process of decreasing the carbon content in steel is known as *decarburization*. Collection of methane gas in the voids of steel develops high pressure, which causes cracking. Thus, steel loses its strength.

- **Liquid metal corrosion:** This occurs due to the chemical action when a liquid flow at high temperature over solid metal or alloy. Such corrosion occurs in devices generally used for nuclear power. The corrosion reaction involves either:
  - dissolution of a solid metal by a liquid, or
  - internal penetration of the liquid into the solid metal.

  Whatever may be the mode of corrosion, ultimately it weakens the solid metal.

- Wet or Electrochemical Corrosion: In aqueous solutions, most of the corrosion reactions are electrochemical in nature. These are governed by the kinetics of the electrochemical reactions occurring at the metal-solution interface. Stern has discussed the concepts of exchange of current, activation polarization and concentration polarization to understand the theoretical electrode kinetics and application to corrosion science and engineering.

  If a metal is immersed in a solution containing its ions, there will be a simultaneous transfer of ions in both directions across the interface. At equilibrium, the half-cell potential of the electrode becomes equal to the potential difference across the metal-solution interface. This half-cell potential is constant at a constant temperature and activity of the reactants for a particular metal. The 'Nernst equation' can be used to determine the potential of the system in which the reactants are not at unit activity,

$$E = E_o + 2.303\frac{RT}{nF}\log\frac{\alpha_{oxid}}{\alpha_{red}}$$

Where, E is the half-cell potential,

$E_o$ is the standard half-cell potential for the reaction, $M \rightarrow M^{n+} + ne^-$

$\alpha_{oxid}$ is the activity of the metal ion, $M^{n+}$

$\alpha_{red}$ is the activity of the metal

R is the universal gas constant in consistent unit

n is the number of electrons transferred

T is the absolute temperature, and

F is the Faraday constant.

However, the following circumstances may be involved during occurrence of the electrochemical corrosion:

- Anodic and cathodic areas are formed when comes in contact with each other,
- A conducting medium is present,
- Only the anodic area corrodes, and
- The corrosion product is formed in between anodic and cathodic areas. As a result, current of electron flows between the anodic and cathodic areas.
- Involves flow of electron-current between the anodic and cathodic areas.

Oxidation reaction takes place (liberation of free electron) at anodic area; hence, anodic metal is destroyed by either dissolving or assuming combined state (such as oxide, etc.). Therefore, corrosion always occurs at anodic areas.

$$M \rightarrow M^{n+} + ne^-$$

$M^{n+} \rightarrow$ Dissolves in solution $\rightarrow$ Forms compounds such as oxide.

At cathodic area, reduction reaction takes place (gain of electrons), usually cathode reactions do not affect the cathode, because most of the metals cannot be further reduced. So, at cathodic part, the constituents get dissolved in the conducting medium and accept the electrons to form some ions like $OH^-$ and $O^{2-}$.

When the cathodic reaction consumes electrons, depending on the nature of the corrosive environment either of the following is observed:

- Evolution of hydrogen, or
- Absorption of oxygen.

- **Oxygen Absorption Type:** If iron remains within a neutral aqueous solution of an electrolytes such as NaCl solution in the presence of atmospheric oxygen, rusting takes place. To prevent corrosion the surface of iron is usually coated with a thin film of iron oxide. However, if this iron oxide film develops some cracks, anodic areas would be created on the surface; while the well metal parts acts as cathodes.

Iron dissolves as ferrous ions with liberation of electrons.

$$Fe = Fe^{2+} + 2e^-$$

**At Cathode:** The liberated electrons are intercepted by the dissolved oxygen.

The $Fe^{2+}$ ions and $OH^-$ ions diffuse and when they meet, the ferrous hydroxide is formed and precipitated.

$$Fe^{2+} + 2OH^- \rightarrow Fe(OH)_2$$

- If enough oxygen is present, ferrous hydroxide is easily oxidized to ferric hydroxide. $4Fe(OH)_2 + O_2 + 2H_2O \rightarrow 4Fe(OH)_3$ (Yellow rust $Fe_2O_3,H_2O$)
- If the supply of oxygen is limited, the corrosion product may be ferric oxide which is black anhydrous magnetite, $Fe_3O_4$.

- **Galvanic (Bimetallic) corrosion:** When two different and dissimilar metals such as zinc and copper are electrically connected and exposed toan electrolyte, the metal of higher electrochemical series undergoes corrosion. In this process, themore active metal having more negative electrode potential acts as an anode and the less active metal having less negative electrode potential acts as cathode.

  In the above example, zinc is of higher electrochemical series acts as the anode and is attacked, gets dissolved; while copper being of lower electrochemical series or more no bleacts as cathode. In acidic solution, the corrosion caused by the hydrogen evolution process. While in neutral or slightly alkaline solution, absorption of oxygen occurs. The electron-current flows from the anode (zinc) to the cathode (copper).

$$Zn \rightarrow Zn^{2+} + 2e^- \text{ (Oxidation)}$$

  Thus, it is understood that the corrosion occurs at the anode metal; while the cathodic part remains
  protected from the attack as shown in Fig 13.3.

  **Example:** Steel screws in a brass marine hardware,

  1. Lead-antimony solder around copper wire;
  2. A steel propeller shaft in bronze bearing
  3. Steel pipe connected to copper plumbing.

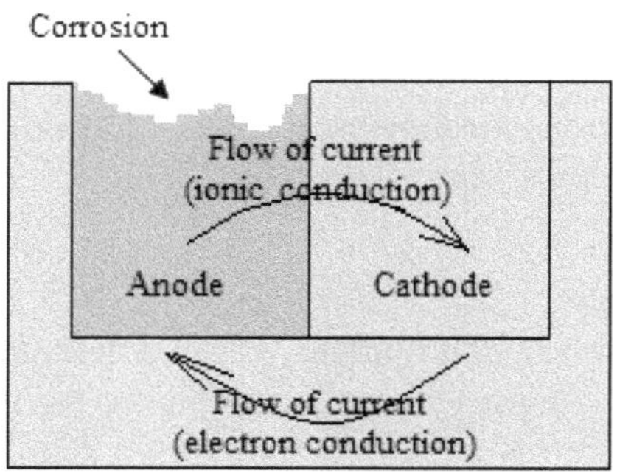


**Fig. 13.3** Galvanic corrosion

- **Filiform Corrosion:** This type of corrosion takes places on painted or plated surfaces, when moisture can penetrate the coating. Long branching filaments of corrosion product spreads out from the original corrosion pit and causes degradation of the protective coating. Filiform corrosion can be reduced by
  - Careful surface preparation before coating,
  - Use of coatings that are resistant to this form of corrosion, and
  - Careful inspection of coatings to ensure that the holes, in the coating are minimized.

- **Intergranular Corrosion:** When a metal or alloy is attacked on or adjacent to the grain boundaries, the intergranular corrosion occurs. The most effective means of prevention is the proper selection of alloy and/or suitable heat treatment.
- **Concentration cell corrosion:** This type of corrosion is due to electrochemical attack on the metal surface, exposed to an electrolyte of different concentrations or of varying aeration (varying concentration of oxygen).It occurs when one part of the metal is exposed to an environment having air concentration different from the other part. As a result, a difference in potential between differently aerated areas takes place. It has been observed experimentally that poor-oxygenated parts are anodic. For example:

  (i) The metal part immersed in water or in a conducting liquid, this is called water line corrosion.

  (ii) The metal part partially buried in soil.

  At Anode, if supply of oxygen is less (less aerated), the corrosion occurs as:

  $M \rightarrow M^{2+} + 2e^-$

  At Cathode, if supply of oxygen is more (more aerated), $OH^-$ ions are produced.

  This type of corrosion also occurs in the following cases:

  - Pitting or localized corrosion,
  - Crevice corrosion,
  - Pipeline corrosion,
  - Corrosion on wire fence

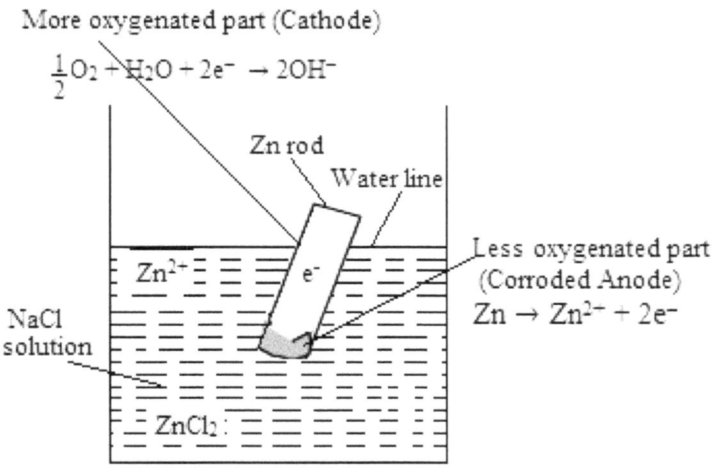


**Fig. 13.4** Concentration cell corrosion

- **Pitting Corrosion:** Pitting is a localized attack. This causes the formation of a hole around which the metal remains relatively un-attacked. The mechanism of this corrosion follows creation of differential aeration or concentration cell. Metal area covered by a drop of water, dust, sand, scale etc. behaves as the aeration or concentration cell. Pitting corrosion can be explained by considering a drop of water or brine solution (aqueous solution of NaCl) on a metal surface, (especially iron).The area covered by the drop of salt solution remains less oxygenated and acts as anode. Hence, corrosion occurs in this area; while the uncovered area acts as cathode, because of relatively higher oxygen content. It has been observed that the rate of corrosion will be more where the area of cathode is larger than that of the anode. Hence, there is more material around the small anodic area which causes the formation hole or pit.

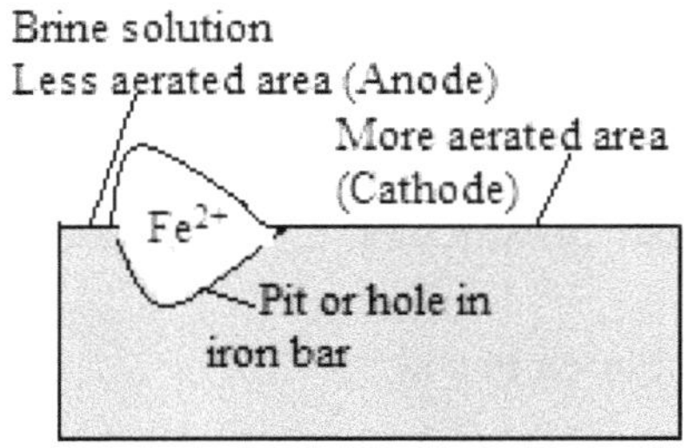


**Fig. 13.5** Pitting corrosion

**At Anode:** Fe is oxidized to $Fe^{2+}$ ion and electron is released.

$$Fe \rightarrow Fe^{2+} + 2e^{-}$$

**At Cathode:** Oxygen is converted into hydroxide ion with consumption of electrons in presence of water.

$$\frac{1}{2}O_2 + H_2O + 2e^{-} \rightarrow 2OH^{-}$$

The net reaction is $Fe + 2OH^{-} \rightarrow Fe(OH)_2$

By using ferroxyl indicator (a mixture containing phenolphthalein and potassium ferricyanide) the above reaction-mechanism can be confirmed. The pink color with phenolphthalein indicator confirms the formation of $OH^{-}$ ions at the cathode. At the anode, iron is oxidized to $Fe^{2+}$and the $Fe^{2+}$ioncombines with ferricyanide and produces a blue color.

- **Stress corrosion cracking (SCC):** Stress corrosion cracking (SCC) is produced by the simultaneous effects of tensile stress and a specific corrosive environment. Stresses may be due to applied loads, residual stresses from the manufacturing process, or a combination of both. The stress corrosion cracking can be avoided by
  - using appropriate heat treatment,
  - selecting the proper alloy for a given environment,
  - putting the equipment in service in a stress-free condition, or
  - using protective coatings.
- **Crevice corrosion:** If a crack, formed by a narrow opening between metallic and non-metallic material, is in contact with a liquid, the crack becomes anodic and undergoes corrosion. Hence, oxygen supply to the crack is less. The exposed area has high oxygen supply and acts as cathode. Bolts, nuts, rivets, joints are examples for this type of corrosion.
- **Pipeline corrosion:** Buried pipelines or cables, passing from one type of soil such as clay soil (clay soil is less aerated) to another soil such as sandy soil (sandy soil is more aerated),may get corroded due to differential aeration.

- **Corrosion in wire fence:** A wire fence is one in which the areas where the wires cross (anodic) are less aerated than the rest of the fence (cathodic). Hence, corrosion takes place at the wire crossing. Corrosion occurring under metal washers and the pipeline passing through clay to cinders(ash) are other examples.
- **Corrosion fatigue:** This is a special case of stress corrosion which is caused by the combined effects of cyclic stress and corrosion. No metal is resistant from some reduction of its resistance to cyclic stressing, if the metal is in a corrosive environment. Control of corrosion fatigue can be achieved by
  - lowering the cyclic stresses, or
  - corrosion control by using protection methods.
- **Fretting corrosion:** This is a rapid corrosion, occurs at the boundary between the highly loaded contacting metal surfaces exposed to slight vibratory motions. Fretting corrosion is greatly reduced by lubricating the contacting surfaces, and similarly in machinery-bearing surfaces so that the direct contact with air is excluded.

## Prevention of Corrosion

The corrosion of metal is very harmful and tremendous losses are experienced. It is necessary to reduce or avoid the corrosion of metal. Only under ideal conditions corrosion can be stopped completely. But complete attainment of ideal conditions is again practically not possible. It is possible only to minimize corrosion up to a considerable extent. Since various types of corrosion occur under different conditions or in environment, different methods are used to control corrosion. As the corrosion is a reaction between the metal or alloy and the environment, any method of corrosion control must focus towards either modifying the metal or the environment. Hence, selection of an appropriate metal which cannot be easily corroded, is necessary. The methods of prevention of corrosion can be classified as:

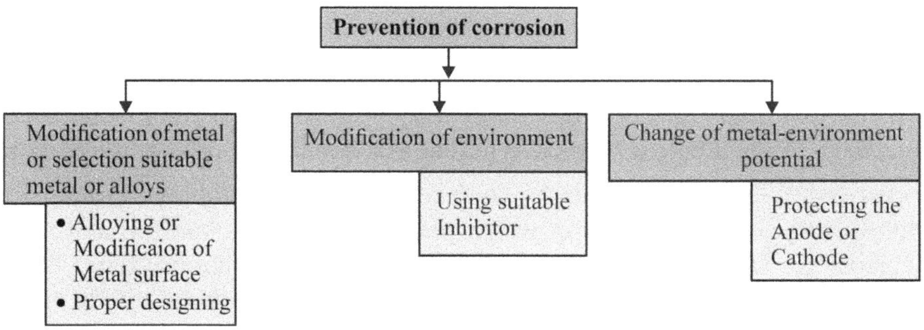


### Selection of Metals and Alloys

1. The noble metals such as gold and platinum are of first choice. They are the most resistant to corrosion.

   Since, these are very costly, they are not used for general purposes.

2. The next choice is the metals of highest purity. But in many cases, it is not possible to produce or get a metal of highest chemical purity. Even a trace amount of impurity results corrosion.
3. Therefore, the next choice is the use of corrosion resistant alloys. Various corrosion resistant alloys have been developed for specific purposes and environment. For example, (a) Stainless steel containing chromium produce an exceptionally coherent oxide film which protects the steel from further attack. (b) Cupro-nickel (70% Cu +30%Ni) alloys are presently used for condenser tubes and for bubble trays used infractionating column in oil refineries. (c) Highly stressed Nimonic alloys, alloy of Ni-Cr-Mo is used in gas turbines are very resistant to hot gases.

**Proper Designing:** Proper geometrical design plays a very important role in the control of corrosion of equipments and structure. The following general guidelines are necessary for the design of materials and components to control corrosion:

(a) The preferred designs and structures are always simple.

(b) The design with more complicated shapes having more angles, edges, corners etc. should be avoided.

(c) The contact between dissimilar metals should be avoided since they may cause galvanic type corrosion, and to overcome this galvanic corrosion, insulation can be used.

(d) When two dissimilar metals are in contact, the anodic area must be kept as large as possible and the cathodic area should be kept as small as possible.

(e) As far as possible the cracks or gaps between two metals, if used, should be avoided between the adjacent parts of a structure.

(f) In place of bolts and rivets proper welding should be done. Metal washers should be replaced by rubber or plastic washers as they do not adsorb water and also act as insulation. Corrosion in pipelines can be prevented by using smooth bends.

(g) Heat treatment like annealing reduces the stress corrosion.

(h) The design of water storage tanks is considered good, when water can be drained from it easily and it can be cleaned easily. Such a design avoids accumulation of dirt etc

## Modifying the Environment-Corrosion Control

Similar to metal, environment plays enormous role in corrosion of the metals. Hence, corrosion can be prevented to a great extent by modifying the environment. Some of the methods used are:

**(i) Deaeration:** When water comes in contact with air, it dissolves oxygen of the air. If the amount of oxygen is increased in water, the water becomes harmful and increases the rate of corrosion. Deaeration involves the mechanical agitation along with increase in temperature; as a result, dissolved oxygen and dissolved carbon dioxide are removed from water; thus, water becomes less corrosive.

**(ii) Use of inhibitors:** Inhibitors are organic or inorganic substances. These decrease the rate of corrosion. Usually, the inhibitors are added in small quantities to the corrosive medium. Inhibitors are classified into following categories:

1. Anodic inhibitors (chemical passivators)
2. Cathodic inhibitors (adsorption inhibitors)
3. Vapor phase inhibitors (volatile corrosion inhibitors)

1. **Anodic Inhibitors:** This type of inhibitors form a sparingly soluble compound witha newly produced metal cations and retards the corrosion of metals. The compound formed is then adsorbed on the corroding metal surface forming a passive film or barrier. Anodic inhibitors are used to repair/prevent the following:
   (a) Formation of the crack of the oxide film over the metal surface,
   (b) The pitting corrosion, and
   (c) Formation of porous oxide film over the metal surface.

   Chromate, phosphate, tungstate, nitrate, molybdate etc. are commonly used for this purpose.
2. **Cathodic Inhibitors:** Depending on the nature of the cathode reaction in an electrochemical corrosion, cathodic inhibitors are classified into following categories;

   **In an acidic solution:** liberation of hydrogen gas is the main cathode reaction; the corrosion can be controlled by reducing the diffusion of $H^+$ ions through the cathode. For example, amines, mercaptans, thiourea, etc.

   $$2H^+ + 2e- \rightarrow H_2\uparrow$$

   **In a neutral solution:** When the medium is neutral, adsorption of oxygen or formation of hydroxyl ions occurs and those indicate the cathodic reaction. Therefore, the corrosion can be controlled either by eliminating oxygen from the corroding medium or by reducing its diffusion to the cathodic area. The dissolved oxygen can be eliminated 1. by adding reducing agents like $Na_2SO_3$ or 2. by controlling the diffusion of oxygen by adding suitable inhibitors like Mg, Zn or Ni salts such as $Na_2SO_3$, $N_2H_4$, salts of Mg, Zn or Ni.

   $$\frac{1}{2}O_2 + H_2O + 2e^- \rightarrow 2OH^-$$
3. **Vapor phase inhibitors:** These organic inhibitors can readily vaporize and can form a protective layer on the metal surface. These can be conveniently used to prevent corrosion in closed spaces, storage containers, packing materials, sophisticated equipments etc.; for example, dicyclohexyl ammonium chromate, nitrate, benzotriazole, phenylthiourea etc. can be used as organic inhibitor.

   **(i)** ***Anodic Protection*:** This is another method used to control the electrochemical corrosion. In this method, an external potential control system, called *potentio-stat*, is used to produce and maintain a thin non corroding, passive film on a, metal or an alloy. The potentio-stat is used to shift the corrosion potential into passive potential so that the corrosion of the metal is stopped. The potential of the object (say acid storage tank) can be controlled by potential controller (potentio-stat) so that under certain potential range, the object becomes passive and further corrosion is prevented. This potential range depends upon the metal as well as on the environment.

   ***Applications***

   1. Used in acid coolers in dilute sulphuric acid plants.
   2. Used in storage tanks for sulphuric acid.
   3. Used in chromium in contact with hydrofluoric acid.

**Limitations**

1. This method cannot be applied in the case of corrosive medium containing destructive chloride salt.
2. This cannot be used if protection breaks down at any point, because it is difficult to reestablish.

**Protective Coatings:** The metal can be protected from corrosion by applying a suitable coating to cover the surface of the metal. Such coating is called protective coating and acts as a physical barrier between the coated metal surface and the environment. The coating improves the physical appearance of the metal and also provides some special properties such as hardness, resistance to oxidation and thermal insulation. For such coating following materials can be used. Protective coatings can be broadly classified into two types.

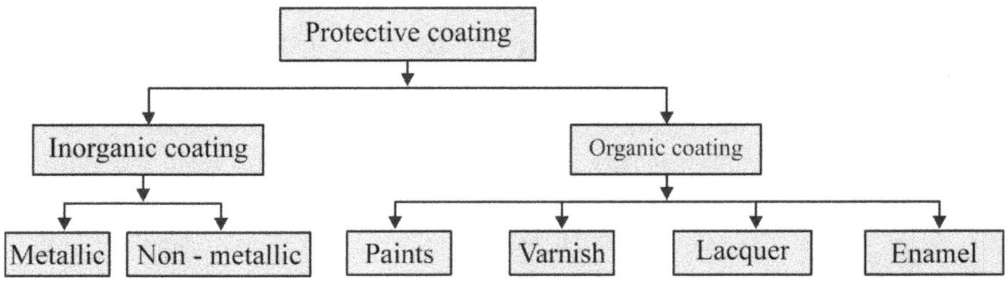


Metallic coating may be done by

1. Hot dipping- Galvanizing, Tinning,
2. Metal cladding,
3. Cementation-Sherardizing, Chromizing, Calorizing, and
4. Electroplating.

Non-metallic coating may be done by

1. Surface coating or chemical conversion coating – Chromate coating, Phosphate coating and Oxide coating,
2. Anodizing,
3. Enamel coating or Vitreous or Porcelain coating.

Organic coatings consist of Paints, Varnishes, Lacquers and Enamels.

## Paint

Paint is most commonly used as coating material. Paint is a viscous, opaque (not clear), mechanical dispersion mixture of one or more pigments(dye) in a vehicle (drying oil). It should have following characteristics:

1. Hiding or covering power
2. A good and uniform film forming capacity on the metal surface
3. The film should not crack on drying
4. Ability to provide a glossy film
5. The film produced should be washable
6. Ability to provide a stable and decent color on the metal surface

7. Good resistance to the atmospheric conditions
8. Should be fluid enough to spread easily over the surface
9. Good adhesion capacity to the material over which it is intended to be applied
10. Ability to dry quickly or in a reasonable duration.
11. The color of the paint should not fade.

A paint is generally composed of the following constituents:

(a) Pigment
(b) Vehicle or medium or drying oil
(c) Thinner
(d) Driers
(e) Fillers or Extenders
(f) Plasticizers
(g) Antiskinning agents

## Electroplating

It is a coating technique, most frequently used in the industrial method of producing metallic coating. Electroplating is the process by which a metal is deposited in the form of coating over the surface of the base metal. The method bypasses a direct current through an electrolytic solution containing the soluble salt of the coating metal. The base metal to be plated is used as cathode and either the coating metal itself or an inert material of good electrical conductivity (like graphite) is used as the anode.

The article to be electroplated is first treated with organic solvent like carbon tetrachloride, acetone, tetrachloro ethylene, etc. to remove organic dirt, oils, greases etc. Then the article is treated with diluted hydrochloric or sulphuric acid (acid pickling) to make it free from surface scale, oxides, etc. After thorough cleaning of the article, it is then used as the cathode of the electrolytic cell. It has been mentioned above that the anode is either the coating metal itself or an inert material of good electrical conductivity. The electrolyte used is a solution of soluble salt of the coating metal. When direct current is passed, coating metal ions migrate from the anode to the cathode and get deposited there. Thus, a thin layer of coating metal is deposited on the surface of the article made as the cathode. To produce strong, adherent and smooth deposit, certain types of additives such as glue, gelatin, boric acid are added to the electrolytic bath. To improve the brightness of the deposit, brightening agents are added in the electrolytic bath. The success of electroplating process depends on the following conditions:

1. Optimum temperature,
2. Optimum current density, and
3. Low metal ion concentration.

### Electroless Plating

Electroless plating is a newer technique used to deposit a noble metal from its salt solution on the surface of a metal to be plated. The surface of the metal to be protected is made active catalytically. Hence, this technique does not consume any electrical energy. Only a suitable

reducing agent is used. The reducing agent reduces the metal ions into metal which deposits over the catalytically activated surface and produces a uniform and thin coating.
Metal ions + reducing agents → Metal (deposited) + Oxidized product

## Materials Used for Pharmaceutical Plant Construction

### Ferrous Metals

Primarily there are three ferrous metals such as cast iron, steels, and stainless steels that are used for construction of pharmaceutical plants and machineries.

### Cast Iron

It consists of iron with some amount of carbon. By varying proportion of carbon and iron, the property of the cast iron prepared can be changed. Cast iron does not react with concentrated sulphuric acid and nitric acid, and with dilute alkalis. But it reacts with both dilute and concentrated hydrochloric acid, with dilute sulphuric acid, and nitric acid. This is very important in pharmacy to note that cast iron is susceptible to ammonium salts and tannins at high temperature. In plants it is commonly used as supports, in making jackets of steam pan, kettle, etc. Cast iron is used because it is cheap. Sometimes, enamel, plastic, and other suitable materials are used to coat the article made of cast iron to make it resistant to acids, alkalis and tannins. Such coated cast iron can replace more expensive resistant materials.

Iron forms alloy with silicon, nickel, chromium. The alloys have typical characteristics different from that of cast iron. Silicon alloys have been found considerable applications in chemical engineering processes, because it is more resistant to acids. These are very hard but brittle; these cannot be machined due to their brittleness.

### Steel

Mild steel is an iron alloy that contains only a small percentage of carbon and it can be welded, machined and so on. On the other hand, cast iron cannot be welded, or machined. Mild steel has much greater mechanical strength than cast iron and is much less brittle.

Like cast iron, mild steel possesses similar capability to resist the chemical but the extent of resistance varies according to its composition. For chemical and pharmaceutical plant construction, mild steel with greater tonnage (heaviness) has been used. Other materials are relatively less used. Mils steel is used to support the structure such as beams, joists, (girders), etc. and bases for industrial vessels. For large machineries, vessels, pipelines and small fittings and fixtures (accessories) such as nuts and bolts, steel is a metal of choice. When the internal surface is required to be non-corrosive, steel is used in place of cast iron to make vessels and industrial pans.

### Stainless Steel

Stainless steels are steel alloys, generally with nickel and chromium. The stainless steels can be categorized by their high resistance to corrosion. For example, '18/8 stainless steel' contains 18% of chromium and 8% of nickel; these have been considerable used in pharmaceutical industry.

Pharmaceutical and chemical plants of different shapes and sizes can be constructed with this material because it can be handled like mild steel. However, substantial skill and knowledge would be necessary to alter its corrosion-resistant properties during heating processes such as welding, because carbide is formed during welding and precipitates at the crystal-grain boundaries. The formation of carbide can be prevented by reducing the carbon content or by adding a suitable stabilizer such as titanium, molybdenum, or niobium.

For construction of most pharmaceutical plant, including storage and extraction vessels, evaporators and fermenting vessels, etc. stainless steel can be used. Small apparatuses that are commonly made of stainless steel are funnels, buckets, measuring vessels and shovels. Sinks and bench tops where a good surface with high resistance to corrosion is necessary are also made of stainless steel.

It is not commonly used because of its high cost, but its performance and durability often justify even on a very large scale. For example, many of the plants used for the production of penicillin have been constructed by using stainless steel because it is by far the most satisfactory, strong enough, corrosion resistant, non-contaminating and readily cleansed and sterilized.

## Nonferrous Metals

This group of metals includes aluminium, tin, lead, silver, nickel, chromium, copper, copper alloys, copper-zinc alloys, copper-tin alloys, etc

### Aluminium

Aluminium can considerably resist corrosion due to many substances but it is susceptible to mineral acids. It can resist strong nitric acid, caustic soda, caustic potash, mercury and its salts. Aluminium forms a film on its surface and becomes resistant. For example, acetic acid forms a film of gelatinous aluminium subacetate which is resistant to acetic acid. Similarly, pure strong ammonia solution forms a resistant film of aluminium hydroxide which is highly resistant to many corrosive conditions. However, aluminium can form a compact oxide film which also makes the aluminium resistant.

Pure aluminium is soft but relatively more resistant to corrosion than most of its alloys such as duralumin. Alloys having adequate corrosion resistance and strength can be improved with small percentages of manganese, magnesium, or silicon. Plant with excellent thermal conductivity can be easily fabricated.

The most valuable advantage of using aluminium in construct of pharmaceutical plant is probably the non-toxicity of its salts whether colored or colorless. Since the metal or the alloy is also non-toxic to micro-organisms, it can be used for biosynthetic processes such as the production of citric, gluconic acids, and of streptomycin by deep culture methods. The metal is also suitable for construction of plants to be used for preparing culture media and for absorption and extraction vessels used in preparing antibiotics (microbiology plant). Because of the formation of resistant films, it is used for acetic acid plant and storage vessels for ammonia. The welded aluminium vessels can also be used for the nitric acid industry. Due to its low density, it is most suitable for transport containers such as drums and barrels, road and rail tankers.

## Lead

Lead is commonly used in the chemical industries. It is remarkably resistant to corrosion. It can also be easily fabricated into complicated shapes. Manufacturing sulphuric acid using lead chamber process is a common example of the use of lead in heavy chemical industries. However, in pharmaceutical industries, it is not preferred because its poisonous salts can contaminate the product. In fact, traces of lead salt are poisonous to health. It is commonly used for preparing cold water pipes, waste pipes and for dilution tanks for laboratories.

## Copper

Copper can be easily fabricated because of its ductility and malleability. It has good thermal conductivity, about eight times greater than steel. Due to its good malleability and excellent thermal conductivity it had been wisely in plant construction. But the most common disadvantage of it is that it is corroded by many substances, particularly oxidizing agents. In all concentrations, nitric acid can react with copper. Hot concentrated sulphuric and hydrochloric acids, and even some organic acids can corrode copper. Ammonia reacts with copper readily and form blue cupro-ammonium salts. Even the constituent of many drugs can react with copper. For this reason, copper is not commonly used in pharmaceutical plant construction; if it is used, it is coated by a layer of tin to protect from corrosion and to protect the product from contamination. It is commonly used for construction of evaporators, pans of different types, stills, fractionating columns, etc. with a lining of suitable material which is resistant to corrosion. Now a days, other materials such as stainless steel is used where corrosion is likely to occur.

## Copper alloys

Alloys of copper commonly with zinc and tin are commonly used; but alloys of copper with aluminium, nickel and silicon have their special applications in pharmaceutical plant construction.

## Copper-zinc alloys (Brasses)

Brass can perform better than other alloys of copper. The major limitation of it is that it is more susceptible to corrosion for which it is not used in pharmaceutical plant construction. Like copper, it is used where rusting is to be avoided. But its tensile strength is more than that of copper.

## Copper-tin alloys (Bronzes)

Bronzes usually contain 2 to 13 percent of tin, small amount of phosphorus, and traces of other elements. Hardness and durability of bronze are more than that of brass. For this reason, the bronzes are used commonly to make filter gauzes, stirrers, valves, pumps, autoclaves, high pressure pipes, and special tableting punches and dies.

### Copper-Nickel Alloy (Monel Metal)

Monel metal is composed of about 67% of nickel and 33% of copper. It is harder and more resistant than nickel. It can be used in place of steel, where corrosion resistance is of prime importance.

### Tin

Tin is more resistant to corrosion and its salts are not toxic. Hence, it has wide applications in food industries. Since it is weaker in strength, it is commonly used to make a protective coating over copper, steel, brass, etc. Coating of other metals with tin had been practiced for about 2000 years and now a days, about half of the materials are being coated with tin. For example, steel coated with tin is used for making containers, condenser tubes, etc.

### Nickel

It is resistant to alkalis and oxidation, but slowly react with dilute mineral acid and rapidly with concentrated acids. It is resistant to weak organic acids such as citric acid, tartaric acid, stearic acid, etc. which are commonly used in pharmaceutical preparations. Nickel is resistant to phenols. Its salts are nontoxic. Hence, it is commonly used to make pans, vats, tanks, mixers, valves, and pumps. Nickel wires can be used to make filter cloths.

### Chromium

It is hard and resistant to corrosion, but not commonly used for construction of plants. It can form alloys with nickel which is more resistant. Due to this property, it is normally used in manufacture of stainless steel. It is also used for plating the steel to make it more resistant.

### Silver

Being costly, silver is only used for construction of special plants. For example, plants where salicylates and acetic acid are manufactured. In crystallization of vitamin, silver-plated basket is used as hydroextractor, for bromination, a solid silver vessel in cast-iron jacket is used. In such plants silver-coated material is used, not the solid silver. It is susceptible to concentrated hydrochloric or sulphuric acid, and to nitric acid of any concentration, sulphur, and sulphur compounds. It is resistant to organic acids and their salts. The malleability and ductility of silver is more than that of copper. Hence, it can be easily fabricated. Compared to all metals it has highest thermal conductivity.

## Inorganic Non-Metals

In this category glass, stone, slate, brick, concrete and asbestos are used as the materials for plant construction.

## Glass

Glass is very resistant to any type of corrosive material. Due to its extensive brittleness, it is widely used to make small-scale apparatus. Although, it was developed as a material of construction for use in large scale.

Ordinary soda glass is used for bottles and other cheap articles, but is not satisfactory for large-scale plant or for containers where alkali is used. For these purposes, borosilicate glass is used. Such glass has several advantages over soda glass. For example, it is less brittle. It has a low thermal expansion and can be used with safety over wide range of temperature. However, its thermal conductivity is low and therefore, it should be heated gradually to avoid fracturing. Pipe line made of glass may be used with pressure up to 8 bars, if the pipe diameter is less than 5 cm and pipe lines with larger diameters are used with pressures up to 4 bars.

Special advantages of glass are that it can be easily cleaned and sterilized. Moreover, the contents of a glass vessel can be readily examined for color and clarity.

A disadvantage is the difficulty of joining sections of glass plant together. Ground-glass joints are sometimes used satisfactorily, in small-scale apparatus, but these are rigid. Gaskets of rubber, plastics, fibre, and asbestos are used to form a more flexible joints but these must be chosen with care because they are normally less resistant than glass.

Glass pipeline is useful for transporting liquids from stage to stage in various operations. The diameter of such pipe line may vary from 15 mm to 0.3 m with fittings for the assembly of complete systems.

All glass still is used for preparing Water for Injections and other distilled preparations. Containers up to 100lt are used and larger tanks can be made by clamping glass plates in frames.

Glass fibres are excellent for heat insulation or refrigeration plant. Such fibre, treated with oil, is used for filtering air for aseptic rooms. Woven fibre may be used for filter cloths and glass may be sintered in the preparation of filters.

## Glass Linings and Coating

Metalscan be coated with glass to give a protective lining. The limitations of such apparatus are:

- Uneven expansion of metal and glass, and
- Accidental chipping of the glass surface.

Great care must therefore be taken in heating and cooling and in protecting the glass lining from accidental damage. Vessels of up to 5000lt capacity, pipe line, fittings, valves, condensers, columns, pumps, stirrers and mixers are among the many glass coated items which are in use. High resistance to corrosion and ease of cleaning make it valuable for pharmaceutical use.

## Stone Ware

Ceramics are reasonably cheaper, but their weight, low thermal conductivity, and fragility give only a low resistance to mechanical and thermal shock. Corrosion resistance is usually due to a surface glaze which may become chipped.

Ceramics are used widely on a small scale, but only to a limited extent on a large scale. Pipe line, tanks, vessels and filters are among the items made from it. Of special interest among ceramic products are bacteria-proof filters.

Stone, slate, brick, and concrete have their particular uses, among which granite is used for certain types of mill, vitrified acid-resistant bricks are used for tanks, drains, culverts, etc., and for structural purposes and sometimes for tanks, concrete is used.

Asbestos is a poor conductor of heat;it is used for heat insulation. Since it is extremely inert, it is used for pipe lining and for pipe jointing. It is fibrous material and may be woven into cloth for filters.

## Organic Non-Metals

### Plastics

According to the use, plastics are considered under the following headings –

Rigid material,

Flexible material,

Coating and linings,

Cements and fillers,

Special cases.

'Keebush' is an example of a rigid material. It is a phenolic resin, used as inert fillers with various inert materials selected for their particular purpose. It may be machined, welded, and worked in other ways and is also used for making gears, bearings, and similar items. These can reduce noise up to two thirds compared with iron. Its weight is about one quarter that of iron.

It is resistant to corrosion, but susceptible to oxidizing substances and strong alkalis. Any items such as vessels, pipes, fittings, valves, pumps, fans, ducts, filter presses and many others may be made from this material. Polyethylene and polyvinyl chloride (PVC) are similar materials and are rigid or flexible, depending upon the amount of plasticizer added. These do not withstand high temperature but are non-resistant only to strong oxidizing acids, halogens, and organic solvents.

Rigid and semi-rigid mouldings may be used for tanks, pipes, ducts, and other similar items and slightly flexible funnels, buckets and jugs are made which are almost unbreakable.

Metallic surfaces may be protected from corrosion by coating with plastics of the polyethylene or PVC type materials. For coating suitable plasticizer is mixed with the plastics. Perfect adhesion of plastic to metal is sometimes difficult. The major disadvantages are the differences in thermal expansion of plastic and metal and the accidental chipping during coating.

These materials are used for lining of tanks and vessels and for coatings on stirrers and fans. Plastic cements are used for ceiling the spaces between acid-resistant tiles and bricks, and for similar purposes. For moving parts of machinery and aseptic screens transparent plastic guards are also used. Nylon and PVC fibres may be woven into filter cloths.

### Rubber

For the purposes similar to those mentioned under plastics, hard rubber may be used. While soft rubber may be used for linings and coatings. Rubber swells in contact with oils; it is subject to oxidation and is attacked by some organic solvents. Synthetic rubbers have been developed with greater resistance.

### Timber

Earlier tanks and vats have been made with wood which has been greatly diminished since it has disadvantage of absorbing the contents. Its advantage is its lightness. For this reason, where parts have to be handled, and filter presses are sometimes made of wood.

## Short Questions

1. Classify the factors to be considered during construction of pharmaceutical plant. What are the different physical factors?
2. Write a note on chemical factors.
3. What are necessities of corrosion studies? What happens when corrosion takes place?
4. Write a note on bimetallic corrosion.
5. What are oxygen absorption type and filiform corrosions?
6. What are electroplating and electroless plating?
7. Write down the applications of stainless steel and aluminium.
8. Write down the application of lead, copper and copper alloys for construction of pharmaceutical plant.
9. How are the paints used for coating the materials used for construction of pharmaceutical plant.
10. Write a note on protective coating.

## Long Questions

1. Explain different physical factors to be considered.
2. What do you understand by the term corrosion? What are the factors that affect corrosion?
3. Explain the theories of corrosion. What are corrosion rates?
4. Explain different types of dry or chemical corrosion.
5. Explain electrochemical corrosion.
6. What is concentration cell corrosion? Explain pitting corrosion.
7. Explain stress corrosion, crevice corrosion, pipeline corrosion, and fretting corrosion.
8. What are various ways by which environment-corrosion can be controlled?
9. Briefly mention the applications of different inorganic non-metals used as materials for plant construction.
10. Explain the uses of organic non-metals for construction of pharmaceutical plant

# CHAPTER 14

# Material Handling System

Objectives & Applications of Material Handling Systems, Different Types of Conveyors such as Belt, Screw and Pneumatic Conveyors.

## Introduction

Materials handling can be defined as '*a function dealing with the preparation, placing and positioning of materials to facilitate their movement or storage*'. Material handling is the art and science involved in the movement, handling and storage of materials during different stages of manufacturing. The value of a product does not change with the material handling system, but the cost of the product definitely changes. If the cost of the product increases, it will affect the customer. Hence, sales may be affected. Thus, the cost of handling of material should be as minimum as possible. In Indian industries the cost pf material handling amounts to about 40% of the cost of the product. About 20% of the total time required for manufacturing a product is actually utilized for actual processing; rest 80% of the time is spent on the movement of the materials from one place to another, waiting for processing, etc. Poor material handling may result in delays and finally results in idling of the equipment. Thus, material handling is an important system that must be considered carefully. The function comprises every consideration of the product except the actual processing operation. In fact, in many cases, the handling is considered and included as an integral part of the processing. By implementing scientific material handling system, considerable reduction in the cost as well as in the production cycle time could be achieved.

Haynes has defined "*Material handling embraces the basic operations in connection with the movement of bulk, packaged and individual products in a semi-solid or solid state by means of gravity manually or power-actuated equipment and within the limits of individual producing, fabricating, processing or service establishment*".

Material handling cost = Cost of transportation + Cost of packaging + Cost of space + Cost of handling equipment (including its operation, maintenance and depreciation, etc)

## Objectives

Therefore, the primary objective of the material handling engineer is to reduce the overall cost of the product. Material handling equipment is not production machinery, but is auxiliary equipment that improves the flow of material which in turn reduces slowdowns or idling of the production machines and thus, increases their utilities in production.

The basic purpose of material handling refers to the movement of material, which was started from the industrial revolution since late eighteenth and early nineteenth centuries.

In industries, supermarkets, offices, construction projects and banks, the movement of things take place. In earlier days, handling of the material was physically done by men; over the passage of time the mechanical principles like lever, wheel, pulley etc. have been used.

Earlier, it was generally believed and accepted that most of this cost is expected and cannot be easily avoided, but now-a-days, the need for reduction in materials handling costs through systems is being realized.

Not only the cost, majority of production time is also consumed in handling materials before, during and after the manufacture. The material handling time and cost can be reduced by proper selection, operation, maintenance and layout of these handling devices.

The materials handling problems must be studied and considered at the time of planning, installation and usage of various machines and tools required and before the erection of the factory building. Materials handling is a major consideration in designing new plants, and the existing plants needs to be modified by the application of modern material handling strategies. These strategies increase output, improve quality, speed up the deliveries and therefore, reduces the production cost.

Therefore, the objectives of material handling can be categorized as mentioned below:

1. Minimizing the cost of material handling.
2. Minimizing the delays and interruptions by making the materials available at the point of use at right quantity and at right time.
3. Increasing the productive capacity of the production facilities by effective utilization of capacity and enhancing productivity.
4. Improvement in safety in material handling through improvement in working condition.
5. Maximizing the utilization of material handling equipment.
6. Prevention of damages to materials.
7. Reduction in the investment in process inventory.

Material handling system can be developed through obtaining the answers to the questions given below:

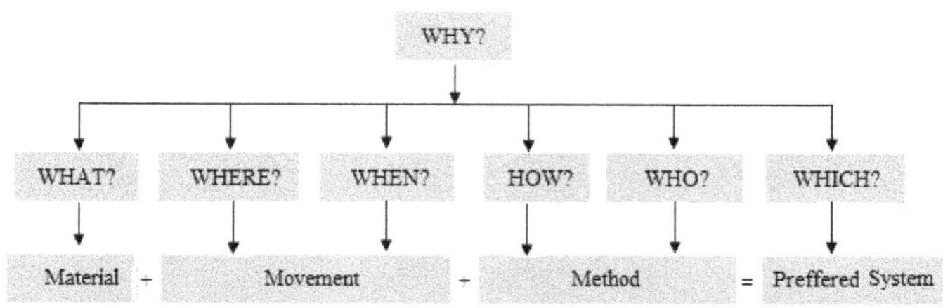

## Designing of the Material Handling System

In the year, 1966 the College-Industry Council on Material Handling Education decided and adopted twenty principles on material handling. In 1981, these were revised in accordance to the changes in industrial operations and made effective since the year first adopted.

The material handling principles provide brief statements of the fundamentals of material handling practice. These provide the guidance and viewpoint to material handling system designers. The applicability of the principles depends on the conditions that occur due to the many different conditions that might exist. It is questionable that any principle can always be relevant. The principles serve as rough guidance or rules of thumb for the material handling systems design. Based on these principles, a number of checklists have been developed to facilitate the identification of improvement opportunities for existing systems. Checklists can be used for the purpose of designing of new and improved systems a valuable to the process. These principles can also be slightly different or modified as per the actual requirement to achieve the objectives. These principles should be compatible with each other.

1. **Orientation:** Identify existing methods and problems with respect to physical and economic limitations.
2. **Planning:** Create a plan to include primary requirements, desirable options, and the considerations of contingencies for all material handling systems and storing activities.
3. **Systems:** Integrate those handling systems and storage activities that are economically viable into a coordinated system of operations, such as receiving, inspection, storage, production, assembly, packaging, warehousing, shipping, and transportation.
4. **Unit Load:** Make a product unit as large as possible which can be handled comfortably.
5. **Space Utilization:** All cubic spaces should be effectively utilized.
6. **Standardization:** Handling methods and equipments are to be standardized wherever possible.
7. **Ergonomic:** During designing of the material handling equipment and procedures, the human capabilities and limitations are to be recognized for effective interaction with the people using the system.
8. **Energy:** Consider and include the energy consumption of the material handling systems and procedures, compare and prepare economic justifications.
9. **Ecology:** Use material handling equipments and procedures that are either ecofriendly or can minimize adverse effects on the environment.
10. **Mechanization:** The material handling equipment and process are mechanized wherever possible to increase the efficiency and economy in handling of materials.
11. **Flexibility:** Use of methods and equipments that can perform a variety of tasks under a variety of operating conditions.
12. **Simplification:** Simplified handling by eliminating, reducing, or combining unnecessary movements and/or equipment.
13. **Gravity:** Utilization of gravity to move material wherever possible, while respecting limitations concerning safety, product damage, and loss.

14. **Safety:** The safe material handling equipment and methods that follow existing safety codes, and regulations in addition to accrued experience are to be provided.
15. **Computerization:** Computerization in material handling and storage systems is required, when circumstances warrant, for improved material and information control.
16. **System Flow:** Integration of data flow with physical material flow in handling and storage.
17. **Layout:** Preparation of operation sequence and equipment layout for all viable system solutions, then select the alternative system which best integrates efficiency and effectiveness.
18. **Cost:** Comparison of the economic justification of alternative solutions in equipment and methods on the basis of economic effectiveness as measured by expense per unit handled.
19. **Maintenance:** Preparation of a plan for preventive maintenance and scheduled repairs on all material handling equipment.
20. **Obsolescence:** Preparation of a long-range and economically sound policy for replacement of obsolete equipment and methods with special consideration to after-tax life cycle costs.

Handling system can be classified into four categories:

1. Mechanical,
2. Semi-automatic,
3. Automatic, and
4. Information-directed

Material handling equipments can be classified into four categories:

1. Containers and unitizing equipment,
2. Material transport equipment,
3. Storage and retrieval equipment, and
4. Automatic identification and communication equipment

The approach for ideal material handling system is shown in Fig 14.1.

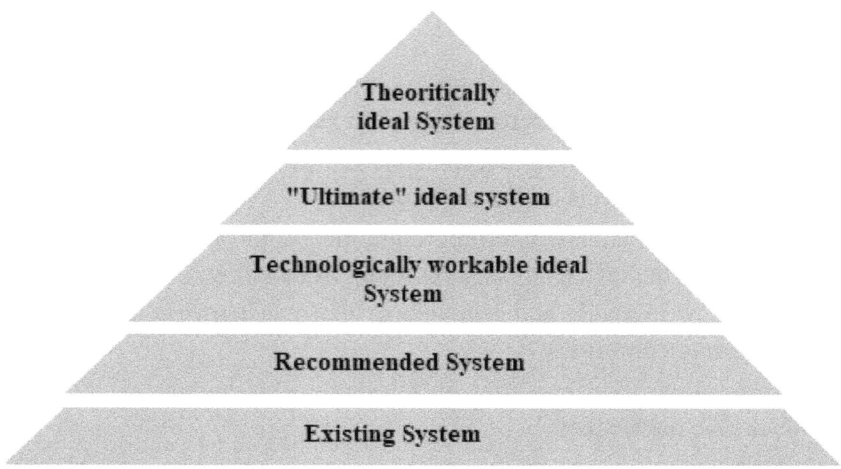


**Fig. 14.1** Ideal approach for material handling system

## Applications of Material Handling Systems

Material handling system is generally applied for five reasons:

1. To reduce cost of the product,
2. To increase the capacity,
3. To improve working conditions,
4. To improve customer service, and
5. To improve productivity.

1. **Reduction in total cost of the product:** Reduction in total cost of production can be achieved by either reducing materials handling or by use of improved handling procedure or both. This can be achieved by implementing the following practices.
   (a) Reducing the material handling labor,
   (b) Skilled or semi-skilled workmen should not be assigned to perform material handling work,
   (c) Indirect labor expenses on activities related to storage, inspection, quality control, repair and maintenance, tool room, shipping, etc. should be reduced.
   (d) Reducing damage or loss of material during handling.
   (e) Better utilization of space,
   (f) Reducing in-process storage of product,
   (g) Increasing productivity,
   (h) Reducing expenditure on packaging and other protective strategies, and
   (i) Reducing the cost of inventory.
2. **Increasing capacity of production:** Use of improved material handling system can increase the production capacity by better utilization of space. The capacity of production is increased by implementing the improved material handling system in the following ways:
   (a) By better utilization of space:
   (b) Air space can be fully utilized by stacking the containers in racks. Overhead cranes, conveyors, lift trucks, etc. can be used satisfactorily for this kind of activity.
   (c) By reducing travel space or excessive wastage of space:
   (d) For this purpose, flow of materials between the operations should be studied with respect to flow paths, volume of material, timing, etc. Such studies may help in reducing travel time and space requirements.
   (e) By improving equipment utilization:
   (f) Utilization of equipment can be improved by ensuring regular supply and distribution of material. This can reduce the idling of machine.
   (g) By faster loading or unloading:
   (h) This can be done by using conveyor systems, cranes, loaders, rail road cars, tipping trucks, etc.
3. **Improvement in working conditions:** Working conditions need to be improved with respect to safety, convenience to work, and systematic operation.

(a) ***Safety aspects:*** Safety of working personnel, material and required equipments are necessary to prevent not only the financial loss, but also to improve the confidence of employees.

(b) ***Easy working:*** Heavy and complicated works can be completed easily and smoothly, if right equipments should be used properly. By doing so, the rate of production can be improved greatly and the works can be done easily. This will bring aboutbetter working environment, high morale of the workers and lower workers turnover.

(c) ***Full-proof operation:*** Manual handling of equipments should be replaced as far as possible by using appropriate equipments or machineries, so that the chances of confusion can be avoided. Right materials can be placed at right places and production can be done undisrupted.

4. **Improved customer service:** Service to the customers can be improved, if the material handling system is improved properly. As a result, the production can be completed timely, and regular and timely supply of the products can be maintained. These are the main sources of good customer services.

## Functions of Material Handling

The primary function of material handling system and the movement of material, are as old as man. The necessity of material handling was realized earlier and was developed with the development of the systems in a factory. In the late eighteenth and early nineteenth centuries, such development took place and started with the industrial revolution.

Movement of material takes place in industries, supermarkets, offices, construction sites, and even in banks. For example, in early days the man was physically carrying big material (stone) which took lot of time and accidents were prone. Over the years, the mechanical principles like lever, wheel, pulley, etc. were used to increase the productivity and facilitate the work.

The material handling does not add value to a product, it reduces the overall cost of the product significantly and results smooth working. With certain exception, about 20 – 35% of the cost of a product is due to the material handling. Earlier, it was believed that most of the elements of production cost cannot be avoided and are inevitable; but presently the cost can be reduced considerably by using appropriate material handling systems at different stages of production, storage and shipment. Repetition of work, manufacturing time can be minimized to a great extent. Proper selection, utilization, operation, maintenance and layout of these handling devices save the time as well as cost.

Material handling is an important factor to be considered while designing a new plant or renovation of an existing plant, since these devices can improve the productivity.

In general, the material handling can be classified into three types irrespective of the type of industry.

- Handling of individual part or unit by men (manually),
- Handling inside a room or in a department or in the plant (production)
- Handling of materials during distribution network up to the ultimate user or customer.

Various steps and stages of the handling system are shown as:

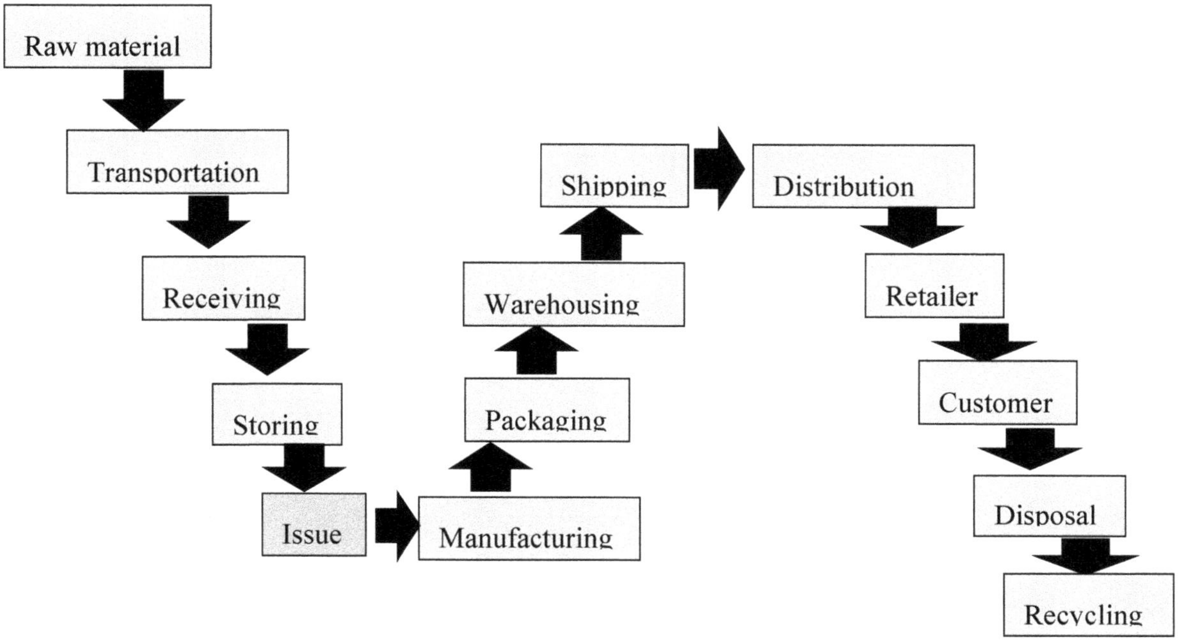


## Different Types of Conveyors

In general, the term conveying is associated to operation of transportation of solid or liquid materials. For this purpose, the selection of equipment depends on various factors; the most important factor is the shape and size of the material to be transported, and whether transportation is vertical, horizontal or inclined.

Whatever may be the purpose or type of the equipment is used, in most cases the design is made on the basis of empirical experience, not on any rational method of calculation. This is mainly due to the two reasons:

- The properties of material to be transported are inherently different,
- Wide range of processes are there, where material handling is involved.

Conveyors can be classified as follows:

## Belt Conveyors

Primarily belt conveyor is a simple equipment. It consists of a belt on which the solid materials are transported. However, a large-scale belt conveyor is relatively complicated. The component parts are available in a wide variety of forms. The design and installation of such a belt becomes difficult even to an expert. If the belt is loaded and unloaded manually (by hand) which is usually done for transportation of packaged items, a belt conveyor consists of the following components:

1. The belt,
2. The drive,

3. Supports, and
4. Tightener.

Otherwise, belt conveyor requires feeding and discharge devices.

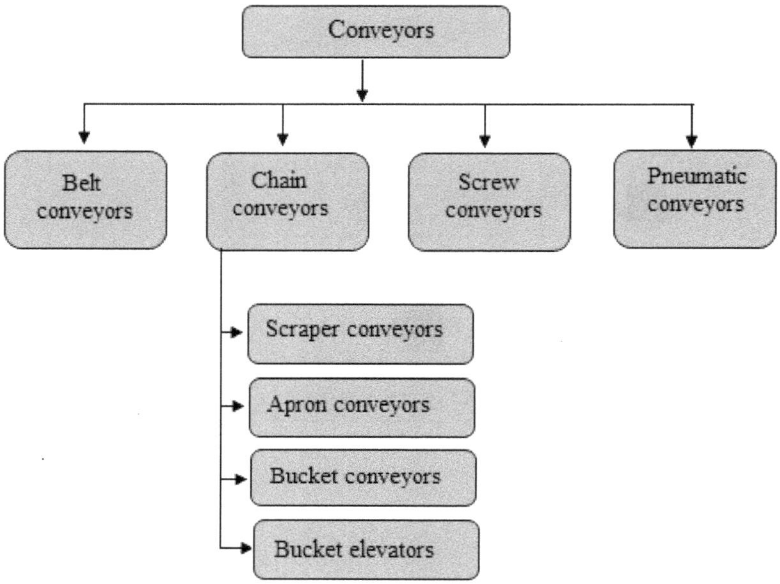


1. **Belt:** The most commonly rubber is used to make a belt. The rubber belt consists of a core, or body, of several plies (layers) of cotton duck. Each layer of cotton is impregnated with rubber and bonded together with rubber. Over the body there is a covering of rubber that binds the whole together. The top cover is thicker than the below. Special grades of rubber can strengthen the belt to resist excessive abrasion, effect of high temperature (121°C), and chemical attack, etc. Such belt can withstand a safe working stress ranging from 4.5 – 7.15kg/cm per ply. Special construction of belt is necessary and available for working at temperature more than 121°C.

   Cord belts are made with cord tires. The cord must be completely surrounded by rubber to form base. The cotton cord is commonly available. For higher strengths, the nylon cord may be used. The safe working stress for cord belts may range from8.9 to 17.9kg/cm per ply. However, the strongest and most expensive belts consist of steel wire in place of fabric cords. Such belts are capable to withstand the strengths more than 525 kg/cm per ply.

2. **Belt-conveyor drive:** There are several methods, as shown in Fig 14.2, for driving the conveyor belt. Drive with a bare steel pulley which is activated by power, is the simplest one. In this method the power which is transmitted is low enough to be carried by the friction of the belt on the pulley, hence it is satisfactory. In this type of drive both the area of contact between the belt and the pulley, and the coefficient of friction are small. In the next step, the pulleys covered with rubber or leather is utilized and the coefficient of friction is increased.

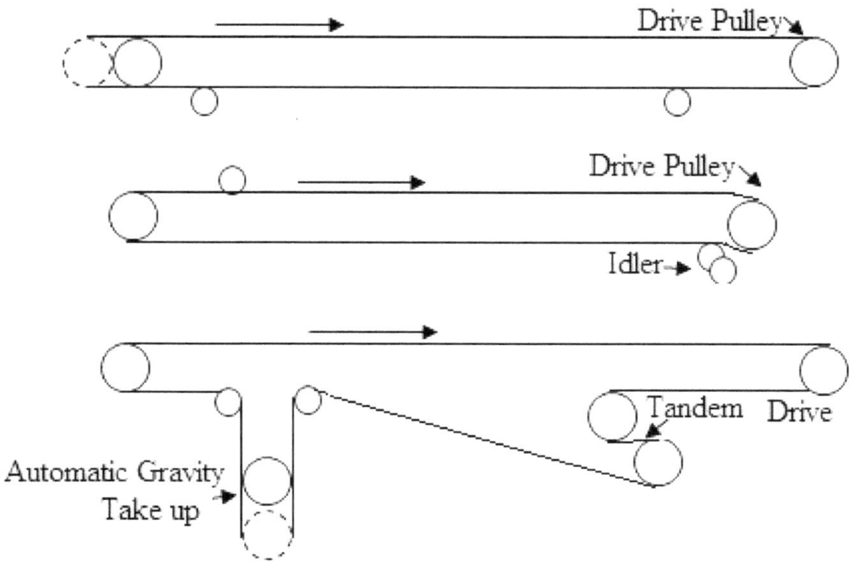


**Fig. 14.2** Belt conveyor drives

Whether there are bare or insulated pulleys, if a snubber idler just behind the drive pulley is attached, it can increase the arc of contact from 180 to 220°.If with this arrangement the power requirement is not met, tandem drive can be used. The tandem drive is used. Which brings the belt around one pulley and back over a second pulley. Although the drive of the belt conveyor is attached to the head or discharge end, but it can be attached to the back (tail) or feed end. For a given power input. This latter arrangement provides a greater stress in the belt and is not ordinarily used.

3. **Belt conveyor support:** For a belt, the rollers on the shaft act as the support and are commonly called *idlers*. These are built in various forms. The idlers carried on roller bearings and fitted with pressure-grease-gun lubrication system are the most expensive. When the idlers are carried on ordinary bushings, these become cheaper. These are lubricated with grease cups. In general, the idlers are troughed to allow the belt to be depressed in the centre and edges are raised. This allows a belt of a given width to carry more material per linear foot without spillage. Usually, the beltreturns on lighter, non-troughing rolls and is sometimes mounted on the same base as the top idlers.
4. **Belt-conveyor tighteners or take-ups:** The length of a belt changes considerably due to the change in load or in temperature and humidity. When this happens to the shortest conveyor and the magnitude of this change in length is greater, and an uneven tension is observed, particularly if the belt is not kept stretched. For this reason, a tightener or take-up should be fitted to keep the belt normal under all conditions, no uneven tension can result.

   The simple form of tighteners consists of a cast-iron bed with a travelling block that moves along a screw. The block consists of a plain bearing box.

## Screw Conveyors

Screw conveyor is used for transportation of solid materials. Primarily a screw conveyor contains following four components:

1. U-shaped trough,
2. Flight (screw type conveying system),
3. Feeding arrangement, and
4. Discharge arrangement or outlet.

### Principle

As per the placement of the motor, the horizontal or inclined or vertical screw conveyor conveys or transport the material in the trough from one point (feed point) to another point (discharge point).

### Construction

**Trough:** The trough is a U-shaped container or vessel as shown in the Fig 14.3 which holds the material to be transported or conveyed. It is made of steel sheet and its length may vary from 8 to 12 ft. The length of the trough can be increased by joining the trough of standard length.

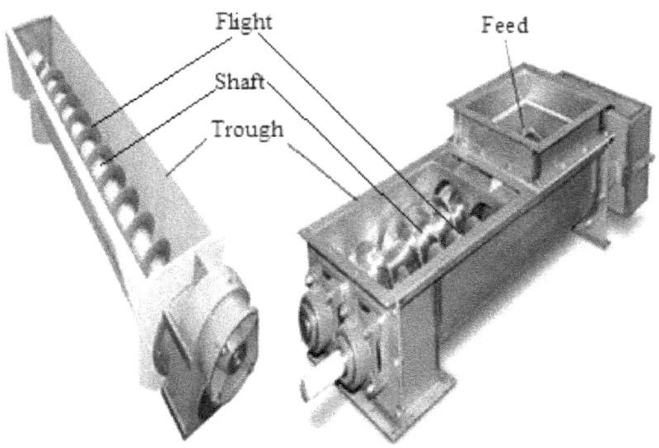


**Fig. 14.3** Screw conveyors

**Flight and power supply system:** The flight is basically a spiral blade, alternatively called as screw element. It is mounted on a pipe or shaft which rotates around an axis in the bottom of the trough.

Power is supplied to the flight through the shaft. The flight may be sectional, helicoid, cast iron, ribbon or cut flight. The Fig 14.4 represents the typical diagrams of different types of flights used in screw conveyor.

The sectional conveyor is made of short sections, each of the sections is in form of a circular disc, cut along one radius and then twisted to make it spiral shape. Each of such discs gives one full turn of the conveyor.

The helicoid flight is made from a single long ribbon, twisted and warped into a spiral shape and then welded to the central shaft. This type of flight is standard flight.

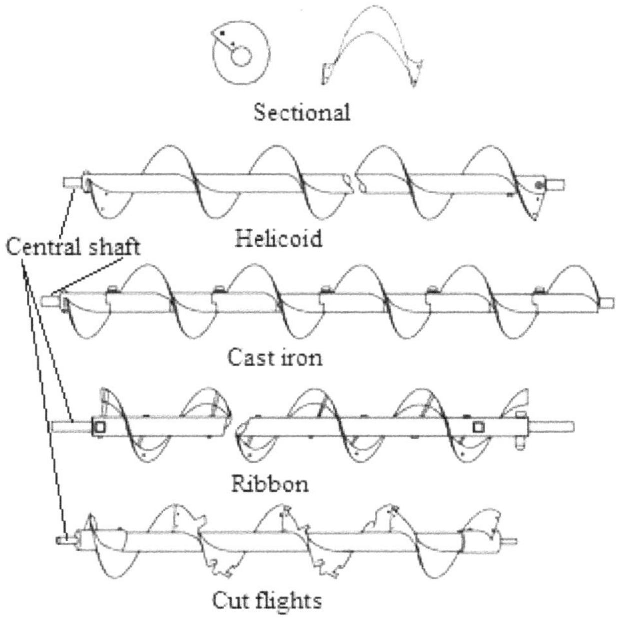


**Fig. 14.4** Schematic diagram of screw-conveyor flights

For working at higher temperature and for transporting abrasive materials, cast iron flights are used. Ribbon type is suitable for sticky materials. Cut flights can be used for any degree of mixing.

The drive end and discharge end are called *box ends*. At the drive end, the shaft is connected to bevel gears. When the flight rotates, it comes closer to the bottom of the trough.

The feed is usually introduced by plain jets, which provides uniform flow of the material. At the discharge end, necessary provision is made to collect the material using open-end trough or open-bottom trough.

At relatively low rotational speed, the screw conveyor can work. The flight rotates on suitable bearings attached to the end plates of the conveyor and is suspended from hangers alongthe length of the trough.

Generally, for each section there is a hanger. Since the bearings are lubricated with oil or grease, there is greater chance of contamination of the material undergoing transportationwith oil or grease. For this reason, bushings of white cast iron which do not require greasing are used. The shaft is brought through and is connected to the drive usually by bevel gears. Construction of various types of screw conveyors depends on:

- The scale of operation,
- Severity of service,
- Value of material, and
- Other requirements.

The design of a screw conveyor depends on the size and the speed of the screw for a particular purpose. Hence, the materials can be classified into following types:

- **Type A:** Materials are of light weight, fine, non-abrasive, andfree flowing such as flour, malt, rice, etc.
- **Type B:** Materials are of medium weight, nonabrasive, and granular such as coffee beans, granular gelatin, etc.
- **Type C:** Materials are non-abrasive, granular or small lumps mixed with fine powders having density more than that of the materials of Type B. For example, dried milk, coarse or fine salt, cocoa, etc.
- **Type D:** Materials are semi-abrasive or abrasive, fines, granular or small lumps with fines having density more than that of the materials of Type C and have fairly linear shape. For example, raw sugar, sulphur, zinc oxide, etc.

The simple and less expensive screw conveyor can be made of any length by joining the sections of spiral and half round liner. The Fig 14.5 demonstrates the standard *coupling* consisting of a short section of the solid shaft fitting into the hollow conveyor shaft. The conveyor pipe is reinforced at the ends, and a part of coupling shaft works as the journal.

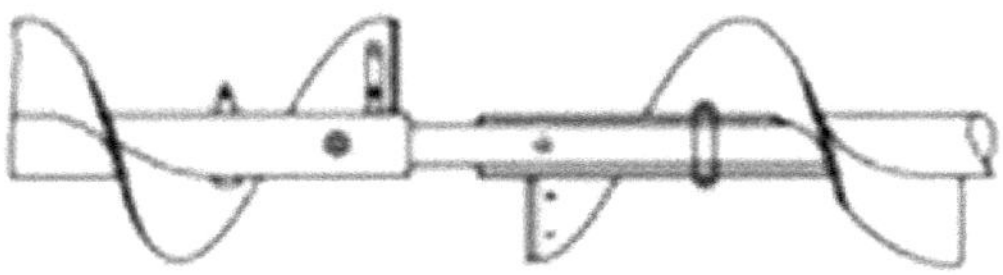

**Fig. 14.5** Schematic diagram of screw-conveyor coupling

## Working

When switched on, the power is supplied.The drive rotates the shaft through the bevel gears; as a result, the screw element starts rotating. The flight rotates round its axis and remained closer to the bottom of the trough. Normally, through plain jet the feed material is introduced into the conveyor. The material is trapped in- between the spiral blade and the trough. The material moves along the movement of the flight. The material is received at the destination through the open-end trough or open-bottom trough.

## Applications of Screw Conveyor

1. For transporting fine powders or paste-like materials screw conveyer is suitable.
2. Screw conveyor has multipurpose utility, it can be used to convey the materials which are light-weight, medium-weight, abrasive, non-abrasive with varied densities.
3. Special flights and casings are available for operation like mixing, heating and cooling, dewatering.
4. Screw conveyors can have larger capacity to handle even up to 2800-meter cube per hour.

## Advantages of Screw Conveyor

- Screw conveyor can transport the materials horizontally, inclined, as well as vertically.
- It is convenient to operate and it occupies relatively less space.

- It can be used for various types of materials and it is available in various types. Different materials such as cast iron, stainless steel can be used for construction of screw conveyors.
- It can work under both positive and negative pressure.
- By insulating the casing suitably, it can be used at both high and low temperature.
- Being a closed system, it does not pollute the environment with dust.

### Disadvantages of Screw Conveyor

- It works at low rotational speed.
- Handling of screw conveyor of very large size is not easy.
- Problem of abrasion is observed when the conveyor works at high speed.
- It consumes relatively more power for transportation of material to higher level.

There are different types screw conveyors,

- Horizontal,
- Inclined, and
- Vertical.

Grain handling equipment is mostly used to transport grains from one location to another. The four types most commonly used for industrial and farm applications are belt, bucket, pneumatic and screw conveyors. Conveyors play an important role in the handling of agricultural materials.

## Horizontal Screw Conveyor

Most commonly horizontal screw conveyors are used to transport bulk materials from one place of aprocessing to another as shown in Fig 14.5A. These are available in a wide range of sizes, lengths, configurations and materials of construction. Depending on the characteristics of the material such as specific bulk material, the screw conveyors are designed to transport bulk materials at 15, 30 or 45-percent trough loading. In general, trough loading of 45-percent can be used for light, free-flowing and non-abrasive bulk materials. Trough loadings of 15 and 30-percent are used for denser, sluggish and more abrasive bulk materials respectively.

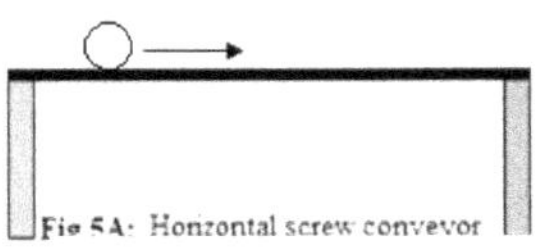

**Fig. 14.5A** Horizontal screw conveyor

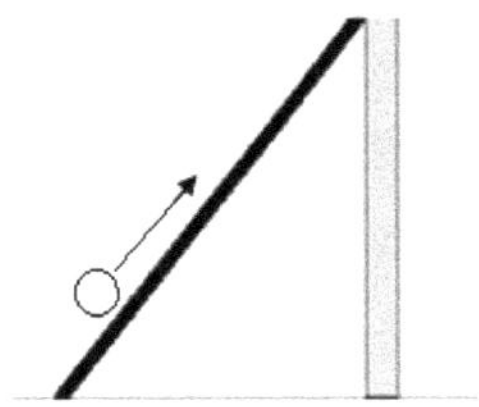

**Fig. 14.5B** Inclined screw conveyor

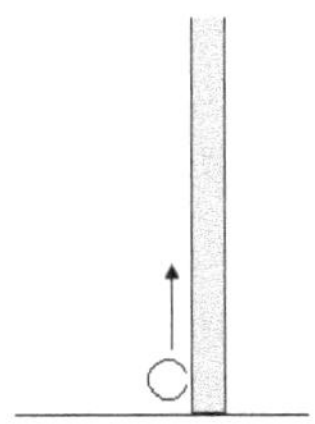

**Fig. 14.5C** Vertical screw conveyor

### Inclined Screw Conveyors

Inclined screw conveyors are suitable for operation at a level, slightly above the horizontal level to 45-degrees from the horizontal position. Above 45-degrees an inclined screw conveyor is considered as a vertical screw conveyor and it must be designed in accordance with the engineering guide for vertical screw conveyors. With the increase in degree of inclination, the conveying efficiency is reduced and the power requirement (horsepower)also increases due to the influence of gravity. Thus, the conveying efficiency is affected by the angle of inclination. The designing of screw conveyors using the lowest possible degree of inclination depends on the characteristics of the specific bulk material, type of screw conveyor trough and screw pitch.

## Vertical Screw Conveyors

For elevating different types of bulk materials at very steep inclines or completely vertical place, this type of screw conveyors is found to be very efficient. Any screw conveyor located on an inclination more than 45-degrees can work as a vertical screw conveyor. The compact design allows the vertical screw conveyor to fit into almost any plant layout with a minimum number of moving parts, the vertical screw conveyor is a cost-effective and reliable component of any bulk material handling process.

## Advantages of Vertical Screw Conveyor

- It is ideal for handling dry to semi-fluid materials,
- Capacity of the conveyor may be up to 6,000 cubic feet per hour.
- It has the ability to elevate bulk materials up to 30-feet without use of internal bearings,
- Totally enclosed design for dust and vapor-tight vertical screw conveyors can meet the needs of many industries, such as chemical, minerals processing, food, wood products and waste-water treatment plant.

## Factors influencing the Design of Screw Conveyor

Design of screw conveyor depends on the following factors:

- Characteristics of the bulk materials such as maximum particle size, lump size, lump size ratio, bulk density, abrasiveness, corrosiveness, flowability, and special characteristics of the bulk material.
- Bearing material such as Nylatron, Gatke, Bronze, Hard iron, etc.
- Trough loading such as 15%, 30%, 45%, etc.
- Generation of static electricity.
- Stability of the bulk material on storage,
- Flammability of the bulk material,
- Temperature/pressure sensitivity of the bulk material,
- Explosiveness of the bulk material,
- Stickiness of the bulk material,

### Selection of Screw Conveyor

Following five steps are considered during selection of a screw conveyor:

1. Establishment of characteristics of the bulk material to be conveyed.
2. Determination of conveyor size and speed on the basis of capacity.
3. Calculation of horsepower requirements.
4. Verification of torque rating of components.
5. Selection of conveyor components.

## Pneumatic Conveyors

A well-designed pneumatic conveying system is a more practical and economical method of transporting materials from one point to another. But it may not be suitable for reactive materials and/or where there is a threat of dust explosions. While the alternative mechanical systems such as belt conveyors, screw conveyors, vibrating conveyors, drag conveyors, etc. are not suitable because of three important reasons

1. Pneumatic systems are relatively economical to install and easy to operate.
2. Pneumatic systems are totally enclosed and can be operated without moving parts coming into contact with the conveyed material. Being enclosed these are relatively clean, more environmentally acceptable and convenient to maintain.
3. They are flexible, can be expanded. A pneumatic system can convey a product at any place where a pipe line can run.

Pneumatic conveyor can be used for particles ranging from fine powders to pellets and materials with bulk densities ranging from0.016 to 3.2 g/cm$^3$ (1 to 200 lb/ft$^3$). Generally, pneumatic conveyor works for particles up to 2 inches in diameter.

To design the pneumatic conveying system the following criteria must be considered such as;

- Design of pipeline diameter, length and the material of the pipe.
- Head loss produced inside the pipeline due to friction and bend section.
- Selection of air mover system, drive system, material feeding system and air-drying system.

All of the above criteria are selected by using the standard design calculations from the 'Pneumatic conveying system design guide' by David Mills. The calculations related to the design depend mainly on three aspects of pneumatic conveying system and these are:

1. Mode of conveying.
2. Conveying capacity.
3. Conveying pressure.

### Principle

The fluidized motion conveyors can offer advantages over other forms of bulk solids transport, particularly where the power consumption is low. In fact, these conveyors are not as widely used as might be expected. This may be due to lack of confidence on the part of the design engineer, since even air-gravity conveying remains something of an art. In order to makethe systems optimally designed, some knowledge about the air-floating system, or fluidized motion conveying system, would be necessary. When a particulate bulk solid is being transported through pneumatic convey or along a duct becomes similar to a liquid flowing in an inclined channel. Apparently, it can be considered that the continuous supply of air that is necessary to maintain the liquid like state of the material has a close affinity to the gas fluidization process.

## Construction

The Fig 14.6 shows the construction of a pneumatic conveyor. For movement of light and bulky materials or material suspended in a stream of air. The household vacuum cleaner is a common example of the pneumatic conveyor. A suitable fan or a cycloidal blower is connected to the conveying system. The material is transferred in a stream of air produced by a fan or a cycloidal blower. The suction of the blower is connected to the conveying system and the material is sucked up through a nozzle. The suspension is admitted to a cyclone separator. The larger particles and finer particles are separated and removed in a bag filter. The system is then connected to the pump.

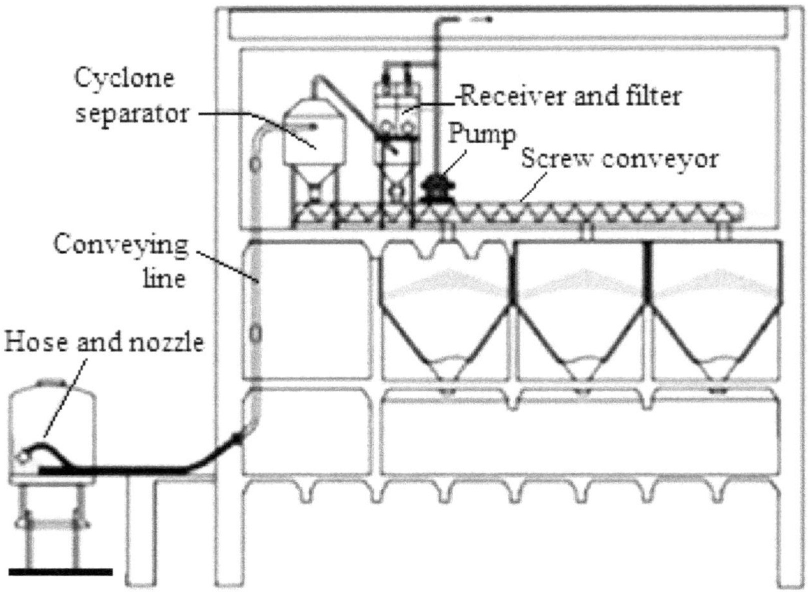


**Fig. 14.6** Schematic diagram of pneumatic conveyor and auxilliary equipment

A pneumatic conveyor is suitable for relatively smaller sizepellet materials (0.6 cm) having bulk densities ranging from 0.3 to 52.55 g/ml. The material can move to few metres to few hundred metres. The conveyor can be operated for horizontal as well as vertical distances. The material can be supplied to the air slide through the rotary feeder valve. The other end of the pipeline is connected to a cyclone separator.

### Working

At a pressure of about 7.0 kilopascals, the fans run and blow the air. The air is blown at a rate of about 1.5m/min into the pipeline. The rotary feeder valve rotates and allows the feed to enter into the pipeline. The solids are suspended in the stream of air in a fluidized state until it reaches the receiving end. The material is then introduced into the cyclone separator to remove larger and fine particles. The larger particles are collected into the bin; while the fine particles are trapped in a bag filter. In a closed system, the gas can be recycled to the blower and thus, the valuable gas is saved.

### Uses

- In a chemical industry, the pneumatic conveyor can satisfactorily work.
- In pharmaceutical industry, it is used during formulation of powdered insufflation.
- Usually, light and bulky materials such as grains can be transported easily through pneumatic conveyor.
- Since the pneumatic conveyor works under closed system, toxic and unpleasant materials can be transported without any problem.

### Merits

- During transportation of material, the path may have turns and lifts. However, other types of transportation are relatively costly.
- Compared to other types of transportation systems, pneumatic conveyor is economical.
- Since there is no movement of mechanical parts, frictional losses would be small.

### Demerits

- This method of transportation requires more power.
- Erosion of internal surface of the vessel and erosion of solids may take place.
- Uneven contact of gas and solids can take place.

### Types of Pneumatic Conveyor

In general, the pneumatic conveying systems can be classified into three main categories:

1. *Dilute-phase conveying* refers to the process of pushing or pulling materials, air-suspended, from one location to another by maintaining a sufficient air-velocity. Basically, dilute phase conveying is a continuous process, characterized by high velocity, low pressure and low product to air ratio.
2. *Dense-phase conveying* depends on a pulse of air to force a slug of material from one place to another. Dense-phase system is basically a batch process. It is characterized by low velocity, high pressure and high product to air ratio unlike dilute phase which requires a low product to air ratio.
3. *Air-activated gravity conveying* is a method of moving product along a conveyor on a cushion of air. These summaries the distinguishing characteristics of dense and dilute phase transport.

## Short Questions

1. Classify the material handling system and material handling equipments.
2. How the total cost of the product can be reduced?
3. How can the capacity of production be increased?
4. How can the working conditions be improved with respect to safety, convenience to work, and systematic operation?
5. Describe the belt-conveyor drive with the help of a suitable diagram.
6. Write down the applications, advantages and limitations of screw conveyor.
7. Write a note on vertical screw conveyor and mention the advantages of screw conveyor.
8. Write down the applications, advantages and limitations of pneumatic conveyor.
9. What are different types of pneumatic conveyor?

## Long Questions

1. Explain the objectives of material handling systems.
2. Discuss the principles of designing the material handling system.
3. Describe the functions of material handling.
4. Describe the construction and working of screw conveyor.
5. Explain pneumatic conveyor. How can you select the screw conveyor?
6. Write down the principle, construction and working of a pneumatic conveyor.
7. Write notes about horizontal, inclined and vertical pneumatic conveyor.
8. Discuss the applications of material handling systems.
9. Briefly discuss the components of belt conveyor.

# Conversation of Units from One System to Another

## Mass

| System | System | Multiplied by |
|---|---|---|
| Kilograms | Pound | 2.2046 |
| Tons | Kilograms | 1000 |
| Tons | Pounds (avoirdupois) | 2204.6 |
| Kilograms | Grams | 1000 |
| Pounds (avoirdupois) | Grams | 453.59 |
| Grams per cu.cm | Pounds per cu. ft | 62.43 |
| Pounds per cu. ft | Grams per cu.cm | 0.016018 |
| Kilograms | Grams | 1000 |
| Pounds per cu. ft | Kilograms per cu. m | 16.018 |

## Length

| | | |
|---|---|---|
| Centimeter | Angstrom | $10^8$ |
| Micron | Angstrom | $10^4$ |
| Centimeter | Micron | $10^4$ |
| Meter | Centimeter | $10^2$ |
| Meter | Millimeter | $10^3$ |
| Foot | Meter | 0.3048 |
| Meter | Foot | 3.2808 |
| Inch | Centimeter | 2.54 |
| Foot per minute | cm. per second | 0.5080 |

## Time

| | | |
|---|---|---|
| Day | Hour | 24 |
| Hour | Minutes | 60 |
| Minute | Second | 60 |

## Area

| Cubic meter | Liters | 1000 |
|---|---|---|
| Cu. ft. | Cu. cm (cc) | 28317 |
| Cu. ft. | Cu. m. | 0.028317 |
| Cu. ft. | Liters | 7.481 |
| Gallon | Cu. m. | 0.003785 |
| US Gallon | Imperial gallon | 0.8327 |
| Gallons | Liters | 3.785 |
| Gallons per minute | Cu. ft. per second | 0.002228 |
| Gallons | Cu. in. | 231 |

## Pressure

| | | |
|---|---|---|
| Cm. of Hg at 0°C | Ft. of water at 39.1°F | 0.4460 |
| Cm. of Hg at 0°C | Pounds per sq. in. | 0.19837 |
| Grams per sq. in. | Pounds per sq. in. | 0.014223 |
| Kg per sq. in. | Pounds per sq. in. | 14.223 |
| Atmosphere | Mm Hg at 32°F | 760 |
| Atmosphere | Ft. of water at 39.1°F | 33.90 |
| Atmosphere | Grams per sq. cm. | 1033.3 |
| Atmosphere | Pounds per sq. in. | 14.696 |
| Bars | Atmospheres | 0.9869 |
| Bars | Pounds per sq. in. | 14.504 |

## Viscosity

| | | |
|---|---|---|
| Centipoise | Poise | 0.01 |
| Centipoise | lb/hr. ft. | 2.42 |
| Centipoise | lb/sec. ft (British unit) | 0.000672 |
| lb/sec. ft (British unit) | Centipoise | 1488 |

## Heat

| | | |
|---|---|---|
| Centigrade heat units | Btu | 1.8 |
| Kilowatt hour | Btu | 3414 |
| Kilowatt | Horsepower | 1.3410 |
| Btu | Calories | 252.16 |
| Btu | Foot-pounds | 777.9 |
| Btu/lb.°F | Cal/g.°C | 1 |
| Btu/hr. $ft^2$.°F | Kg.cal/hr.$m^2$.°C | 4.88 |
| g.cal/hr.$cm^2$.°C/cm | Btu/hr.$ft^2$.$^2$F/in | |

## Energy

| | | |
|---|---|---|
| Foot-pounds | Kilowatt hours | $3.766 \times 10^{-7}$ |
| Foot-pounds/sec | Kilowatts | 0.0013558 |
| Horsepower (British) | Btu/hr | 2545 |
| Horsepower (British) | Ft.lb/sec | 550 |
| Horsepower (British) | Horsepower(metric) | 1.0139 |
| Watts | Btu/hr | 3.413 |
| Kilowatt hour | Btu | 3413 |
| Tons (refrigeration) | Btu/hr | 12000 |

## Units in SI systems

| | | | | | | | |
|---|---|---|---|---|---|---|---|
| Exa | E | gram/meter | $10^{18}$ | gram/meter | Deci | d | $10^{-1}$ |
| Peta | P | gram/meter | $10^{15}$ | gram/meter | Centi | c | $10^{-2}$ |
| Tera | T | gram/meter | $10^{12}$ | gram/meter | Milli | m | $10^{-3}$ |
| Giga | G | gram/meter | $10^{9}$ | gram/meter | Micro | $\mu$ | $10^{-6}$ |
| Mega | M | gram/meter | $10^{6}$ | gram/meter | Nano | n | $10^{-9}$ |
| Kilo | K | gram/meter | $10^{3}$ | gram/meter | Pico | p | $10^{-12}$ |
| Hect | h | gram/meter | $10^{2}$ | gram/meter | Fem'o | f | $10^{-15}$ |
| Deca | da | gram/meter | 10 | gram/meter | Atto | a | $10^{-18}$ |

# Abbreviations

| | |
|---|---|
| Numerical value of x | [x] |
| Common logarithm | $\log_{10}$ or log |
| Natural logarithm | $\log_c$ or ln |
| Function of x | f(x) |
| Increase of x | Δx |
| Summation of | Σ |
| Differential of x | dx |
| Derivative of x with respect to y | dx/dy or x' |
| Integral of | ∫ |
| Plus or minus | ± |
| Less than | < |
| Not less than | $\nless$ |
| Approximately equal | ≅ |
| Equivalent to | ⟺ |
| Approaches to | ≐ |

*Contd...*

| | |
|---|---|
| Infinity | $\infty$ |
| Square root | $\sqrt{}$ |
| nth root | $\sqrt[n]{}$ |
| Integral between the limits a and b | $\int_b^a$ |
| Ratio | : |
| More than | > |
| Not more than | $\not>$ |
| Similar to | ~ |
| Not equal to | $\neq$ |
| Varies as | $\propto$ |
| Therefore | $\therefore$ |

## Symbols

| | | | | | |
|---|---|---|---|---|---|
| Alpha | $\alpha$ | Epsilon | $\varepsilon$ | Iota | $\iota$ |
| Beta | $\beta$ | Zeta | $\zeta$ | Kappa | $\kappa$ |
| Gamma | $\gamma$ | Eta | $\eta$ | Lambda | $\lambda$ |
| Delta | $\delta$ | Theta | $\theta$ | Mu | $\mu$ |
| Nu | $\nu$ | Xi | $\xi$ | Pi | $\pi$ |
| Rho | $\rho$ | Sigma | $\sigma$ | Tau | $\tau$ |
| Upsilon | $\upsilon$ | Phi | $\phi$ | Chi | $\chi$ |
| Psi | $\psi$ | Omega | $\omega$ | | |

## Viscosities of Common Gases and Water Vapor

| Air | $H_2$ | $O_2$ | $N_2$ | CO | $CO_2$ | $H_2O$ vapor |
|---|---|---|---|---|---|---|
| 0.0163 | 0.00805 | 0.01816 | 0.01579 | 0.01561 | 0.01283 | |
| 0.0172 | 0.00842 | 0.01919 | 0.01665 | 0.01650 | 0.01368 | |
| 0.0177 | 0.00862 | 0.01976 | 0.01711 | 0.01698 | 0.01416 | |
| 0.0190 | 0.00915 | 0.0213 | 0.01838 | 0.01830 | 0.01545 | |
| 0.0203 | 0.00967 | 0.0228 | 0.01960 | 0.01958 | 0.01672 | 0.01192 |
| 0.0215 | 0.01017 | 0.0242 | 0.0208 | 0.0208 | 0.01794 | 0.01296 |
| 0.0227 | 0.01064 | 0.0256 | 0.0219 | 0.0220 | 0.01913 | 0.01398 |
| 0.0238 | 0.01111 | 0.0269 | 0.0230 | 0.0231 | 0.0203 | 0.01498 |
| 0.0250 | 0.01155 | 0.0282 | 0.0240 | 0.0242 | 0.0214 | 0.01598 |
| 0.0260 | 0.01198 | 0.0295 | 0.0250 | 0.0253 | 0.0223 | 0.01595 |
| 0.0271 | 0.01240 | 0.0307 | 0.0260 | 0.0264 | 0.0236 | 0.01792 |
| 0.0281 | 0.01281 | 0.0318 | 0.0270 | 0.0274 | 0.0246 | 0.01886 |

## Specific Heats of Gases, Btu/lb(°F)

| Temp (°F) | Air | $H_2$ | $O_2$ | $N_2$ | CO | $CO_2$ | $H_2O$ vapor |
|---|---|---|---|---|---|---|---|
| 0 | 0.239 | 3.364 | 0.218 | 0.248 | 0.248 | 0.190 | 0.443 |
| 32 | 0.240 | 3.390 | 0.218 | 0.248 | 0.248 | 0.195 | 0.444 |
| 50 | 0.240 | 3.395 | 0.219 | 0.248 | 0.248 | 0.197 | 0.445 |
| 100 | 0.240 | 3.425 | 0.220 | 0.248 | 0.249 | 0.205 | 0.446 |
| 150 | 0.241 | 3.437 | 0.221 | 0.248 | 0.249 | 0.211 | 0.448 |
| 200 | 0.241 | 3.449 | 0.222 | 0.249 | 0.249 | 0.217 | 0.450 |
| 250 | 0.242 | 3.455 | 0.224 | 0.249 | 0.250 | 0.222 | 0.454 |
| 300 | 0.243 | 3.461 | 0.226 | 0.250 | 0.251 | 0.228 | 0.457 |
| 350 | 0.244 | 3.464 | 0.228 | 0.250 | 0.252 | 0.233 | 0.460 |
| 400 | 0.245 | 3.466 | 0.230 | 0.251 | 0.253 | 0.238 | 0.464 |
| 450 | 0.246 | 3.468 | 0.232 | 0.252 | 0.254 | 0.243 | 0.468 |
| 500 | 0.247 | 3.469 | 0.234 | 0.254 | 0.256 | 0.247 | 0.471 |

## Thermal Conductivities of Some Common Gases

| Temp (°F) | Air | $H_2$ | $O_2$ | $N_2$ | CO | $CO_2$ | $H_2O$ vapor |
|---|---|---|---|---|---|---|---|
| 0 | 0..0131 | 0.0912 | 0.0133 | 0.0131 | 0.0126 | 0.0076 | |
| 32 | 0.0140 | 0.0965 | 0.0142 | 0.0139 | 0.0134 | 0.0084 | |
| 50 | 0.0144 | 0.0994 | 0.0147 | 0.0143 | 0.0138 | 0.0088 | |
| 100 | 0.0157 | 0.1072 | 0.0160 | 0.0155 | 0.0150 | 0.0100 | |
| 150 | 0.0169 | 0.1149 | 0.0173 | 0.0167 | 0.0162 | 0.0112 | 0.0120 |
| 200 | 0.0181 | 0.1222 | 0.0185 | 0.0177 | 0.0173 | 0.0125 | 0.0133 |
| 250 | 0.0192 | 0.1293 | 0.0198 | 0.0190 | 0.0184 | 0.0138 | 0.0145 |
| 300 | 0.0204 | 0.1362 | 0.0210 | 0.0201 | 0.0195 | 0.0151 | 0.0158 |
| 350 | 0.0214 | 0.1429 | 0.0221 | 0.0211 | 0.0205 | 0.0165 | 0.0171 |
| 400 | 0.0225 | 0.1493 | 0.0232 | 0.0221 | 0.0215 | 0.0179 | 0.0184 |
| 450 | 0.0236 | 0.1557 | 0.0244 | 0.0231 | 0.0225 | 0.0193 | 0.0198 |
| 500 | 0.0246 | 0.1618 | 0.0254 | 0.00241 | 0.0235 | 0.0207 | 0.0211 |

## Atomic Number, Atomic Mass, Symbol and Name of Element

| Element | Symbol | Atomic number | Atomic mass | Element | Symbol | Atomic number | Atomic mass |
|---|---|---|---|---|---|---|---|
| Hydrogen | H | 1 | 1.008 | Promethium | Pm | 61 | 145 |
| Lithium | Li | 3 | 6.94 | Samarium | Sm | 62 | 150.36 |
| Beryllium | Be | 4 | 9.0122 | Europium | Eu | 63 | 151.96 |
| Boron | B | 5 | 10.81 | Gadolinium | Gd | 64 | 157.25 |
| Carbon | C | 6 | 12.011 | Terbium | Tb | 65 | 158.93 |

*Contd...*

| Element | Symbol | Atomic number | Atomic mass | Element | Symbol | Atomic number | Atomic mass |
|---|---|---|---|---|---|---|---|
| Nitrogen | N | 7 | 14.007 | Dysprosium | Dy | 66 | 162.50 |
| Oxygen | O | 8 | 15.007 | Holmium | Ho | 67 | 164.93 |
| Fluorine | F | 9 | 18.998 | Erbium | Er | 68 | 167.26 |
| Neon | Ne | 10 | 20.180 | Thulium | Tm | 69 | 168.93 |
| Sodium | Na | 11 | 22.99 | Ytterbium | Yb | 70 | 173.05 |
| Magnesium | Mg | 12 | 24.305 | Lutetium | Lu | 71 | 174.97 |
| Aluminium | Al | 13 | 26.982 | Hafnium | Hf | 72 | 178.49 |
| Silicon | Si | 14 | 28.085 | Tantalum | Ta | 73 | 180.95 |
| Phosphorous | P | 15 | 30.974 | Tungsten | W | 74 | 183.84 |
| Sulphur | S | 16 | 32.06 | Rhenium | Re | 75 | 186.21 |
| Chlorine | Cl | 17 | 35.45 | Osmium | Os | 76 | 190.23 |
| Argon | Ar | 18 | 39.948 | Iridium | Ir | 77 | 192.22 |
| Potassium | K | 19 | 39.098 | Platinum | Pt | 78 | 195.08 |
| Calcium | Ca | 20 | 40.078 | Gold | Au | 79 | 196.97 |
| Scandium | Sc | 21 | 44.956 | Mercury | Hg | 80 | 200.59 |
| Titanium | Ti | 22 | 47.867 | Thallium | Tl | 81 | 204.38 |
| Vanadium | V | 23 | 50.942 | Lead | Pb | 82 | 207.2 |
| Chromium | Cr | 24 | 51.996 | Bismuth | Bi | 83 | 208.98 |
| Manganese | Mn | 25 | 54.938 | Polonium | Po | 84 | 209 |
| Iron | Fe | 26 | 55.845 | Astatine | At | 85 | 210 |
| Cobalt | Co | 27 | 58.933 | Radon | Rn | 86 | 222 |
| Nickel | Ni | 28 | 58.693 | Francium | Fr | 87 | 223 |
| Copper | Cu | 29 | 63.546 | Radium | Ra | 88 | 226 |
| Zinc | Zn | 30 | 65.38 | Actinium | Ac | 89 | 227 |
| Gallium | Ga | 31 | 69.723 | Thorium | Th | 90 | 232.04 |
| Germanium | Ge | 32 | 72.630 | Protactinium | Pa | 91 | 231.04 |
| Arsenic | As | 33 | 74.922 | Uranium | U | 92 | 238.03 |
| Selenium | Se | 34 | 78.971 | Neptunium | Np | 93 | 237 |
| Bromine | Br | 35 | 79.904 | Plutonium | Pu | 94 | 244 |
| Krypton | Kr | 36 | 83.798 | Americium | Am | 95 | 243 |
| Rubidium | Rb | 37 | 85.468 | Curium | Cm | 96 | 247 |
| Strontium | Sr | 38 | 87.62 | Berkelium | Bk | 97 | 247 |
| Yttrium | Y | 39 | 88.906 | Californium | Cf | 98 | 251 |
| Zirconium | Zr | 40 | 91.224 | Einsteinium | Es | 99 | 252 |
| Niobium | Nb | 41 | 92.906 | Fermium | Fm | 100 | 257 |
| Molybdenum | Mo | 42 | 95.95 | Mendelevium | Md | 101 | 258 |
| Technetium | Tc | 43 | 98 | Nobelium | No | 102 | 259 |
| Ruthenium | Ru | 44 | 101.07 | Lawrencium | Lr | 103 | 266 |
| Rhodium | Rh | 45 | 102.91 | Rutherfordium | Rf | 104 | 267 |

*Contd...*

| Element | Symbol | Atomic number | Atomic mass | Element | Symbol | Atomic number | Atomic mass |
|---|---|---|---|---|---|---|---|
| Palladium | Pd | 46 | 106.42 | Dubnium | Db | 105 | 268 |
| Silver | Ag | 47 | 107.87 | Seaborgium | Sg | 106 | 269 |
| Cadmium | Cd | 48 | 112.41 | Bohrium | Bh | 107 | 270 |
| Indium | In | 49 | 114.82 | Hassium | Hs | 108 | 270 |
| Tin | Sn | 50 | 118.71 | Meitnerium | Mt | 109 | 278 |
| Antimony | Sb | 51 | 121.76 | Darmstadtium | Ds | 110 | 281 |
| Tellurium | Te | 52 | 127.60 | Roentgenium | Rg | 111 | 282 |
| Iodine | 1 | 53 | 126.90 | Copernicium | Cn | 112 | 285 |
| Xenon | Xe | 54 | 131.29 | Nihonium | Nh | 113 | 286 |
| Caesium | Cs | 55 | 132.91 | Flerovium | Fm | 114 | 289 |
| Barium | Ba | 56 | 137.33 | Moscovium | Mc | 115 | 290 |
| Lanthanum | La | 57 | 138.91 | Livermorium | Lv | 116 | 293 |
| Cerium | Ce | 58 | 140.12 | Tennessine | Ts | 117 | 294 |
| Praseodymium | Pr | 59 | 140.91 | Oganesson | Og | 118 | 294 |
| Neodymium | Nd | 60 | 144.24 | | | | |

# Exercises

## Multiple Choice Questions

### Chapter 1

1. The pressure measured by a manometer is
   (a) Absolute pressure
   (b) Atmospheric pressure
   (c) Gage pressure
   (d) None of the above.
2. Reynolds number is the ratio of
   (a) Inertia force by gravitational force
   (b) Viscose force by inertia force
   (c) Inertia force by viscose force
   (d) None of the above
3. If the Reynolds number in a flow is 1500, which type of flow is it.
   (a) Laminar flow
   (b) Turbulent flow
   (c) Viscose flow
   (d) Transition flow
4. Bernoulli's equation is
   (a) All types of flow
   (b) Only non-viscose flow
   (c) Only viscose flow
   (d) None of the above
5. The energy loss occurs in a fluid flow due to pipe bend is an example of
   (a) Minor loss
   (b) Major loss
   (c) Both
   (d) None of the above
6. The energy loss occurs in a fluid flow sudden expansion or contraction of pipe is
   (a) Major loss
   (b) Minor loss
   (c) Both
   (d) None of the above
7. Friction factor is associated to which type of energy losses.
   (a) Major loss
   (b) Minor loss
   (c) Both
   (d) None of the above
8. A practical application of Bernoulli's theorem is
   (a) Venturimeter
   (b) Orifice meter
   (c) Pitot tube
   (d) All of the above
9. Coefficient of discharge varies between
   (a) 0 to 1
   (b) 0 to 10
   (c) 0 to 100
   (d) None of the above
10. If the coefficient of discharge is 1 for a fluid flow, which type of flow is it.
    (a) Real flow
    (b) Ideal flow
    (c) Laminar flow
    (d) Turbulent flow
11. Darcy-Weishbach law is applicable to
    (a) Energy loss due to friction
    (b) Momentum loss
    (c) Both
    (d) None of the above

12. Energy loss that occurs due to friction is categorized under
    (a) Major loss
    (b) Minor loss
    (c) Both
    (d) None of the above
13. Bernoulli's equation is based on
    (a) Conservation of mass
    (b) Conservation of momentum
    (c) Conservation of energy
    (d) None of the above
14. The absolute pressure in a fluid increases with depth of the fluid.
    (a) True
    (b) False
    (c) Cannot be determined
    (d) None of the above
15. The dimension of Reynolds Number is
    (a) Dimensionless
    (b) [MLT]
    (c) $[ML^2T]$
    (d) $[ML^2T^{-2}]$
16. The dimension of energy head in Bernoulli's theorem is
    (a) $[M^0LT^0]$
    (b) $[M^0L^2T^0]$
    (c) $[M^0L^2T^0]$
    (d) Dimensionless
17. If the Reynolds Number in fluid flow through a pipe is measured as 5000, the flow can be classified as -
    (a) Laminar flow
    (b) Turbulent flow
    (c) Ideal flow
    (d) Transitional flow
18. In a turbulent fluid flow, which one of the following forces dominate the flow.
    (a) Inertia force
    (b) Pressure force
    (c) Viscose force
    (d) None of the above
19. In a laminar fluid flow, which one of the following forces dominate the flow.
    (a) Inertia force
    (b) Pressure force
    (c) Viscose force
    (d) None of the above
20. A flow can be called as ideal if
    (a) Absolute viscosity is zero
    (b) Coefficient of discharge is zero
    (c) Both
    (d) None of the above

## Chapter 2

21. Comminution of drug can result
    (a) Increased therapeutic effectiveness
    (b) Any effect on therapeutic effectiveness
    (c) Increases the compressibility of the drug
    (d) No effect on extraction
22. Size reduction imparts a positive effect on
    (a) Content
    (b) Uniformity of content
    (c) Uniformity of weight
    (d) Chemical stability
23. For producing coarse particles which type of crusher and grinder is used
    (a) Roller mill
    (b) Cutter mill
    (c) Dodge mill
    (d) Ball mill
24. "The work required for size reduction is directly proportional to the new surface created"- a statement known as
    (a) Kick's law,
    (b) Bond's law.
    (c) Newton's law,
    (d) Rittinger's law.
25. Which of the following properties of a material can affect the size reduction?
    (a) Color
    (b) Bulk density
    (c) Solubility
    (d) Bioavailability
26. Which of the following is considered as a factor that influence the size reduction?
    (a) Dissolution rate
    (b) Disintegration time
    (c) Ratio of feed size to product size
    (d) Product size

27. Ball mill contains the balls of
    (a) Larger size only
    (b) Smaller size only
    (c) Mixture of larger and smaller size
    (d) None of the above
28. Which of the following statements is correct?
    (a) Larger balls crush the feed and the smaller ones form the fine product
    (b) Smaller balls crush the feed and the larger ones form the fine product
    (c) The balls of a Ball mill do not wear regularly
    (d) The balls are not required to be replaced.
29. Which of the following statements is correct?
    (a) The hammer mill works by impact
    (b) The hammer mill works by attrition
    (c) The hammer mill works by compression
    (d) The hammer mill works by cutting
30. Which of the following statements is correct?
    (a) For grinding toughness and hardness of the material are equally important.
    (b) For grinding toughness is more important than hardness of the material
    (c) For grinding toughness is less important than hardness of the material
    (d) All of the above
31. Which of the following statements is correct?
    (a) Hardness of a material can be reduced after treating with liquified gas, such as liquid nitrogen
    (b) Hardness of a material would be increased after treating with liquified gas, such as liquid nitrogen
    (c) Toughness of a material can be increased after treating with liquified gas such as liquid nitrogen
    (d) Toughness of a material can be reduced after treating with liquified gas such as liquid nitrogen
32. Treatment of a material with liquid nitrogen causes
    (a) Increase of decomposition of thermolabile material
    (b) Reduction of decomposition of thermolabile material
    (c) No change in decomposition of material
    (d) Immediate explosion
33. Which of the following statements is correct?
    (a) Comminution results in uniformity of content.
    (b) Comminution fails to improve the physical stability.
    (c) Size reduction improve the uniformity of weight.
    (d) Size reduction does not have any effect on extraction of drug.
34. The principle of compression used for size reduction by
    (a) Hammer mill
    (b) Cutter mill
    (c) Roller mill
    (d) Ball mill
35. "The work required for crushing a given mass of material is constant for given reduction ratio irrespective of the initial size." – a statement known as
    (a) Poiscelle's law
    (b) Newton's law
    (c) Darcy's law
    (d) Kick's law
36. 'The work required for size reduction is directly proportional to the new surface created.' – a statement known as
    (a) Kick's law
    (b) Stoke's law
    (c) Bond's law
    (d) Rittinger's law
37. In a ball mill, for better grinding the balls in the mill should occupy
    (a) More than 60% of the mill volume
    (b) More than 60 – 70% of the mill volume
    (c) 30 – 50% of the mill volume
    (d) Less than 10% of the mill volume
38. When fluidized energy mill is used for particle size reduction
    (a) The particles size of the product is independent of the speed of air/inert gas.
    (b) The particles size of the product depends on the feed size.

(c) There is no chance of formation aggregates after milling.
(d) The particles size of the product is independent the position of the nozzle.

39. Which of the following statements is correct?
(a) The edge runner mill is useful for tough and fibrous materials.
(b) The edge runner mill cannot be used to grind paint, clays and sticky materials.
(c) The edge runner mill is not useful for grinding wet materials.
(d) The edge runner mill cannot produce very fine powders.

40. Which of the following statements is correct?
(a) The end runner mill is suitable for grinding sticky materials.
(b) The end runner mill requires more attention during running.
(c) The end runner mill produces less noise.
(d) The end runner mill can produce fine particles.

## Chapter 3

41. Which of the following statement is correct?
(a) Tailing is the fraction that passes through the mesh after final grinding.
(b) Tailing is the fraction that retains over the mesh after final grinding.
(c) Tailing is the fraction that passes through the mesh after initial grinding.
(d) Tailing is the fraction that retains over the mesh after final grinding.

42. The mesh no. is assigned on the basis of
(a) Number of perforations present in one cm of the sieve.
(b) Number of perforations present in per sq cm of the sieve.
(c) Number of perforations present in per sq inch area of the sieve.
(d) Number of perforations present in two sq cm area of the sieve.

43. The mechanism of size separation of particles by centrifugal method involves
(a) Oscillation
(b) Vibration
(c) Gyration
(d) None of the above

44. The mechanism of size separation of particles by agitation method involves
(a) Oscillation
(b) Vibration
(c) Gyration
(d) All of the above

45. When all the particles pass through mesh number 10, these are called
(a) Coarse powders
(b) Moderately coarse powders
(c) Fine powders
(d) Moderately fine powders

46. Moderately coarse powders pass through must pass through
(a) 22
(b) 10
(c) 85
(d) 44

47. Sieve Number is defined by
(a) The nominal aperture size,
(b) The nominal diameter of the wire,
(c) The number of holes in each inch, in each direction parallel to each wire.
(d) None of the above.

48. Dry sieving is done by
(a) Elutriation
(b) Vibration
(c) Settling method
(d) Sedimentation

49. Micromerograph is an instrument that can measure
(a) Sedimentation of particles in water
(b) Sedimentation of particles in air
(c) Particle porosity
(d) None of the above

50. Sieving divides the powders into
(a) Two fractions
(b) Three fractions
(c) Four fractions
(d) Zero fraction

51. A sieve shaker can separate the particles
(a) Excellently in dried condition

(b) Even after aggregation
(c) Under humid condition
(d) Without any maintenance

52. The rate of size separation through a sieve shaker can be increased by
(a) Gravitation
(b) Mixing
(c) Agitation
(d) Compression

53. Brush is used to improve the separation of particles, if the particles are
(a) Very dry
(b) Very fine
(c) Coarse
(d) Sticky in nature

54. In a cyclone separator the material is introduced into the equipment
(a) From the top
(b) From the bottom
(c) At a very high speed
(d) Tangentially

55. The size separation of fine particles can be done by using
(a) Air separator
(b) Cyclone separator
(c) Sieve shaker
(d) Bag filter

56. Air separator can be used to separate
(a) Fine particles
(b) Coarse particles
(c) Large particles
(d) None of the above

57. Which of the following separators can separate the particles into different and defined size ranges?
(a) Cyclone separator
(b) Air separator
(c) Sieve shaker
(d) Bag filter

58. Which of the following separators requires large areas of space?
(a) Sieve shaker
(b) Bag filter
(c) Cyclone separator
(d) Air separator

59. Elutriation method is suitable
(a) For the separation of coarse particles of oversize from a powder sample.
(b) For the separation of extra coarse particles of oversize from a powder sample
(c) For the separation of fine particles of oversize from a powder sample
(d) None of the above.

60. Which of the following statements is correct?
(a) The process cannot be made continuous
(b) Compared to sedimentation, the time for separation of the particles is large in this method.
(c) As per the necessity, the number of stages cannot be increased.
(d) Apparatus is very simple and compact.

## Chapter 4

61. Mixing is important in pharmacy for
(a) Obtain a simple physical mixture,
(b) Avoiding a physical change
(c) Promoting a chemical reaction,
(d) Facilitate a photolytic degradation reaction.

62. Which of the following statements is NOT correct?
(a) The mixing of gases or the mixing of gas and liquid may take place through diffusion.
(b) In through diffusion, the process does not cause any problem.
(c) The process is reversible in nature.
(d) The mixture obtained is stable.

63. Which of the following statements is NOT correct?
(a) Positive mixing takes place slowly and there is no work done, if it happens during a long period.
(b) Sufficient work must be done to produce a negative mixture.
(c) Negative mixtures are relatively more difficult to obtain.
(d) Neutral mixtures are dynamic in nature.

64. Equipment used to mix the liquid and liquid is
    (a) Shear mixer
    (b) Shaker mixer
    (c) Tumbling mixer
    (d) Agitator mixer
65. A homogenous powder mix cannot be prepared, if the powders have
    (a) Similar weights
    (b) Dissimilar size range
    (c) Similar densities
    (d) Similar sizes
66. Which of the following statement is correct?
    (a) The homogeneous mixing does not depend on the volume of mixer.
    (b) The homogeneous mixing does not depend on the duration of mixing.
    (c) The homogeneous mixing does not depend on the type of mixer used.
    (d) The homogeneous mixing depends on the volume of mixer.
67. Mixing of semi-solid materials depends on the following property
    (a) Particle size
    (b) Particle shape
    (c) Particle charge
    (d) All of the above
68. Which of the mechanisms is involved in mixing of solids
    (a) Convection
    (b) Conduction
    (c) Radiation
    (d) None of the above
69. Which of the mechanisms is involved in mixing of solid in liquid
    (a) Convection
    (b) Diffusion
    (c) Conduction
    (d) Radiation
70. Segregation of particles from the mixture can occur due to
    (a) Larger particles descend down the bed of particles.
    (b) Particles of lighter density descend down the bed of particles.
    (c) Fall of smaller particles through the voids between the larger particles.
    (d) Shear mixing of particles.
71. Which of the following statements is NOT correct?
    (a) Mixing of plastic materials are usually difficult.
    (b) Dilatant materials can be easily mixed
    (c) Thixotropy can make mixing of plastic or dilatant materials easier
    (d) Pseudoplastic materials are easy to mix.
72. The tumble blender is also available in the shape of
    (a) Double cone blender
    (b) Ribbon blender
    (c) Sigma blade blender
    (d) Turbine
73. Both convective and dispersive flow properties of powders within a tumbler mixer can be expressed as:
    (a) $\sigma^2 - K.e^{-kN}$
    (b) $k^2 - A.e^{-\sigma N}$
    (c) $\sigma^2 = A.e^{-kN}$
    (d) $\sigma^2 = K.e^{-AN}$
74. Which of the following statements indicates the limitation of a V-blender?
    (a) Particle size reduction and attrition are minimized due to the absence of any moving blades.
    (b) V-blender can be used for fragile materials.
    (c) The V-blenders require high head-room for installation and operation.
    (d) Charging and discharging of material is easy.
75. Which of the following statements is correct?
    (a) Ribbon blender is an efficient mixer.
    (b) Shearing action in a ribbon blender is less than that in a planetary mixer.
    (c) Ribbon blender has variable speed drive
    (d) Dead spots are not found in ribbon blender.

76. Which of the following components is not attached to a planetary mixer?
   (a) A bowl with varying capacity.
   (b) An agitator
   (c) Moveable bowl
   (d) Moveable agitator
77. Which of the following statements is NOT correct?
   (a) Planetary mixer cannot be cleaned easily.
   (b) Planetary mixer saves energy.
   (c) Planetary mixer can be used to whip and blend.
   (d) The blades on a mixer is also variable.
78. Among the following mixers which is not suitable for mixing liquids?
   (a) Turbine mixer
   (b) Propeller mixer
   (c) Planetary mixer
   (d) Paddle mixer
79. Which of the flow pattern is found with propeller impeller
   (a) Radial
   (b) Tangential
   (c) Radial and tangential
   (d) Axial
80. Silverson mixer is used for preparation of
   (a) Emulsions
   (b) Capsules
   (c) Tablets
   (d) Elixir

## Chapter 5

81. Which of the following crystallizers brings about supersaturation on cooling?
   (a) Tank crystallizer.
   (b) Vacuum crystallizer.
   (c) Krystal evaporator
   (d) Salting evaporator.
82. In pharmaceutical industries crystallization technique is used to
   (a) Purify and separate the product obtained
   (b) Synthesis of components
   (c) All of the above
   (d) None of the above
83. Which of the following property is not modified by crystallization technique?
   (a) Physical stability
   (b) Bioavailability
   (c) Drug release characteristics
   (d) Therapeutic activity
84. Which of the following processes responsible for formation of crystals in a supersaturated solution?
   (a) Fermentation of solution
   (b) Formation of nucleus
   (c) Decomposition of solution
   (d) Chemical reaction
85. For crystallization to occur the solution must be
   (a) Unsaturated
   (b) Saturated
   (c) Super saturated
   (d) None of the above.
86. Which of the following statements is correct as per Mier's theory of crystallization?
   (a) The solute and solvent molecules move separately in different molecular paths.
   (b) The solute and solvent molecules move in the same molecular path.
   (c) The solvent molecules force the solute molecules to unite to form crystal
   (d) None of the above.
87. In crystallization, the stable equilibrium state of a solution refers to
   (a) The state of a solution at its supersaturated state before crystallization
   (b) The state of a solution at its supersaturated state
   (c) The state of a solution at its saturation state before crystallization
   (d) The state of a solution at its saturated state after crystallization
88. Usually the crystallization pan is attached to
   (a) A heat exchanger for heating or cooling
   (b) A mechanical agitator
   (c) Both
   (d) None
89. Which of the following statements is correct?
   (a) Agitation increases the rate of heat transfer

(b) Agitation produces large crystals in the crystallizing solution
(c) Agitation makes the solution supersaturated
(d) Agitation decreases the rate of heat transfer

90. Which of the following statements is correct?
(a) Decrease in temperature increases the viscosity of the solution containing solute with reverse solubility.
(b) Decrease in temperature increases the viscosity of the solution.
(c) Maximum supersaturation will take place in the hottest point.
(d) Agitated batch crystallizer cannot produce crystals of uniform size.

91. Which of the following statements is correct?
(a) Krystal crystallizer consists of a vapor head and a crystallization chamber.
(b) The vapor head of Krystal crystallizer is short tube.
(c) The vapor head of Krystal crystallizer is constricted towards upper end.
(d) The lower end of the vapor head of Krystal crystallizer is connected to a vacuum pump.

92. Which of the following statements is NOT correct?
(a) Vacuum crystallizer is very complicated.
(b) Vacuum crystallizer does not contain any moving parts.
(c) Vacuum crystallizer consists of a cylindrical body.
(d) The bottom portion of the vacuum crystallizer is conical in shape.

93. The feed solution which is introduced into a vacuum crystallizer should be
(a) Saturated solution
(b) Hot saturated solution
(c) Supersaturated solution
(d) Unsaturated solution

94. Which is a serious problem usually occurs during handling of crystals
(a) The crystalline products are stored in bulk
(b) The loose aggregates break easily
(c) During storage, the crystals surfaces can break
(d) During storage, crystals may form cake

95. Caking of soluble crystalline substances does not depend on
(a) Humidity and temperature
(b) Impurity content and its nature
(c) Method used for preparation of crystalline particles
(d) Particle size and shape of the crystals

96. Caking of crystals depends on
(a) Size, shape and porosity of the heap of the crystals
(b) Crystallizer used to produce crystals
(c) Method used to produce crystals
(d) Conditions employed during crystallization

97. When the crystals do not form cake
(a) The crystals are of uniform size with maximum number of voids
(b) The crystals should be exposed to moist atmosphere
(c) The shape of the crystals should be irregular
(d) Melting point of the crystals should be low

98. Growth of crystals can be prevented by
(a) Decreasing the rate of heat transfer
(b) Suspending the fine crystals in the supersaturated solution
(c) Nucleation should be avoided
(d) Maintaining the minimum super-saturation

99. Which of the following statements is correct?
(a) Crystals are not formed and deposited on the cooling surface
(b) Solutes do not precipitate as hydrates
(c) Agitated batch crystallizer produces the crystals in batches
(d) Maximum supersaturation should take place in the coldest point

100. Maximum superstation takes place at
(a) The hottest point
(b) The coldest point
(c) The boiling point of the solvent
(d) None of the above

## Chapter 6

101. The process of evaporation is used in pharmaceutical industries for
    (a) Manufacturing bulk drugs, biological products.
    (b) Manufacturing tablets and capsules
    (c) Manufacturing ointments
    (d) None of the above
102. Which of the following does not influence the process of evaporation?
    (a) Temperature
    (b) Photosensitivity of the component
    (c) Heat sensitivity of substance
    (d) Duration of evaporation
103. Which of the following statement is correct?
    (a) The evaporating pan produces solid powder
    (b) The evaporating pan is economic.
    (c) The residue obtained is a concentrated liquid
    (d) The evaporating pan is difficult to clean and maintain.
104. The characteristic property of an evaporating pan is
    (a) Suitable for organic solvent also.
    (b) Suitable for the materials that produce the foam on heating
    (c) Heating efficiency increases with increase in pan size
    (d) The overall heat transfer coefficient is poor
105. Horizontal tube evaporator is constructed in such a way that
    (a) The tubes are horizontally placed in the evaporator.
    (b) The feed liquid is introduced into the tubes.
    (c) Steam is passed around the tubes.
    (d) Heat is transported from steam to the tubes.
106. Which of the following statements is correct?
    (a) Horizontal tube evaporator is not suitable nonaqueous solutions.
    (b) Horizontal tube evaporator is suitable for viscous solution also.
    (c) Horizontal tube evaporator is not suitable for producing highly thick concentrate.
    (d) Horizontal tube evaporator can be cleaned easily.
107. Horizontal tube evaporator is suitable for
    (a) Viscous liquids
    (b) Producing highly thick concentrate
    (c) Aqueous and non-aqueous solutions
    (d) Quick drying of a liquid
108. Which of the following statements is correct?
    (a) Long-tube evaporator can work efficiently with a wide difference in temperature.
    (b) Long-tube evaporator can work efficiently even with a small difference in temperature.
    (c) Heat transfer is not efficient in case of long-tube evaporator due to minimum boundary layer.
    (d) Contact time between the liquid and heating surface is more in case of long-tube evaporator.
109. Which of the following statements is correct?
    (a) The long-tube evaporator is not economical.
    (b) The long-tube evaporator is easy to clean and maintain.
    (c) The long-tube evaporator is not suitable for materials that form foam on heating
    (d) The efficiency of separation of liquid concentrate and vapor is less.
110. Forced circulation evaporator is suitable for
    (a) Thermostable substances
    (b) Viscous solution
    (c) Solution that does not deposit solids
    (d) Preparing crystals that does not remain suspended in the liquid.
111. In which evaporator the liquid is held-up for long period?
    (a) Evaporating pan
    (b) Horizontal tube evaporator
    (c) Climbing film evaporator
    (d) Forced circulation evaporator

112. Multiple effect evaporator is generally used for
    (a) Crystallization
    (b) Concentrating the liquid at high temperature
    (c) Reducing the volume of the solvent of a solution
    (d) Conducting the process with extra steam pressure
113. The economy of a multiple effect evaporator depends on
    (a) Temperature of the product
    (b) Ratio of product weight to the feed weight
    (c) Pressure difference
    (d) Amount of product produced in unit time
114. Which of the following is a factor influencing the rate of evaporation
    (a) Rate of decrease in temperature of the product
    (b) Moisture content of the circulating air
    (c) Rate of increase in temperature of the product
    (d) All of the above
115. The process of evaporation usually depends on the temperature
    (a) 75 – 75°C
    (b) 100 – 110°C
    (c) 80 – 85 °C
    (d) 90 – 95°C
116. Which of the following materials is heat sensitive?
    (a) Enzymes, hormones
    (b) All the antibiotics
    (c) Crude drugs
    (d) None of the above
117. The evaporating can be used to concentrating the solution containing
    (a) Blood products
    (b) Hormones
    (c) Plant extract
    (d) Enzymes
118. Non-aqueous solutions can be concentrated by using
    (a) Evaporating pan
    (b) Horizontal tube evaporator
    (c) All of the above
    (d) None of the above

## Chapter 7

119. Which of the following processes takes place without transfer of heat?
    (a) Evaporation
    (b) Drying
    (c) Crystallization
    (d) Dilution of very dilute solution.
120. Which of the following processes indicate the mechanism of heat transfer?
    (a) Convection
    (b) Distillation
    (c) Conduction
    (d) Radiation
121. Which of the following statements is correct?
    (a) The rate of heat transfer is proportion to the density of the material
    (b) The rate of heat transfer is proportion to the density of the material
    (c) The rate of heat transfer is proportion to the surface area of the material
    (d) The rate of heat transfer is proportion to the quantity of the material
122. Which of the following statements expressing thermal conductivity is correct?
    (a) Copper > Aluminium
    (b) Stainless steel > Steel
    (c) Silver > Copper
    (d) Air > water
123. When heat passes through the scale deposited on the heating surface in the form of film, it follows the mechanism of
    (a) Conduction
    (b) Convection
    (c) Radiation
    (d) Absorption
124. With respect to the wavelength,the types of electromagnetic waves can be arranged as
    (a) Cosmic rays < Gamma rays
    (b) Ultraviolet rays > X rays
    (c) Infrared rays < Gamma rays
    (d) Radio waves < Visible rays

125. Which of the following statements is correct?
    (a) A body colored black is called black body
    (b) A body which has black holes is called black body
    (c) A body which radiates maximum possible amount of energy at a given temperature is called black body.
    (d) A body which absorbs all energy radiated X rays at a given temperature is called black body.
126. If the energy radiated per hour is q at absolute temperature T and the area of the radiating surface is A; the total amount of radiation emitted by a black body would be expressed as:
    (a) $q = 1.74 \times 10^{-9}$ AT
    (b) $q = 1.74 \times 10^{-9}$ $AT^2$
    (c) $q = 1.74 \times 10^{-9}$ $AT^3$
    (d) $q = 1.74 \times 10^{-9}$ $AT^4$
127. According to the Fourier's law
    (a) The rate of heat transfer through a material is proportional to the area, the temperature, and inversely proportional to the length of the path of flow of heat.
    (b) The rate of heat transfer through a uniform material is proportional to the area, the temperature drop, and inversely proportional to the length of the path of flow of heat.
    (c) The rate of heat transfer through a material is proportional to the area, the temperature, and to the length of the path of flow of heat.
    (d) The rate of heat transfer through a uniform material is inversely proportional to the area, the temperature drop, and to the length of the path of flow of heat.
128. Which of the following statements is correct?
    (a) Heat exchanger is used in wet granulation
    (b) Heat exchanger is used in dry granulation
    (c) Heat exchanger is used in evaporation
    (d) None of the above
129. Heat interchanger is used to
    (a) Transfer the heat from one liquid to another liquid
    (b) Transfer the heat from a solid to another solid
    (c) Transfer the heat from one liquid or gas to another liquid or gas
    (d) Interchange the heat between two substances
130. Radiation of electromagnetic waves follows the
    (a) Laws of light
    (b) Laws of motion
    (c) All of the above
    (d) None of the above
131. Which of the following statements is correct?
    (a) A substance thatcan radiate the energy even at a lower temperature is called black body.
    (b) A black body radiates the minimum possible amount of energy at a higher temperature.
    (c) A substance that can radiate the energy is called black body.
    (d) A black body radiates the maximum possible amount of energy at a given temperature.
132. In liquid – liquid heat interchanger, heat transfer takes place
    (a) Slowly
    (b) Rapidly
    (c) Moderately
    (d) Very slowly
133. To determine the efficiency of the process of evaporation
    (a) The flow of heat is determined qualitatively
    (b) The flow of heat is determined quantitatively
    (c) The flow of heat is determined
    (d) The flow of heat is not determined
134. The mechanism of heat transfer by conduction can be expressed as
    (a) The rate of heat transfer, $\frac{dQ}{d\theta} = \frac{\text{Driving force}}{\text{Resistance}} = \frac{k \times A \times dt}{dL}$

(b) $\frac{dQ}{d\theta} = \frac{k \times A \times dt}{dL}$

(c) $\frac{dQ}{d\theta} = -\frac{k \times A \times dt}{dL}$

(d) $\frac{dQ}{d\theta} = \frac{A \times dt}{dL}$

135. In most cases, the wavelength of radiation ranges from
 (a) 0.8 – 40 μm
 (b) 0.8 – 25 μm
 (c) 2.5 – 40 μm
 (d) 10 – 25 μm

136. Which one of the following is not a heat exchanger?
 (a) Shell-and-tube heater
 (b) Multi-pass heater
 (c) Two pass floating head heater
 (d) Steam

137. Shell-and-tube heater is
 (a) A single-pass heater
 (b) A two-pass heater
 (c) A three-pass heater
 (d) A four-pass heater

138. In a shell-tube heat exchanger, the tubes and shell may expand due to
 (a) The pressure differences
 (b) The temperature differences
 (c) The concentration differences
 (d) The temperature and concentration difference

## Chapter 8

139. Removal of small amount of water from solid or almost solid materials is called
 (a) Evaporation
 (b) Distillation
 (c) Drying
 (d) Centrifugation

140. For drying granular or loose materials, which of following dryer is chosen?
 (a) Rotary dryer
 (b) Tunnel dryer
 (c) Agitator dryer
 (d) Festoon dryer

141. Heat is transferred by convection method in
 (a) Contact dryer
 (b) Direct dryer
 (c) Microwave oven
 (d) Radio frequency electromagnetic field

142. Transfer of moisture in a solid takes place following which mechanism?
 (a) Diffusion of vapor
 (b) Hydrostatic pressure difference
 (c) Knudsen diffusion
 (d) All of the above

143. Which of the following statement is correct?
 (a) The moisture content of a wet solid in equilibrium with air of given humidity and temperature is its equilibrium moisture content.
 (b) The moisture released by a wet solid at a given humidity and temperature is its equilibrium moisture content.
 (c) The moisture gained by a wet solid at a given humidity and temperature is its equilibrium moisture content.
 (d) The moisture content of a wet solid in equilibrium with air is its equilibrium moisture content.

144. The equilibrium moisture content of a material depends on
 (a) Temperature
 (b) Temperature, pressure and humidity
 (c) Temperature and pressure
 (d) Humidity

145. The most preferred experimental methods for determining adsorption-desorption isotherm is:
 (a) Barometric method
 (b) Manometric method
 (c) Hydrometric method
 (d) Falling-rate method

146. Tray dryer can be used to dry the material
 (a) In batches
 (b) Continuously
 (c) All of the above
 (d) None of the above

147. In a drum dryer, the rate of drying is more when
 (a) The drum rotates at high speed

(b) The temperature of drum-wall is less
(c) The drum rotates at low speed
(d) Humidity of the environment is high

148. In a fluidized bed dryer
(a) The rate of powder flow in upward direction is not more than its settling rate
(b) The rate of powder flow in downward direction is more than its settling rate
(c) The rate of powder flow in upward direction is more than its settling rate
(d) The rate of powder flow in upward direction is equal to its settling rate

149. In spray drying process, the particle size of the material to be dried depends on
(a) The rate of evaporation of the solvent
(b) The rate at which the product is removed
(c) Size of the dryer
(d) Speed of atomization

150. In drying the temperature of the material is raised to
(a) The temperature equivalent to boiling point of water
(b) The temperature more than the boiling point of water
(c) The temperature less than the boiling point of water
(d) None of the above

151. Which of the following statements is correct?
(a) Unbound moisture exerts its vapor pressure equivalent to that of the free liquid (water).
(b) Unbound moisture exerts its vapor pressure not equivalent to that of the free liquid (water).
(c) Unbound moisture exerts its vapor pressure is less than that of the free liquid (water).
(d) Unbound moisture exerts its vapor pressure more than that of the free liquid (water).

152. Which of the following statements is correct?
(a) Bound moisture is the liquid (water) whose vapor pressure is more than that of the pure liquid (water) at the same temperature and atmospheric pressure.
(b) Bound moisture is the liquid (water) whose vapor pressure is less than that of the pure liquid (water) at the same temperature and atmospheric pressure.
(c) Bound moisture is the liquid (water) whose vapor pressure is equivalent to that of the pure liquid (water) at the same temperature and atmospheric pressure.
(d) Bound moisture is free moisture.

153. Constant drying of a material depends on
(a) Constant velocity of air
(b) Temperature of the circulating air
(c) Relative humidity of air
(d) All of the above

154. According to the diffusion theory, the rate of flow of water depends on
(a) The gravitational force
(b) The effect of capillary
(c) The effect of frictional forces
(d) The moisture gradient

155. The diffusion theory can explain
(a) The drying rate at various ranges of moisture gradients,
(b) Decrease in diffusivity with decreasing moisture content and humidity,
(c) Increase in diffusivity with increasing pressure.
(d) None of the above

156. Freeze drying or lyophilization is a process in which
(a) Water is removed as liquid water
(b) Water is removed as water vapor
(c) Water is removed as solid water
(d) Water is removed as liquid water and water vapor

157. Which of the following statements is correct?
(a) Freeze drying can minimize the chemical decomposition
(b) Freeze drying can increase the chemical decomposition
(c) In freeze drying the rate of drying is high
(d) Freeze drying is not suitable for sterile product

158. Freeze drying process is the most suitable for
(a) The substances which are not stable under ambient conditions of temperature and pressure

(b) The substances which are not stable at lower temperature
(c) The substances which are stable at higher temperature
(d) The substances which are not hygroscopic

## Chapter 9

159. Which of the following statements is correct?
(a) Distillation is a process of separation of one component at a time
(b) Distillation is a process of separation of one liquid component at a time
(c) Distillation is a process of separation of one liquid component from non-volatile solute
(d) Distillation is a process of separation of one liquid component of a solution in form of vapor from non-volatile solute present in the solution by boiling the solution

160. Which of the following statements is correct?
(a) Distillation and evaporation are same process
(b) Distillation is a process where the vapor of a liquid is condensed and collected
(c) Distillation is a faster evaporation process
(d) By distillation only volatile comment can be separated, not the non-volatile one.

161. Which the following statements is correct?
(a) The liquid or liquid mixture which is distilled is called distill and
(b) The liquid mixture which is distilled in the process of distillation is called distillate
(c) The liquid which is collected in the receiver is called distill and
(d) The liquid mixture which is collected is called distillate

162. Which the following statements is correct?
(a) Volatile oils from the extract of cloves, anise seeds and eucalyptus leaves can be separated by simple distillation.
(b) Boiling range of a liquid can be determined by steam distillation
(c) Solvents from extracts of drugs of plant origin or from synthetic reaction mixture can be separated by distillation.
(d) Purification of petroleum products in the petroleum industry is done by simple distillation.

163. Purification of petroleum products in the petroleum industry is done by
(a) Simple distillation
(b) Destructive distillation
(c) Flash distillation
(d) Steam distillation

164. During preparation of an ideal solution
(a) Heat should neither be produced nor absorbed
(b) Heat should only be generated
(c) Heat should only be absorbed
(d) Heat can be generated or absorbed

165. Distillation process can be applied to separate a component only when
(a) The mixture is an ideal one
(b) The mixture is a real one
(c) The mixture contains two liquids
(d) The mixture is a solution

166. The characteristics of a good condenser should be
(a) The material of construction of the condenser should not be a good conductor of heat
(b) It should have minimum cooling surface
(c) The inner surface of a condenser should be very smooth
(d) The outer surface of a condenser should be very smooth

167. Water cooled condenser is suitable when the liquid boils at a temperature
(a) More than 130°C
(b) Less than 130°C
(c) More than 230°C
(d) Less than 250°C, but more than 150°C

168. Which of the following condensers has maximum efficiency of condensation?
(a) Spiral single-surface condenser

(b) Plane tube single-surface condenser
(c) Bulb type single-surface condenser
(d) Double-surface condenser

169. Baffles are attached to distillation units at a place
(a) Within the sill
(b) Within the condenser
(c) In between sill and condenser
(d) In between condenser and receiver

170. When the mixture is suddenly vaporized by passing the mixture from a high pressure zone to a low-pressure zone, the process is called as
(a) Flash distillation
(b) Fractional distillation
(c) Bubble-cap distillation
(d) Simple distillation

171. Flash distillation is suitable for separating two components when
(a) The difference between the boiling point of two components is narrow
(b) The difference between the boiling point of two components is wide
(c) The components have similar volatility
(d) There are only two components in the system

172. Which of the following characteristics must be possessed by a fractionating column?
(a) Heat must be supplied to the top of the column to re-vaporize the liquid.
(b) A condenser is attached to the bottom of the column to return liquid refluxed in sufficient quantity.
(c) The column should have a high pressure-drop
(d) The liquid should be held by the column for a minimum period.

173. The bubble cap plate fractionating column is the most popular one, because
(a) The contact between liquid and vapor is poor
(b) The contact between liquid and vapor is excellent
(c) Throughout the column hold-up time is considerably very less
(d) The column does not drain off the liquid

174. Turbogrid plate fractionating column is suitable, because
(a) Wide range of operations can be done
(b) Minimum liquid goes down the plate
(c) Pressure drop is not low
(d) Liquid hold-up is much less

175. The distillation under vacuum is suitable for
(a) Liquids of high boiling pointunder atmospheric pressure
(b) Making a product which is not to be processed further
(c) Making a semi-solid or solid extract
(d) Active constituent which stable at higher temperature

176. Steam distillation cannot be used for
(a) Separation of immiscible liquids
(b) Extracting volatile oils from plant parts
(c) Preparation of aromatic water.
(d) The material that can react with water

177. If the viscosity of the material and pressure are low,
(a) The mean free path of the molecules of the material becomes long.
(b) The mean free path of the molecules of the material becomes short.
(c) The distillation becomes complicated.
(d) None of the above.

178. If λ is the mean free path, η is the viscosity and ρ is the density of the material, p is the pressure; then
(a) $\lambda = \eta\sqrt{\frac{1}{p.\rho}}$
(b) $\lambda = \eta\sqrt{\frac{3}{p.\rho}}$
(c) $\lambda = \eta\sqrt{\frac{p.\rho}{3}}$
(d) $\lambda = 3\sqrt{\frac{\eta}{p.\rho}}$

## Chapter 10

179. Filtration is applicable to separate the undissolved material from a solution or fluid, t

may the fluid may be
(a) Gas
(b) Liquid
(c) Vapor
(d) All of the above

180. If V is the volume of filtrate, t is the time of filtration (time duration), K is the constant for filter medium and the filter cake, A is the area of the filter medium through which filtration takes place, ΔP is the pressure drop across the filter medium or filter cake, μ is the viscosity of the filtrate, and $l$ is the thickness of the cake; then the rate of filtration, $\frac{dV}{dt}$ can be expressed as:
(a) $\frac{dV}{dt} = \frac{K \times A\Delta P}{\mu \times l}$
(b) $\frac{dV}{dt} = \frac{K \times \mu \times \Delta P}{A \times l}$
(c) $\frac{dV}{dt} = \frac{K \times A \times \mu}{\Delta P \times l}$
(d) $\frac{dV}{dt} = \frac{K \times A \times l}{\mu \times \Delta P}$

181. The rate of filtration depends on
(a) Shape of the undissolved solid,
(b) Type of filter medium used
(c) Ultimate application of filter medium
(d) Color of solvent

182. The process of filtration is repeated because
(a) The filter medium resists the passage of fine particles
(b) To block the pores of the filter medium
(c) To prevent the particles to pass through the filter medium
(d) To get a clear filtrate

183. Filter aid is a substance that
(a) Bleaches the solution and make the filtrate clear
(b) Dissolves into the solution and help to improve the filtration rate
(c) Makes a layer over the filter medium and reduce the size of the pores
(d) Facilitate the solution to pass through the filter medium

184. Plate and frame filter is alternatively called as
(a) Flush plate
(b) Filter leaf
(c) Meta filter
(d) Cartridge filter

185. The filter cake produced over the frame of filter press consists of
(a) Kieselguhr powder
(b) Insoluble solids present in the feed
(c) Calcium sulphate powder

186. The rate of filtration through the filter press
(a) Is increased with the increase of the thickness of filter cake
(b) Is increased with the use of filter aid powder
(c) Is decreased with the increase of thickness of the filter cake
(d) Is increased by addition of more amount of filter aid powder

187. Which of the following statements is correct?
(a) Filter press has a 'down-time'
(b) Filter press requires a re-useable filter cloth
(c) Filter press can be operated easily
(d) Filter press is suitable for filtering large quantity of slurries

188. Which of the following statements is correct?
(a) Filter leaf requires a greater number of labors
(b) Initial cost of a filter leaf filtration is relatively less
(c) The filtration through the leaf filter does not follow surface filtration
(d) The rate of filtration increases if filter leaf is operated under vacuum.

189. The mechanism of filtration followed by rotary drum filter is
(a) Surface filtration
(b) Sieve-like filtration
(c) Both of the above
(d) None of the above

190. Rotary drum filter is able to filter the slurries containing
(a) Maximum up to 5% of solids
(b) Maximum up to 10% of solids

(c) Up to 15 – 30 % of solids
(d) Up to 5 – 10 % of solid

191. Which of the following statements is correct?
(a) Rotary drum filter is labor extensive
(b) Rotary drum filter cannot be operated automatically
(c) Rotary drum filter can filter at a lower rate only
(d) The capacity of rotary drum filter is high

192. Which of the following statements is correct?
(a) Rotary drum filter is cheap
(b) Rotary drum filter is a simple equipment
(c) There is no chance of boiling of the hot filtrate
(d) The filter obtained can form porous cake

193. Which of the following statements is correct?
(a) Meta filter can withstand high pressure, if applied.
(b) The running cost of meta filter is high
(c) Meta filter is not an economic filter
(d) The cake cannot be removed or washed effectively by back-flushing with water.

194. Which of the following statements is correct?
(a) For preparation of solution for ophthalmic and parenteral dosage forms, the cartridge filter cannot be used.
(b) The cartridge filter cannot be easily assembled or disassembled.
(c) The cartridge filter can be used as in-line continuous filtration.
(d) The cartridge filter increases the chance of contamination.

195. Membrane filters are available with different porosity
(a) From 1 – 5 μm
(b) From 5 – 10 μm
(c) From 0.2 – 3.0 μm
(d) From 10 – 25 μm

196. For filtration of aerosol membrane should have the porosity of
(a) 0.2 – 0.45 μm
(b) 1.2 – 4 μm
(c) 1.8 – 5 μm
(d) 0.8 – 3.0 μm

197. Which of the following statements is correct?
(a) Seidtz filters are similar to other depth filter
(b) Seidtz filter cannot filter at a high rate.
(c) Seidtz filter chocks frequently.
(d) Seidtz filter cannot be used for longer period.

198. Which of the following statements is correct?
(a) Seidtz filter are made of mixed cellulose nitrate esters
(b) Seidtz filter are made of asbestos.
(c) There is a chance of shedding of loose fibres
(d) Seidtz filter are not useful for filtration of air or water

## Chapter 11

199. The rate of filtration through a filter medium is
(a) Inversely proportional to the thickness of the cake produced
(b) Directly proportional to the viscosity of the liquid being filtered
(c) Inversely proportional to the pressure drop across the filter medium
(d) Inversely proportional to the area of the filter medium

200. Centrifugal effect is expressed as
(a) The ratio of centrifugal force to gravitational force
(b) The ratio of gravitational force to centrifugal force
(c) Difference between centrifugal force and gravitational force
(d) Difference between gravitational force and centrifugal force

201. During centrifugation, the force, F acts on the body being centrifuged is expressed as
(a) $F = \frac{\text{Mass of the body} \times (\text{radius of circular path})^2}{\text{velocity of the body}}$
(b) $F = \frac{\text{Mass of the body} \times \text{radius of circular path}}{\text{Velocity of the body}}$
(c) $F = \frac{\text{Mass of the body} \times (\text{Velocity of the body})^2}{\text{Radius of circular path}}$
(d) $F = \frac{\text{Mass of the body} \times \text{Velocity of the body}}{\text{Radius of circular path}}$

202. Centrifugation is not used for
(a) Isotope separation
(b) Separation of solution
(c) Assessing tolerance of pilots
(d) Assessing tolerance of astronauts

203. Which of the following statements is correct?
(a) Vacuum filtration is carried out when solid concentration is more
(b) Vacuum filtration is carried out when filtration capacity of the filter is more
(c) Vacuum filtration system requires less space
(d) Vacuum filtration is not cheaper than centrifugation

204. On which of the following, centrifugation process depends?
(a) Color of the slurry
(b) Surface charge of the insoluble solid
(c) Polarity of the solvent
(d) Aqueous miscibility of the solvent

205. Centrifugation cannot be used for
(a) Evaluation of suspension and emulsion
(b) Determination of molecular weight of colloids
(c) Determination of solubility of a substance
(d) Production of biological products

206. Which of the following statements is correct?
(a) Centrifugation methods cannot handle slurries containing high proportion of solids.
(b) Centrifuges are not very compact; hence, more floor space would be required.
(c) Centrifugation process is not expensive because of low labor cost.
(d) The moisture content of the product is less than that obtained in filtration.

207. If F is the relative centrifugal force, m is the mass of the particle, r is radius of rotation (cm) i.e., the distance of particle from the axis of rotation, and ω is the average angular velocity (radians/se(c); then
(a) $F = m^2\omega^2r$
(b) $F = m\omega^2r$
(c) $F = m^3\omega^2r$
(d) $F = m\omega^2r^2$

208. If at a point equivalent to 4 cm from the centre of rotation and if the angular velocity is 2500 rad $s^{-1}$, then the value of centrifugal field, G would be:
(a) $2.5\times10^7 cm\ s^{-2}$.
(b) $2.5\times10^7 cm\ s^{-2}$.
(c) $2.5\times10^7 cm\ s^{-2}$.
(d) $2.5\times10^7 cm\ s^{-2}$.

209. If an ultracentrifuge is run at a speed of 37500r.p.m. the angular velocity, ω would be:
(a) 3027 rad $s^{-1}$
(b) 3279 rad $s^{-1}$
(c) 3927 rad $s^{-1}$
(d) 3792 rad $s^{-1}$

210. Which of the following does not have effect on centrifugation?
(a) Viscosity of the liquid
(b) Concentration of solid
(c) Particle size distribution
(d) Density of the solid

211. Which of the following statements is not correct?
(a) Centrifugation can recover maximum amount of the liquid than filtration.
(b) Centrifugation removes the water of crystallization of crystallized solid.
(c) Centrifugation can remove the unwanted solids from a liquid.
(d) Compared to filtration, centrifugation can recover maximum amount of the liquid.

212. Which of the following statements is correct?
(a) Centrifugation by using perforated basket centrifuge is expensive.
(b) Moisture content of the final product is more than that obtained in filtration.
(c) Usually centrifugation done using perforated basket centrifuge is a continuous.
(d) The process of charging, separation of phases, washing, drying and removal of cake in a perforated basket centrifuge are very slow.

213. Which of the following statements is correct?
(a) Non-perforated basket centrifuge removes the solid from the slurry on the basis of density difference between two phases.

(b) Non-perforated basket centrifuge is used when the solid content of the slurry is less.
(c) Non-perforated basket centrifuge consists of a rectangular or square bowl.
(d) The bowl of non-perforated basket centrifuge rotates around the horizontal axis.

214. Non-perforated basket centrifuge can be used
(a) For batch wise centrifugation only.
(b) To separate the particles on the basis of density difference between two phases.
(c) To separate the particles on the basis of viscosity difference between two phases.
(d) To rotate the basket at a speed varying from 5000 to 20000 per sec.

215. Which of the following statements is correct?
(a) Semi continuous centrifuge acts as a surface filtration.
(b) Semi continuous centrifuge acts as a sieve filtration.
(c) Semi continuous centrifuge acts as a filtration centrifuge.
(d) Semi continuous centrifuge contains a non-perforated basket.

216. Which of the following statements is correct?
(a) Semi continuous centrifuge requires more labor.
(b) More power is required by semi continuous centrifuge
(c) Semi continuous centrifuge requires more time for completion of a cycle.
(d) In semi continuous centrifuge, crystals may break during discharge.

217. Which of the following statements is correct?
(a) In tubular bowl centrifuge, the centrifugal force exerted on a particle is directly proportional to the radius of the basket.
(b) In tubular bowl centrifuge of laboratory scale, the rotation varies from 22000 to 50000rpm.
(c) In tubular bowl centrifuge of laboratory scale, the rotation varies from 2200 to 5000rpm.
(d) Super centrifuge is alternatively known as tubular bowl centrifuge.

218. Which of the following statements is correct?
(a) Super centrifuge is not used for continuous separation of phases.
(b) Super centrifuge is used for separation of two immiscible liquid phases of an emulsion.
(c) Super centrifuge is not rotated with the help of drive-assembly.
(d) Super centrifuge contains two liquid outlets at the bottom of the bowl of same radii.

## Chapter 12

219. Which of the following is not an ancillary area?
(a) Climate
(b) Maintenance work shop
(c) Utilities
(d) Stores

220. Storage of raw materials, packaging materials and finished products come under
(a) Transportation area
(b) Manufacture area
(c) Utility area
(d) Ancillary area

221. Which of the following is not a factor to be considered during layout of a plant?
(a) Convenience of maintenance
(b) Safety
(c) Education of employees
(d) Future expansion

222. Which of the following does not come under safety programs?
(a) Encouragement to adhere to safety measures and practices.
(b) Evaluation of work-efficiency of the employees.
(c) Safety at design level and equipment installation stage
(d) Education of employees in safety practices.

223. Which of the following is not the purpose of plant layout?
   (a) The streamline movement of materials throughout the plant
   (b) Facilitating the manufacturing activities.
   (c) Designing the site for change room
   (d) Minimizing the overall production time.
224. Which of the following does not come under classification of plant layout?
   (a) Group layout
   (b) Process layout
   (c) Product layout
   (d) Organization structure
225. Which of the following does not come under utility?
   (a) Availability of labor
   (b) Cool water supply
   (c) Electricity
   (d) Refrigeration
226. Which of the following category of materials does not match with others with respect to application?
   (a) Raw materials
   (b) Inflammable materials
   (c) Intermediate products
   (d) Recycle materials
227. Which of the followings is considered as a biological hazard?
   (a) Noise
   (b) Vibration
   (c) Dust
   (d) Radiation
228. Which of the followings is considered as a general hazard?
   (a) Noise
   (b) Fire
   (c) Pressure
   (d) Fibres
229. Which of the followings is considered as a chemical hazard?
   (a) Toxins
   (b) Heat
   (c) Fire
   (d) Payment system
230. Mechanical hazard may be caused due to
   (a) Shearing
   (b) Entanglement
   (c) Collision
   (d) Crushing and cutting
231. Occurrence of hazards may be prevented by
   (a) Poor maintenance
   (b) Proper planning of the building
   (c) Poor house keeping
   (d) Falling on a pointed object
232. Which of the following belongs to class A chemical hazard?
   (a) Flammable gas
   (b) Organic peroxides
   (c) Compressed gas
   (d) Poisons
233. Which of the following belongs to class D chemical hazard?
   (a) Compressed gas.
   (b) Combustible gas
   (c) Oxidizing material
   (d) Poisons
234. Which chemical of the following can cause green tongue salivation?
   (a) Mercury
   (b) Sulphur dioxide
   (c) CNS depressant
   (d) Hydrogen sulphide
235. Which of the additives can cause leukemia?
   (a) Azo dyes
   (b) Benzene
   (c) Caustic soda
   (d) Lead
236. Which of the following is not a method used for control of dust pollution?
   (a) Inertial separation,
   (b) Electrostatic precipitation
   (c) Friction and abrasion
   (d) Filtration
237. Which of the following may be considered as preventive measure for fire?
   (a) Providing personal protective cloth
   (b) Installation of machines with emergency shutdown system.

(c) Controlling and eliminating hazards
(d) Stop and lock button for machines.

238. Which of the following actions is not to be monitored for industrial safety?
(a) Treatment
(b) Medical examination
(c) Education
(d) Industrial lay out

## Chapter 13

239. Which of the following is not the factor to be considered during construction of pharmaceutical plant?
(a) Physical
(b) Chemical
(c) Biological
(d) Economic

240. Which of the following does not influence the corrosion process?
(a) pH of the solution
(b) Aeration
(c) Temperature
(d) Pressure

241. Which of the following does not belong to dry corrosion?
(a) Electrochemical corrosion
(b) Oxidation corrosion
(c) Corrosion by hydrogen
(d) Liquid metal corrosion

242. Which of the following are anodic inhibitors used to repair corrosion
(a) The crack of the oxide film over the metal surface
(b) The pitting corrosion
(c) The porous oxide film formed on the metal surface
(d) Fretting corrosion

243. For protection of metal from corrosion which of the following method is not used?
(a) Metal cladding
(b) Chromate coating
(c) Cementation
(d) Electroplating

244. Which of the following is metallic coating?
(a) Calorizing
(b) Varnishes
(c) Enamel
(d) Oxide coating

245. Which of the following is non-metallic coating?
(a) Electroplating
(b) Tinning
(c) Enamel coating
(d) Chromizing

246. Which of the following is not a constituent of a paint?
(a) Drier
(b) Plasticizer
(c) Thinner
(d) Varnish

247. Which of the following is not a condition for good electrodeposit
(a) Optimum temperature
(b) Concentration of antimasking agent
(c) Optimum current density
(d) Low metal ion concentration

248. Which of the following is a ferrous metal used for construction of pharmaceutical plant?
(a) Cast iron
(b) Lead
(c) Copper
(d) Tin

249. Which of the following is an inorganic non-metal?
(a) Plastics
(b) Rubber
(c) Stone ware
(d) Timber

250. Which of the following is a subsidiary factor to be considered during construction of pharmaceutical plant?
(a) Strength
(b) Ease of cleaning
(c) Thermal conductivity
(d) Thermal expansion

251. The pharmaceutical plant should be constructed with material that are
(a) Susceptible to alkali
(b) Susceptible to tannins
(c) Susceptible to acid
(d) Resistant to acid

252. Which of the following statements is correct?
   (a) The efficiency of a machine is reduced due to corrosion.
   (b) The corroded machine can be used
   (c) Corrosion does not cause health hazards
   (d) Corrosion does not release the toxic product.

253. The corroding metal consists of
   (a) An electron sink area where electronation reaction occurs
   (b) An electron sink area where de-electronation reaction occurs
   (c) An electron source area where de-electronation reaction occurs
   (d) An electron sink area where metal does not dissolve

254. According to Wagner and Traud, the metal becomes unstable because
   (a) Metals becomes stable because of similar electronic charge transfer reactions
   (b) Electronic charge transfer reactions occur simultaneously in the same direction
   (c) The impurities or any other heterogeneous substance present on the surface are not solely responsible for corrosion reaction
   (d) The impurities or any other heterogeneous substance present on the surface are solely responsible for corrosion reaction.

255. If W is the weight loss (grams), a is the area of the specimen (sq. in), t is the time (hrs.), and d is the density of the specimen (g/cm$^3$); then the rate of corrosion in mpy is expressed as
   (a) $\text{mpy} = \dfrac{534 \times W \times d}{a \times t}$
   (b) $\text{mpy} = \dfrac{82.75 \times W}{a \times t \times d}$
   (c) $\text{mpy} = \dfrac{53.4 \times W}{a \times t \times d}$
   (d) $\text{mpy} = \dfrac{534 \times W}{a \times t \times d}$

256. Corrosion due to oxidation reaction can be expressed as
   (a) $2M + \frac{n}{2} O_2 \rightarrow 2M^{n2+} + nO^{2-}$
   (b) $M + \frac{n}{2} O_2 \rightarrow 2M^{n2+} + nO^{2-}$
   (c) $M + \frac{n}{2} O_2 \rightarrow M^{2+} + nO^{2-}$
   (d) $M + O_2 \rightarrow M^{2+} + \frac{1}{n}O^{2-}$

257. The Nernst equation can be written as
   (a) $E_o = E + 2.303\frac{RT}{nF}\log \frac{a_{oxid}}{a_{red}}$
   (b) $E = E_o + 2.303\frac{RT}{nF}\log \frac{a_{oxid}}{a_{red}}$
   (c) $E_o = E + 2.303\frac{nT}{nR}\log \frac{a_{red}}{a_{oxid}}$
   (d) $E_o = E + 2.303\frac{RT}{nF}\log \frac{a_{oxid}}{a_{red}}$

258. In which of the following circumstances the electrochemical corrosion occurs?
   (a) A conducting medium is not present.
   (b) The corrosion product is formed at cathodic area.
   (c) The corrosion product is formed at anodic area.
   (d) The corrosion product is formed in between anodic and cathodic areas.

## Chapter 14

259. Which one of the following statements is correct?
   (a) Material handling is involved in the movement of materials.
   (b) Material handling is involved in the movement and storage of materials.
   (c) Material handling is involved in the movement, handling and storage of materials.
   (d) Material handling is involved in the movement, handling and storage of materials during different stages of manufacturing.

260. Which one of the following statements is correct?
   (a) Material handling cost = Cost of material + cost of handling of material
   (b) Material handling cost = Cost of handling + cost of transportation
   (c) Material handling cost = Cost of material handling equipment + cost of transportation + cost of packaging + cost of space
   (d) Material handling cost = Cost of material + cost of storage of material + cost of transportation + cost of packaging + cost of space
261. The objectives of material handling is
   (a) Minimizing the cost of material handling.
   (b) Minimizing the delays and interruptions by making available the materials at the point of use at right quantity and at right time.
   (c) Increasing the productive capacity of the production facilities by effective utilization of capacity, enhancing productivity and improvement in safety.
   (d) All of the above
262. Handling system can be classified into:
   (a) Mechanical,
   (b) Semi-automatic,
   (c) Automatic
   (d) All of the above
263. Material handling equipments can be classified as
   (a) Containers and unitizing equipment,
   (b) Material transport equipment,
   (c) Storage and retrieval equipment,
   (d) All of the above
264. Reduction of in-process storage of products leads to
   (a) Improvement in working conditions
   (b) Reduction in total cost of the product
   (c) Improved customer services
   (d) Improved ease of production
265. Irrespective of the purpose and type of equipments to be used, the design is based on an empirical decision, because
   (a) The properties of material to be transported are inherently different,
   (b) Wide range of processes are there where material handling is involved.
   (c) All of the above
   (d) None of the above
266. Scraper conveyor and bucket conveyor belong to
   (a) Belt conveyor
   (b) Chain conveyor
   (c) Screw conveyor
   (d) Pneumatic conveyor
267. Idler is the alternative name of
   (a) Belt conveyor support
   (b) Belt
   (c) Belt conveyor drive
   (d) Belt conveyor tightener
268. Which of the following fails to reduce the total cost of the product?
   (a) Reducing the material handling labor
   (b) Using the skilled and semi-skilled labor for material handling
   (c) Increasing productivity
   (d) Better utilization of space.
269. Capacity of production cannot be increase by
   (a) Increasing the space for travel
   (b) Better utilization of space
   (c) Reducing the wastage of space
   (d) Improving the utilization of equipment
270. Improvement of working conditions can be affected by
   (a) Full-proof operation
   (b) Easy working
   (c) Complicated working
   (d) Safety aspect
271. Which of the following is not a class of material handling system?
   (a) Handling of individual unit by men
   (b) Handling of products at its selling point.
   (c) Handling inside a department
   (d) Handling of materials during distribution

272. Which of the following is not a component of belt conveyor?
   (a) Chain
   (b) Belt
   (c) Drive
   (d) Tightener
273. Which of the following is not a component of screw conveyor?
   (a) U-shaped trough
   (b) Flight
   (c) Feeding arrangement
   (d) Belt

274. Which of the following is a limitation of screw conveyor?
   (a) It can transport the material horizontally, vertically, and in inclined direction
   (b) Handling of large size screw conveyor is not easy
   (c) It works at low rotational speed
   (d) It does not pollute the environment with dust
275. Vertical screw conveyor is suitable for
   (a) Handling of dry to semi solid material
   (b) Handling of liquid material
   (c) Lifting of materials up to 100 feet high per hour
   (d) Elevate the material maximum up to 10 feet high per hour
276. Which of the following statements is an advantage of a pneumatic conveyor?
   (a) The pneumatic conveyor consumes more power
   (b) The pneumatic conveyor is not economical
   (c) The pneumatic conveyor causes even contact of gas and solids.
   (d) When the pneumatic conveyor is used, frictional losses would be more.
277. Which of the following statements is correct?
   (a) There is greater erosion of internal surface of the vessel.
   (b) The method requires relatively less power
   (c) Pneumatic conveyor is not economical
   (d) Frictional loss es would be small.
278. A method of moving product along a conveyor on a cushion of air is called.
   (a) Dilute-phase conveying
   (b) Dense-phase conveying
   (c) Air-activated gravity conveying
   (d) None of the above

# Answers

| | | | | | | |
|---|---|---|---|---|---|---|
| 1. (c) | 2. (c) | 3. (a) | 4. (b) | 5. (a) | 6. (b) | 7. (a) |
| 8. (d) | 9. (a) | 10. (b) | 11. (a) | 12. (a) | 13. (c) | 14. (a) |
| 15. (a) | 16. (a) | 17. (b) | 18. (c) | 19. (a) | 20. (a) | 21. (a) |
| 22. (b) | 23. (c) | 24. (d) | 25. (b) | 26. (c) | 27. (c) | 28. (a) |
| 29. (a) | 30. (b) | 31. (d) | 32. (b) | 33. (a) | 34. (c) | 35. (d) |
| 36. (d) | 37. (c) | 38. (b) | 39. (a) | 40. (d) | 41. (b) | 42. (c) |
| 43. (d) | 44. (d) | 45. (a) | 46. (a) | 47. (c) | 48. (b) | 49. (b) |
| 50. (a) | 51. (a) | 52. (c) | 53. (d) | 54. (d) | 55. (a) | 56. (a) |
| 57. (c) | 58. (b) | 59. (c) | 60. (d) | 61. (a) | 62. (c) | 63. (d) |
| 64. (b) | 65. (b) | 66. (d) | 67. (d) | 68. (a) | 69. (b) | 70. (c) |
| 71. (b) | 72. (a) | 73. (c) | 74. (c) | 75. (b) | 76. (c) | 77. (a) |
| 78. (c) | 79. (d) | 80. (a) | 81. (a) | 82. (c) | 83. (d) | 84. (b) |
| 85. (c) | 86. (a) | 87. (d) | 88. (c) | 89. (a) | 90. (b) | 91. (a) |
| 92. (a) | 93. (b) | 94. (d) | 95. (c) | 96. (a) | 97. (a) | 98. (b) |
| 99. (d) | 100. (b) | 101. (a) | 102. (b) | 103. (c) | 104. (d) | 105. (a) |
| 106. (c) | 107. (d) | 108. (b) | 109. (a) | 110. (b) | 111. (d) | 112. (a) |
| 113 (c) | 114. (b) | 115. (d) | 116. (a) | 117. (c) | 118. (b) | 119. (d) |
| 120. (b) | 121. (c) | 122. (a) | 123. (a) | 124. (b) | 125. (c) | 126. (d) |

| | | | | | | |
|---|---|---|---|---|---|---|
| 127. (b) | 128. (c) | 129. (c) | 130. (a) | 131. (d) | 132. (b) | 133. (b) |
| 134. (a) | 135. (b) | 136. (d) | 137. (a) | 138. (b) | 139. (c) | 140. (a) |
| 141. (b) | 142. (d) | 143. (a) | 144. (b) | 145. (b) | 146. (a) | 147. (c) |
| 148. (c) | 149. (d) | 150. (c) | 151. (a) | 152. (b) | 153. (d) | 154. (d) |
| 155. (d) | 156. (b) | 157. (a) | 158. (c) | 159. (d) | 160. (b) | 161. (a) |
| 162. (c) | 163. (c) | 164. (a) | 165. (d) | 166. (c) | 167. (b) | 168. (d) |
| 169. (c) | 170. (a) | 171. (b) | 172. (d) | 173. (b) | 174. (d) | 175. (a) |
| 176. (d) | 177. (a) | 178. (b) | 179. (d) | 180. (a) | 181. (b) | 182. (d) |
| 183. (c) | 184. (a) | 185. (b) | 186. (c) | 187. (a) | 188. (d) | 189. (b) |
| 190. (c) | 191. (d) | 192. (d) | 193. (a) | 194. (c) | 195. (c) | 196. (d) |
| 197. (a) | 198. (b) | 199. (a) | 200. (a) | 201. (c) | 202. (b) | 203. (d) |
| 204. (b) | 205. (c) | 206. (d) | 207. (b) | 208. (a) | 209. (c) | 210. (d) |
| 211. (b) | 212. (a) | 213. (a) | 214. (b) | 215. (c) | 216. (d) | 217. (d) |
| 218. (b) | 219. (a) | 220. (d) | 221. (c) | 222. (b) | 223. (c) | 224. (d) |
| 225. (a) | 226. (b) | 227. (c) | 228. (b) | 229. (a) | 230. (d) | 231. (b) |
| 232 (c) | 233. (d) | 234. (a) | 235. (b) | 236. (c) | 237. (a) | 238. (d) |
| 239. (c) | 240. (d) | 241. (a) | 242. (d) | 243. (b) | 244. (a) | 245. (c) |
| 246. (d) | 247. (b) | 248. (a) | 249. (c) | 250. (b) | 251. (d) | 252. (a) |
| 253. (b) | 254. (c) | 255. (d) | 256. (a) | 257. (b) | 258. (d) | 259. (d) |
| 260. (c) | 261. (d) | 262. (d) | 263. (d) | 264. (b) | 265. (c) | 266. (b) |
| 267. (a) | 268. (b) | 269. (a) | 270. (c) | 271. (b) | 272. (a) | 273. (d) |
| 274. (c) | 275. (a) | 276. (b) | 277. (d) | 278. (c) | | |

# Bibliography

1. Allanou, R, Hasen, B.G. and van der Bilt. Y. Public availability of data on EU high production volume chemicals. EU 18996 EN European chemicals Bureau, Ispra, Italy.
2. Aubin, J.; Kresta, S.M.; Bertrand, J.; Xuereb, C.; Fletcher, D.F. Alternate Operating Methods for Improving the Performance of a Continuous Stirred Tank Reactor. Chem. Eng. Res. Des. 2006, 84, 569–582.
3. Badger, W.L. and Banchero, J.T.; Introduction to Chemical Engineering; Tata McGraw-Hill Publishing Co. Ltd., New Delhi, 2005
4. Badger,W. L. and Banchero, J. T. Introduction to Chemical Engineering.; ($13^{th}$ reprint); Tata McGraw-Hill Publishing Co.
5. Bartolomai, A. (ed.): Food Factories: Processes, Equipment and Costs.; VCH, New York, 1987.
6. Bentur, A., Diamond,S. and Berke, N.S.; Corrosion of Steel in Reinforced Concrete, E&FN Spon, London, (1996).
7. Beveridge, T., Large-Scale Centrifugation, Minister of Public Works and Government Services Canada; 2000.
8. Bruin, S. (ed.): Preconcentration and Drying of Food Materials (Elsevier, New York, 1988).
9. Buckley, H. E.: Crystal Growth.; Wiley, New York, 1951.
10. Carter, S. J.; Cooper and Gunn's Tutorial Pharmacy, $1^{st}$ Indian Edition, 1986; CBS Publishers & Distributors, New Delhi.
11. D. Derle and M. Bele. Essentials of Pharmaceutical engineering, Pharma med Press, pp.135-144.
12. Dangerous substances and explosives atmospheres Regulation 2002. Approved code of Practice and guidance l136 HSE Books, 2003.
13. Dara, S.S.; Engineering Chemistry, 1st Edition, S. Chand & Co, New Delhi.
14. David Mills - Pneumatic conveying design guide 2004.
15. Dodge, J.; Procedure for transportation of materials in conveying channels using pressurized air. DRP88402, 1895. German Patent.
16. E.A. Rawlins. Bentley's Text book of pharmaceutics, 8th edition, published by Elsevier, a division of Reed Elsevier India Private Limited, pp. 398-410.
17. Faktor, M. M. And Garrett, D. E.: Growth of Crystals from the Vapour.; Chapman and Hall, London, 1974.
18. Fincher, J. H.: J. Pharm. Sci., 57:1825, 1968.7. Tingstad, J, E.: J. Pharm. Sci., 53:955, 1964.
19. Findlay, A. and Campbell, A. N.: The Phase Rule and its Applications 9th. edition.; Longman, London,
1951.

20. Fontana, M. G. and Green, N. D.; Corrosion Engineering, Mc Graw Hill, New York, Ed., (1978).
21. Gaihua Zhao, Weiyin Luo. New concept physics tutorial: 1st edition of mechanics [M]. Beijing: education press, 1995, 235—244.
22. Gu,L. and Liu, Y.; Physics; M. Henan: Elephant Press, 2007, 10—11
23. Holtbrügge, J., Kunze, A. K., Niesbach, A., Schmidt, P., Schulz, R., Sudhoff, D., & Skiborowski, M. Reactive and Membrane-Assisted Separations. P. Lutze, & A. Górak(Eds.). Walter de Gruyter GmbH & Co KG.; 2016
24. Hong Wei. Working principle of motor sprayer [0L]. http: //www. chinabaik, 2008
25. Hong Wei. Working Principle of Motor sprayer; http: //www. chinabaik, 2008
26. Isabela, M.P.; Leandro, S.O. CDF Modelling and Simulation of Transesterification Reactions of Vegetable Oils with an Alcohol in Baffled Stirred Tank Reactor. Appl. Mech. Mater. **2013**, 390, 86–90.
27. Jain and Jain, Engineering Chemistry, 15th Edition, Dhanpat Rai Publishing Co., New Delhi.
28. James Sorbick. Encyclopedia of Pharmaceutical Technology, 3rd edition.
29. Jancic, S. J. and Grootscholten, A. M.: Industrial Crystallization.; Reidel, Dordrecht, 1984.
30. JoVE Science Education Database. General Laboratory Techniques. An Introduction to the Centrifuge. JoVE, Cambridge, MA, doi: 10.3791/5019, 2016
31. Kaldis, E. and Scheel, H. J.: Crystal Growth and Materials.; North-Holland, Amsterdam, 1977.
32. Kanig, J.: J. Pharm. Sci., 52:513, 1963.
33. Kraml, M., Dubue, J., and Gaudry, R.: Antibiot. Chemother., 12:232, 1962.
34. Laguzzi, G., Tommesani, L., Luvidi, L., Bucci, R., Brunoro, G., Corros. Sci. 41,197(1999).
35. Larson, R.: Constitutive Equations for Polymer Melts and Solutions.; Butterworth, London, 1988).
36. Lawson, W. D. and Nielsen, S.: Preparation of Single Crystals.; Butterworths, London, 1958.
37. Leitzel, R.E. and Morrisey, W.M.; Air-float conveyors. Bulk Materials Handling, Vol 1, pp 307-325, Ed M.C. Hawk, Univ Pittsburgh, Sch Mech Eng. 1971.
38. Li xin Gu, Yuqing Liu. physics [M] . Henan: Elephant press, 2007, 10—11
39. Lui, Y. A., McGee, H. A. and Epperly, W. R. (eds.): Recent Developments in Chemical Process and Plant Design.; Wiley, New York, 1987.
40. MacDonald, L.H., and Himelick, R. E.: J. Am. Pharm. Assoc., Sci. Ed., 37:368, 1948.
41. Mak, A.T.C. Solid-Liquid Mixing in Mechanically Agitated Vessels. Ph.D. Thesis, University of London, London, UK, 1992.
42. Mathur, P.B. and Vasudevan T, Corrosion, 38 (3), 171 (1982).
43. Ober, S.S., Vincent, H.C., Simon, D.E., and Frederick, K.J.: J. Am. Pharm. Assoc., Sci. Ed., 47:667, 1958
44. Pandiamnnal, M., Vincent, S., Kumar, K., Muralidharan, V.S., and lyer Y.M., Ninth Nat. Cong. Corros. Control Souvenir, Goa,37,16 (1999).
45. Parrott, E. L.: J. Pharm. Sci., 64:878, 1975.
46. Parrott, L.J.; A review of carbonation in reinforced concrete. Rep., Cement and Concrete Association/Building Research Establishment, Wexham Springs, U.K, 1986.
47. Reavell, B.N. and Goodwin, G. A.; Evaporation of Heat -Sensitive Materials.; Chemistry and Industries, 1450 – 1458; 1958.
48. Robert H. Perry Don. W. Green. Perry's chemical engineering handbook, 7th edition, pp. 26-49.
49. Rose, H. E. and Sullivan, R. M. E.; A Treatise on the Internal Mechanics of Ball, Tube and Rod Mills.; London, Constable, 1958.

50. Rose, H. E. and Sullivan, R. M. E.; Vibration Mils and Vibration Milling.; London, Constable, 1961.
51. Sambamurthy, K.; Pharmaceutical Engineering; New Age International (P) Ltd., Publishers, New Delhi, 2008 Santhanam, M.; Conc. Matt., 1(3) (2011) 1.
52. Seyed, H.; Dineshkumar, P.; Farhad, E.M.; Mehrab, M. Study of Solid-Liquid Mixing in Agitated Tanks through Computational Fluid Dynamics Modeling. Ind. Eng. Chem. Res. 2010, 49, 4426–4435.
53. Subrahmanyam, C.V.S., Thimma Setty, J., Suresh, S. and Kusum Devi, V.; Pharmaceutical Engineering (Principles and Practices); Vallabh Prakashan, Delhi; 2010
54. Tatterson, G.B. Fluid Mixing and Gas Dispersion in Agitated Tanks; McGraw-Hill: New York, NY, USA, 1991.
55. Thornton, J.W., McCally, M, and Houlihan, J.; Biomonitoring of Industrial pollutants: Health and policy Implications of the chemical body burden. Public health reports, 117, 315-323
56. US Department of Health and Human Services (DHHS), National Institute of Occupational Health and Safety (NIOSH), September, 2004, 165.
57. Versteeg, H.K.; Malalasekera, W. An Introduction to Computational Fluid Dynamics. In The Finite Volume Method, 2nd ed.; Pearson Education: New York, NY, USA, 2007.
58. Wilson, Ian D. Poole, Colin F.; Handbook of Methods and Instrumentation in Separation Science, Volume 1 - Centrifugation to Covalent Chromatography. Elsevier, 2009.
59. Woodcock, C.R. and Mason, J.S.; Bulk Solids Handling - An Introduction to the Practice and Technology. Blackie and Son Ltd.; 1987.
60. Zadghaffari, R.; Moghaddas, J.S.; Revstedt, J. A Study on Liquid-Liquid Mixing in a Stirred Tank with a 6-Blade Rushton Turbine. Iran. J. Chem. Eng. 2008, 5, 12–22.
61. Zhao,G. and Luo, W.; New concept physics tutorial: 1st edition of mechanics; Beijing: Education Press, 1995, 235—244.

www.ingramcontent.com/pod-product-compliance
Ingram Content Group UK Ltd.
Pitfield, Milton Keynes, MK11 3LW, UK
UKHW050953290926
15470UKWH00006B/1794

9 789391 910662